THE CENTER FOR PUBLIC INTEGRITY

February 22, 1999

Mr. Clarke Thacker
5003 Butternut Road
Durham, NC 27707-5218

Dear Mr. Thacker:

Thank you for joining the Center for Public Integrity with your gift of $50, received on 12/31/98. Your generous contribution allows us to continue our efforts to investigate and expose ethical wrongdoing to help educate and empower American citizens.

In addition to the signed copy of *The Buying of the Congress*, during the next year you will receive each new issue of our award-winning investigative newsletter, *The Public i*. You may also take advantage of our 30% member discount when ordering any of our reports.

Please feel free to call with any questions or comments you have about our work over the next year.

Pearl Stewart
William Julius Wilson

Executive Director
Charles Lewis

Director of the
International Consortium of
Investigative Journalists
Maud S. Beelman

Director of
Investigative Projects
Bill Hogan

Director of
State Projects
Diane Renzulli

Director of Development
Barbara W. Schecter

Sincerely,

Charles Lewis
Executive Director

Encl.

<u>Memo:</u>
This letter may be used as a receipt for tax purposes. Since every copy of *The Buying of the Congress* costs the Center for Public Integrity $12.50, $37.50 of your contribution is tax-deductible.

910 17th Street, NW 7th Floor   Washington, DC 20006   (202) 466-1300   Fax: (202) 466-1101   e-mail: contact@publicintegrity.org
http://www.publicintegrity.org

THE **BUYING** OF THE **CONGRESS** | | | | | | | |

To Anita Thacker —
Best wishes!

— [signature]

Also by

**Charles Lewis
and The Center for Public Integrity**

THE BUYING OF THE PRESIDENT

THE
BUYING
OF THE
CONGRESS

**How Special Interests Have Stolen Your Right
to Life, Liberty, and the Pursuit of Happiness**

*Charles Lewis
and
The Center for Public Integrity*

AVON BOOKS  NEW YORK

AVON BOOKS, INC.
1350 Avenue of the Americas
New York, New York 10019

Copyright © 1998 by The Center for Public Integrity
Interior design by Kellan Peck
Visit our website at **http://www.AvonBooks.com**
ISBN: 0-380-97596-3

Library of Congress Cataloging in Publication Data:

Lewis, Charles, 1953–
    The buying of the Congress : how special interests have stolen your right to life, liberty, and the pursuit of happiness / by Charles Lewis and the Center for Public Integrity.
        p.   cm.
    Includes bibliographical references (p. 390) and index.
    1. Lobbying—United States.   2. Pressure groups—United States. 3. United States. Congress—Ethics. I. Center for Public Integrity. II. Title.
JK1118.L47   1998   98-4032
328.73'078—dc21   CIP

First Avon Books Printing: October 1998

AVON TRADEMARK REG. U.S. PAT. OFF. AND IN OTHER COUNTRIES, MARCA REGISTRADA, HECHO EN U.S.A.

Printed in the U.S.A.

FIRST EDITION

QPM   10   9   8   7   6   5   4   3   2   1

For my father

||||||||||||

The Investigative Team

||||||||||||

Executive Director
Charles Lewis

Director of Investigative Projects
Bill Hogan

Chief of Research
Bill Allison

Senior Editor
William O'Sullivan

Senior Researcher
David Engel

Writers
Paul Cuadros
Alan Green
Patrick J. Kiger
John Kruger
Sam Loewenberg
Curtis Moore
Jeff Shear
Ken Silverstein
Nancy Watzman

Researchers
Angela Baggetta
Lloyd Brown
Justin Buchler
Gayle Collins
Josh Dine
Deirdre Fernandes
Nicole Gill
Jennifer Goldstein
Matthew Greller
Adrianne Hari
Jamie Heisler
J. D. LaRock
Matthew Lash
Abigail Lounsbury
Myra Marcaurelle
Carolyn Mueller
Christopher Rosché
Sadia Shirazi
Mary-Catherine Sullivan
Ellen Sung
Russell Tisinger
Orit Turé
Eric Wilson

The Center for Public Integrity
Myra Marcaurelle
Julie Mathers

The Center for Responsive Politics
Kent Cooper, Executive Director
Larry Makinson, Deputy Director
Sheila Krumholz, Project Director

Contents

||||||||||||

CONTENTS

YOUR FREEDOMS ||||||||||||||||||||||||||||||

Suppose you go to Washington and try to get at your government. You will always find that while you are politely listened to, the men really consulted are the men who have the biggest stake—the big bankers, the big manufacturers, the big masters of commerce. . . . The government of the United States at present is a foster child of special interests.

—WOODROW WILSON

||||||||||||

Congress meets tomorrow morning. Let us all pray: Oh Lord, give us strength to bear that which is about to be inflicted upon us. Be merciful with them, oh Lord, for they know not what they're doing. Amen.

—WILL ROGERS

THE BUYING OF THE CONGRESS | | | | | | |

Introduction

||||||||||||

THE CZECH PRESIDENT AND WRITER VÁCLAV HAVEL ONCE OBSERVED: "They say a nation has the politicians it deserves. In some sense that's true: Politicians are truly a mirror of the society and a kind of embodiment of its potential."

In many ways, this book is not so much about Congress as it is about us. You and me. We all have our own daily realities; we worry about our health, our safety, our jobs, our monthly mortgage or rent, our children's educations, our financial future. It is difficult for us as a society to realize our full potential if our most basic concerns are not first met.

As Americans, of course, we take some pride and comfort in knowing that we live in the most powerful, developed nation on earth, and we generally accept that our imperfect, still-evolving experiment in democracy has the most fairness and freedom of any type of governance on earth. In our representative form of government, we elect politicians to protect and to promote our interests, the broad public interest. A mere 535 men and women in Congress somehow must reflect the collective cares and needs of 269 million Americans, a dynamic people growing and changing each day, with one birth every eight seconds, one death every fourteen seconds, a new immigrant every thirty-nine seconds. These elected representatives are our employees, our public servants. Responding to our most basic concerns is their job. They work for us.

Or do they?

This book is the result of a yearlong investigation into just how responsive Congress is to our most basic concerns. Think of it as a giant employee evaluation. We found that in general, Members of Congress moonlight for themselves and their wealthy patrons more than they work for us, the American people. This fundamental betrayal of the employer-employee relationship is, unfortunately, quite serious to us all. Indeed, it directly affects the air we breathe, the water we drink, the food we eat, our safety in the workplace, the health care we receive, the prices we are charged for a wide array of goods, the taxes we pay. We have organized *The Buying of the Congress* by many of the most basic concerns confronting each and every American—and precisely how our employees in Congress have reacted to those concerns. Once we discuss our findings, the historical and contemporary context of Congress today, and the latest ways in which influence is wrought, the book is divided into three parts: "Your Health and Safety," "Your Money," and "Your Freedoms."

Our investigation—conducted by three dozen writers, editors, and researchers—concluded that our elected officials seem to have forgotten for whom they are working. Too frequently, on the most important public-policy issues of our time, at critical forks in the road between the broad public interest of the American people and the narrow, economic agenda of a few vested interests, our elected officials have taken the wrong path. Along the way, they have picked up hundreds of millions of dollars in campaign contributions from companies, labor unions, and individuals bent on influencing them, dollars documented throughout this book by the Federal Election Commission and by the Center for Responsive Politics, a nonpartisan research organization.

For most Americans, Congress is a distant abomination, out of sight and out of mind. We don't think about it much, we barely know what it does, and we can hardly even name our elected representatives. The jarring reality, however, is that Congress is directly involved with your life every single day. You literally cannot go to your supermarket, the local drugstore, the hospital emergency room, or the nursing home where your loved one is being cared for without being directly affected by decisions made in Congress. You cannot watch TV, take a flight on an airplane, pay your taxes, or eat dinner without being affected by laws enacted by Congress. You simply cannot tune out or escape the fact that Congress is a significant, relevant force in your life.

For example, we found that:

• For years, Congress has protected the food industry from tougher safety standards. At the same time, from 1987 through 1996, the food industry has fed Members of Congress more than $41 million in campaign contributions. Meanwhile, thousands of Americans die each year from poisoned food, and many millions more become ill.

• Even though 400,000 Americans die each year from tobacco-related illnesses, and despite new evidence that company executives lied about smoking for decades, Congress has protected the tobacco industry, and it continues to allow the U.S. government itself to operate programs to help grow tobacco, insure it, export it, and protect it against foreign imports. From 1987 through 1996, the tobacco companies have blown smoke and more than $30 million in contributions to Members of Congress and the two major political parties.

• Roughly 10 to 20 percent of all drug treatments cause adverse reactions, which may kill as many as 160,000 Americans a year and cause more than 1 million people to be hospitalized. Congress has done nothing about this problem, except to protect the pharmaceutical industry by proposing weaker regulations. From 1987 through 1996, the pharmaceutical and medical device companies injected nearly $28 million into the re-election coffers of Capitol Hill lawmakers.

• In minor accidents, airline seats frequently are deathtraps. More than half of the commercial aircraft flying today have seats built to 1952 safety standards, designed for the Propeller Age, before jets. These seats can withstand only *half* the crash impact of the seats in your car. Members of Congress accept not only campaign contributions—$7.5 million from 1987 through 1996— but also free and discounted tickets from the airline industry. Not surprisingly, Congress ultimately has done nothing to improve airline seat safety standards.

• When it comes to preserving the worrisome future of Social Security, Congress has also done nothing. Meanwhile, your elected representatives have used the Social Security money to help pay for the annual federal budget. Since 1980, at the same time Congress has slashed federal income taxes for the wealthy and for corporations, it has increased the FICA tax that pays for all the Social Security benefits seven times. It is revealing that Members of Congress indexed their own guaranteed retirement pension to inflation in 1962, but they did not bother to adjust millions of Americans' Social Security benefits for inflation until 1975.

• In 1980, 54 percent of workers at large and medium-size U.S. firms had the full cost of their families' health insurance paid by their employers; by 1993, the number had dropped to 20 percent. Meanwhile, we pay the full health-insurance costs for Members of Congress. It has been "visiting hours only" for Congress on this and many other worsening health-care issues, and the health-care industry has inoculated Congress against any reform or regulatory tendencies by giving Members more than $72 million from 1987 through 1996.

• The food you buy at the grocery store costs more because Congress has done sweetheart deals for some of its major patrons. For example, the price of milk went up by twenty cents a gallon in New England in 1997 because of a special subsidy for the region's dairy farmers passed by Congress. Dairy interests in general poured $10 million into Congress from 1987 through 1996.

• Have you noticed that your monthly cable TV bills are higher? You can thank Congress for that. When the historic Telecommunications Act became law in 1996, the industry and Congress said that cable rates would fall because of the new law and market competition. Well, so far, cable prices are 8.5 percent higher than before the law was enacted. And millions of dollars in new revenue have accrued to the cable companies. The cable television industry invested $15.9 million in political contributions to Members of Congress from 1987 through 1996.

• Each year 27,000 children who live and work on farms are injured and 300 are killed. Overall, an estimated 64,000 adolescents aged fourteen to seventeen required treatment in hospital emergency rooms for work-related injuries in 1992—and only a third of work-related injuries are generally seen in emergency rooms. Congress has failed consistently to protect children from their exploiters. Well-heeled groups such as the American Farm Bureau Federation, the National Council of Chain Restaurants, the National Restaurant Association, the Food Marketing Institute, the National American Wholesale Grocers' Association, and the corporate-funded Labor Policy Association have contributed millions of dollars to Members of Congress and spent millions more lobbying to weaken current child labor laws.

• As ranked on the Fortune 500, the nation's largest corporations—from number-one General Motors Corporation through number-500 Vencor, Inc.—contributed at least $182 million to Members of Congress from 1987 through 1996 through their political action committees (PACs). "Soft money" contributions to both parties during the same period totaled more than $73 million. It is hardly surprising, then, that over the years Congress has repeatedly cut taxes for corporations and wealthy individuals. In 1956, corporate income taxes accounted for 28 percent of all federal tax revenue. Today that number is down to 10 percent.

How do these things happen? Naturally, money greases the skids, but there are several other ways to make a favorable impression on Congress. For example, we found that 443 Members of Congress and 2,020 congressional aides accepted at least $8.6 million in all-expenses-paid trips all over the United States and around the world in 1996 and the first half of 1997. California and Florida were the two favorite destinations inside the United States, and we noticed that no one journeyed to such places as Dubuque, Iowa, and El Paso, Texas. The two most frequently visited countries were Taiwan and China. Who paid for these freebies? Various business and labor interests that want Congress to adopt their public-policy agendas.

Another way for special interests to ingratiate themselves with Congress is to hire former lawmakers and their aides. We found that of the most important nonelected officials on Capitol Hill from 1991 to 1996, 15 percent of senior Senate aides became registered lobbyists in Washington, and 14 percent of the senior

House aides similarly cashed in. The revolving door practically came unhinged on some of the "money" committees, such as the Senate and House Commerce Committees, where 36 and 40 percent of senior staffers there, respectively, left to become registered lobbyists. All of this—hobnobbing with major contributors at fund-raising events, traveling with them to interesting locales as their guests, schmoozing with former Hill colleagues who have doubled or tripled their previous government salaries—creates an incestuous, mercenary culture in which the lines between personal, private, and public interests become hopelessly blurred.

|||||||||||||||||||||||||||||||||||||||

In 1996 the average cost of winning a seat in the U.S. Senate was $4.7 million. This kind of cash does not come from community bake sales but almost entirely from deep-pocketed donors with business before the federal government.

|||||||||||||||||||||||||||||||||||||||

Nonetheless, the fact remains that Members of Congress are our employees, whom we can fire on Election Day. Why, then, are our representatives in Washington so aloof and unresponsive to our concerns? In some ways, it is because they are, as Havel put it, a mirror of society. Like us, they are first and foremost worried about themselves, their jobs, their monthly mortgage or rent payments, their financial futures. Like us, they know what side their bread is buttered on. To them, survival means getting elected and staying elected, and there are a few ways to help ensure that. Of course, whether they are Republican or Democrat, they must always appear to be on the side of the angels, always consonant with God, country, and apple pie. They are generally against new taxes and for some kind of reform. Beyond the posturing, their public positions, and thousands of votes cast, there is one other imperative that all incumbents fully recognize: preserving the current campaign finance system that places nonmillionaire challengers in their districts or states at a distinct disadvantage. Political campaigns today cost more and more, and without achieving high recognition among voters via television, radio, and newspaper advertising, a candidate has no real chance of getting his or her message before the voters.

In the 1996 congressional elections nationwide, candidates

raised $791 million and spent $766 million, more than ever before, all from private sources. According to the Center for Responsive Politics, in 1996 the average cost of winning a seat in the U.S. Senate was $4.7 million, and the average cost of winning a seat in the U.S. House of Representatives was $674,000. This kind of cash does not come from community bake sales or backyard barbecues but almost entirely from deep-pocketed donors—companies, labor unions, individuals—with business before the federal government. It is a very exclusive game. According to the Center for Responsive Politics, in the 1996 federal elections, less than one-tenth of 1 percent of the American people wrote checks for $1,000 or more, and money from such privileged interests accounted for 40 percent of all money raised. One-quarter of 1 percent of the population gave $200 or more to congressional candidates or the political parties in 1995–96.

Many good, talented people decide not to enter politics because so much money-grubbing is required. What we are left with, then, are millionaires deciding to seek public office or the kind of candidates who are willing to dial for dollars and shake strangers' hands at fund-raising events incessantly, because thousands of dollars must be raised practically every single day they are candidates and after they are in office.

In this demeaning exercise, a debilitating dependency develops. Just as we generally do not lambaste or seek to undermine our bosses, politicians and their political parties are not usually antagonistic to their financial sponsors. Indeed, over the years, the politicians and their patrons develop a mutually beneficial relationship, in which the former desperately need cash in order to function and the latter have plenty of cash to invest in the political actors most strategically relevant and amicable to their economic agendas. The result is a predictable confluence of interests.

The consequences of this arrangement are hugely significant to the public at large. The twenty-eighth President of the United States, Woodrow Wilson, noticed them many decades ago. "The government, which was designed for the people, has got into the hands of their bosses and their employers, the special interests," he wrote. "An invisible empire has been set up above the forms of democracy."

As lawyer-novelist Scott Turow put it in a *New York Times*

op-ed article in 1997, "Is it entirely coincidental that . . . as the cost of political campaigns has skyrocketed, historical patterns have reversed themselves and the incomes of the top quintile of earners have risen faster than the earnings of other Americans?" Since the 1970s, Congress has substantially reduced both the top income-tax rate and the tax on capital gains, among many other sops to the rich. The incomes of the top 1 percent more than doubled in real terms from 1977 to 1989, and while the median income remained approximately the same, the bottom 20 percent of wage earners saw their incomes drop by 10 percent. Of those under twenty-five years old with full-time jobs, the proportion who earned only a poverty-level income jumped from 23 percent in 1980 to 47 percent in 1992. Investigative journalists Donald Barlett and James Steele, two-time winners of the Pulitzer Prize, found that 45 percent of all tax returns submitted to the Internal Revenue Service in 1993—44 million out of the total 98 million returns showing wage or salary income—were filed by individuals and families reporting income under $20,000.

Many Americans are working harder than before just to make ends meet. Author Jeffrey Madrick has reported that the average full-time male employee today works about a week and a half longer each year now than in 1973, the first significant increase in hours worked in this century. Today 7 million workers hold at least two jobs, the highest proportion in half a century. The United States now has the widest gap between rich and poor of any industrialized country. Indeed, the gap shrank continually between 1929 and 1969; since then, it has been steadily widening. According to essayist John Ralston Saul in *The Unconscious Civilization,* the income of 75 million Americans is lower today than it was in 1966.

There are social ramifications, of course, to the growing disparity in wealth and opportunity. Today, for example, more than 5 million Americans are in jail or under judicial supervision—three times as many as in 1980. Affluent Americans are increasingly buying out of what they perceive to be inadequate public services, placing their children in private schools as urban public schools continue to deteriorate, utilizing private "pay-per-use" playgrounds instead of public playgrounds. By 1990, the number of private security guards nationwide had surpassed the number of public police officers. More than 3 million households in the United States today live in walled and fenced residential areas, and gated communities now can be found in every major metropolitan area. This is a stunning increase since 1985. Conservative historian Edward Luttwak has predicted that, if current inequalities keep worsening, the United States will be a Third World country by 2020.

In 1996, out of 196.5 million Americans who were eligible to vote, 146.2 million people registered, and less than half of the voting age population, 96.4 million people, actually voted. It was the lowest voter turnout for a presidential election year since 1924. The greatest disengagement in our democracy is occurring among the most economically disadvantaged. It is also clear that anger and disgust toward politicians in general has deepened discernibly. Could it be that the American people intuitively recognize that politicians represent the financial elites, and not them? Is it entirely coincidental that public participation in the political process is at a record low?

In 1996, as part of a national survey conducted with the Kaiser Family Foundation and Harvard University, *The Washington Post* published a series of articles about cynicism. The findings were remarkable. In 1964, three in four Americans trusted the federal government all or most of the time. Today that view is shared by only one in four people.

> **People are tuning politics right out of their lives. . . . Four in ten Americans surveyed could not identify the current Vice President of the United States.**

Part of the alienation of the American people manifests itself in how much time is actually spent reading and thinking about government. People are tuning politics right out of their lives. The *Washington Post*/Harvard University/Kaiser Family Foundation survey found that two-thirds of those interviewed did not know the name of their Representatives in Congress. Four in ten Americans surveyed could not identify the current Vice President of the United States. Almost half—

46 percent—could not name the speaker of the U.S. House of Representatives.

Members of Congress are aware of this lack of interest and disillusionment. Senator Richard Lugar of Indiana, who ran unsuccessfully for the Republican presidential nomination in 1996, told the Center: "The mail is down; it's unprecedentedly low. After twenty years, I've never seen so little mail coming through on any subject." Although he ascribed the fall-off to the economy ("They would [write] if we were in a recession"), Lugar also acknowledged that "the perception is we're not very relevant."

Most Capitol Hill lawmakers are not millionaires, but at least thirty-six Senators—more than a third of the institution—are. Compare that with the proportion of millionaires to the general U.S. population: less than 1 percent.

Former Representative Patricia Schroeder of Colorado, a Democrat who also once ran unsuccessfully for President, told us: "I now have a feeling that a higher percentage of people think [Congress] is irrelevant, doesn't make a difference, that they [Members of Congress] are debating how many angels can dance on the head of a pin. And when you look at some of the legislation, I mean, it really is kind of a joke. . . .

"What I see people saying is that they've so given up on this institution that they're not willing to invest their energy in demanding a change. Now, that is very dangerous to me, because if you've given up on the institution, you've almost given up on the form of government. I think there has just been this huge shift in the last ten years. America is going gated, and no one wants to talk about it. But there isn't an 'America' in the old sense of the word. Everyone is trying to get as much money as they can to get behind the biggest gates they can and then they're going to develop their own community, with their own schools, their own legal systems, their own parks, and they aren't going to want to participate in a greater civic good."

Scott Klug, a former Emmy Award-winning television journalist who is retiring after four terms in the House of Representatives, told us that cynicism "has always been there, and frankly I think that's part of the American psyche." He cited the famous line by

Mark Twain that "there is no distinctly native American criminal class except Congress."

Klug, a Republican, also said that when he's back in his Wisconsin district, "one of the first questions I'll get asked when I go to talk to a school class, to second or third or fourth graders, is: 'Thank you for coming to talk to us today. Have you ever met the President?' And then the next question is usually 'Do you have a limousine, and can I ride in it?' Well, I think that gives you an idea of what people's attitudes are like toward Congress—the sense that we're privileged, we're above it all, most people here are millionaires."

Most Capitol Hill lawmakers are not millionaires, but at least thirty-six Senators—more than a third of the institution—are. Compare that with the proportion of millionaires to the general U.S. population: less than 1 percent. How has Congress taken care of itself in relation to the nation at large? While the median household income of Americans has risen only slightly in twenty years (7.7 percent, from $32,943 in 1975 to $35,492 in 1996, both in 1996 dollars), the income of Members of Congress has risen dramatically (50 percent, from $89,034 in 1975 to $133,600 in 1997, both in 1997 dollars). In other words, over the past two decades the incomes of our employees (a.k.a. public servants) have risen six times more than those of their constituents, their employers. Members of Congress are a privileged class with more benefits and perks than the American people. For example, in a nation in which 41 million Americans can't afford health insurance and many retired Americans have no pension except for Social Security, Members of Congress have superb health-insurance benefits and one of the best retirement plans in the nation.

"The great thing about America is that the people are still the

> **In a nation in which 41 million Americans can't afford health insurance and many retired Americans have no pension except for Social Security, Members of Congress have superb health-insurance benefits and one of the best retirement plans in the nation.**

sovereigns, and the governors still understand that they must submit to the will of the governed," veteran muckraker Jack Anderson, who has spent half a century investigating Congress and many other subjects, told us. "But if the governed do not express their will, that leaves our leaders free to tend to the desires and will of the special interests, which is what they spend most of their time doing."

Harkening back to Václav Havel's wise remarks about a nation getting the politicians it deserves, I believe that we deserve better, although we seem to have accepted much less. In recent decades, by voting or by not exercising our right to vote, we have sent candidates to Congress who later have substantially improved their own positions and that of their financial patrons. At the same time, the ranks of the poor have grown and gotten poorer, and the shrinking middle class has barely kept even with inflation. And that is not even considering what Congress has done to protect polluters, cigarette manufacturers, food producers, the airline industry, the insurance industry, corporate welfare cheats, and hundreds of other moneyed interests—endangering our health, diminishing our financial security, and encroaching upon our hard-earned freedoms in this supposed democracy of the people, by the people, and for the people.

With all that in mind, *The Buying of the Congress* is not a bouquet of roses that celebrates the legislative branch of government, with puffy features about the various leaders, their tireless "constituent service," and their other achievements—there are hundreds of press secretaries on Capitol Hill putting out that stuff on our nickel. Nor is it a pontificating memoir by a former lawmaker, nor a scholarly tome readable only by political scientists, nor a sensational, behind-closed-doors exposé about Members' sex lives or their latest ethical mishaps.

Rather, this book is an investigative report about Congress: the lawmakers we have hired to protect our right to life, liberty, and the pursuit of happiness, and what they—our employees— have actually done on our behalf. We hope you will use it as a new measure of accountability from those who call themselves public servants.

1

∣∣∣∣●∣∣∣∣

The Death of Conscience

Woodrow Wilson, the only political scientist to become President, wrote about the bewildered citizen in his first book, *Congressional Government,* published in 1885. His words could well have been written today. A prospective voter, he said, "distrusts Congress because he feels that he cannot control it. The voter, moreover, feels that his want of confidence in Congress is justified by what he hears of the power of corrupt lobbyists to turn legislation to their own uses. He hears of enormous subsidies begged and obtained; of pensions procured on commission by professional pension solicitors; of appropriations made in the interest of dishonest contractors; and he is not altogether unwarranted in the conclusion that these are evils inherent in the very nature of Congress."

Americans—those who vote as well as the increasing numbers who do not—are still bewildered today and as distrustful as ever about the evils inherent in Congress. So too was President and renowned trustbuster Theodore Roosevelt. He railed against the "robber barons" while simultaneously depending upon their campaign contributions, and he relied on his Justice Department to break up trusts rather than turn to Congress for new antitrust legislation. Capitol Hill lawmakers were simply too close to the big corporations themselves, even then. Of all the Presidents in this century, Roosevelt was possibly the most outspoken about corporate influence on the political process. Indeed, business leaders were outraged by his frequent attacks. "We bought the son of a bitch," steel magnate Henry Frick complained, "and then he did not stay bought."

For years, investigative journalists exposed—and progressive reformers decried—the influence of money on elections. In 1905 and 1906, President Roosevelt called for political reform in his annual messages to Congress. In 1907, with mounting public pressure for change, Congress passed the Tillman Act, which prohibits corporations and national banks from making any contributions to candidates for federal office. Although the law is still on the books, politicians and their political parties have ignored it for decades. In 1996, the two major national political parties exploited the biggest loophole in the Federal Election Campaign Act, the post-Watergate reform law, by raising roughly $262 million in "soft money," three times the total just four years earlier. "Soft money" is shorthand for funds raised and spent outside the reach of federal election law—the direct, sky's-the-limit contributions from corporations, labor unions, and individuals that would be flatly illegal in congressional or presidential campaigns. In 1995 and 1996, both parties spent tens of millions of dollars of "soft money" on television commercials that were specifically designed to benefit their respective presidential candidates, Bill Clinton and Robert Dole.

In 1910, after his second term in the White House, Teddy Roosevelt declared: "We must drive the special interests out of politics. . . . The citizens of the United States must effectively control the mighty commercial forces which they have themselves called into being. There can be no effective control of corporations while their political activity remains. To put an end to it will neither be a short nor an easy task, but it can be done. . . . Corporate expenditures for political purposes, and especially such expenditures by public service corporations, have supplied one of the principal sources of corruption in our political affairs."

Roosevelt, who coined the word "muckrakers," was the first and perhaps the last President to invite investigative reporters into the White House. The Progressive Era marked the dawn of investigative journalism in the United States, in which magazines such as *Arena, The Atlantic Monthly, Forum,* and *McClure's* published articles about various political, social, and economic ills. Lincoln Steffens wrote magazine stories about corrupt urban political machines that became the classic book *The Shame of the Cities:* Ida Tarbell exposed Standard Oil Company; and Upton Sinclair's 1906 novel *The Jungle* revealed the filthy conditions of Chicago's slaughterhouses. The documented outrages prompted new laws to safeguard the public. It was in this milieu of investigation and exposure that journalist David Graham Phillips wrote a series of articles entitled "The Treason of the Senate," which ran in *Cosmopolitan* magazine in 1906.

The first article asserted: "The treason of the Senate! Treason is a strong word, but not too strong, rather too weak, to characterize the situation in which the Senate is [the] eager, resourceful, indefatigable agent of interests as hostile to the American people as any invading army could be, and vastly more dangerous: interests that manipulate the prosperity produced by all, so that it heaps up riches for the few; interests whose growth and power can only mean the degradation of the people, of the educated into sycophants, of the masses toward serfdom. . . . The Senators are not elected by the people; they are elected by the 'interests.' "

In his stories, Phillips named names and included much detail. He revealed, for example, that Senator Chauncey Depew, a Republican from New York, was on the boards of directors of seventy corporations and received more than $50,000 a year in fees from them. He said that Senator Thomas Collier Platt, a Republican from New York, had a "long . . . unbroken record of treachery to the people in legislation of privilege and plunder promoted and in decent legislation prevented."

|||||||||||||||||||||||||||||||||||||||||||

In 1975, when the Gallup Organization asked a representative sample of Americans how much confidence they had in Congress, 40 percent responded: "A great deal" or "Quite a lot." By 1995, only 21 percent responded that way.

|||||||||||||||||||||||||||||||||||||||||||

The series ended with the following observation: "Such is the stealthy and treacherous Senate as at present constituted. And such it will continue to be until people think instead of shout about politics; until they judge public men by what they do and are, not by what they say and pretend. However, the fact that the people are themselves responsible for their own betrayal does not mitigate contempt for their hypocritical and cowardly betrayers. . . . The stupidity or negligence of the householder in leaving the door unlocked does not lessen the crime of the thief."

The articles were roundly condemned by politicians, and Phillips himself was disheartened by the response. He did not live long enough, though, to realize what he had accomplished. As journalists Arthur and Lila Weinberg note in their book *The Muckrakers,* Phillips's series on the Senate was a catalyst in the passage of the Seventeenth Amendment, which gave the American people the direct election of Senators.

At the time Phillips wrote his exposés, candidates for federal office were not required to disclose the sources of either their campaign funds or their personal incomes. There were no rules governing outside income. Today, after hundreds of grim reports over the years of personal excesses by our elected officials, including the Watergate scandal in the 1970s, we have various mechanisms to try to hold our employees more accountable to us. As we have learned to our consternation, however, these rules—mandating that the money moving to our officials be observable and transparent to the public—are not by themselves sufficient to safeguard us from betrayal.

Since the late 1980s, we have seen more sustained disgrace and disrepute fall on Congress than in any other decade this century. In 1975, when the Gallup Organization asked a representative sample of Americans how much confidence they had in Congress, 40 percent responded: "A great deal" or "Quite a lot." In 1985, the total was 39 percent. But by 1995, only 21 percent of the respondents expressed "a great deal" or "quite a lot" of confidence in Congress.

It is not particularly mysterious why people have soured on their elected officials. In June 1989, House Majority Whip Tony Coelho resigned from Congress rather than face formal ethics hearings and charges over the favors he had received from a savings-and-loan operator who had helped him buy a $100,000 junk bond. Within days, House Speaker Jim Wright also resigned after a year and a half of constant revelations of ethical improprieties. In November 1990, in hearings led by Democrat Henry Gonzalez of Texas, then chairman of the Committee on Banking, Finance, and Urban Affairs, five Senators—Democrat Alan Cranston of California, Democrat Dennis DeConcini of Arizona, Republican John McCain of Arizona, Democrat John Glenn of Ohio, and Democrat Donald Riegle, Jr., of Michigan—were accused of taking a total of $1.4 million from Lincoln Savings and Loan Association operator Charles Keating and pressuring federal regulators on his behalf. (Crantson was severely reprimanded; the others were found either to have given the appearance of impropriety or to have exercised poor judgment.) As we look back today, it is interesting to note that more than 80 percent of the money that Keating raised for or on behalf of the five Senators was unregulated, almost impossible to discern "soft money." In its final report in November 1991, after months of hearings, the Senate Select Committee on Ethics urged Congress "to address the urgent need for comprehensive campaign finance reform," adding: "The reputation and honor of our institutions demand it."

Keating, whose savings and loan defrauded thousands of people and was shut down, was convicted and sent to prison. (He has been released by an appeals judge, and a retrial is pending.) "[Reporters have asked] whether my financial support in any way influenced several political figures to take up my cause," Keating once said. "I want to say in the most forceful way I can: I certainly hope so."

And the Senators themselves were unrepentant. Cranston, who had committed the most egregious offenses of the five, told his colleagues that his campaign fund-raising practices and "constituent service" for Keating "were not fundamentally different from the actions of many other Senators." He went on to say: "The present system makes it virtually impossible—virtually impossible—for a Senator to avoid what some will assert is a conflict of interest. . . . How many of you, after really thinking about it, could rise and declare you have never, ever helped—or agreed to help—a contributor close in time to the solicitation or receipt of a contribution?"

From July 1988 to October 1991, more than half the Members of the House of Representatives—269 in all—were found to have written thousands of overdraft checks with no penalties. Why? Because they had their own unregulated "bank" on the premises.

In 1996, a poster child for Washington excesses and insiderism, Dan Rostenkowski, former chairman of the House Ways and Means Committee, pleaded guilty to fraud and went to prison. He had been charged in 1994 in a seventeen-count indictment of using government employees to remodel his house, of illegally exchanging postage stamps for cash at the House Post Office, of pocketing federal funds and campaign money, of using merchandise in the House Stationery Store as gifts to friends and constituents, and so on. The sentencing judge, Norma Holloway Johnson, branded Rostenkowski's actions "reprehensible," adding: "In your important position, you capriciously pursued a course of personal gain for you, your family, and your friends. You have stained them, as well as yourself and the high position you held."

> From July 1988 to October 1991, more than half the Members of the House of Representatives—269 in all— were found to have written thousands of overdraft checks with no penalties.

Rostenkowski's response was the same thing that Cranston had said in 1991, the same thing that the Clinton White House would say in 1997 amid the campaign fund-raising scandals: Everybody does it. "I personally have come to accept the fact," Rostenkowski said, "that sometimes one person gets singled out, to be held up by law enforcement as an example."

In 1994, after years of scandal involving members of the Democratic majority, the Republicans took over Congress for the first time in four decades. Newt Gingrich of Georgia became the new Speaker of the House. Gingrich and House Republicans had campaigned successfully on a "Contract with America," but change never begat change. The seventy-three freshmen "reform" Republicans elected in 1994, who had pledged to clean up Washington, took in $11 million toward their reelections from special interests in just their first six months in office. Once they were in power, some minor alterations were made—committees were renamed and certain procedural reforms were enacted, but one thing that stayed the same was the access of Big Money to their favorite politicians. Campaign finance reform, of course, had never been in the fine print of the highly publicized "Contract with America." Indeed, months into his Speakership, Gingrich and some of his Republican colleagues announced that the problem with politics was actually that there was not enough money! In the 1996 congressional elections, the Republicans retained control of the House and Speaker Gingrich ran one of the most expensive campaigns in the nation. He spent more than $4.5 million, and his opponent, a millionaire cookie mogul, spent more than $2.3 million.

When Gingrich first ran for Congress in 1974, the year the Watergate scandal was engulfing America, he said: "I have no desire to curry favor with lobbyists or accumulate power for my own sake. I will not play the game of special-interest politics." But over the next two decades, he excelled at the game, raising millions of dollars from virtually every conceivable special interest (except labor unions) for his own campaigns and for scores of other Republicans nationwide. It is fair to say that without substantial money raised to obtain power, Gingrich would not be Speaker today. Along the way, he used charitable organizations for political purposes, possibly in violation of federal tax laws, and lied to his House colleagues. The House formally reprimanded Gingrich and penalized him $300,000. Gingrich had the chutzpah to make sure that the $300,000 assessment was officially called not a "fine" but a "cost assessment" or "reimbursement" to the House Committee on Standards of Official Conduct for its investigation. Why? So that he could deduct the amount as a "work-related" expense on his income taxes.

Gingrich opposes any legislation that would reduce the role of money in politics, and throughout 1995, 1996, and 1997, he and his Republican leadership team in the House kept any serious political campaign-reform legislation off of the floor. Thus, there could be no recorded roll-call vote identifying which Members of Congress were for or against "reform" of any kind. The issue just never made it onto Congress's agenda. Bluntly stated, Gingrich; Senate Majority Leader Trent Lott of Mississippi; Mitch McConnell of Kentucky, chairman of the Republican Senatorial Campaign

Committee; and other GOP congressional leaders have made the cold-blooded calculation that campaign cash—and lots of it—is essential to their hold on power.

It has been difficult for the Democrats to make cleaning up our political system an issue, although they have tried. To put it charitably and to paraphrase former California Governor Jerry Brown's marvelous description of himself, President Clinton is a "flawed vessel" on the subject of integrity in government and keeping an arm's length from special interests. He has been one of the most investigated Presidents in this century, alongside Warren Harding and Richard Nixon. In the 1996 presidential election, the most expensive and possibly the most corrupt in U.S. history, Clinton essentially had a continuous yard sale for special interests, selling off access to the White House in the most shameless manner the nation has ever seen. In his first term, 938 guests, many of them campaign donors, slept over in the White House, including in the Lincoln Bedroom. Patrons were invited to fly with the President on Air Force One, and 1,544 people, many of them contributors, attended 102 "coffees" in the White House from January 1995 to August 1996. Vice President Albert Gore, Jr., spoke at a fund-raising event in a Buddhist monastery in Los Angeles, and everyone from Colombian drug traffickers to Chinese arms dealers passed through the White House, obtaining access for cash.

Like sleazy telemarketing salesmen, the President and Vice President each made cash-seeking telephone solicitations from their offices in the White House—calls that, regardless of whether there is a "controlling legal authority," to use Gore's Orwellian phrase, were unprecedented and crass at best. From White House videotapes that did not exist and then somehow later surfaced, we know that the President personally solicited contributions from foreign nationals, who are prohibited from contributing to U.S. elections. Perhaps most serious of all, we know that the President was personally involved in raising and diverting tens of millions of dollars in Democratic Party contributions to his own reelection campaign, spent on television commercials that he personally approved and that aired more than a year before the 1996 election.

When the Republican Congress tried to investigate all this in 1997, the challenge was to find the truth in a few months' time, without the full cooperation of the White House or the Justice

Department and despite the fact that, according to the Senate Governmental Affairs Committee, more than forty-five key figures fled the country or pleaded the Fifth Amendment. Months of hearings were held, somehow without ever really mentioning the money-in-politics transgressions by Members of Congress. Indeed, the very lawmakers entrusted with investigating the many allegations of impropriety had a few skeletons in their own closets. For example, five of the sixteen members of the Senate Governmental Affairs Committee that in 1997 investigated political corruption have, through their campaign committees, violated election laws (Senators Robert Bennett, Carl Levin, Arlen Specter, Robert Smith, and John Glenn). The hypocrisy was just as thick in the House, where the chairman of the Government Reform and Oversight Committee, Republican Dan Burton of Indiana, reportedly had shaken down an American lobbyist for Pakistan for campaign cash. Weeks before his campaign-finance hearings began in 1997, Burton flew to California to play golf in an AT&T-sponsored golf tournament at Pebble Beach with the company's chairman and chief executive officer, Robert Allen. At the time, Burton's committee was overseeing the awarding of a $10 billion government telephone contract being bid upon by AT&T, Sprint Corporation, and MCI Communications Corporation.

Five of the sixteen members of the Senate Governmental Affairs Committee that in 1997 investigated political corruption have, through their campaign committees, violated election laws.

With such an addictive dependency on special-interest money and perks by both Democrats and Republicans in Washington, it was not particularly surprising that Congress just could not seem to find proof of systematic illegality or even determine the extent of wrongdoing by either party in the 1996 elections. It also was not surprising that, at the same time, Congress could not reform the way in which its own elections are financed.

What we are talking about, then, is a corrupt system that perpetuates itself and besmirches all participants. So, in this debased milieu, who has the credibility to lead? Whom can we trust? Are all politicians crooks?

Most people are not scoundrels, and in this regard Václav Havel is right: Congress is a mirror. Just as there are many exemplary citizens in our society, the same is also true of Congress. To be fair to the men and women who work tirelessly, trying to serve their constituents and preserve some semblance of a personal life, the pace and the daily pressures are intense. As then-Senator John F. Kennedy wrote in his 1956 Pulitzer Prize-winning book, *Profiles in Courage,* a Member of Congress

> *cannot ignore the pressure groups, his constituents, his party, the comradeship of his colleagues, the needs of his family, his own pride in office, the necessity for compromise and the importance of remaining in office. He must judge for himself which path to choose, which step will most help or hinder the ideals to which he is committed. He realizes that once he begins to weigh each issue in terms of his chances for reelection, once he begins to compromise his principles on one issue after another for fear that to do otherwise would halt his career and prevent future fights for principle, then he has lost the very freedom of conscience which justifies his continuance in office. But to decide at which point and on which issue he will risk his career is a difficult and soul-searching decision.*

Fairly or unfairly, the public perception today is that most politicians will not risk their careers for anything. Indeed, the word "conscience" together with the word "politician" seems an oxymoron. But there are many outstanding men and women serving in Congress, dedicated public servants conducting the public's business in as honest a manner as the present system allows. I had the great privilege of meeting or watching two of this century's real "profiles in courage." Two Senators, one a Republican and the other a Democrat, were each frequently referred to as "the conscience of the Senate," and both were enormously respected by their peers for their strength of character, their principled independence, and their humility. From the Capitol Senate gallery, I watched Philip Hart, a Democrat from Michigan, during floor debates and roll-call votes. I met and interviewed John Williams, a Republican from Delaware, in 1974, three years after he retired from Congress. At the time, during the peak of the historic Watergate scandal, I was working in Washington as a Senate intern.

When Williams retired from the Senate after four terms in 1970, Democrat Sam Ervin of North Carolina, who later became a household name for his masterful stewardship of the Senate Watergate Committee, said that Williams "did more to expose mismanagement and even corruption in government than any other Senator in the history of the United States. He always prepped himself before he said anything, and then he displayed unparalleled courage in fearlessly exposing whatever the corruption or mismanagement was, regardless of the way it was found."

Williams, a chicken farmer and feed dealer from southern Delaware, had never gone to college. He spoke so quietly on the Senate floor that the news media dubbed him "Whispering Willie." But when he spoke, people listened as he exposed the biggest corruption scandals of the late 1940s, 1950s, and 1960s—sending hundreds of government officials to prison, saving taxpayers hundreds of millions of dollars—without a sleuthing staff, without the power of subpoena, without a special counsel serving as prosecutor. Congress never appropriated a penny for his investigations, and Williams paid all expenses, such as necessary travel, out of his own pocket. He always informed the subject of an investigation of his findings personally before he announced them publicly, and never once in twenty-four years did he falsely accuse anyone. He also never had a press secretary, something practically unheard of in Washington even then. "I always figured that if there was something newsworthy, the press people would find it, and if they don't find it, then it isn't newsworthy," he once told me. "I didn't need public relations."

Williams helped uncover wrongdoing by William Boyle, the chairman of the Democratic National Committee, and, separately, Guy Gabrielson, the chairman of the Republican National Committee; both men resigned. Such evenhandedness caused Peter Wyden of *Coronet* magazine to call Williams the "politician without politics." As Williams put it, "A man that's going to be crooked is not going to be crooked just because he's a Republican or a Democrat."

In March 1949, Williams announced on the Senate floor, "Mr. President, I have information that, if the books of the Commodity Credit Corporation were examined, we would find that over $350 million is unaccounted for." The Secretary of Agriculture, Charles Brannan, publicly rebuked Williams, but it turned out that Williams was dead right. Eventually, 131 warehousemen who had converted millions of dollars' worth of grain to their own use were charged with criminal conversion or embezzlement.

When the Internal Revenue Service informed Williams that he had been delinquent in paying his income taxes, he investigated and discovered that not only had he properly paid his taxes, but an IRS employee had juggled taxpayer accounts (Williams's among them) and embezzled $30,000. Williams kept asking questions, and eventually 125 IRS employees were convicted and 388 were fired or quit, including the top five IRS officials. *Look* magazine called Williams "the taxpayer's unofficial prosecutor." Williams, according to the magazine, "single-handedly has unearthed so many administration scandals that thousands of taxpayers have come to regard him as their personal ambassador."

Williams was one of the first to raise questions about suspicious ties between Sherman Adams, President Eisenhower's closest adviser, and Bernard Goldfine, a wealthy Boston industrialist. Adams later resigned. Years later, in the 1960s, Williams exposed the criminal exploits of Bobby Baker, the powerful secretary to the Senate Democrats and Lyndon Johnson's protégé. Baker had amassed a personal fortune of $2.1 million by the age of thirty-four on an annual salary of $19,600. Johnson's close association with Baker never became a significant political issue for the President, but in 1964 LBJ was terribly agitated about Williams's pursuit of the Baker matter. We now know from Michael Beschloss's 1997 book *Taking Charge* and its transcripts of the Johnson White House tapes that at one point Johnson got Senate Majority Leader Mike Mansfield to shut down the Senate's investigation of Baker. Johnson also said to Mansfield on May 14, 1964, "We'll just have to go after Mr. Williams. . . . He's a mean, vicious man." Whether Johnson actually followed through is unknown, but as John Barron reported in *Reader's Digest* back in 1965, the heat directed at Williams was enormous. Baker and his cronies tried to "silence Williams's sources, to deceive him with false leads, to smear his character, even involve his family." Strangers from Washington began showing up in tiny Millsboro, Delaware, asking questions about Williams. The IRS summoned the Senator to explain his 1963 tax return, which of course had been properly computed and filed. *The Washington Evening Star* reported that Williams's mail was even intercepted. "The Senate should be totally outraged," the newspaper said in an editorial. "Obviously, someone high in the Executive branch issued the instructions for this monitoring. Nothing of the sort, as far as anyone knows, has ever been done before."

"I have plenty of time . . . and I am not about to be intimidated," the beleaguered Williams, sounding a bit like Jimmy Stewart in *Mr. Smith Goes to Washington,* warned his colleagues. "In fact, my curiosity and determination grow as resistance intensifies." Eventually, Bobby Baker was convicted of theft, income-tax evasion, and conspiracy.

E. I. du Pont de Nemours and Company has been the biggest employer in Delaware for as long as anyone can remember. When special legislation was introduced to help the huge, multibillion-dollar corporation avoid taxes after Du Pont lost a court decision, the man who led the fight against Du Pont was Delaware Senator Williams.

Williams was willing to stand up to any President, Republican or Democrat, and the most powerful corporate interests in his own backyard. Throughout his political career, he refused to accept political contributions but instead ran his campaigns through the state Republican Party. He had no campaign manager and no campaign organization. Today if a person of Williams's modest background expressed an interest in running for Congress, he or she would probably have trouble getting anyone in either party to listen.

John Williams and Philip Hart could not have been more different from each other politically (a conservative Republican and a liberal Democrat), geographically (Delaware and Michigan), and professionally (the owner of a small business and a big-city lawyer). But both men were dead honest, modest, and unpretentious.

An infantryman wounded on D-Day during World War II, Hart had earlier earned a bachelor's degree at Georgetown University and a law degree at the University of Michigan. Before entering politics, he worked in a Detroit law firm. As a novice political candidate in 1950, biographer Michael O'Brien noted in *Philip Hart: The Conscience of the Senate,* Hart did not interact well with strangers, was reluctant to ask people to vote for him, and sometimes even apologized for running for office. Hart lost his first election, for Secretary of State, and following a stint as a U.S. Attorney, he was elected to statewide office as Michigan's lieutenant governor in 1954 and was reelected in 1956. He was elected to the Senate in 1958 and served there until his death from cancer in 1976.

Today a Senate office building is named after Hart, and inscribed in marble is the following: "This building is dedicated by his colleagues to the memory of Philip A. Hart with affection, respect, and esteem. A man of incorruptible integrity and personal courage strengthened by inner grace and outer gentleness, he elevated politics to a level of purity that will forever be an example to every elected official. He advanced the cause of human justice, promoted the welfare of the common man, and improved the quality of life. His humility and ethics earned him his place as the conscience of the Senate."

Hart was known as an author and sponsor of important legislation in the areas of civil rights (he was a leader in the fight for the 1956 Voting Rights Act), antitrust enforcement, and consumer and environmental protection. But most unusual, then and today, Hart frequently took difficult, courageous stands on issues directly against his own political self-interest. In late 1968, for example, a staff aide on the Senate Antitrust and Monopoly Subcommittee, which Hart chaired, proposed that the subcommittee investigate the automobile industry. As recounted in O'Brien's book, Hart met the aide, Donald Randall, in the hallway:

" 'Don, I understand you're recommending we go into investigation of the automobile business,' Hart observed.

" 'Yes, sir,' said Randall.

" 'Do you know that I'm running for reelection next year?'

" 'Yes, sir.'

" 'Do you know I'm from Michigan?'

" 'Yes, sir.'

" 'You know that the biggest business in my state is the auto industry, don't you?'

" 'Yes, sir.'

" 'And do you know that if I lose, you lose?'

" 'Yes, sir.'

" 'Do you still want to do it?' Hart asked.

" 'Yes, sir,' Randall replied.

" 'Well,' Hart said, 'go do it.' "

For more than a year, Hart's subcommittee held hearings on abuses in the automobile-repair business. Hundreds of angry car owners, frustrated mechanics, and auto-industry experts testified about the rampant incompetence and exploding costs in the multibillion-dollar business. The owner of an automobile-diagnostic center in Denver testified that tests on 5,000 cars in his shop revealed that only one of every 100 cars was being repaired properly.

One of the outcomes of Hart's hearings was the 1970 Motor Vehicle Information and Cost Savings Act, which mandated fragility standards for assembling automobiles. *Motor Trend* magazine said, "Senator Hart is a man of courage. To attack a problem as large and politically explosive as automobile repair, especially for a Senator from Michigan, the home of the auto industry, is no small undertaking."

Hart was also upset by monopolistic practices in the communications and newspaper industry, and he held hearings on the subject. He was one of the few dissenting voices against the Newspaper Preservation Act in 1970, which gave a special exemption to competing newspapers that merged their business operations and fixed their advertising rates. "Swift congressional rescue of the publishers," Hart observed, "must make fascinating reading for the blacks who, until the 1964 Civil Rights Act, had waited decades for relief from court convictions for eating in certain restaurants and hotels."

The principled actions of Williams and Hart were gutsy and unusual in their time, but today they are almost unimaginable. In 1996, for example, Congress passed the historic Telecommunications Act, a big wet kiss to media corporations, cable companies,

II

Investigative reporter Morton Mintz remembers former Democratic Senator Philip Hart as "so principled, he even went up against his own constituents."

telephone companies, and the computer industry. In 1997, Congress agreed to a multibillion-dollar giveaway of our digital airwaves, after receiving $7.6 million in campaign contributions from the national broadcasting industry in the previous campaign cycle. The broadcasting industry also deployed a platoon of more than 174 lobbyists to twist arms on Capitol Hill. And legislation requiring the television networks to offer free time to political candidates somehow never made it anywhere near the House or Senate floor.

What politician today would so frontally take on the news media? Or the most powerful economic interest in his or her state? There are occasional, inspiring glimpses of steely independence, as when Henry Gonzalez of Texas, who then chaired the House Banking Committee, held hearings into the savings-and-loan fiasco that was abetted by so many of his fellow Democrats. Or when Jim Leach of Iowa, the chairman of the House Banking Committee, voted not to reelect Newt Gingrich, a fellow Republican, as House Speaker because of his ethical improprieties—one of only nine Republicans, and the only committee chairman, to stand up to Gingrich.

But fairly or unfairly, in the grand picture we have of Capitol Hill, such moments seem fleeting. Veteran investigative reporter Morton Mintz, who broke many important stories for *The Washington Post* over nearly three decades and who is the author of ten books, remembers Hart as one of "a significant number, even if a small minority, of outstanding human beings" in the Senate in the 1960s and early 1970s. "Hart was so principled," Mintz told the center, "he even went up against his own constituents." Mintz assessed the issue of courage in Congress by saying, "Things are a hell of a lot worse today."

Whether we are talking about the investigative aggressiveness and thoroughness of congressional hearings or the willingness of

Members of Congress to take on the huge economic interests, today our elected representatives generally are gutless in both word and deed.

With literally thousands of multibillion-dollar multinational giants making the world their playground, and with Washington beset by thousands upon thousands *more* lobbyists representing these and many other interests, Congress is increasingly in danger of becoming an auction house where public policies are sold to the highest bidder. That is why America desperately needs courageous, independent leadership and integrity in the political process—elected officials who are not cowed by the interests, and who have the backbone and conscience to do the right thing for the country.

We desperately need leaders in the mold of Philip Hart and John Williams.

2

||||||●||||||

Going, Going, Gone

N OT EVERYTHING IS FOR SALE IN WASHINGTON. IT IS REASSURING, for example, that you can still stroll on the Mall among the visual symbols of our democracy, visiting the Lincoln Memorial, the Washington Monument, and the Jefferson Memorial for free. They, of course, belong to us and sit on public land.

Are these the last bastions of propriety, dignity, and honor left in our nation's capital? Apparently they are, when you consider how red-carpet access to many of the nation's other precious landmarks has been sold.

According to investigative reporter Sheila Kaplan, in the summer of 1995, Republican Party "Eagles"—donors giving $20,000 or more—were led on private "midnight tours" inside the Capitol, which is closed to the public at that hour. Robert Dole spoke to the "Eagles" and even gave them a special tour of his State Majority Leader office. We all know that many of the Democratic Party's wealthiest donors were invited to sleep overnight in the Lincoln Bedroom of the Clinton White House (the family quarters are off-limits to the public). Less well known is Senate Minority Leader Tom Daschle's 1997 fund-raising event at Mount Rushmore in South Dakota. According to Ruth Marcus of *The Washington Post*, for $5,000 each, a group of well-heeled Democratic party donors, along with Daschle, were led on a hike up to the top of George

Washington's head by the national park superintendent himself. If ordinary folks try that, they're fined $500.

Just as these magnificent memorials are symbols to the rest of the world of the United States' remarkable success, our politicians' exploitation of them to raise campaign cash and to reward their patrons symbolizes what's wrong with our political process. Laws and rules are bent to accommodate the wealthy—and the American people are excluded, bystanders to their own democracy. There was a time when our politicians had more dignity and respect for the public trust, when former officials would never have contemplated hawking corn chips and other products on television commercials. Now more than ever, our elected officials and their political parties are in a headlong, unabashed rush for money—anywhere, anytime, from anyone. Their coarse ambition cheapens them, demeans their offices, and further diminishes public respect for politicians generally. And if they will sell exclusive access to our most famous, sacred national treasures, what else do you think they will sell in closed-door, committee markup sessions and on page 823 of some almost unreadable tax bill in conference at two o'clock in the morning?

But it is not only the special goodies given out selectively and secretively that are the problem. One of the things that surprised us the most is how often Congress simply leaves matters of critical importance to millions of Americans off its agenda. Sometimes that plainly happens because of the money and power of the interests involved. As political scientist and author Michael Parenti once wrote, "One of the most important aspects of power is not to prevail in a struggle but to predetermine the agenda of struggle—to determine whether certain questions ever reach the competition stage."

As we illustrated in *Place Your Bets,* a Center report published in June 1996, the legalized gambling industry in the United States is exploding in revenue and importance and already has managed to predetermine the policy agenda. By one estimate, Americans spent $482 billion on legal wagers in 1994, an increase of 2,800 percent since 1974. By 1994, gross revenues in the gambling industry trumped box-office receipts from motion pictures and revenues from spectator sports, theme parks, cruise ships, and recorded music combined. More than 200 Native American tribes have set up gambling operations. Not surprisingly, campaign contributions from gambling interests have shot up, with at least $6 million given to the two major political parties, presidential candidates, and congressional candidates in the 1995–96 election cycle alone.

Not only is there no policy about gambling today at the federal level, but there is also no serious legislative proposal to tax gambling profits as a potential new source of revenues at the federal level. In 1994, when President Clinton proposed a 4 percent excise tax on gambling revenues to help pay for his plan to overhaul the nation's welfare system, it died before the dice were even rolled. The gambling industry kicked into high gear, forming the American Gaming Association, headed by Frank Fahrenkopf, the former chairman of the Republican National Committee. The association's first organizational meeting, in Beverly Hills, was attended by executives from twenty companies in the gambling industry, including Hilton Hotels Corporation; Mirage Resorts, Inc.; and Circus Circus Enterprises, Inc. "They had billion-dollar investments in casinos," Fahrenkopf told us, "and they had no representation [in Washington]." Alas, that is no longer a problem for them. By 1995, gambling interests had, in addition to the American Gaming Association, at least seventeen firms lobbying on their behalf in Washington. According to 1996 lobbying registration records, the gambling industry employs more than 180 lobbyists.

Representative Frank Wolf, a Republican from Virginia, has waged a lonely, losing fight against the pro-gambling forces. He told us that he thinks the industry "has attempted to corrupt the process up here." Not only did he cite the remarkable sums of money going to both political parties and to presidential candidates, and all of the lobbyists, but Wolf also said that there is now a Congressional Gaming Caucus. "Twenty years ago, a Member of Congress wouldn't have taken [gambling-industry money], wouldn't have wanted to be in the room with a gambler, and now there's a gambler caucus," Wolf said. "Now they don't call it gambling, they call it gaming. But gaming is kind of the respectable name for it. It's gambling."

But important subjects sometimes never make it to the Senate or House floor, to public view and discourse in Washington, because there are no moneyed interests pushing them. Take, for example (as we do in Chapter 19), children, who do not have a say in what goes on in Washington. Today many child labor laws are all but ignored. Old classrooms and school and public libraries have decaying walls, pipes, lights, and electrical systems. Programs that feed millions of hungry children have been downsized. Public-health immunization programs for childhood diseases have been cut. The voices and cries of children today, particularly poor children, are lost in the well-orchestrated din of Washington.

Several of the Members of Congress we interviewed have noticed who gets heard in Washington and who doesn't.

"When I served on the Banking Committee . . . and I used to look around the room, I'd see all the big financial interests represented," Democratic Representative Marcy Kaptur of Ohio recalled. "But you think about all the consumers who are angry with the fees that are being placed on their transactions, the whole question of competition in the industry—now we're moving into this world where we have banking and insurance becoming an integrated operation. And you didn't get anybody out there who worried about that. Citicorp had its witness, and you had the big banks from Ohio [that] would come in, but never the customers." Kaptur also discovered that she had received about the least amount of campaign money from banking interests of any member on the committee, which wasn't much of a mystery to her. "I knew it was because I didn't always vote their position."

Senator Paul Wellstone of Minnesota noticed the similarly disproportionate influence of vested interests:

||||||||||||||||||||||||||||||||||||||||||||||||

Now Members of Congress have become "direct marketers and retail salesmen, as opposed to legislators," lobbyist Tommy Boggs said.

||||||||||||||||||||||||||||||||||||||||||||||||

"Take the telecommunications bill. The anteroom, the room outside the Senate chamber, was lined wall to wall with people. I couldn't find truth, beauty, and justice anywhere. It was like one group representing billions here and another group representing billions there. Maybe there were one or two people trying to fight for consumers.

"It is, I think, a very, very distorted pattern of power, and in that sense there is real corruption. But it is not the wrongdoing of individual officeholders. It is systemic—a huge imbalance between elites, whether it be the political class or the economic notables, and the vast majority of people. That is what's so scary. I mean that the whole standard of each person counting as one and no more than one is so seriously violated, not just in terms of money, but in terms of who pays lobbyists, who is here in Washington, who has the expertise, who has access to media, who has prestige."

It is worth exploring when and how the patterns of power in the nation's capital changed. The most seismic shift of the latter half of this century came in the mid-1970s. The Watergate scandal proved to be a watershed in which a new generation of reformers was elected to Congress. After years of bottled-up frustration over the Vietnam War and Watergate, an astounding number of fresh majority faces, seventy-five Democrats (then more than a quarter of all House Democrats), entered the House of Representatives in 1975, just months after President Nixon resigned. The class of '74 included such now-recognizable names as Max Baucus, Christopher Dodd, Tom Harkin, George Miller, the late Paul Tsongas, Henry Waxman, and many more. As Miller told political analyst William Schneider in *The Atlantic Monthly:* "We had a real sense of urgency. We thought we were special. We came here to take the Bastille."

What they did was provide the votes to enable veteran reformers to finally end the seniority system and make committee chairpersons responsible to the party caucus. The reformers took over the party caucus and passed a rule that committee chairpersons had to be confirmed by secret ballot in the caucus. Three powerful Southern committee chairmen were ousted. The number of subcommittees increased substantially, and the entire committee system became more democratized.

Just months earlier, the most significant political reforms in U.S. history had become law. Limits of $1,000 were placed on how much individuals could contribute to congressional candidates for each primary or general election. Public-disclosure requirements were improved, and the new information was administered centrally by a newly created Federal Election Commission.

Over the past two decades, however, the most powerful economic interests have successfully adapted to the new Washington landscape. The well-intentioned reforms have been rendered all but ineffectual. Even though there are limits on campaign contributions and internally Congress is more democratic and there is more sunshine than in the past—from C-SPAN television coverage of House and Senate proceedings to campaign and personal financial disclosure records—one fundamental reality has never changed: Then and now, the nation's most powerful interests control Congress.

Not everyone, of course, sees it that way, and who better to consult about what has been going on inside the hen house than the fox himself?

Named after his famous father—Thomas (Hale) Boggs, the House Majority Leader whose airplane went down in Alaska in 1972—Tommy Boggs first registered as a lobbyist in September 1967 or 1968. "The reason I remember that," he said, "was (a) I did it myself, which I haven't done since, and (b) I was like the sixty-first or sixty-second person to register that year." He went on to say: "The reason you had sixty-some-odd lobbyists in the late sixties is because you had about ten people who ran the government. Each of them had about six friends. . . . Now you have five hundred and thirty-five Congressmen who think they run the government and you have fourteen thousand lobbyists. The system is totally different." Today, as the managing partner of a firm that bears his name—Patton, Boggs—Tommy Boggs makes at least $1 million a year. The firm represents more than 180 corporate clients and employs approximately 100 registered lobbyists.

These days, political power in Washington is much more diffuse than it was three decades ago, and not only the number but also the importance of lobbyists has increased. To Boggs, ending seniority and bringing sunshine into the process of government was "probably the worst thing [Congress] could do," he said. "That totally destroyed the leadership and buddy system. When they did things behind closed doors—you know, 'I'll vote for your levy in Louisiana if you vote for my potato crop in Vermont'—there was no rationale to that. It was a buddy system and a leadership system. And all of a sudden there were cameras and they had to justify why they're from Vermont voting for a levy in Louisiana. So they didn't vote for it."

There remains considerable secrecy today in Congress, making public accountability quite difficult, but a new dynamic involving information has evolved. The more public scrutiny, the greater the need to develop logical rationales for public positions, to marshal facts in a compelling fashion. "Now even the old guard had to look smart," Boggs said. "It created a great demand for information, which probably changed the system more than anything else. . . . The Washington lobbying community learned how to start conveying information, and Members [of Congress] started learning that they could get a lot quicker, better info from the outside than the inside."

> In 1997 freshman lawmaker Jerry Weller of Illinois offered a check from his own PAC to any Republican colleagues who would attend a special breakfast promoting his candidacy for a leadership post in the House. Weller, who lost his bid, gave out $118,000.

Patton, Boggs and other Washington lobbying firms provide up-to-the-minute information to Capitol Hill lawmakers and Executive Branch officials on every conceivable issue from utility deregulation to nuclear-waste disposal. Information is indeed power and telling a Member of Congress—gratis—what his or her constituents think based on the latest, expensive tracking poll is valuable intelligence. And there is a macro political effect of this deluge of data, in which substance is subordinated to the superfluous.

Leon Panetta—former Representative, director of the Office of Management and Budget, and White House chief of staff—believes that the "Information Age explosion" has helped erode interpersonal relationships among Members of Congress and the overall respect for Congress as an institution. "There is this instantaneous ability now . . . to be able to 'spin' a story," Panetta said. "Whether you're using the Internet or talk shows or CNN, there is a remarkable capacity to move information quickly. I think both parties have viewed that as an opportunity to gain an advantage over the other, [one] that moves them away from the substance of the issue that they're dealing with to kind of 'hit-and-run' quickly on issues and try to score their thirty-second sound-bite advantage. And if they've done that, that becomes their mark of success, rather than: Have they done something important for the country?"

Because of the need to move information quickly and the increased competition for power and position, Panetta said that a politician has to raise a lot of money. "You need to hire your consultants and your pollsters and your focus groups," he said, adding that Members of Congress "now more than ever turn to these consultants and pollsters that basically tell them what the public wants, and then that's what they do." It is disconcerting that politicians cannot figure out what the public thinks without such latter-day, expensive soothsayers, many of whom are simultaneously making millions working for their other clients in the private sector—mammoth corporations bent on influencing government decisions.

Who helps Members of Congress raise all that money? The lobbyists, of course. Boggs said he considers "ludicrous" the amount of time candidates have to spend ingratiating themselves with lobbyists because of the money chase. He said that in the old days—pre-1974—Members of Congress would rely on the chairmen or ranking minority members of important committees, such as House Ways and Means, to raise a couple of hundred thousand dollars for them. "You didn't have to go out there and bust your hump raising money from every grandmother in your district," he said. "You were beholden to the chairman of the committee or the Speaker or what have you." Now Members of Congress have become "direct marketers and retail salesmen, as opposed to legislators," he said. "So their relationship to the leadership evaporated when they started to have to raise their own money, build their own constituencies, and go out and hustle."

But lobbyists are not the only people helping Members of Congress raise money from special interests. The bad old days of back rooms, cigar smoke, and a handful of men of privilege running the country may be gone, but leaders of both chambers in both parties actually continue to ingratiate themselves by dispensing campaign cash to their colleagues. One of the ways in which campaign money passes from Member to Member is via "leadership" political action committees. According to the Center for Responsive Politics, at least fifty-one lawmakers have such PACs today. In the 1995–96 election cycle, House Speaker Newt Gingrich dispensed at least $751,500 to Republican candidates from his Monday Morning PAC. House Majority Leader Dick Armey gave at least $733,558 to Republican candidates from his Majority Leader's Fund PAC. House Minority Leader Richard Gephardt gave at least $508,645 to Democratic candidates from his Effective Government Committee PAC. Senate Majority Leader Trent Lott, through his New Republican Majority Fund, gave at least $655,142 to GOP candidates.

Just as Harry Truman once said, "People just don't give money away for no reason," Capitol Hill lawmakers just don't spread campaign money around to one another to be generous. *The Chicago Tribune* reported in 1997, for example, that a freshman lawmaker, Jerry Weller of Illinois, offered a check from his own PAC to any Republican colleagues who would attend a special breakfast promoting his candidacy for a leadership post in the House. Weller, who lost his bid, gave out $118,000.

Congressional leaders are perfectly willing to pass out special-interest money as well. Take the case of John Boehner of Ohio, the chairman of the House Republican Conference. His leadership PAC, Freedom Project, distributed $202,721 in the 1995–96 election cycle. But in the summer of 1995, he passed out half a dozen checks from tobacco interests to his fellow Members on the floor of the House. The matter enraged some of his fellow Republicans but stayed hushed up for nearly a year. When Bob Herbert, a columnist for *The New York Times,* found out about it and asked Barry Jackson, Boehner's chief of staff, why his boss had committed the sacrilege of handing out checks in the House chamber of the Capitol, Jackson said matter-of-factly, "The floor is where the Members meet with each other." Unfortunately, this practice was common for years; new House rules now forbid it.

Besides both national political parties, each party has campaign committees in the House and Senate that cumulatively raised at least $196.1 million in the 1995–96 election cycle, compared with $137.8 million in 1993–94 and $147.3 million in 1991–92. The National Republican Congressional Committee raised by far the most money, $74.2 million, followed by the National Republican Senatorial Committee, at $64.5 million. The Democratic Senate Campaign Committee raised $30.8 million, while the Democratic Congressional Campaign Committee raised $26.6 million.

Representative John Linder, the current chairman of the National Republican Campaign Committee, is opposed to any limits on political contributions. "You have to have money to get your ideas out," he told us. "You can have all the brilliance in the world, and if you can't get to a broader audience, you're not going to win. We urge people to make phone calls for us and to help us sell tables for major fund-raisers, and we have senior leadership people going around the country to campaign for other Members. . . . For the most part, we ask people to contribute, and we don't make any threats." When it was pointed out that House Majority Whip Tom DeLay is well known as "The Hammer" for his repeated directives to contributors as to how much to give and to which party's candidates, Linder replied: "What Tom did was not very wise in my judgment, and he probably wishes he hadn't done it. I don't do that. I'm the chairman of the committee."

But we found that the involvement of legislative leaders in the money chase is relevant to the dynamic of who becomes or does not become a party leader in Con-

> **H**ouse Majority Whip Tom DeLay is known as "The Hammer" for his repeated directives to contributors as to how much to give and to which party's candidates.

gress—and has permeated the internal daily discourse itself. "Early on in my time in the Congress, I used to go to these very small whip meetings with [House Speaker] Tip O'Neill, [where we would] basically talk about the issues that were coming up that week, the votes, who had to work the votes, etcetera," Panetta told us. "As time went on . . . they spent more and more time at each of those whip meetings talking more about who had

|||||||||||||||||||||||||||||||||||||||||||||||||||||||||||||||||||||||||

Marcy Kaptur, a Democratic Representative from Ohio, said, "Sometimes I feel crestfallen as a Member because I've thought of running for positions in leadership, but I don't. I'm not a big money-raiser [for the party]. You see why people rise in these institutions."

raised what as opposed to dealing with particular issues that were coming up."

The Center for Public Integrity obtained an internal tally sheet of the Democratic Congressional Campaign Committee, headed "DCCC 1997 Members' Participation" with five columns below— "Member," "Date," "1997 Dues," "Indiv Mny [Money] Raised," and "Non Trdtnl PAC/Corp"—and the names of 210 Democratic Representatives.

"You're publicly embarrassed on a regular basis if you're not one of the funders," Kaptur told us. "I don't like being made to feel like I'm a lesser Member because I can't muster the money. And that's how you're made to feel. . . . The money is absolutely central to what happens in here. And I have to tell you, sometimes I feel crestfallen as a Member because I've thought of running for positions in leadership, but I don't. I'm not a big money-raiser. . . . You see why people rise in these institutions."

Kaptur is immensely popular in her working-class district in Toledo, Ohio: She was reelected in 1996 with 77 percent of the vote. For her own reelection campaigns, she consistently raises half of what the average successful race for the House costs today. (She spent less than $300,000 in 1996.) Besides her interest and prowess in fund-raising, however, she would seem to have all the necessary other credentials for leadership. A respected, hardworking, former urban planner and Carter White House aide serving her eighth term in the House, Kaptur is best known for leading the opposition to the North American Free Trade Agreement in 1993 and the "fast-track" trade legislation in 1997. In August 1996, Ross Perot asked her to be his running mate. She declined.

Another veteran lawmaker from across the aisle also expressed outrage at the leadership-money equation. Jim Leach of Iowa, a twenty-year veteran of the House who chairs the Banking Committee, told us that it "is deeply offensive to me when leadership raises money from PACs all over America and then gives it out to other Members seeking election or reelection, therefore indebting those Members to them as they reseek leadership positions." What is particularly troubling to him, Leach said, is the fact that these are not only the people "who are setting the agenda for Congress, but some are [in line] to be President of the United States in certain emergency situations."

One point on which virtually everyone agrees is that because of the diffusion of power, the proliferation of lobbyists, the increasingly sophisticated manipulation of information and the news media, and the unprecedented amounts of money now pouring into Washington, it is infinitely easier today for special interests to stop legislation than it was in the past.

There is no better example of this phenomenon than the failed attempt at comprehensive health-care reform. Presidents Truman, Nixon, and Carter talked about reforming the nation's health-care system, only to be frustrated by the entrenched medical establishment. Now add President Clinton to that list. From 1989 to 1992, scores of polls said that the American people supported major health-care reform. The then-governor of Arkansas made it a key issue in his 1992 presidential campaign, and in September 1993 he unveiled his plan for a comprehensive overhaul of the nation's health-care system. Exceedingly complicated and poorly packaged, the plan was proposed to the American people by the Clinton White House. In the end, the Clinton health-care team was hoisted on its own petard of arrogance. But that aside, what happened during the debate epitomizes how Washington—and specifically Congress—really works.

In 1993 and 1994, as we documented in our study *Well-Healed: Inside Lobbying for Health-Care Reform,* hundreds of special interests cumulatively spent well in excess of $100 million to influence the outcome of this public-policy issue. At least ninety-seven lobbying, public-relations, and law firms were hired to influence the debate. Those firms and their clients hired at least eighty former Capitol Hill lawmakers and aides and Executive Branch officials to help do their bidding. In the same two-year span, organizations with health-care-related interests have given more than $25 million to congressional campaigns. In 1992 and 1993, more than eighty-five Members of Congress went on 181 trips sponsored by the health-care industry to seventy-three cities in the United States, as well as to Puerto Rico, France, and Jamaica. The largest trip-giver by far was the American Medical Association, which sponsored fifty-five junkets to "educate" Members of Congress on health-care issues. We also found that more than forty lawmakers (including their spouses or their dependent children) held health-care-related stock in 1993 while serving on committees with jurisdiction over health-care legislation.

The health-care interests added a new weapon to their public-relations and lobbying arsenal: television advertising. Groups such as the Democratic and Republican National Committees, the National Restaurant Association, the Health Care Reform Project, the American Association of Retired Persons, and the Families USA Foundation bought airtime. Altogether, according to Kathleen Hall Jamieson, the dean of the Annenberg School of Communication at the University of Pennsylvania, forty-nine groups spent more than $50 million on TV, print, and direct-mail campaigns about health-care reform. No series of commercials was more successful than the "Harry and Louise" ads paid for by the Health Insurance Association of America (HIAA), a trade group of more than 300 small and medium-sized insurance companies. Indeed, these ads—in which an angst-ridden husband and wife discussed the real-life pitfalls of health-care reform—are widely considered to have been a key reason why public support for Clinton's health-care plan dropped by a precipitous eighteen points in the six months after it was introduced.

The Health Insurance Association of America was led by Willis Gradison, a former nine-term Representative from Ohio who in early 1993 literally left the House on Sunday and became a well-paid insurance lobbyist on Monday. Gradison and his organization were determined to dampen the nation's enthusiasm for health-care reform and used the commercials as a blunt instrument to affect public policy. How? In the spring of 1994, Dan Rostenkowski, then the chairman of the House Ways and Means Committee, asked for a meeting with his old committee colleague Gradison, and after fifteen hours of conversation over many weeks, they struck a deal. The HIAA would refrain from running the devastating "Harry and Louise" commercials in key states that might be detrimental to certain committee members, and in exchange Rostenkowski agreed to modify health-care policies affecting the insurance industry. The deal unraveled when Rostenkowski was indicted, the ads resumed immediately, and months later Clinton's health-care plan itself was dead. The episode was the first time anyone can remember that there was a quid pro quo relationship between advertising and specific provisions in legislation.

Another intensely focused group, the National Federation of Independent Business (NFIB), opposed the Clinton plan from the beginning and devoted about two-thirds of its annual budget—approximately $40 million—to killing it. According to John Motley, who was then the NFIB's top lobbyist, the 600,000-member organization mounted "the largest single focused grassroots lobbying campaign we have ever done, which spans two years and two million pieces of mail." Motley boasted that he had ten lobbyists working the Senate and House. "Our structure is very similar to the White House," he said. "I copied it, back in the early eighties. . . . Actually, I've got more people working in the House than they do . . . I think they have about four. I've got six, and we'll probably expand."

More than 600 interest groups gnawed away at Clinton's health-care plan, but the HIAA and the NFIB were the most effective. "Some groups aren't well represented here at all," Gradison acknowledged to us in a reflective moment. "I don't mean there are zero advocates, but there aren't a lot of advocates for the poor." Or as his archrival in the health-care drama, White House senior adviser Ira Magaziner, told us: "The real issue is not all the groups that made their voices heard. It is all the people without an organized voice." He went on to explain that few groups represented the roughly 40 million Americans without health-care insurance or the 80 million Americans with existing medical conditions. "There was no lobbyist for the one hundred and twenty million Americans with lifetime limits on their insurance policies that could cause their insurance to run out when they need coverage most."

The poor and the uninsured do not organize "phone trees"

and action alerts, mobilizing tens of thousands of activists nation-wide in a matter of hours and days. They do not have millions of dollars to spend on television commercials. They do not have the cold cash to descend upon our nation's capital from all over the nation, buttonholing Members of Congress about their concerns.

The pharmaceutical companies, insurance companies, and other powerful multibillion-dollar health-related interests were delighted that the latest resident of 1600 Pennsylvania Avenue to carp about health-care reform had been silenced. They have seen Presidents and Members of Congress come and go, and they view them smugly as amateur interlopers. Two years of national discussion and thousands of news-media stories resulted in . . . nothing. Once again, the status quo was preserved by the interests. And the most expensive health-care system in the world—unaffordable to millions of American families—was left intact and immensely profitable for its industry proponents.

In general, the interests and their big-time Washington lobby-ists are as happy as pigs in slop these days, and they have nothing but the highest praise for their reliable friends in Congress. Tom Donohue, president and chief executive officer of the U.S. Chamber of Commerce, told us, "I want to treat these ladies and gentlemen with great respect. They have a harder job than I do. . . . You can't buy the Members of this Congress. You can buy some access and some concern, but you can't buy them." Veteran tax lobbyist Charls Walker said, "Congress today is head and shoulders over Congress when I came to town—that would have been in 1959—in terms of intelligence, in terms of working hard, in terms of dedication, in terms of integrity, and . . . in terms of sobriety, which I mean both literally and figuratively. Because in the old days, liquor was an important ingredient."

But all the praise belies the grim reality that the interests and their lobbyists are in control perhaps as much as they have ever been. "I think Congress is more manipulable today than it was in the seventies," Abner Mikva—former Representative, U.S. Court of Appeals Judge, and White House counsel to President Clinton—told us. "I think it responds to grosser and more corrupting influences than it did back in the seventies. By corrupting, I don't just mean money."

Nevertheless, Leach told us, he does worry about the corrupting influence of money. "I think it's increased and it's becoming accepted," he said. "The more it's become accepted, the more rotten it is because you have an assumption that that's the system and therefore there are no issues of right or wrong."

In the peculiar ethos of Washington today, it is not right or wrong to lead wealthy patrons on "midnight tours" of the Capitol, to give fat-cat donors a night in the White House Lincoln Bedroom, or to hold a fund-raising event at Mount Rushmore. Those and many more serious, substantive favors are merely the price of power.

3

|||||●|||||

The Ways, the Means,
and the Ends

IN THE MERCENARY CULTURE OF WASHINGTON, THERE ARE MANY WAYS to win friends and influence people on Capitol Hill—the net effect of which is to initiate, change, or prevent public-policy decisions that have direct relevance to our daily lives. Here are a dozen of the most common approaches used by special interests to worm themselves into the lives of lawmakers and get their way—the effects of which are likely to be felt by you:

• **Campaign Cash.** The 1996 congressional elections were the most expensive in U.S. history, and overall, candidates and parties raised a record $2.4 billion, according to the Center for Responsive Politics. The longer a lawmaker is in Washington, the more the campaign cash comes from outside his or her state or congressional district. For example, only one of then-Senator Robert Dole's top ten career patrons was actually from his home state of Kansas. In 1996, a fourth of the $791 million in campaign contributions raised by Members of Congress came from political action committees operated by corporations, trade and professional associations, labor unions, and the like. Although each PAC can give a candidate no more than $5,000 for a primary election and another $5,000 for the general election, PACs tend to run in packs, and a single industry can easily channel $100,000 or more to a single lawmaker. And even though individuals can give no more than $1,000 per election, employees of a single firm—the partners, say, in a Washington law firm—can "bundle" their checks together and deliver them to a grateful lawmaker. Former Democratic Senator Bill Bradley of New Jersey, a self-proclaimed campaign reformer, was the "King of Bundling" in his last reelection campaign, according to the Center for Responsive Politics. The reports that candidates file with the Federal Election Commission are sprinkled with the inexplicable examples of six-year-old children writing $1,000 checks to congressional campaigns. Capitol Hill lawmakers also benefit in a big way from "soft money," the unlimited money that flows to the national political parties and the congressional campaign committees under the ruse of "party-building activities" and such. Much of this money comes from interests with business before Congress, and their in-house and hired-gun lobbyists host fund-raising events for Capitol Hill lawmakers practically every night.

In the appendix section titled Top Ten Career Patrons of Congressional Leaders, we identify the career patrons of thirty-two of the most powerful lawmakers on Capitol Hill. Using data from the Federal Election Commission and the Center for Responsive Politics, we have studied, sorted, and otherwise scrutinized a full decade's worth of campaign contributions to Members of Congress. Politicians often like to say that they just do not know who their financial supporters are, but it is virtually unfathomable that a lawmaker does not know his or her ten most significant benefactors over five election cycles.

||||||||||||||||||||||||||||||||||||||||||||

The reports that candidates file with the Federal Election Commission are sprinkled with the inexplicable examples of six-year-old children writing $1,000 checks to congressional campaigns.

||||||||||||||||||||||||||||||||||||||||||||

House Speaker Newt Gingrich, for example, knows how to take care of his patrons. Over the past ten years, Terry Kohler and his wife, Mary, have been Gingrich's most generous supporters, contributing a total of $816,107 to Gingrich's campaign; to his new PAC, the Monday Morning PAC; and to GOPAC, which for years managed to skirt federal election laws, keeping its top donors secret. The Kohlers, who are from Sheboygan, Wisconsin, own Windway Capital Corporation. Windway

Capital has diverse interests, including Enzopac, Inc., a maker of packaged food products; Vollrath Company, Inc., which manufactures stainless-steel ware for households and institutions; and North Marine Group, Inc., which makes sails and other components for luxury yachts. Windway also owns companies that make sailboats. Its boat businesses reflect Terry Kohler's interest in yachting; he owns a seventy-foot yacht, the *Cynosure*.

Kohler and fellow members of the leisure class were dealt a blow in 1990, when the budget deal added a 10 percent tax on purchases of luxury yachts valued at more than $100,000. Which perhaps explains why Newt Gingrich—then a back-bencher—took to the floor in July 1991 with, among others, two of his loyal lieutenants, Richard Armey and Tom DeLay. Gingrich purportedly wanted to talk about tax fairness and to dispel misconceptions about who really paid the luxury taxes. He said, "As we are all learning—for example, from the boat builders—if you raise taxes on people who buy a product, then you lay off people who are making the product, and it is not very fair to the thousands of boat workers who are not working today."

Gingrich did not mention, however, that repealing the luxury tax—which Congress did in 1994—was more than fair to Terry Kohler, his number-one patron.

House Minority Leader Richard Gephardt of Missouri has an especially cozy relationship with his number-one patron. St. Louis-based Anheuser-Busch Companies, Inc., the nation's largest brewer, turned to Gephardt when President Clinton proposed in 1993 to boost "sin taxes" on alcohol and tobacco products to pay for his health-care plan. Gephardt wangled an invitation for August A. Busch III, Anheuser-Busch's chairman, to attend Clinton's preinaugural economic summit in Little Rock, Arkansas, in December 1992. In February 1993, while traveling with Clinton aboard Air Force One, Gephardt broached the sin-tax subject, telling the President that he opposed any increase in the tax on beer. At a White House press conference on February 25, 1993, with Busch standing by his side, Clinton suggested that higher tobacco taxes would be used to help pay for his health-care plan. Asked whether higher taxes on alcohol would also be part of the equation, Clinton replied, "I specifically passed up a chance to say that today."

Going that extra mile for a constituent has earned Gephardt more than just August Busch's vote. Busch has urged his employees in writing to contribute money to Gephardt's campaigns. Over the past ten years, Anheuser-Busch and its employees have sent at least $215,000 Gephardt's way. Busch has also written letters to Anheuser-Busch distributors around the nation, urging them to support Gephardt, and they have—to the tune of at least $103,650. That pushes the total up to at least $318,950.

Senate Majority Leader Tent Lott of Mississippi owes his position in no small measure to the National Association of Realtors, which has sent at least $367,498 his way in the past ten years. In return, Lott has been an especially ardent advocate of the organization's pet issues. He cosponsored several measures that the realtors had lobbied for, including the Wetlands Regulatory Reform Act of 1995, which would have gutted environmental-protection laws by opening huge tracts of pristine wilderness to suburban subdivisions, and the Omnibus Property Rights Act of 1995, which would have forced the federal government to compensate private-property owners whose land is deemed environmentally sensitive and thus off-limits to developers.

It does not always take six-figure contributions for patrons to get what they want in Washington. Senate Minority Leader Tom Daschle of South Dakota cosponsored legislation in 1996 that would require the federal government to pay for hospice care for terminally ill veterans—on its surface, a laudable measure. Miami-based Vitas Healthcare Corporation, a for-profit company that derives 85 percent of its revenues from the Medicare program, has long been angling to tap into yet another huge pool of taxpayer dollars. Hugh Westbrook, the CEO of Vitas Healthcare, and other top executives at the company come in at number four on Daschle's list, having contributed $23,000.

In 1993, Republican Senator William Roth, Jr., of Delaware requested a legal opinion from the Federal Deposit Insurance Corporation (FDIC) for the benefit of his top patron, MBNA Corporation. MBNA, the world's second-largest issuer of credit cards, is based in Wilmington, Delaware, and not just by chance. Delaware is among the few states that have no antiusury laws, which limit the interest rates that banks can charge. MBNA's top executives were concerned that the Interstate Banking and Branching Efficiency Act, then being considered by the Senate Banking Committee, of which Roth was a member at the time, would subject the company to the antiusury laws of other states. Roth, in effect, got the FDIC to act as legal adviser to MBNA. This was not part of the mission that Congress envisioned when it created the FDIC in 1933; on the contrary, the FDIC is supposed to promote and preserve public confidence in financial institutions and ensure that they comply with consumer-protection laws. Nowhere in its charter is the FDIC instructed to ensure that credit-card companies in a given state can charge 22 percent interest to their customers around the country. The legal advice was not free, of course; MBNA has poured at least $143,839 into Roth's reelection campaigns since 1987.

> Senate Majority Leader Trent Lott owes his position in no small measure to the National Association of Realtors, which has sent at least $367,498 his way in the past ten years.

In June 1994, Charles Rangel of New York, now the ranking Democrat on the House Ways and Means Committee, went to bat for his top patron, Goldman, Sachs & Company, which has invested at least $55,000 in the New York City lawmaker. (Rangel's district doesn't even include Wall Street.) He proposed a bill that would have provided "payroll tax relief" for Wall Street investors, capping at $135,000 the amount of their income that is subject to Medicare taxes. Had it passed, Rangel's bill would have robbed the Medicare Trust Fund of millions of dollars at a time when the system faces insolvency. A similar measure was sponsored by Daniel Patrick Moynihan of New York, then the chairman of the Senate Finance Committee. Goldman, Sachs & Company has been Moynihan's seventh-most generous patron since 1987, accounting for at least $45,050 in contributions to his reelection account.

At the behest of his top patron, Houston-based energy giant Enron Corporation, House Republican Whip Tom DeLay of Texas introduced legislation in January 1996 that would have completely deregulated the electricity industry. DeLay's legislation was known on Capitol Hill as the "Enron bill," and not just because Kenneth Lay, the company's chairman and chief executive officer, and other Enron executives personally consulted with DeLay as he drafted the bill. DeLay's proposal was a veritable legislative wish list for the company, which had already planned its market expansion around industry deregulation. And all it cost was $51,550 in contributions to DeLay's reelection campaigns and to his PAC.

• **In-Kind Contributions.** Membership organizations such as labor unions, the Christian Coalition, and the National Rifle Association, to name just a few, routinely flex their muscles on behalf of political candidates. Unions, for example, are famously effective at getting voters to the polls to support Democrats on Election Day, and 1998 will be no different. "We'll have thousands more activists in each congressional district than we had in '96," AFL-CIO president John Sweeney told us. "I really think that we are going to be able to have a major effect in enough districts to take back the Congress." In 1996, the Christian Coalition disseminated to 45 million Americans "voter guides" that favored Republican candidates. The Federal Election Commission filed suit against the Christian Coalition in July 1996, alleging that it had made illegal in-kind contributions and independent expenditures on behalf of GOP candidates for the 1990, 1992, and 1994 elections. Specifically, the lawsuit charged that the Christian Coalition coordinated, cooperated with, or consulted with candidates in spending money on voter-identification drives, get-out-the-vote efforts, and voter guides. Over the years, the National Rifle Association's PAC has made millions of dollars of in-kind contributions to its favorite candidates by operating phone banks, staffing campaign offices, and giving mailing lists to candidates.

• **Issue Advertising.** The new frontier in subverting the spirit and the letter of federal election laws is the "issue ads" that don't implore the public to "vote for" or "vote against" a specific candidate—at least not explicitly. In 1996, the Supreme Court ruled that political parties may spend unlimited amounts on behalf of their own candidates, a ruling that set the stage for what was to follow. As journalist Elizabeth Drew first disclosed in *Whatever It Takes,* the Republican National Committee laundered $4.6 million in 1996 through Americans for Tax Reform, which spent it "independently" on 4 million phone calls and 17 million pieces of mail. In 1997, in the New Jersey gubernatorial election, the Virginia gubernatorial election, and the special election to fill the seat vacated by Republican Representative Susan Molinari of New York, the GOP made $5 million in "independent expenditures," five times as much as the Democrats. During the 1996 congressional campaigns, the AFL-CIO announced a $35 million drive to return control of the House of Representatives to the Democrats. The labor union sent activists into 102 congressional districts and placed $25 million in ads in about forty-four congressional districts. Conservative groups favoring Republican candidates rallied by Election Day, spending millions of dollars on the other side. The University of Pennsylvania's Annenberg Public Policy Center in Washington has estimated that in 1996 more than two dozen organizations spent up to $150 million on issue-advocacy advertising "that looked and sounded like campaign ads"—an ominous harbinger of the 1998 and 2000 elections.

Studies have shown that viewers cannot distinguish between these supposedly independent ads and commercials aired by the candidates themselves. Equally troubling, the public generally has no idea who is behind these ads, which feature split-second, small-print tag lines with such unrevealing, apple-pie names as Citizens for Reform and Coalition for Change. There are no contribution limits or disclosure requirements. Nonetheless, issue ads have become the method of choice for special interests to dump millions of dollars into a single election without risk of detection.

• **Power Meals.** Special interests can also curry favor with lawmakers by paying ludicrous amounts of money, in the form of campaign contributions, just to share a meal with them. Back in the late 1980s, Lloyd Bentsen of Texas, then the chairman of the Senate Finance Committee, breakfasted every month with a group of forty lobbyists, charging each of them $10,000 for the privilege. Three other Republicans on the Senate Finance Committee—John Chafee of Rhode Island, Bob Packwood of Oregon, and William Roth, Jr., of Delaware—all had their own $5,000-each "breakfast clubs." In 1994, just weeks before Republicans won control of the House of Representatives, at an exclusive dinner of lobbyists in Washington, Newt Gingrich reminded his audience that he and the Republicans had helped block lobbying reform legislation. According to *The Atlanta Journal and Constitution,* Gingrich made it very clear that he expected the lobbyists to cough up more campaign money for GOP congressional candidates, telling them, "For anybody not on board now, it's going to be the coldest two years in Washington."

• **The Back Door.** Sometimes lobbyists do far more than merely host fund-raising events. Consider the case of Republican Bud Shuster of Pennsylvania, the chairman of the powerful House Transportation and Infrastructure Committee. (Want a bridge or a new road in your congressional district? Call Bud.) As this book went to press, Shuster was under federal criminal investigation by the Justice Department regarding possible improprieties in the $10 billion Boston Central Artery construction project. Ann Eppard, an aide to Shuster for more than two decades, has been indicted by a federal grand jury for allegedly receiving $230,000 in illegal payments and with embezzling $27,500 from Shuster's campaign committee. She resigned as his chief of staff in late 1994. Within weeks, she became a lobbyist for several interests with business before the Transportation Committee. In so doing, she hit the jackpot: Ann Eppard Associates took in more than $1 million in its first year, including more than $600,000 from transportation clients. As *The Washington Monthly* and others reported, thanks to Eppard and Shuster, such companies as Federal Express Corporation and Frito-Lay, Inc., were exempted from regulations on mid-weight delivery trucks, over the objections of truck-safety advocates. Carnival Cruise Lines, also thanks to Eppard and Shuster, got a "technical amendment" added to a Coast Guard reauthorization bill that would shield cruise companies from lawsuits by women raped aboard their ships unless the women had also incurred "substantial physical injury."

It is illegal for senior congressional aides who leave Capitol Hill to lobby anyone in their former offices for one year, and both Shuster and Eppard are shocked, *shocked,* that anyone would suggest that any law was broken. At the same time as all this, Eppard was also pulling down $3,000 a month as the assistant treasurer of Shuster's 1996 reelection campaign, for which she helped him raise more than $655,000. Of her twenty-three clients, five with business before Shuster's committee wrote PAC checks totaling $22,500: the Washington law firm of Dyer, Ellis, Joseph & Mills; Federal Express; Union Pacific Corporation; United Air Lines, Inc.; and the Washington law firm of Verner, Liipfert, Bernhard, McPherson & Hand. Separately, Eppard chaired a fund-raising event to pay for a $40,000 oil portrait of Shuster to be hung in the Transportation Committee's hearing room. By the way, Eppard's $850,000 waterfront town house in Alexandria is where Shuster's campaign records were kept, where she did her campaign fund-raising, where she ran her lobbying business, and where Shuster often slept while Congress was in session. (In 1997, Eppard sold her town house and bought a home nearby for $1.4 million.)

This cozy arrangement has benefited everyone but the public—Eppard, who has a lucrative business; her corporate clients, who have access to power and special favors because of Eppard's uniquely close relationship with the chairman of the Transportation Committee; and Shuster, who gets all the money he needs and a portrait to boot. In November 1997, the House Committee on Standards of Official Conduct, after taking off almost a full year to develop and implement new procedures, opened a formal investigation of the matter. Shuster, Eppard, and Republican Nancy Johnson of Connecticut, who chairs the ethics committee, all declined the Center's requests for interviews.

• **All in the Family.** There is a time-honored tradition in Washington in which special interests hire the spouses or children of lawmakers. You cannot get any better access and influence than that. Joan Lowy of Scripps Howard News Service reported in 1993, for example, that then-Senator Bennett Johnson, a Democrat from Louisiana, had gone to China on privately financed trips with two of his sons, Hunter and J. Bennett III, who represented separate companies wanting to do business there. Or take the case of former Representative Sam Gibbons of Florida. He was the ranking Democrat on the House Ways and Means Committee at the same time his son Clifford Gibbons was a registered foreign agent representing before Congress clients that had a stake in tax and trade matters. Among them were Lloyd's of London, the Ministry of Ontario, Toyota Motor Corporation, and Aermacchi, S.p.A.

Then there is the matter of House Speaker Newt Gingrich, his wife Marianne, and former Representative Vin Weber, a close friend. Weber, a Republican from Minnesota, left office in January 1993 to become a lobbyist, representing, among others, the Israel Export Development Company Ltd. Within months, Weber personally lobbied Gingrich and several other Members of Congress on behalf of the company, and he also got his client to hire Marianne Gingrich. She was eventually given the position of vice president of business development, even though she had no experience in international business or trade and at the time of her hiring was selling cosmetics from her home. "Her relationship with Newt Gingrich had zero impact [on the decision to hire her]," David Yerushalmi, the chairman of the Israel Export Development Company, insisted to us in a telephone interview from Israel. Speaker Gingrich, Marianne Gingrich, and Weber all declined to be interviewed, although in an "I am incensed" letter to the Center, Weber said he took great umbrage at any suggestion that his lobbying activities might have been improper. In fact, they appear to violate the federal law that prohibits former Members of Congress from lobbying their colleagues during their first year out of office. There has been no sign that the Justice Department has any interest in pursuing the matter. Meanwhile, according to Gingrich's financial disclosure form for 1996, his wife is no longer working for the company.

Finally there is the story of Randy DeLay, a Houston lawyer and failed businessman who filed for bankruptcy in 1992 and is the younger brother of the third most powerful Member of the House, former pest exterminator Tom DeLay. Randy DeLay, according to Frank Greve, an investigative reporter for Knight-Ridder Newspapers, became a Washington lobbyist within days of his brother's ascension to House Majority Whip. He suddenly turned successful as a businessman, grossing more than $550,000 in his first year as a lobbyist. Randy DeLay met with his big brother twenty-one times on behalf of his client, Cemex, a Mexican cement company. Majority Whip DeLay went to bat in Washington for Cemex and several of his brother's other new clients. This apparently is not worthy of investigation under the current rules of the House of Representatives. The DeLays, of course, have denied doing anything wrong, and Representative DeLay declined our request for an interview.

• **Financial Favors.** Throughout the 1990s, we have seen that special interests like to do things that hit lawmakers right where they notice it the most—in the wallet. Senator Alfonse D'Amato, a Republican from New York, made $37,000 in a single day. From 1989 to 1992, then-House Speaker Thomas Foley, a Democrat from Washington, cleared more than $100,000 in profit. In a 1992 stock deal, then-Representative Robert Torricelli, a Democrat from New Jersey, picked up a cool $70,000. How did they all do it? As the Capitol Hill newspaper *Roll Call* and others reported, they invested in initial public offerings. Most Americans and even most investors don't get the opportunity to invest in IPOs.

A savings-and-loan swindler who's now doing time in federal prison sought—and got—political favors from Republican Senator Phil Gramm of Texas; he subsequently thanked Gramm by doing $53,586 worth of free construction on the Senator's vacation home on Maryland's Eastern Shore. Dwayne Andreas, the chairman of Archer Daniels Midland Company, with billions of dollars in agriculture subsidies before Congress, sold Senator Robert Dole's wife and brother-in-law an oceanfront condominium in Bal Harbour, Florida, below the market value and allowed them to make the first payment seven months after the purchase date. And who can forget the book deal that was to pay Speaker Newt Gingrich $4.5 million up front—offered by a publishing company owned by Rupert Murdoch, who had major business before Congress at the time. In the wake of the public furor, Gingrich decided against taking the advance. And then there was Republican Bob Packwood of Oregon, who, before he resigned in disgrace from the Senate, revealed in his now-infamous diaries that he had approached four different lobbyists and asked them to help him find work for his ex-wife, in order to substantially ease his monthly alimony payments.

• **All-Expenses-Paid Trips.** How would you like to go just about anywhere you want and not have to pay for your trip? Members of Congress and their top aides, if they so choose, are offered such freebies—in the name of "fact finding," of course— all the time. We entered into a computer database every trip report filed in 1996 and the first half of 1997 by Members of Congress and congressional aides. In all, 443 members of Congress—eighty-seven Senators and 356 Representatives—and 2,020 congressional employees accepted "free" trips worth a total of at least $8.6 million from various special interests, finding essential facts in such places as Athens, Greece; Auckland, New Zealand; Bordeaux, France; Katmandu, Nepal; Kuala Lumpur, Malaysia; and St. Moritz, Switzerland, to name just a handful.

Congress's most frequent flier was Kenneth Kies, the staff director of the Joint Committee on Taxation. He accepted forty-eight trips (valued by their sponsors at a total of $66,743) from numerous parties seeking tax favors from Congress, including his old law firm, Baker & Hostetler, which had him speak to its current and prospective clients in Columbus, Ohio; Houston, Texas; and Orlando, Florida. In November 1996, Kies journeyed to Cannes and Paris, France, courtesy of the European-American Tax Institute. Cost: $9,700. Three weeks later, Kies was back in Paris, followed by Stockholm, Sweden, and Prague, Czechoslovakia, courtesy of the Tax Foundation. Cost: $6,537. Kies has defended his trips in the past and did not respond to the Center's inquiries. His boss, Republican William Archer of Texas, personally approved all of Kies's trips. Archer told a reporter for *The Wall Street Journal*: "I have total confidence in his integrity and his noncorruptibility."

The second most-frequent traveler was Democrat Patricia Schroeder of Colorado, who retired from the House in 1996. She took forty-five trips paid for by others that were worth a total of $51,503. In August 1996, for example, she traveled to a conference sponsored by the Aspen Institute in St. Petersburg, Russia. Cost: $5,436. Next was then-senator Bill Bradley of New Jersey,

||||||||||||||||||||||||||||||||||||||||||||||||||||||||||||||||||

From 1996 to 1997, Representative Maxine Waters took twenty-six free trips, worth $35,862, more than any other current Member of Congress.

who took twenty-nine such trips (total cost: $42,031), including a $10,462 trip to Davos, Switzerland.

Representative Maxine Waters, a Democrat from California, took twenty-six trips worth a total of $35,862, more than any other current Member of Congress. She went to the Bahamas in January 1996, courtesy of the National Newspaper Publishers Association, and again in February 1996, courtesy of the National Bar Association. Her husband, Sidney Williams, a former professional football player who most recently sold Mercedes-Benzes in Los Angeles, was tapped by President Clinton to be the U.S. Ambassador to—you guessed it—the Bahamas. Waters also journeyed in the wintertime to Hawaii and Jamaica, the latter trip courtesy of the Caribbean Banana Exporters Association.

The top sponsor of trips for Members of Congress and those who work for them was the Aspen Institute, a nonprofit organization based in Washington. The Aspen Institute, by our count, sponsored no fewer than 394 trips in 1996 and the first half of 1997, to such venues as Barcelona, Spain; Elbow Beach, Bermuda; Lanai, Hawaii; Lisbon, Portugal; Rome, Italy; West Palm Beach, Florida; and St. Petersburg, Russia. The total cost of these excursions was $747,122. (Former Democratic Senator Dick Clark of Iowa, the Aspen Institute's director of congressional programs, told the Center that the trips and associated seminars are designed "to help educate Members of Congress primarily on foreign-affairs issues.") The second-ranking trip sponsor was the Center for Market Processes, a nonprofit organization funded by undisclosed corporations and foundations and affiliated with George Mason University, in Fairfax, Virginia. It paid for 185 trips, at a total cost of $84,695. The Nuclear Energy Institute, underwritten by utility companies, took Members of Congress and congressional aides on 101 trips, to such locales as Belgium, France, and Sweden.

Members of Congress must approve, in advance, any such trips they or their employees take, with a signature under the statement: "I have determined that all of the expenses listed above were necessary and that the travel was in connection with the employee's official duties and would not create the appearance that he/she is using public office for private gain." Who signed the most on the dotted line? Republican Thomas Bliley of Virginia, the chairman of the House Committee, was first, approving 196 trips by his employees. Archer was second, at 195 trips. And third was Shuster, who approved 112 trips.

While these Members and staffers are gallivanting around the globe, who is tending to the public's business?

• **Writing Legislation.** This is about as good as it gets if you are a special interest, far better than making a contribution or underwriting a vacation. And what a public service to those over-worked lawmakers, who need all the help they can get. This practice has been going on for years by corporations, labor unions, and interest groups for Republicans and Democrats alike, but we were all reminded of it in the early months of the Republican Revolution in the House of Representatives. Majority Whip Tom DeLay unabashedly invited certain business lobbyists to write legislation deregulating the very same industries they represented, and during congressional hearings some of the lobbyists were spotted up on the dais, where Members of Congress and their staff customarily sit. Similarly, also in 1995, then-Senate Majority Leader Robert Dole asked corporate lobbyist C. Boyden Gray, former White House counsel to President George Bush, to write his regulatory-reform legislation. Gray doubles as the chairman of Citizens for a Sound Economy, an antiregulation outfit financed by major U.S. corporations.

• **Secrecy.** Special interests and the politicians who cater to them like to keep the American people in the dark. If the public does not really know what is going on and who got what behind closed doors, there will never be any outrage and resistance. Even in this age of the Internet it is impossible to obtain copies of discussion drafts and committee drafts of legislation, either on-line or on paper. As Gary Ruskin of the Congressional Accountability Project has noted, "While Washington lobbyists read the relevant working drafts of bills, the rubes back home" are left in the dark. Congress still has not established a nonpartisan, easily searchable database of congressional voting records, indexed by bill name, subject, bill title, Member's name, and so forth.

When Congress passed the landmark Freedom of Information Act of 1966, it naturally exempted itself from the law, so internal Capitol Hill correspondence, appointment calendars (how many lobbyists did your Senator meet with last week?), and the like are not publicly obtainable. The House GOP's "Contract with America" promised to place Congress under the same rules and regulations as everyone else in the nation. But the Freedom of Information Act wasn't amended to cover Congress. "It was seriously discussed in '92, '93, '94, and then it's kind of tended to fade, unfortunately," Representative Scott Klug, a Republican from Wisconsin, told us.

||||||||||||||||||||||||||||||||||||||||

When Congress passed the Freedom of Information Act in 1966, it exempted itself from the law, so internal Capitol Hill correspondence, appointment calendars (how many lobbyists did your Senator meet with last week?), and the like are not publicly obtainable.

||||||||||||||||||||||||||||||||||||||||

Meanwhile, the Senate still has an archaic practice in which each Senator has the power to place what is known as a "hold" on a bill or nomination. This remarkable power is exerted in secrecy. In 1997, reformers in the Senate tried to require "holds" that blocked legislation or a presidential nomination to be placed in public, but their antisecrecy amendment was killed— in secret, of course.

At least we have disclosure of campaign contributions, you say. In 1995–96, however, three-fourths of the Members of Congress failed to comply with the requirement to list the occupations and employers of their campaign contributors, according to the Center for Responsive Politics.

• **Front Groups.** The essence of lobbying in Washington is cloaking the most crass, narrow, commercial concern in the altruistic nobility of the broad public interest. Controversial groups such as pesticide manufacturers form and finance third-party, cutout groups such as the Center for Produce Quality. Sounds as if your friendly greengrocer works there, doesn't it? In our 1997 book *Toxic Deception: How the Chemical Industry Manipulates Sci-*

ence, Bends the Law, and Endangers Your Health, written by Dan Fagin and Marianne Lavelle, we examined various front groups established by the chemical industry, including the Center for Indoor Air Research (the tobacco industry), the Risk Science Institute, and the Council for Agricultural Science and Technology (the pesticide industry). Sometimes good reporters who ought to know better get snookered by front groups and their dramatic new research findings. In 1996, for example, *The Wall Street Journal* had egg on its face after running a prominently placed article based on a report issued by an unknown group called Contributions Watch. Weeks later, *Washington Post* reporter Ruth Marcus discovered that it was a front group for Philip Morris Companies, Inc.

These nonprofit, tax-exempt organizations, which are not required by law to disclose their sources of funds, flood Congress with their propaganda, hold conferences, and finance trips for Members and their staff. In 1997, Marcus reported that the Ripon Educational Fund—which is affiliated with the Ripon Society, a haven for moderate Republicans—took fourteen Members of Congress on a trip to Prague for discussions about the Czech Republic's possible entry into NATO. Undisclosed in the trip reports filed with the Senate and House was the fact that sixty-seven corporate lobbyists had actually underwritten the costs of the expensive trip and physically accompanied the lawmakers, thereby securing a week of almost entirely unfettered access.

Another important purpose of front groups is creating the illusion of broad public support. One of the most notorious growers of artificial grass roots—known as "AstroTurf lobbyists"—is Jack Bonner, the president of Bonner & Associates. As journalist Ken Silverstein and others have revealed, Bonner's telemarketers get citizens upset on a subject, encourage them to speak out, and then immediately patch the citizen through to congressional offices. So Members of Congress receive thousands of irate calls and letters from ordinary folks who frequently have no idea that they are speaking on behalf of powerful interests such as Browning-Ferris Industries, Inc.; Northrop Grumman Corporation; the coal industry; the oil industry; and many others.

• **Revolving Door.** One of the most reliable standbys for

influencing the public-policy process is hiring as lobbyists the very people who have been inside that process. This is such a pervasive practice in Washington that it is widely regarded as a permanent part of the political landscape. In *The Trading Game,* our 1993 study about lobbying for the North American Free Trade Agreement, for example, we found that Mexican interests had hired at least thirty-three former U.S. officials who had worked in the White House, the Treasury and State Departments, and congressional offices.

By comparing financial disclosure reports filed by senior congressional aides from 1991 to 1996 (employees with annual salaries of $83,160 or more in 1996, for example) and lobbying registration reports filed in 1996, we were able to get one of the clearest pictures to date of the migratory patterns from Capitol Hill into Washington's high-priced lobbying firms. In all, we found that at least 15 percent of senior Senate aides left to become registered lobbyists, with the real action in such key venues as the Commerce Committee (site of the bonanza known as telecommunications legislation), where 45 percent went on to become lobbyists, and the Finance Committee, where 40 percent went on to become lobbyists. In the House, 14 percent of the top aides became registered lobbyists, including 41 percent of the Commerce Committee's senior staff and 39 percent of the Ways and Means Committee's senior staff. These numbers are conservative, because not everyone who works in a law, public-relations, or lobbying firm in Washington formally registers as a lobbyist, even though his or her work is helpful to corporate clients.

Sometimes the things former lawmakers are willing to do for financial gain are almost beyond belief. In 1997, for example, three former Senate Majority Leaders—Democrat George Mitchell and Republicans Howard Baker, Jr., and Robert Dole—went to work for the tobacco industry. The most surprising was Baker, whose 200-lawyer firm, based in Huntsville, Tennessee, took on as clients Philip Morris, R. J. Reynolds Tobacco Company, Brown & Williamson Tobacco Corporation, Loews Corporation (the parent of Lorillard Tobacco Company), and U.S. Tobacco. Baker's first wife, Joy, died of lung cancer, as did her famous father, the late Senator Everett Dirksen. Physicians at the prestigious Mayo Clinic, where one of Joy Baker's surgeries was performed, were upset that Baker—the chairman of the nonprofit Mayo Foundation, which manages the clinic—had agreed to help an industry whose products kill an estimated 400,000 Americans annually. In response, Baker resigned from the foundation's board of directors. Although he declined to talk to us, Baker defended his actions in an interview with Jim Warren, the Washington bureau chief of *The Chicago Tribune*. "It's a legitimate representation by a big firm," he told Warren. "It doesn't mean you approve of tobacco. It's a legal product, a legal business."

Dole and Mitchell are among the marquee names at the Washington law firm of Verner, Liipfert, Bernhard, McPherson and Hand. The law firm's PAC and partners contributed $684,354 to congressional campaigns in the 1995–96 election cycle, and it reportedly earned $4.7 million from the tobacco industry in the first half of 1997.

The Constitution makes ironclad post-employment prohibitions on government officials virtually impossible, with a few exceptions. There are laws on the books to establish a "cooling off" period so that public servants cannot become private mercenaries within minutes of leaving office. But these laws have not perceptibly slowed the spinning of the revolving door.

With all of these complicating circumstances and inducements made possible by inordinate sums of cash, it is easy to understand how policy decisions affecting the broad public interest often turn out badly, favoring some narrow economic concern. It was not surprising, for example, that a $50 billion tobacco-industry tax break quietly slipped through both the Senate and the House and was signed into law in the summer of 1997, considering who was pushing for it from the outside and from the inside and considering the millions of dollars that have passed from the industry to Congress and both political parties, especially the Republicans. Secrecy was also invaluable to the outcome. A single sentence consisting of forty-six words, apparently written by a tobacco lobbyist, was added to a mammoth tax bill on July 31. No one admitted paternity or ever took responsibility for the classic maneuver, and the tax break was approved in both chambers without any public debate.

Eventually, lawmakers and journalists discovered that Senate Majority Leader Trent Lott and House Speaker Newt Gingrich had personally insisted on the provision. The White House also had agreed to it. "There was no sneaking in the middle of the night, there was no skullduggery," Lott told a reporter for *The Washington Post.* "The White House knew what was going down. [White House Chief of Staff] Erskine [Bowles] was in the room. [White House lobbyist John] Hilley was in the room, and either [Treasury Secretary Robert] Rubin or [Office of Management and Budget Director Franklin] Raines was in the room at all times."

The public outrage was palpable and immediate. Six weeks later, the Senate voted ninety-five to three to kill the tax break. With a full gallery and the national television cameras of C-SPAN looking on, Lott reversed his position and voted to end the short-lived provision, with no comment. Christina Martin, Gingrich's press secretary, said: "The Speaker's one and only objective is to protect America's children, and he has no interest in protecting tobacco companies or trial lawyers."

Words in Washington are frequently untethered to truth, and the people who utter them do so with a straight face, without blushing. What is most alarming is how commonplace such "spin" is every day in our nation's capital and how admired it is as an art form. In this era of increased scrutiny, lawmakers must be able to maintain a veneer of innocence should their quiet roles as handmaidens for industry be found out.

In researching this book, we did not try to read every page of every bill (neither did the Members). We did, however, exhaustively analyze the legislative activities of Congress over the past decade. As stated earlier, there is no question that many votes cast by elected officials had little or nothing to do with the influence of money. Two widely publicized bills that became law in 1997, for example, are interesting to us not because of the cash component, but for the insight they provide into Congress itself.

When thousands of Americans in thirty-three Midwestern and Western states were left homeless after spring flooding in 1997, Congress was unable to agree on disaster-relief legislation. Worse, with flood victims left to ponder their future, Members of Congress went off on their ten-day Memorial Day recess. President

Clinton said, "Disaster doesn't take a holiday," and editorial pages across the country agreed with him. Eventually, Congress passed a disaster bill loaded up with dozens of amendments that had nothing to do with flood relief, some of them just plain petty, partisan Republican maneuvering. Clinton vetoed the bill because of its "extraneous" provisions. *The Record* (Bergen, New Jersey) said the GOP Members had acted "with amazing, barefaced impudence." Clinton, *The Chicago Tribune* reported, "had an apt description for this failure: unconscionable." Eventually, a clean disaster-relief bill was passed and signed, but the experience left the nation angry, and even Republicans were frustrated at their own destructive tendencies.

Playing politics and public relations with people's lives at such a desperate time was a metaphor in some ways for how Congress—and Washington—works. Former Republican Senator Warren Rudman of New Hampshire echoed to us the nation's frustration over the disaster-relief debacle. "Call it political integrity, call it intellectual integrity," he said. "Those kinds of things, I think, [are] where the public sees a lack of integrity."

The so-called minimum-wage bill that passed in the summer of 1996 is another case in which integrity took a backseat to political expediency. Ostensibly, the minimum wage in the United States went from $4.25 to $5.15 an hour. On the South Lawn of the White House, Clinton proudly signed the legislation, announcing that it was a major victory for the "working people of America." Across Lafayette Square, overlooking the White House, a copy of that signed bill is proudly framed on the wall of the top-floor office of AFL-CIO president John Sweeney. What most people do not know is that we got stuck with the bill that ought to be paid by the nation's employers. As Eric Pianin of *The Washington Post*

> When thousands of Americans in the Midwest and West were left homeless after spring flooding in 1997, Congress was unable to agree on disaster-relief legislation. Worse, with flood victims left to ponder their future, Members went off on their ten-day Memorial Day recess.

reported, "Under pressure from companies and trade groups, the 104th Congress converted a straightforward wage bill into a $21 billion bonanza of tax breaks for corporate America—from pharmaceutical companies and soft-drink makers to pizza chains and convenience-store operators." In the 1995–96 election cycle, members of the tax-writing Senate Finance and House Ways and Means Committees received more than $36 million in campaign contributions from corporations.

The name of this new 146-page law? The Small Business Job Protection Act of 1996. "It wasn't even called a minimum-wage bill," Sweeney complained in our interview. "They don't even have the courage to address the tax issue as a tax issue and to address the minimum-wage issue as an increase for people who are at the lowest level of the economic ladder."

But perhaps there is no better example of the smoke-and-mirrors posturing by both parties in Congress than the widely ballyhooed balanced-budget agreement. In May 1997, President Clinton and Republican leaders in Congress announced that both parties had reached a historic agreement that would balance the federal budget by 2002 for the first time in more than three decades. "We have," Clinton declared, "put America's fiscal house in order again." Speaker Gingrich called the agreement "a great victory for all Americans." Republican John Kasich of Ohio, the chairman of the House Budget Committee, said, "This is a golden moment for America."

Despite the hoopla and hyperbole, a poll taken at the time by the Gallup Organization found that 81 percent of the American people did not think the agreement would result in a balanced federal budget. There was good reason for the skepticism. Few of the hard choices had been made. The agreement is based on a rosy assumption that there will be no break in the past six-plus years of economic growth. At the same time, Congress passed a tax cut mostly for the wealthy. And the politicians also postponed, instead of confronting, difficult but crucial entitlement issues such as Social Security, Medicare, and Medicaid.

What we have, then, is a Congress enormously susceptible to the influence of the nation's most wealthy, powerful interests, a Congress that also is too frequently incapable of candor, courage, and integrity. In the coming chapters, you will see how these serious character flaws have affected us in our daily lives, in terms of our health, our safety, our personal finances, and our democratic freedoms.

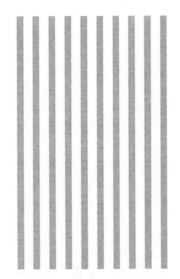

YOUR HEALTH
AND SAFETY

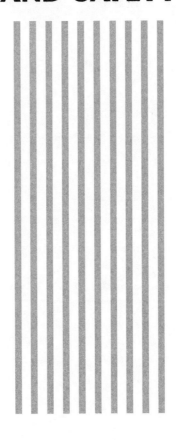

4

|||||||||||

The Killing Fields

As she exhaled for the last time, Sandra Cornwall Mero could not have known that her life was part of the price that elected officials had decided should be paid for cheaper produce, their own job security, and the continued prosperity of two U.S. chemical companies.

The politicians would deny it, of course—and it is true that, in some respects, Sandra Mero's death was an accident. As it happened, the studio next door to her apartment in Toluca Lake, California, was being fumigated with methyl bromide to kill insects and the odorless gas seeped through seven empty pipes leading into Mero's home. Unaware that the virulent pesticide had invaded her body, Mero went to sleep, awoke the next day feeling ill, telephoned friends to let them know, and went back to bed. She never got up again, and on March 25, 1997, after two and a half weeks in a coma, the thirty-six-year-old entertainment-company assistant was pronounced dead at a Burbank hospital.

If chemicals are dangerous enough—and, by almost any measure, methyl bromide is as dangerous as they get—bans on their production or use can be adopted by state or federal governments, or even agreed to internationally. Methyl bromide has been, at one time or another, subject to bans at all of those levels. Exposure to this toxin may cause everything from inflammation of organs to eye damage, convulsions, and death. Exposure of pregnant women may result in fetal defects. The release of the chemical into the atmosphere has been found to severely damage the earth's ozone layer, which protects humans from cancer-causing ultraviolet radiation. By all measures, methyl bromide is a deadly menace.

Although there are safe alternatives, millions of pounds of the deadly pesticide methyl bromide are still produced and sold each year—a testament to the adroit manipulation of the political system by the handful of companies that are the poison's principal manufacturers and users.

Although there are safe alternatives, millions of pounds of methyl bromide are still produced and sold each year—a testament to the adroit manipulation of the political system by the handful of companies that are the poison's principal manufacturers and users.

One of the deadliest weapons in the exterminator's arsenal, methyl bromide is used primarily to sterilize soil before strawberries, tomatoes, and other crops are planted. The poison gas is injected into the ground to a depth of one to two feet, after which the earth is covered with massive tarpaulins that are removed twenty-four to seventy-two hours later. During this interval, methyl bromide kills insects. It kills weeds. It kills worms. It kills fungi. Because it effectively rids the soil of unwanted life forms, methyl bromide is a favorite of the agricultural community, which might otherwise have to use a more expensive combination of chemicals. It is also a major source of revenue for Great Lakes Chemical Corporation and Albemarle Corporation, two of the three firms (along with the Israeli company Dead Sea Bromine Company Ltd.) that collectively produce more than 75 percent of the world's supply of the chemical.

The bottom line: 152 million profit-producing pounds of the stuff is used annually around the world, a global trade that has been estimated in excess of $50 billion. When the choice is health or wealth, big corporations—and the politicians who cater to them—frequently have little trouble deciding on the latter.

*   *   *

The story of methyl bromide illustrates the ease with which corporate polluters not only manipulate the nation's political system at all levels, but also hammer U.S. policy into a weapon to fend off international efforts to regulate the chemical. As usual, money is their principal tool and Congress their target, although in this instance California's governor also played a pivotal role.

Under California's Birth Defects Prevention Act of 1984, manufacturers of potentially harmful chemicals were required to submit health studies to the state by 1991 or face a ban on their products. The manufacturers of methyl bromide did not submit the required studies on time, and for their laxity they were granted a five-year extension until March 30, 1996. When the poison producers were on the verge of missing another deadline, Republican Governor Pete Wilson, acting at the behest of powerful farm groups, called a special session of the state legislature to ask that the ban be postponed until December 1997. Less than three weeks before the lethal chemical was to have been rendered illegal in California, lawmakers granted Wilson his wish.

Later that same month, Wilson was flanked by pesticide-industry lobbyists and legislators representing farm districts as he signed into law the provision that would result in Sandra Mero's death. At the time, Wilson was heavily in debt from his failed campaign for the Republican presidential nomination in 1996. He was thus a prime target for the Methyl Bromide Working Group, a somewhat mysterious Washington, D.C., trade association whose members have worked tirelessly—and, for the most part, secretly—to ensure that the world will not be deprived of this lethal chemical. Perhaps more important, Wilson had a long-standing relationship with one of the largest and most politically aggressive of methyl bromide's defenders, Sun-Diamond Growers of California. Formed as an umbrella group for five agricultural cooperatives in California, New Mexico, Oregon, and Illinois, Sun-Diamond had been a top contributor to Wilson's campaigns for governor, weighing in with more than $190,000 from 1989 to 1996. And Sun-Diamond's member co-ops wanted to keep using methyl bromide.

Of course, neither Governor Wilson nor those who did his legislative bidding could have known that, twelve months later, Sandra Mero would be the nineteenth resident of Southern Cali-

||||||||||||||||||||||||||||||||||||||||||||||||||||||||||||||||||||||||||||||||

In Fremont, California, more than 1,200 people were forced to flee their homes when methyl bromide fumes drifted off a gladiolus field.

fornia in thirteen years to be killed by methyl bromide. But it was clear that additional tragedies caused by this poisonous fumigant were as inevitable as the Pacific tides.

Consider the evidence: At nonlethal levels of exposure, methyl bromide causes nausea, vomiting, dizziness, headaches, skin injuries, chest pains, shortness of breath, numbness, loss of muscle control, and blurred vision. At higher levels, it produces tremors, agitation, convulsions, coma, and such neurological problems as inflammation of the nerves. Ratchet up the exposure, and death soon follows.

At the time the California legislature acted, more than 400 bromide-related poisonings had been reported in the state since the early 1980s. The poison was, and still is, routinely applied within breathing distance—sometimes as close as thirty feet—of schools, homes, and day-care centers. In Fremont, California, more than 1,200 people were forced to flee their homes when methyl bromide fumes drifted off a gladiolus field. In the San Joaquin valley town of Ceres, 1,500 people were evacuated—and thirty-five received medical treatment—after methyl bromide was improperly applied to a spice field. A jogger fell ill after passing a field owned by the University of California at Davis that was being fumigated with the chemical. And if lawmakers were interested enough to look across the state line for corroborating evidence, they would have unearthed countless horror stories like the one in Miami: Seventy-five-year-old Caridad Clausell, who was trying to exterminate dry-wood termites, died two days after being accidentally trapped in her house as it was being treated with methyl bromide. A neighbor who heard Claussel's screams and vainly tried to rescue her suffered a skin rash from contact with the fumes.

But with an economy so dependent on crop production, Wilson and his minions clearly considered the benefits of methyl bromide much greater than the costs—even if Sandra Mero's friends and family might have ultimately felt otherwise. So they toed the line and did agriculture's dirty work.

Despite their success in California, the methyl bromide manufacturers still had a fight in Washington on their hands. There a troublesome ban on the production and importation of methyl bromide had been adopted—not because of the threat to human life, which Congress did not deem worthy of action, but because it is one of the most powerful destroyers of stratospheric ozone.

In 1990, Congress decreed that any chemical listed by the Environmental Protection Agency as a Class I ozone destroyer be banned within seven years. The EPA listed methyl bromide on December 10, 1993, triggering a prohibition on its production and importation as of January 1, 2001.

If that was not enough of a headache for the methyl bromide industry, there was yet another obstacle to overcome. Pursuant to the Montreal Protocol—an international agreement entered into in 1987 to eliminate the emissions of ozone-destroying chemicals—the production of methyl bromide is slated to be phased out in developed nations, including the United States, by 2005 and in developing nations by 2015. To keep the poison flowing, the methyl bromide industry needed to find a way both to overcome U.S. law and to circumvent the treaty.

||||||||||||||||||||||||||||||||||||||||||||||

The methyl bromide industry's first step was to emulate other besieged polluters and form an ambiguous-sounding front organization—in this case the Methyl Bromide Working Group. Such front groups are now invented on a regular basis in Washington by high-powered lobbyists and public-relation firms.

||||||||||||||||||||||||||||||||||||||||||||||

Its first step was to emulate other besieged polluters and form an ambiguous-sounding front organization—in this case, the Methyl Bromide Working Group. Such front groups, virtually unheard of before 1980, are now invented on a regular basis in Washington by the high-powered lobbyists and public-relations firms hired by corporations to fend off new laws, cloud scientific findings, and quell public outcry. An official of the Federal Election Commission estimates that there are more than 1,000 such outfits, although it is often impossible to identify a group's beliefs from its name—a devious strategy that helps corporations blur the distinctions between themselves and the public-interest groups that oppose them.

In the case of acid rain, for example, the coal and utility industries relied on an organization called Citizens for Sensible Control of Acid Rain. About 125 coal and electric companies collectively pumped more than $5 million into the organization, which in 1986 spent more on lobbying than any other such outfit in Washington. Although its name suggests that it is a broad-based, grassroots organization, not one of the "citizens" that were members were real human beings—all were corporations.

Similarly, Responsible Industry for a Sound Environment, which fronts for the nation's pesticide manufacturers, has lobbied to kill proposals that lawn-care companies be required to post warnings after spraying chemicals that can cause cancer and nervous-system damage. The Safe Buildings Alliance, a triumvirate of former asbestos manufacturers, peddles the feel-good message that "you have more of a chance of being hit by lightning than dying from asbestos," in the words of its vice president, Jeff Taylor. Never mind that some experts put the number of Americans killed by exposure to the cancer-causing mineral in the hundreds of thousands over the past several decades.

The goals of the Methyl Bromide Working Group—whose letterhead and promotional materials carefully guard the identity of its backers, officers, directors, members, and staff—are to directly influence the political process, build coalitions with other politically powerful interests, discredit the feasibility of alternatives to methyl bromide, and raise fears of economic ruin and crippling job losses. The group also seeks to cast doubt on scientific consensus, no matter how credible the source or how urgent the findings. NASA, the National Oceanic and Atmospheric Administration, the World Meteorological Organization, and the United Nations Environment Programme jointly concluded in a 1994 report, for example, that bromine, an element in the compound methyl bromide, is fifty times as destructive of stratospheric ozone as chlorine, found in such compounds as chlorofluorocarbon (CFC). The report, published by the WMO, said that eliminating methyl bromide emissions from agricultural, structural, and industrial activities was one of the most important steps that the world's governments could take to reduce future levels of ozone depletion.

To counter such findings, the methyl bromide industry undertook a joint study with the U.S. Department of Agriculture. When the results were tabulated, this report concluded that "relatively little is known about where methyl bromide comes from . . . where it goes . . . and what happens to the methyl bromide which escapes to the atmosphere."

Why would the Agriculture Department undertake a study with such a biased front group, and how could it reach conclusions that are so directly at odds with the findings of other government agencies and the global scientific community? A possible explanation rests in the relationship between Sun-Diamond Growers—Governor Wilson's generous benefactor—and then-Secretary of Agriculture Mike Espy, who was a Democratic Representative from Mississippi when President Clinton picked him for the post in 1993.

Not all the money that Epsy received as a public servant was disclosed to those who paid his salary. In September 1996, a federal jury found Sun-Diamond guilty on eight out of nine counts of making illegal gifts to Espy while he was Secretary of

> **In 1993, when President Clinton was pressing Congress to approve the North American Free Trade Agreement, several members of the Florida delegation extracted, as the price for their votes, a promise from him to keep methyl bromide on the market.**

Agriculture. A year later, Richard Douglas, a lobbyist and senior vice president of Sun-Diamond, was found guilty of delivering $7,600 in gifts to his onetime college roommate and frequent social companion, including top-of-the-line Hartmann luggage, seats at the U.S. Open tennis matches, and $655 in meals. According to the grand jury, one of the things Sun-Diamond sought was the help of Espy and the Agriculture Department in persuading the Environmental Protection Agency not to ban methyl bromide.

The disgraced Espy resigned his post in late 1994 as questions multiplied about his relationships with Sun-Diamond and other interests regulated by the Agriculture Department. But if the methyl bromide industry had lost one friend in high places, it still had plenty of others willing to act as its mouthpiece. In Congress, the chief ally of the Methyl Bromide Working Group proved to be Representative Dan Miller, a Republican whose Florida district is home to some of the nation's largest tomato growers and packers—ergo, fans of methyl bromide.

Some from the Sunshine State learned to use the poison as a legislative bargaining chip. In 1993, for example, when President Clinton was pressing Congress to approve the North American Free Trade Agreement, several members of the Florida delegation extracted, as the price for their votes, a promise from him to keep methyl bromide on the market. Then-U.S. Trade Representative Mickey Kantor penned assurances to the Florida Fruit and Vegetable Association that no restrictions on the manufacture or use of the toxic chemical would be imposed until the year 2000—even though just one week earlier, the EPA had proposed to freeze production of the chemical at its 1991 levels. Beyond that, Kantor promised his personal involvement in the matter to ensure that the commercial interests of the Florida growers would not be affected by future restrictions beyond the new millennium. Miller's press secretary told the Center there was "no truth" to the suggestion that Miller bargained for his vote, saying that the lawmaker has been a consistent supporter of free trade.

But Kantor's assurances were not enough for the industry or for Miller, who on August 4, 1995, introduced legislation to reverse the federal ban on the production of methyl bromide and to withdraw U.S. participation in international curbs under the Montreal Protocol. Miller's proposal also would have, among other things, created a set of certification procedures for alternatives to methyl bromide and stripped the EPA of its authority to force agricultural products treated with methyl bromide to be so labeled. In short, Miller was out to ensure that his tomato-growing constituents would be forever free to wreak environmental havoc as they saw fit, with only a modicum of government oversight or intrusion.

Miller's proposal was branded "dead wrong" by John Passacantando, the executive director of Ozone Action—a public-interest group focused on global climate change and ozone depletion—but the two-term lawmaker nonetheless managed to line up some three dozen cosponsors. Among them was Majority Whip Tom DeLay of Texas, an exterminator by trade, who, seven months earlier, had unsuccessfully introduced his own bill that proposed an outright repeal of all the 1990 amendments to the Clean Air Act.

Support for Miller's bill increased after September 1995, when President Clinton went to electoral-vote-rich California and repeated his softened stance on the methyl bromide ban to a gathering of farmers. Under pressure from Congress, his backpedaling translated into a U.S. retreat at international negotiations. At a meeting in Austria that December, the U.S. delegates pressured their fellow negotiators to back away from the tough phase-out dates that had been in place since 1987. As a result, the ban on the production or importation of methyl bromide for industrialized nations that was supposed to go into effect in 2001 was replaced by a goal of achieving a token 25 percent reduction in its use. Meanwhile, the complete ban on production was pushed back to 2010—or perhaps never, because for the first time the concept was broached of exempting agricultural uses altogether, on the grounds that they constitute a "critical use." Because roughly 95 percent of U.S. methyl-bromide production is dedicated to agricultural uses, the chemical could remain in production essentially forever.

The public's health notwithstanding, the political tide was turning in the direction of the methyl bromide industry. Credit that change in circumstance to the able work of Peter Sparber, a Washington lobbyist whose clients include the Methyl Bromide Working Group and Great Lakes Chemical, the world's largest producer of methyl bromide. The overlap, as it turns out, is not coincidental. Sparber is the president of the Methyl Bromide Working Group, whose headquarters are in the offices of his lobbying firm, Sparber and Associates. The group's chairman, Richard Landrum, works for Great Lakes Chemical in West Lafayette,

Indiana. The tax returns filed by the Methyl Bromide Working Group were prepared in Indiana and had to be sent to Sparber's office in Washington when the Center asked to inspect them, as the law requires. They show that the tax-exempt organization has no employees and pays no rent; the biggest single expense in 1995 and 1996 was the payment of $276,000 a year in "professional fees," presumably to Sparber or his firm.

The Methyl Bromide Working Group was formed, in the words of its tax return, to promote an "awareness and understanding of the essential and critical need" for the chemical that killed Sandra Mero and others. And it is not the only deadly product that has found an effective advocate and ally in Peter Sparber. His lobbying firm also counts R. J. Reynolds Tobacco Company among its clients.

One "critical use" loophole allows methyl bromide to stay on the market if its absence would result in "significant market disruption."

A sure sign of Sparber's effectiveness came in January 1996, when Mary Nichols, the EPA's assistant administrator for air and radiation, told the House Commerce Subcommittee on Health and Environment that the Clinton Administration supported a legislative approach to the issue—an apparent reference to Miller's bill. The stage was thus set for methyl bromide to be permanently exempted from both the Clean Air Act and international regulation.

In the meantime, aides to Clinton and EPA Administrator Carol Browner were pressuring health, environmental, and labor organizations to support the Administration in its efforts to stave off the Methyl Bromide Working Group's offensive on Capitol Hill. The public-interest groups were told that they should line up behind a quid-pro-quo agreement within the Administration: The EPA would maintain the listing of methyl bromide under the Clean Air Act, and the Agriculture Department would be repaid with exemptions for continued methyl bromide use.

But the public-interest groups balked. They not only rejected the demand to support Clinton, they also threatened to launch a high-visibility attack, citing the EPA's own estimates that leaving methyl bromide on the market longer would lead to additional cancer deaths from increased solar radiation. The Environmental Working Group was setting in motion a campaign in California to track complaints in areas where methyl bromide was being sprayed close to homes, schools, and day-care centers, triggering a sudden surge in public awareness. Faced with a unified and unyielding public-interest community and in the midst of a presidential campaign in which Clinton was bludgeoning Republicans for their dismal record on the environment, the Administration backed down.

(Through all this, Vice President Albert Gore, Jr., who in 1992 had blasted the Bush Administration for moving too slowly to phase out methyl bromide and other ozone-depleting chemicals, was mute—a silence all the more conspicuous because Gore, in his best-selling book, *Earth in the Balance,* had written, "The integrity of the environment is not just another issue to be used in political games.")

The Clinton Administration's retreat seemed to signal the end of effective efforts to relax the regulation of methyl bromide. Miller's bill died with no action. The impending ban on production remained undisturbed. And even though the California legislature sided with Governor Wilson and extended use of methyl bromide, a new deadline of December 1997 was set. In September 1997, the signatories to the Montreal Protocol met on the tenth anniversary of the landmark agreement, again in Montreal. Methyl bromide was at the top of the agenda, and the Clinton Administration's position was that production of the chemical should be halted globally by 2001. After all the lobbying, maneuvering, and political showboating, attention was at last being paid to the environment and the public health.

Or so it seemed.

Clinton's negotiators may have asked on paper for a global production ban starting in 1997, but what they ultimately agreed to was entirely different. In fact, the amendments to the Montreal Protocol that were finally adopted effectively guarantee Great Lakes Chemical and Albemarle Corporation a market for methyl bromide until at least 2015, and possibly forever. A phased reduction in production within the United States and other industrialized countries starts in 1999, reaching full effect in 2005.

Developing nations, such as Mexico, have until 2015 to end production. But most important, there are a range of "critical use" loopholes. One, for example, allows methyl bromide to stay on the market if its absence would result in "significant market disruption."

Among those attending the Montreal negotiations was the Methyl Bromide Working Group's Peter Sparber, who aimed to leverage support in Washington into an outcome that locked in a global market for the makers and users of one of the world's deadliest chemicals.

The methyl bromide saga is an all-too-familiar routine in Washington. Time after time, highly toxic chemicals remain on the market, illogically, long after they have been shown to be lethally dangerous. And, more often than not, chemical manufacturers have no more helpful or sympathetic allies than Capitol Hill lawmakers—in whom they invested more than $20 million in campaign contributions from 1987 to 1996.

In October 1997, Miller reintroduced his legislation with some five dozen cosponsors. This time around, what the bill seeks—the repeal of the Clean Air Act's prohibition on methyl-bromide production—is consistent with international agreement, not at odds with it. So in Washington, Sparber has been able to use the multinational agreement as a rationale for repealing U.S. law.

That means if Sparber and his allies have their way, farmers will likely be able to inject the earth with methyl bromide in perpetuity, and that the agribusiness constituents of Dan Miller will be able to conduct business as usual. When more names are added below Sandra Mero's on the list of fatalities attributable to methyl bromide, Miller, Wilson, and politicians like them will no doubt offer up the same refrain: What's that got to do with the price of beans?

5

||||||●||||||

The Tainted Table

I N FEBRUARY 1982, PHYSICIANS AT ROGUE VALLEY MEDICAL CENTER
and Providence Hospital in Medford, Oregon, puzzled over the
cases of more than two dozen people who had been hospitalized
with frightening but inexplicable symptoms: stomach cramps so
intense that one patient described them as being more painful
than childbirth and diarrhea so bloody that patients appeared to
be hemorrhaging. A mysterious invader was destroying massive
numbers of platelets that promote coagulation. Patients' intestines
were swelling, and their kidneys were failing. One doctor was so
mystified that he operated on two victims thinking that they might
be suffering from appendicitis. Finally, after days of interviews,
authorities hit on the one thing that the patients had in common:
They had all eaten hamburgers at a local McDonald's restaurant.

Scientists at the Centers for Disease Control and Prevention
soon discovered that the mysterious outbreak in Medford was the
first sign of a major public-health threat spreading through the
nation's food supply. E. coli O157:H7 was a relatively new strain
of a ubiquitous, normally benign intestinal bacterium that produced a dangerous chemical: the Shiga toxin. Although O157:H7
originated in cattle, it has since been discovered in fruits, vegetables, and water.

The microbe was capable of transforming a hamburger, that

staple of the American diet, into a lethal hazard. When cows were slaughtered, their carcasses were contaminated with bacterium-laden fecal material. As the carcasses were turned into ground beef, the bacterium spread through the packages of hamburger that went to restaurants and supermarkets. Consumers had no way of knowing whether ground beef was contaminated because O157:H7 didn't affect the look or smell of the product. Heat could eradicate the bacterium, but only if a patty was carefully and thoroughly cooked inside and out. Otherwise, a medium-rare burger at a restaurant or from a backyard barbecue had the potential to kill. In about 5 percent of the cases of O157:H7 contamination, the toxin secreted by the bacterium caused hemolytic uremic syndrome (HUS), an illness that attacks the kidneys and other organs. Those who did not die might be left with permanent damage, such as epilepsy, blindness, or lung damage, and might even require organ transplants to survive.

This was precisely the sort of public-health threat that cried out for the intervention of the federal government. Although people could not spot the microbe in the burgers on their plates, it was possible to stop O157:H7 before it got that far. The U.S. Agriculture Department has the authority to regulate the meat-processing industry, and in 1982 it already had an extensive system in place, including thousands of inspectors at packing plants across the nation. Tests to detect the bacterium existed, making it possible to intercept tainted beef before it was shipped to restaurants and supermarkets.

Instead, amazingly, it took another decade and a half for the federal government to protect citizens against the menace of O157:H7. By then, an estimated 8,000 to 16,000 people were being sickened by the microbe each year, and as many as 500 were dying.

As frightening as E. coli O157:H7 is, the microbe is just one of numerous threats to health in our food. A 1996 report by the General Accounting Office, the investigative arm of Congress, noted more than thirty disease-producing agents present in the nation's food supply, and scientists believe that the number is growing. They range from familiar bogeymen—parasites such as trichinella in undercooked pork and viruses such as hepatitis A, passed through infected food handlers or food tainted by sewage—to an increasing number of strange new threats, bacteria with exotic names such as *Listeria monocytogenes* and *Campylobacter jejuni.*

Although the GAO noted in its report that the available data probably did not give the full picture of the epidemic, there are ample signs that the threat of food-borne sickness is rapidly increasing.

• Across the nation, as journalist Nicols Fox notes in *Spoiled,* a recent book on food-borne illnesses, there are mass outbreaks of disease triggered by pathogens that were scarcely mentioned in the scientific literature fifteen years ago. The once-obscure bacterium campylobacter, for example, spread chiefly by contaminated poultry, is now the most common food-borne pathogen in the United States. It may cause as many as 3,830 cases of Guillain-Barré syndrome, one of the leading causes of paralysis, each year. In 1994, 224,000 people across the country became sick after eating ice cream contaminated with *Salmonella enteritidis,* a new, more virulent strain of a familiar microbe, which went from being a rarity in 1980 to the most prevalent form of salmonella.

• The GAO estimates that as many as 81 million cases of food-borne illness occur in the United States every year and that more than 9,000 of the victims die. The economic cost—in hospital and physician bills and lost productivity—may amount to $22 billion.

An estimated 25 percent of all broiler chickens sold in the United States are tainted with salmonella.

However, because not everyone who is a victim of food poisoning seeks medical help and because there is no federal reporting requirement for food-borne illness, there is no way to know the full extent of the problem.

• Poultry sold in the United States is frequently contaminated with salmonella and campylobacter, which each year cause an estimated 5.5 million illnesses and 4,350 deaths nationwide. An estimated 25 percent of all broiler chickens sold in the United States are tainted with salmonella. A 1996 report by the Center for Science in the Public Interest put the blame in part on federal regulations that allow poultry plants to rinse contaminated carcasses rather than discard them. The regulations also permit processors to include the skin—the portion of the chicken most likely to harbor bacteria—in ground poultry products. When the meat and poultry industry complained in 1996 about a proposed new regulation that would have required daily salmonella inspections, the Agriculture Department abandoned it in favor of a test for a more benign strain of bacterium.

• Some raw oysters—especially those from Gulf Coast waters—contain the bacterium *Vibrio vulnificus,* which kills 40 percent of the people it infects. In 1994, FDA regulators tried to ban the sale of raw Gulf Coast oysters during the peak danger period of April through October. But Members of Congress, including Republican Robert Livingston of Louisiana, the powerful chairman of the House Appropriations Committee, forced the FDA to back down. In 1996, there were thirty-five separate reported cases of poisoning from the *Vibrio vulnificus*-contaminated shellfish, and twenty-four victims died.

• Increasingly, fruits and vegetables can also be a source of dangerous illnesses. Cyclospora, a single-celled parasite that invades the small intestine and causes diarrhea, vomiting, weight loss, fatigue, and muscle aches, sickened nearly 1,500 people in the United States in 1996. In 1997, an outbreak that sickened hundreds of people was caused by contaminated basil in pesto sauce sold by a gourmet market in Alexandria, Virginia. In the spring of 1997, more than 150 children and schoolteachers in Michigan contracted hepatitis A after eating contaminated strawberries in school cafeterias. Thousands of children in six other states had to be inoculated after possible exposure to the disease through the fruit as well.

• Cases of E. coli and salmonella have also increased as more food from overseas is imported into the United States. Contaminated water, parasites, and pesticides banned in the United States but used elsewhere have contributed to outbreaks involving Ugandan alfalfa sprouts carrying salmonella, Guatemalan raspberries infected with cyclospora, and Peruvian carrots tainted with E. coli. In 1996, the FDA inspected less than 1 percent of the 2.2 million food shipments. That number may drop even further as the United States forms new trade pacts with Central and South America and Congress puts the squeeze on the FDA's budget.

• Fish and crabs are at increasing risk of carrying disease. A 1997 outbreak of *Pfiesteria piscicida,* a bacterium that thrives on waste materials, killed thousands of fish and put dozens of people in the hospital after they were exposed to the contaminated waters in the Mid-Atlantic region. Victims suffered from memory loss, skin rashes, and respiratory problems. Health officials blamed runoff of waste from nearby chicken farms. Such conditions, which can affect drinking water, may also exist in waterways near North Carolina's hog farms and the Midwest's beef-processing centers. Although in 1993 the Clinton Administration proposed changes to the Clean Water Act to include these "nonpoint," or indirect, sources of contamination, Congress has not acted.

If America's food supply is increasingly fraught with risks, a big part of the problem is Congress. Again and again, when faced with the choice between protecting the public safety and protecting the industry, Capitol Hill lawmakers have chosen the latter. Although Americans are eating more imported fruits and vegetables than ever, federal inspectors screen only one or two of every 100 shipments. The lack of oversight allowed cyclospora-tainted Guatemalan raspberries to make their way into grocery stores, sickening hundreds of people across the country in 1996.

But perhaps the most blatant example of how Congress has abdicated its responsibility with regard to food safety is the case of E. coli O157:H7.

When Congress passed the first meat-inspection law in the late nineteenth century, it was to help the meat industry rather than to protect the public. Meatpackers needed the government seal of approval so that they could export their products to other nations. It wasn't until 1906 that Congress, shamed by the scan-

Although Americans are eating more imported fruits and vegetables than ever, federal inspectors screen only one or two of every 100 shipments. The lack of oversight allowed cyclospora-tainted Guatemalan raspberries to make their way into U.S. grocery stores, sickening hundreds in 1996.

dalous filth in the meatpacking industry as depicted in Upton Sinclair's novel *The Jungle,* passed the Federal Meat Inspection Act, empowering the government to ensure that meat was fit for public consumption.

But after the public furor died down, Congress gradually stopped paying attention. "Meat and poultry inspection was an arcane subject that ninety-nine percent of Members [of Congress] knew nothing about," Carol Tucker Foreman, a former assistant Agriculture Secretary in the Carter Administration, told a reporter from *The Washington Post.* Instead, the responsibility for meat fell to the Agriculture Department, which had a natural conflict; its main mission was to promote agribusiness by helping farmers produce and sell more food, including animals for slaughter. Oversight of the inspection system fell to the Senate and House Agriculture Committees, whose members typically came from states where farms and meat production were big business.

Over the years, the meat industry accumulated considerable political clout. In 1906, even before the passage of the Federal Meat Inspection Act, the biggest companies in the industry set up the American Meat Packers Association, which later became the American Meat Institute (AMI). In the 1970s, as consumer activism and the specter of further government regulation grew, the trade group moved its headquarters from Chicago to Washington, D.C., and worked hard to build influence with the Agriculture Department, the White House, and Congress. The institute represents about 800 companies in various parts of the beef and poultry trade, and its $8.5 million budget is modest by Washington standards. But the meat lobby includes lots of other players, including the cattlemen who raise the cows and the grocers who sell the packaged beef. The big meatpacking outfits such as Excel Corporation, a subsidiary of the multinational food-processing giant Cargill, Inc., and Monfort, Inc., a part of ConAgra, Inc., have their own Washington political operations. Smaller companies have the National Meat Association and the American Association of Meat Processors. All told, individuals, companies, and trade organizations connected with the meat industry gave more than $12.3 million in campaign contributions to congressional campaigns from 1987 to 1996. From 1991 to 1996, these groups chipped in another $945,840 to party organizations, and over the last decade they donated another quarter of a million dollars in speaking fees.

Not surprisingly, the government hasn't so much policed the industry as it has served it. At last count, the Agriculture Department's Food Safety and Inspection Service (FSIS) had more than 7,400 inspectors in the nation's 6,200 meat-processing plants. But as a former Agriculture Department official noted, meatpackers came to see the inspectors in their plants as an "inspection service" whose purpose was to serve the industry. "The inspector was there to put the government stamp of approval on meat, because they needed the stamp to sell products to the public." Inspectors relied on sight and smell to determine whether meat was fit for consumption—a method that revealed more about how appetizing the food would be than whether it was free of contamination.

FSIS had such a close relationship with the industry that when Lester Crawford, the service's administrator from 1987 to 1991, left the government, the National Food Processors Association hired him as its executive vice president for scientific affairs. FSIS officials sometimes go to work for the AMI after they retire, helping companies they once regulated negotiate with their own former government coworkers. Patrick Boyle, the AMI's president, for example, served in the late 1980s as the administrator of the USDA's Agricultural Marketing Service, which oversees the grading, inspection, and regulatory programs for the agency. Little wonder, too, that the industry gets its way so often on Capitol Hill; many of its top lobbyists used to work there. Of the 124 lobbyists whom the Center for Public Integrity identified as working for the meat industry in 1997, twenty-eight came from Capitol Hill, including one former Representative.

||||||||||||||||||||||||||||||||||||||||||||||

Officials from the Agriculture Department's Food Safety and Inspection Service sometimes go to work for the American Meat Institute after they retire, helping companies they once regulated negotiate with their own former government coworkers.

||||||||||||||||||||||||||||||||||||||||||||||

As far back as the 1960s, scientists warned of dangers that eluded the federal government's outdated inspection methods. Microbes such as salmonella and campylobacter are tasteless, odorless, and invisible, and modern food-industry practices promote the spread of such diseases. Animals are massed in tight quarters, where they more easily become contaminated with excrement and are slaughtered at a furious pace in mechanized plants. Modern shipping systems make it possible for meat from distant and diverse sources to be combined in ground beef, increasing the likelihood that pathogens will spread. In her book *Spoiled,* Nicols Fox quotes Robert Tauxe, the chief of the Foodborne and Diarrheal Diseases Branch of the Centers for Disease Control and Prevention, describing today's hamburger as "a mixture of one hundred different cattle from four different countries."

Nevertheless, the Agriculture Department clung to its turn-of-the-century inspection methods. As far back as 1974, it resisted calls for labels on meat warning of the danger of salmonella if it was improperly cooked. Instead, the department argued that the presence of dangerous microbes on food did not fit the definition of "adulterated" in federal food-safety laws. This was the meat industry's long-held position: that it is impossible, or at least impractical, to rid meat of microbes in the packing plant and that consumers can protect themselves through proper cooking methods. In 1994, the General Accounting Office concluded that the inspection program was "only marginally better today at protecting the public from harmful bacteria than it was even eighty-seven years ago."

But O157:H7 put the Agriculture Department under more intense pressure. In 1984, an outbreak at a nursing home in Nebraska killed four elderly patients and sickened thirty-four others. The following year the National Research Council, a private scientific organization financed with a combination of public and private money, urged the federal government to start microbial testing in packing plants.

But the Agriculture Department took no action, and neither did Congress. It is not that Congress was uninterested in the meat industry; in the five years following the O157:H7 outbreak of 1982, Capitol Hill lawmakers put nearly twenty meat-related bills in the hoppers. One sought to limit the importation of lamb; another exempted from federal inspection standards restaurant kitchens that used ready-to-eat meat products. Lawmakers declared the last week in January "National Meat Week" and considered a Senate resolution urging Americans to eat more meat. But even as more of their constituents died, they blithely ignored E. coli O157:H7. In October 1986, in Walla Walla, Washington, thirty-seven people got sick and two died as a result of O157:H7 in a taco mix. In June 1987, at a barbecue at a home for the mentally retarded in Salt Lake City, thirteen-year-old Kip Nicodemus ate a hamburger and spent the next five weeks in the hospital suffering the agonies of kidney failure. Fortunately, he survived, but his young roommate and three other children didn't. "We had no idea it was linked to hamburger until he got out of the hospital," his mother later told a reporter.

In October 1987, Senator Patrick Leahy, a Democrat from Vermont, introduced legislation that would have required the Agriculture Department, for the first time, to test samples of meat for microbial contamination; packing plants where dangerous microbes were found would be subjected to closer scrutiny and, if they were unable to meet standards, shut down. But the American Meat Institute helped keep Leahy's bill bottled up in the Senate Agriculture Committee.

In 1988, more than 100 schoolchildren in Minnesota and Wisconsin got sick from tainted beef. Three years later, the Centers for Disease Control and Prevention warned that "the geographic distribution of outbreaks are evidence that this pathogen is widespread in the United States . . .

> **In the five years following the E. coli O157:H7 outbreak of 1982, Capitol Hill lawmakers put nearly twenty meat-related bills in the hoppers. One sought to limit the importation of lamb; another exempted from federal inspection standards restaurant kitchens that used ready-to-eat meat products. But they ignored O157:H7.**

[and] the dimensions of this problem may be substantial." That year the Agriculture Department finally took its first cautious step to respond, asking supermarkets to voluntarily put safe-cooking instructions on beef.

In December 1992, disaster struck. Six people in the San Diego area became ill after eating fast-food hamburgers tainted with O157:H7; one, a six-year-old girl, died. A few weeks later, in January 1993, eighteen young patients at Children's Hospital in Seattle displayed the same grisly symptoms that Oregon physicians had observed a decade before; tests confirmed the presence of O157:H7. Luckily, a physician at the hospital called Dr. John Kobayashi, Washington state's chief epidemiologist. Within days, Kobayashi had traced the bacterium to tainted hamburger meat at Jack-in-the-Box restaurants and then to a shipment of beef in the chain's warehouse in Tukwila, Washington. The restaurant chain recalled and destroyed 28,000 pounds of frozen hamburger patties.

But about 40,000 patties from the tainted shipment had already been sold to Jack-in-the-Box patrons. Some 600 of them became ill, and ninety-two patients developed life-threatening hemolytic uremic syndrome. On January 22, two-year-old Michael Nole of Tacoma died of heart failure, caused by the damage to his kidneys from the infection. In the next month, two other children died—two-year-old Celina Shribbs and seventeen-month-old Riley Detwiler, who was infected through contact with a day-care classmate who had eaten a tainted hamburger.

The sheer numbers of O157:H7 victims and the news media's coverage of their agony finally caught the attention of Congress. On February 5, 1993, at a hearing of the Senate Agriculture Subcommittee on Agricultural Research, Conservation, Forestry, and General Legislation, Robert J. Nugent, the president of Jack-in-the-Box, appealed to the federal government to do something. Just like McDonald's in 1982, Jack-in-the-Box had used federally inspected beef. "The meat-inspection system and federal food-preparation standards," Nugent complained, "are not providing the protection Americans deserve." (Although it may have sounded as if Nugent were seeking to dodge blame, his complaint was validated in 1994 by John Harman, the GAO's director of food and agricultural issues, who told Congress that "the present inspection system cannot effectively identify and prevent meat contaminated with pathogenic bacteria like E. coli from entering the nation's food supply.")

Also testifying that day in 1993 was James Marsden, the AMI's vice president of science and technical affairs, who pushed the industry line that ultimately it was up to consumers to protect themselves by carefully cooking meat. "Even if some new technology were approved to eliminate pathogens from raw meat . . . there would be no guarantee that pathogens could not be reintroduced to that product in the retail store, food-service establishment, or home," he assured the Senators. Two weeks after the first child died in Seattle, the American Meat Institute put out a press release in which its president, Patrick Boyle, was quoted as saying, "This recent outbreak sheds light on a nationwide problem: inconsistent information about proper cooking temperatures for hamburger."

That argument, however, was flawed. Killing off the lethal bacteria meant cooking beef much more thoroughly than most consumers were accustomed to doing. Furthermore, restaurant patrons had no way of protecting themselves unless they were willing to barge into the kitchen with a meat thermometer. Even restaurants were not willing to rely on cooking alone to kill the microbe. Jack-in-the-Box, Wendy's, and other chains soon began testing the beef they bought for the presence of E. coli.

Nearly four months and several congressional hearings after the Jack-in-the-Box outbreak, Agriculture Secretary Mike Espy finally acted. In March 1993, the Agriculture Department tightened its guidelines on the fecal contamination of carcasses, the mode by which O157:H7 apparently spread. Instead of merely washing off the feces, as packers had been allowed to do in the past, they now had to trim any tainted areas from the carcass. But the outbreaks continued, and in August 1993 Espy announced an emergency rule requiring a label on each package of meat, giving instructions on proper cooking and refrigeration and warning about the dangers of contamination from mishandling.

Although the meat industry argued that consumers needed to cook beef properly, the grocery industry balked at putting labels on the packages telling them to do it. In late September, the National American Wholesale Grocers' Association, the National Grocers Association, and the Texas Food Industry Association filed suit in federal court to stop the cooking-instruction labels, arguing that their legal right to comment on the rule had been ignored. A federal judge agreed, and the Agriculture Department had to go through the standard public-comment process, causing a five-month delay.

As the federal government and the grocery industry fought over the labels, more people became sick from O157:H7. In January 1994, there were twenty new cases in Oregon and Washington. Late that month, Espy appeared at a press conference held by the Lois Joy Galler Foundation for Hemolytic Uremic Syndrome, a research organization named for one of O157:H7's child victims. (The American Meat Institute has been one of the foundation's financial supporters.) Espy had spoken with the girl's parents a month before and had been moved by the experience. With photographs of the three-year-old as a backdrop, he gave an emotional speech in which he described the aggressive attack he wanted to launch on O157:H7. Espy said that he hoped technology would come to the rescue—genetic engineering that would produce cattle immune to O157:H7 infection. In the shorter term, he wanted to revamp his department's inspection system. "We simply must move our inspection into the twenty-first century," he said. "You can't see germs. You can't see food-borne bacteria. . . . It can't be detected by the human eye. We have to introduce microbial testing."

Restaurant patrons had no way of protecting themselves unless they were willing to barge into the kitchen with a meat thermometer.

By then, some Members of Congress were also calling for something to be done. In January 1994, Representative Robert Torricelli, a Democrat from New Jersey, introduced legislation to mandate microbial testing. (Torricelli is now in the Senate.) In addition, he wanted to create an independent federal agency to inspect food. The Clinton Administration, which in 1993 had proposed moving meat inspection over to the Food and Drug Administration, also wanted to change the system. In September, Representative Charles Stenholm, a Democrat from Texas, introduced the Administration's Pathogen Reduction Act, which would have established standards for microbial contamination and set civil penalties for selling tainted meat. In a speech, Stenholm said that he was frustrated by the "seemingly slow pace and direction of change in general within USDA."

Through the spring and summer of 1994, as those bills awaited action in Congress, there were more O157:H7 outbreaks across the nation. Twenty-one cases appeared in Nebraska in April. The next month, health officials in Bismarck, North Dakota, reported seventeen cases of food-borne illness. In June and July, more than 120 cases of E. coli poisoning were reported in New York, New Jersey, and Connecticut. The outbreaks underscored the grim situation faced by the American Gastroenterological Association when it convened a conference on O157:H7 in the nation's capital. At the conference, a panel of industry and government experts concluded that the microbe had become so prevalent that it was no longer possible to guarantee the safety of ground beef. To kill the potentially deadly bacterium, they urged irradiation of hamburger with cobalt—a solution that many food-safety activists, fearing it would cause toxic substances to form in the meat, thought was as harmful as the disease itself.

While Congress stalled, someone finally took action. In the summer of 1994, Espy appointed Michael Taylor, who had been the FDA's deputy commissioner for policy, to head the Agriculture Department's Food Safety Inspection Service. Unlike his predecessor, Russell Cross, a meat-industry favorite who was an opponent of microbial testing, Taylor assessed the E. coli menace and concluded that something had to be done. He decided to confront the meat industry head-on.

On September 29, Taylor dropped his bombshell at a speech to the American Meat Institute. Federal inspectors, he announced, would immediately begin testing meat for O157:H7, with 5,000 random samples taken from both supermarkets and meat-processing plants. Because the bacterium was so virulent, any shipments of beef found to be contaminated would be seized or recalled.

Taylor figured that he did not need to wait for Congress to act; instead, breaking with long-standing official policy, he simply classified the microbe as an adulterant so that FSIS could assert the authority to regulate it. Taylor thought he was on solid ground. After all, although nobody called O157:H7-contaminated beef adulterated, everyone already acted as if it was; if FSIS received information that an outbreak had been traced back to a lot, inspectors quietly impounded whatever meat remained. But from now on, FSIS's inspectors would go looking on their own.

Taylor's bold move quickly raised a storm of protest in the cattle, meatpacking, and grocery industries. The American Meat Institute went over Taylor's head to Deputy Agriculture Secretary Richard Rominger in an attempt to get the testing stopped. "The whole slaughter industry felt that Mike Taylor was sitting in an ivory tower," Sara Lilygren, the AMI's senior vice president for legislative and public affairs, told the Center for Public Integrity.

On November 1, the AMI and other industry groups filed suit in federal court in Austin, Texas, to stop the testing. At a press conference in Washington, D.C., Patrick Boyle, the AMI's president, said the tests were so unreliable that "we have had tests that come up positive on one side of a hamburger patty and negative on the other," and he complained that it would cost packing plants a ruinous $1 million each time they had to recall a shipment of beef. An AMI press release warned, "This program has the potential to mislead consumers with promises of a safer food supply, and as a result they may relax their own cooking and handling standards." John Block, who had been Agriculture Secretary in the Reagan Administration and was now president of the National American Wholesale Grocers' Association/International Foodservice Distributors Association, complained that the department he once ran was proceeding "recklessly with a bureaucratic policy that is unfair and unwise."

Taylor made a small concession to the industry: He agreed to allow hot-water rinses of carcasses, a process that had been shown to reduce the incidence of O157:H7, before the federal inspectors performed their tests. But he wouldn't back down.

The industry remained adamant. The day after its lawsuit was filed the American Meat Institute held an industry briefing on O157:H7 in a hotel outside Chicago. One speaker was Dennis Johnson, a partner in the Washington law firm of Olsson, Frank, and Weeda. He advised the several hundred meatpackers in attendance not even to test ground beef for the microbe themselves, as some had quietly begun to do. "Your exposure is too great," Johnson warned. "You don't want to know."

Relatives of E. coli victims had formed a picket line outside the conference. Carrying signs emblazoned with such messages as "Infected Meat Maims and Kills Thousands" and "Industry Obstructs Again," members of an organization called Safe Tables Our Priority (STOP) insisted that something be done about the deadly microbe. One of the activists, Nancy Donley, held up a photograph of her six-year-old son Alex, who had died from an O157:H7 infection in 1993, a condition, she later said, in which "his insides [were] shredded, his brain liquefied by a pathogen . . . that I can only describe as evil." "How dare you oppose microbial testing that, if used, could have prevented Alex's death?" she demanded.

Shortly thereafter came evidence that testing could prevent tainted beef from reaching restaurant grills and consumers' plates. Florida officials, dissatisfied with the federal inaction on the O157:H7 front, had started its own random-testing program. When Florida inspectors discovered the microbe in one sample of beef, they promptly notified the Agriculture Department, which in turn traced it to a processing plant in Colorado. Nine thousand pounds of possibly contaminated beef were recalled before the meat could cause sickness.

But O157:H7 continued to cut a treacherous swath through the nation. In December 1994, twenty children in New Mexico became ill, apparently after eating tainted beef. In the Northwest, more than thirty people across three states became sick eating contaminated salami. Two weeks later, a federal judge in Texas threw out the lawsuit by the meat industry and grocers.

In January 1995, preschoolers in Ohio, South Dakota, Virginia, and Washington State were hospitalized after eating O157:H7-tainted beef. Meanwhile, after losing its legal battle against microbial testing, the meat industry turned to another ally: Congress. Several industry groups, including the AMI, the National Food Processors Association, and the National Broiler Council, sent a letter to the newly installed chairman of the House Agriculture Committee, Pat Roberts, a Kansas Republican. The letter outlined five legislative components essential to inspection reform. Indeed, the five-month public-comment period for the Agriculture Department's proposal to revamp the system was to begin in February. Both the USDA and many in the industry favored replacing the

|||||||||||||||||||||||||||||||||||||||||||||||||||||||||||||||||||||||

Nobody in the meatpacking industry wanted government inspectors doing daily tests and documenting the presence of a dangerous microbe such as salmonella. Some companies, especially the smaller meatpackers, didn't want to be forced to test for microbes at all.

old pass-fail system with a modern approach known as Hazard Analysis of Critical Control Points, or HACCP ("Have a Cup of Coffee and Pray," as government inspectors refer to it) in which the processors promise to check meat at various points in the process.

But the industry's vision of HACCP was a bit different from what Taylor had in mind. Meatpackers—especially smaller companies—did not like Taylor's push to impose mandatory antimicrobial measures, such as standard times for the chilling of carcasses. Rather than have federal inspectors looking at carcasses and performing pass-fail microbial tests, the industry wanted to have them spend more time reviewing paperwork to verify that a company's own controls were working. "They wouldn't have been looking at every single carcass anymore," the AMI's Sara Lilygren explained. But an industry memo obtained by the *Seattle Post-Intelligencer* proposed more radical changes. The Agriculture Department, the memo noted, would "no longer be responsible for the hands-on review of products, nor for the evaluation for disease or esthetic defects; this should be the facilities' responsibility." In other words, the industry would largely police itself.

More important, Taylor wanted to make testing for microbes a regular part of the federal inspection system. In addition to the sporadic spot tests for E. coli O157:H7, his plan called for daily samples from meatpacking plants to be tested for harmful microbes. Initially, the government planned to start by screening for another, easier-to-detect pathogen: salmonella, the leading cause of food-borne illness. Taylor wanted to measure the incidence of dangerous microbes at plants and eventually set a national performance standard that plants would have to meet. In the shorter term, he proposed interim goals for reducing the incidence of contamination.

The meat industry didn't like Taylor's ideas. Some companies were willing to demonstrate that their plants were maintaining cleanliness and curbing bacterial contamination through testing, but they wanted to test for a benign microbe such as generic E. coli. Nobody wanted government inspectors doing daily tests and documenting the presence of a dangerous microbe such as salmonella. Some companies, especially the smaller meatpackers, didn't want to be forced to test for microbes at all. They feared that if meat from their plants was found to be contaminated, they could be held liable for any resulting illnesses. ("If you do get a positive, will you ship?" James Hodges, the AMI's senior vice president for regulatory affairs, asked at a February 1996 panel discussion by industry officials and an FSIS representative. "What are your liability concerns?")

Some in the industry saw a chance to go even further. In the House and Senate, members of the new Republican majority pushed for a moratorium on new federal regulation of all sorts—including the Agriculture Department's proposed rules on O157:H7. In the Senate, the GOP's antiregulatory package was championed by Robert Dole of Kansas, the newly installed Senate Majority Leader and presidential hopeful, who bristled at the suggestion that he might be acting at the behest of meat-industry lobbyists. (In fact, Dole received more than $400,000 from agriculture PACs from 1989 to 1994, including at least $30,000 from meat and poultry processors and another $83,000 from the processed-food industry.)

Food-safety activists looked on in alarm. In the House, Torricelli and Democratic Representative George Brown of California introduced the Family Food Protection Act, which would have set standards for microbial contamination and explicitly classified O157:H7 and other microbes as adulterants. (Torricelli proposed the legislation after a constituent died of food poisoning. "The simple truth is," Torricelli said, "in some cases, the lucky ones die.") Bill Bradley, another New Jersey Democrat, introduced a similar bill in the Senate. But the proposals went nowhere. Representatives Louise Slaughter, a Democrat from New York, and Cardiss Collins, a Democrat from Illinois, tried another approach, offering an amendment that would have allowed the Agriculture Department to go forward with its proposed rules on pathogens.

"I completely disagree with the proponents of this regulatory moratorium bill that we should delay for one minute, much less six months, the implementation of USDA's regulations to reduce the number of deaths and illnesses that occur each year from food poisoning," Collins said in a February 14 speech to her colleagues. "For the Republican majority that now controls this Congress to not allow the proposed meat and poultry food-safety rule to be implemented is a callous disregard for human health and life."

But not a single Republican voted for the amendment. Former Senator Howard Metzenbaum, a Democrat from Ohio who had long advocated stricter food-safety laws, was outraged. At a press conference held by the Safe Food Coalition, a collection of senior-citizen, consumer-advocacy, labor, and whistle-blower organizations, Metzenbaum complained that there were "not one, not five, not ten, but maybe a hundred and two meat lobbyists lobbying against the [Agriculture Department's] proposed rule." Meat-industry officials, he said, should be "ashamed of themselves."

The debate continued, even as thirty-three people in North Carolina were stricken that May after eating hamburger. Food-safety activists couldn't make much headway against the GOP's antiregulatory juggernaut, but away from Capitol Hill, consumer activists and the well-organized, energetic lobby of families victimized by O157:H7 had more luck. They zeroed in on Dole's vulnerable presidential aspirations. In June, the Safe Food Coalition aired a television commercial in New Hampshire, the crucial primary state, in which Kansas resident Sonya Fendorf told of how her son had suffered permanent kidney damage after being exposed to O157:H7. "America's meat-inspection standards are dangerously out of date," she said in the ad. "Yet our Senator, Bob Dole, is pushing a bill that would block tougher standards—trying to please contributors instead of protecting kids."

An obviously irked Dole shot back from the floor of the Senate, denouncing as "Chicken Littles" those who warned that his bill would increase the O157:H7 risk. Nevertheless, Dole eventually backed down by exempting emergency food-safety threats from the regulatory cost-benefit analysis he wanted to impose.

The meat industry had plenty of allies in the House, too. At its behest, the House Appropriations Committee attached to the 1996 agricultural appropriations bill a rider by Republican James

Walsh of New York, who since 1988 had received at least $66,000 in campaign contributions from agribusiness. His rider—which, according to *The Washington Post,* was drafted in part by Philip Olsson, an attorney for the National Meat Association—would have tossed out the Agriculture Department's plan and forced it to negotiate with industry over the new rule. "It could have cost dearly in human health and lives," Caroline Smith DeWaal, director of the program on food safety at the Center for Science in the Public Interest, a nonprofit health-advocacy organization, told the Center.

In July, as another fifteen people in Georgia, New York, and Tennessee fell victim to O157:H7-tainted beef, the meat industry's strategy proved to be a costly one. Newspaper cartoonists had a field day with the meatpackers. "We took a beating in terms of public opinion," the AMI's Sara Lilygren told the Center. "Instead of stalling the regulations, we were just trying to get a seat at the table."

Meanwhile, the cracks in the meat-industry alliance had deepened. Some executives thought that the growing public fear over microbes was bad for business. IBP, Inc., the nation's biggest meat firm, abruptly quit the American Meat Institute and broke ranks with the industry to oppose the Walsh amendment. Robert Peterson, the company's chairman and chief executive officer, said in a letter to Agriculture Secretary Dan Glickman (who had succeeded Espy) that the delay sought by others in the industry was "not acceptable."

Finally, on July 18, Glickman met with Walsh, members of the House Agriculture Committee from both parties, and Richard Durbin of Illinois, the ranking Democrat on the House Appropriations Subcommittee on Agriculture. Late that night they negotiated a compromise. Walsh withdrew his amendment without a floor debate, and the revamping of the meat-inspection system moved forward. Glickman agreed to hold a series of meetings over the ensuing year, to solicit input from all sides in the debate, before publishing a final inspection plan in mid-1996. Glickman also agreed that as the new regulations were added to the Agriculture Department rule book, he would streamline the system by eliminating as many old regulations as possible.

As the year drew to a close, people were still being stricken by E. coli. In Montgomery, Alabama, a three-year-old child's kidneys were ravaged by hemolytic uremic syndrome; he had apparently eaten a tainted hot dog. Other cases showed up in Kansas, Ohio, and Pennsylvania. At last, however, the government seemed to be doing something about the menace.

Nevertheless, the battle over what to do about O157:H7 still wasn't over. In February 1996, Boyle fired off a testy letter to Taylor in which he complained that a publication of the Food Safety and Inspection Service described O157:H7 as having reached "epidemic proportions." Taylor refused to back down. "We believe that the increasing number of reported E. coli O157:H7 cases in the United States clearly fits the definition of an epidemic," he replied in a letter. In addition, at a February meeting with Patricia Stolfa, the acting deputy administrator of FSIS, representatives of the meat industry made it clear that they still didn't like the idea of government-mandated microbial testing. One told Stolfa that he'd like the agency "to forgo micro testing" altogether.

More significantly, some powerful Capitol Hill lawmakers still were willing to throw a wrench into the modernization of the meat-inspection process. In March 1996, the Senate rejected Taylor's request for an additional $9.5 million to spend on computers that were a key part of modernization plans, and instead adopted an amendment introduced by Senator Thad Cochran, a Republican from Mississippi, forcing the agency to spend an additional $13 million on salaries and benefits for inspectors. Taylor warned that the cuts would send a "powerful signal" that meat safety was again on the back burner.

In the House, Roberts, in his new role as chairman of the Agriculture Committee, slipped through an amendment that would have created a panel of experts from the meat and poultry industry to whom all meat-inspection rules and procedures would have to be submitted for review and comment. Food-safety activists were angry and disheartened. "Our faith in Congress's commitment to safer meat and poultry," Nancy Donley told a House subcommittee, "is just about zero."

By late spring, however, the funds for modernization were

restored to FSIS's budget and the industry review panel was cut. One possible reason: The lurid publicity about bovine spongiform encephalopathy, the "Mad Cow Disease" that was frightening Europe, made it a political nightmare to oppose meat regulation in any form. Subsequently, in July 1996, the Clinton Administration was able to unveil with much hoopla the final meat-inspection rules. "Families shouldn't have to fear the food they eat is unsafe," President Clinton proclaimed in a radio address. "With the tough steps we're taking today, America's parents should be able to breathe a little easier."

Clinton didn't mention, however, some of the significant concessions the industry had obtained. As part of the Walsh compromise, the government had agreed to hold additional informal negotiations with the industry. The cost of complying with the government's new regulations was drastically cut—from the $260 million a year that the Agriculture Department originally estimated in 1995 to about $100 million, or about one-tenth of a cent per pound of meat. This cost reduction was accomplished, in part, by the Agriculture Department's yielding on certain requirements. Instead of requiring packing plants to use an antimicrobial rinse known to be effective against O157:H7, for example, the Agriculture Department would simply require them to show that they could keep contamination below a certain level by whatever means they chose—such as trimming carcasses or slaughtering animals more carefully. Smaller plants weren't required to test as frequently for bacteria, and they had additional time—as much as two years past the January 1998 deadline for the biggest plants—in which to upgrade their practices.

> **The Agriculture Department still relies on hit-or-miss testing of a tiny portion of the nation's ground beef.**

There are questions about whether the federal government's safeguards against O157:H7 are sufficiently stringent. In the HACCP system, government inspectors will test samples daily for salmonella, and plants will be required to test and control levels of generic E. coli, which is an indicator of fecal contamination. But as for detecting the dangerous strain of E. coli O157:H7, the

Agriculture Department still relies on hit-or-miss testing of a tiny portion of the nation's ground beef. In the three years after Taylor instituted random O157:H7 testing, inspectors found only five samples that were positive for O157:H7 out of more than 15,000 samples. But that may give a false sense of security, because finding the O157:H7 bacterium on carcasses can be like looking for a needle in a haystack. It takes only a very small amount of O157:H7 to cause illness—100 to 200 bacteria in a quarter-pound burger—and the approximately 5,000 samples tested each year amount to only a tiny fraction of the 7 billion pounds of ground beef sold in the United States every year. And there are signs that tainted beef is slipping through. When Foodmaker, Inc., the parent company of Jack-in-the-Box, began vigorously testing its own meat supply for O157:H7 in the wake of the 1993 outbreak, it initially found about five positives per 1,000 beef patties—a rate twenty-five times higher than the government's testers found.

Meanwhile, in May 1997, a little more than fifteen years after the first major O157:H7 outbreak, an eighteen-month-old boy named Cody Edge and his half-brother, two-year-old Jason McKinnies, were admitted to Riley Hospital for Children in South Bend, Indiana, for the treatment of what appeared to be the gastrointestinal flu. Soon, however, the boys' conditions took a sharp turn for the worse, and after suffering kidney failure, both needed to undergo dialysis treatments to save their lives. Test results from Cody revealed the culprit: E. coli O157:H7. Like the victims in Oregon in 1982, the boys had apparently become ill after eating at a fast-food restaurant. "You hear about this on TV," the boys' mother, Jody Edge, told a reporter for *The Indianapolis Star*. "But you never think this could happen to you."

Sadly, because of Congress's dereliction of duty, it still can.

6

||||||●||||||

Cash Crop

ON APRIL 14, 1994, SEVEN CORPORATE EXECUTIVES STOOD BEHIND a table in Room 2123 of the Rayburn House Office Building in Washington, D.C., and raised their right hands. The hearing room exploded with flashes of light and the sound of clicking cameras as a standing-room-only crowd of journalists, lobbyists, public-health officials, congressional aides, and others watched the much-anticipated showdown. The executives swore to tell the truth, on penalty of perjury, and sat down to be questioned.

Democrat Henry Waxman of California, then the chairman of the House Energy and Commerce Subcommittee on Health and the Environment, had waited a long time for this moment. The chief executive officers of America's largest tobacco companies might finally admit what the Surgeon General of the United States, the World Health Organization, the American Medical Association, the U.S. Public Health Service, and countless other organizations—not to mention most ordinary Americans—had been saying for decades: Nicotine is addictive, and smoking kills.

Following the opening statements, Waxman fired a question at James Johnston, the chairman and chief executive officer of R. J. Reynolds Tobacco Company, the maker of Camel cigarettes:

"Do you agree that smoking causes heart disease?"

"It may," Johnston replied.

"Okay. They [the public-health community] agree that smoking causes lung cancer. Do you agree?"

"It may."

"Do you know whether it does?"

"I do not know."

Waxman moved on to Andrew Tisch, the chairman and chief executive officer of Lorillard Tobacco Company. Tisch had been questioned by the subcommittee's lawyers earlier and had said that he did not believe smoking caused cancer.

"Do you understand how isolated you are in the belief from the entire scientific community?" Waxman asked.

"I do, sir."

And so it went. Under oath, the executives denied knowing whether their products caused various diseases and death. They denied that nicotine was addictive—the addiction is so strong that the Surgeon General has likened it to that of cocaine or heroin—instead comparing it to the caffeine in coffee or the sugar fix from eating Twinkies. They denied targeting children in their advertising campaigns, likening their Joe Camel ads to ones using Snoopy to sell insurance and Garfield the Cat to hawk rooms at Embassy Suites Hotels.

In short, the seven executives denied knowing very much at all about the nation's single most preventable cause of premature death.

Each year, according to the Centers for Disease Control and Prevention, smoking kills more than 400,000 Americans. The practice is linked to cancers of the pharynx, larynx, esophagus, lungs, bladder, kidney, and pancreas. Environmental, or "secondhand," tobacco smoke may cause up to an additional 3,000 deaths from lung cancer each year, a result of the nearly sixty carcinogens and other substances in it that promote tumors.

Such deaths are not pretty. Cancerous tumors, Sherwin Nuland writes in his bestselling book *How We Die,* "tend to ulcerate and bleed, sometimes producing thick, slimy deposits of [dying] tissue. . . . This is precisely why the ancients referred to *karkinoma* as the 'stinking death.' "

Smoking can also lead to emphysema, a hyperinflation of the lung's air sacs that keeps oxygen from getting into the lungs. There is no cure for emphysema. Many victims spend the rest of their lives hooked up to an oxygen tank eighteen to twenty-four hours a day, gasping painfully for each breath. Some will have part or all of a lung removed.

Dr. Angelo Taviera Da Silva, a pulmonary specialist at Georgetown University Medical Center in Washington, D.C., advises his emphysema patients that the most important thing to do to slow the sickness is to stop smoking. "I tell them, 'If you do not quit, you will not be able to walk, to run, to make love to your wife—you will slowly fade away.'"

Each day in the United States 3,000 new addicts are born among the teenagers who take their first halting puffs of a cigarette. One of three will die of smoking-related diseases; others may quit or die of untreated causes. But the industry must attract young smokers to replace the old smokers who die.

At current prices, the typical pack-a-day smoker will spend about $32,000 on cigarettes in his or her lifetime (and that's not counting the associated higher costs for life insurance, lost wages, and the like). Society pays, too—from $38 billion to $95 billion a year, it is estimated, in added medical costs and lost productivity.

How has the tobacco industry been able to profit so handsomely for so long from the misery of tens of millions of Americans? By investing part of its profits in Congress.

In 1996, the tobacco industry spent nearly $26 million just to lobby Capitol Hill lawmakers. From 1987 to 1996, it gave $17.7 million to

|||||||||||||||||||||||||||||||||||||||||||||

Each day in the United States 3,000 new addicts are born among the teenagers who take their first halting puffs of a cigarette. One of three will die of smoking-related diseases; others may quit or die of unrelated causes.

|||||||||||||||||||||||||||||||||||||||||||||

congressional candidates and poured at least another $12.7 million into the accounts of the two major political parties. In addition, the industry has paid Members of Congress nearly $2 million in speaking fees since 1987 and has provided lawmakers and their employees with all-expenses-paid trips all over the world. To cover its tracks, the industry has set up an elaborate network of front groups that manufacture studies and statistics in support of tobacco.

When compared, however, with what the tobacco industry

has gotten in return—$1 billion a year in subsidies and virtually no real regulation—such costs seem puny indeed.

Tobacco's influence can be felt in almost every aspect of American life. Acre for acre, it is the most profitable legal crop grown in the United States. Approximately 124,000 farms in sixteen states grow tobacco. Convenience stores bring in a quarter of their incomes selling it. Many arts programs, from ballets to museums, are financed in part with tobacco money. Federal excise taxes raised $5.7 billion in 1996, much of it going either to health-care programs or to reducing the deficit. States collected another $7.6 billion, the bulk of it going again to health-care programs. NASCAR stock-car racing, the fastest-growing sport in America, is sponsored in large part by tobacco money. The U.S. government itself runs programs to help grow tobacco, insure it, export it, and guard it against foreign imports. Josh Cooper, a legislative specialist with the American Lung Association, told the Center for Public Integrity: "From museums to philanthropic organizations, everybody is addicted to the money."

> From 1987 to 1996, the tobacco industry has showered more than $30 million on Capitol Hill lawmakers and their national party committees. When it comes to tobacco money, almost every Member of Congress has inhaled.

So is Congress. From 1987 to 1996, the tobacco industry has showered more than $30.4 million on Capitol Hill lawmakers and their national party committees. Legislators from tobacco-producing states such as North Carolina and Kentucky support bills that benefit the industry and lay waste to those that might hurt it. Less likely recipients such as Democratic Representatives Charles Rangel and Edolphus Towns have been reluctant to raise excise taxes on cigarettes because doing so would disproportionately affect the poor people in their New York City districts. When it comes to tobacco money, almost every Member of Congress has inhaled.

The flow of cash into Congress is not new, and its effects

have been lasting. Around the turn of the century, James (Buck) Duke, the founder of American Tobacco Company, persuaded members of the Senate Finance Committee to lower the tax on cigarettes. It did not hurt that several members of the committee held tobacco stock, including one Senator from Rhode Island who owned more than $1 million worth.

In 1906, Congress passed the Pure Food and Drug Act, which subsequently led to the establishment of the Food and Drug Administration. The idea was to ensure the health and safety of products sold to Americans. Lobbyists got Congress to exclude tobacco from the list of goods to be regulated, thus ensuring that an entire class of products, known even then to be harmful, would remain effectively unregulated to this day.

It wasn't until changes were made in 1938 that the Food and Drug Administration had the authority to monitor the quality of tobacco products. And even then it did not do so, except in narrow circumstances in which companies had made false claims about the benefits of smoking.

Since then, Congress has passed no more than a handful of laws regulating tobacco. And little wonder: Using its vast financial resources, Big Tobacco—cigarette manufacturers, makers of smokeless tobacco, farmers, trade associations—has all but bought Capitol Hill.

Big Tobacco has bought the Democratic and Republican National Committees, too. Since 1991, tobacco companies have given $12.7 million in unregulated "soft money" to various national party committees. In the first half of 1997 alone, as the tobacco companies began to push for a nationwide settlement, the industry wrote an unprecedented $2 million in checks to the two major political parties.

When the Republicans won control of Congress in 1994, the tobacco companies won, too. After forty years of Democratic rule in Congress—the previous decade under almost constant attack by Waxman—the industry now had Tom Bliley, a Republican from Virginia, in command of the House Commerce Committee, which oversees some tobacco legislation. Bliley's main corporate constituent and prime financial backer has been Philip Morris and its employees. The tobacco industry's agenda included an end to the pounding they had taken on the health issue. For years, Bliley, a former funeral director, had been one of the top recipients of tobacco money. From 1987 to 1996, in fact, he had taken in at least $138,140 of it.

Soon after his ascension to the chairmanship of the Commerce Committee, Bliley let it be known that Big Tobacco now had a friend in the driver's seat. "My own hunch . . . and it's just a hunch," he said coyly, "is that we're going to be busy [with other things]." Bliley was true to his word. Until November 13, 1997—nearly three years after the Republicans took control of Congress—Bliley's committee did not hold hearings on tobacco.

Senator Mitch McConnell, a Republican from Kentucky, a big tobacco state, makes no apologies for accepting money from tobacco companies. (Three of his top ten career patrons are tobacco companies.) In response to a letter the Center for Public Integrity sent to every Member of Congress asking if he or she would continue accepting contributions in light of admissions that the industry had lied about the addicting nature of nicotine, McConnell wrote: "Yes, and I will strive to be, for the first time, the top recipient. I will accept these contributions because I am proud to have the support of a legal industry that is of great importance to my state."

Other times, holding a leadership position has it privileges. Representative Richard Gephardt, a Democrat from Missouri who was House Majority Leader from 1989 to 1995, collected at least $133,748 in campaign money from the tobacco industry from 1991 to 1996. Gephardt's leadership PAC, the Effective Government Committee, raked in an additional $66,000.

In 1996, following President Clinton's lead—and his own political instinct as he contemplated a presidential campaign in 2000—Gephardt came out for the first time in favor of government restrictions on tobacco. He canceled a September $1,000-a-plate fund-raiser for his Effective Government Committee to be held by Philip Morris in New York City. After the election, Gephardt announced that he would no longer accept money from the industry.

"Mr. Gephardt didn't believe the industry was doing enough to stop children from smoking," Eric Smith, Gephardt's spokesman, told the Center. "Things had built up to the point where he felt it was an appropriate move to make."

Maybe so. But the Minority Leader had changed his mind quickly. On August 27, 1996—the day before Vice President Albert Gore, Jr., delivered an emotional speech at the Democratic National Convention about his sister's death from smoking—Gephardt collected thirty-three checks, totaling $17,000, from employees of Philip Morris Companies, Inc. Over the next three weeks, the period leading to Gephardt's September decision, he got another sixty such checks, totaling $29,500.

A year earlier Gephardt had lobbied against the Clinton Administration's support of new restrictions on advertising and promotions. He called instead for the tobacco companies to take voluntary action.

"Mr. Gephardt realizes the importance of holding the Democratic Party together and helping some of us more conservative Southern Members when we have problems with the Administration," Representative Charlie Rose, a Democrat from South Carolina, said at the time.

Gephardt reversed his position in 1996 when it became apparent that the tobacco companies weren't going to move voluntarily.

The Republican leadership has also allied itself with Big Tobacco. Tom DeLay of Texas, the third-ranking Republican leader in the House, runs Americans for a Republican Majority Political Action Committee, or ARMPAC. In 1995, DeLay hired Karl Gallant, a lobbyist advising the Ramhurst Corporation, a grassroots consulting firm that boasts R. J. Reynolds as its biggest client, to be ARMPAC's executive director. Ramhurst pulled out the stops to defeat a 1996 New Jersey proposal that would have raised tobacco taxes to help finance school programs. Soon after DeLay hired Gallant, R. J. Reynolds reportedly gave $73,000 in "soft money" to ARMPAC.

Around the turn of the century, James (Buck) Duke, the founder of American Tobacco Company, persuaded members of the Senate Finance Committee to lower the tax on cigarettes. It did not hurt that several members of the committee held tobacco stock.

But John Boehner of Ohio, the chairman of the House Republican Conference, may offer the most striking example of what strange bedfellows Congress and the tobacco companies have become.

During the last week of June 1995, Boehner distributed three to six campaign checks from Louisville-based Brown and William-son Tobacco Corporation on the floor of the House while Congress was in session. The action, which he later said he would not repeat, was not illegal. In fact, Barry Jackson, Boehner's chief of staff, said that it was quite a common occurrence.

"For five years, he had seen Members on both sides of the aisle come to the floor—which is where they see each other—to exchange information and sometimes hand each other campaign contributions," Jackson told a reporter for the Associated Press.

In a letter to House Speaker Newt Gingrich asking him to stop the practice, three freshmen Democrats—Lloyd Doggett of Texas, Bill Luther of Minnesota, and Lynn Rivers of Michigan—wrote: "If members of the House are allowed to pass around special-interest checks in the very room where they are sworn to conduct the people's business, it is only a matter of time before the United States Capitol is bought and paid for." The House has since banned the practice.

In February 1997, the Tobacco Institute flew lawmakers to a posh resort for a conference on new tobacco advertising legislation. An idyllic vacation spot outside of Scottsdale, Arizona, the Phoenician Resort boasts a twenty-seven-hole championship golf course, swimming pools, Jacuzzis, tennis courts—including a Wimbledon-style grass court—and magnificent views of Camelback Mountain. Rooms start at $370 a night and can cost as much as $1,650. In an interview with the Center, a spokesman for the Tobacco Institute emphasized that the conference was "a normal part of our working relation with Congress" and that it was designed "to give Members the opportunity to tell what is on their minds." While few lawmakers were forthcoming about their presence at the event, which afforded them time for golf and other activities, federal disclosure records show that at least seventeen Members attended.

One of those was Ed Cassidy, an administrative assistant for Representative Richard (Doc) Hastings, a Republican from Washington State. Cassidy told the Center that he spent a significant portion of his time at the Phoenician Resort in meetings. But why were the meetings closed to the public? "Open meetings have a legitimate purpose, but not all of them can be in public. . . . There are decisions that have to be made that cannot be done in public," Cassidy said. "And to focus on the trips that Members and their staffs make to meet with officials overlooks the hundreds of closed-door meetings that take place all the time."

Representative Scotty Baesler, a Democrat from Kentucky, and John Townsend, his communications director, also went to the Phoenician. "It's one of the few opportunities to get all of the principals—the majors [the big cigarette manufacturers], the farmers, producers, warehousers—in under one roof," Townsend told the Center. "It's a case of: Do you bring the mountain to Mohammed, or does Mohammed go to the mountain?" Townsend said that he also went on an industry-financed trip to Williamsburg, Virginia, late in the summer of 1997, but did not participate in the golf tournament. "The prizes were lousy, I heard—cigars or something," he told the Center.

In 1993, at least twenty Members of Congress traveled to the Boca Raton Beach and Resort Club in Florida for the Jack Africk Invitational Tennis Tournament.

Jack Africk, as it turns out, was a vice chairman of UST, Inc.—a manufacturer of smokeless and pipe tobacco, among other products—which sponsored the charity event. The company's charitable activity apparently extended to at least three Capitol Hill lawmakers who collected $1,000 apiece in "speaking fees" for appearing at the tournament.

Philip Morris paid for Bliley and his wife to take a "fact-finding" trip to Sweden in 1991 and paid for McConnell to spend two nights in Singapore in 1992, according to financial disclosure reports.

In all, from 1991 to 1997, at least fifty-four lawmakers went on 142 industry-paid trips to such places as San Juan, Puerto Rico; Las Vegas, Nevada; Palm Springs, California; and Boca Raton, Florida. Often spouses went along on the free trips. Over the years, the tobacco industry has also organized hundreds of all-expenses-paid trips for congressional aides. In 1996, for example, the tobacco industry arranged eighteen such trips for Mem-

||||||||||||||||||||||||||||||||||||||||||||||||||||||||||||||||||||||||||

On August 27, 1996—the day before Vice President Albert Gore, Jr., delivered an emotional speech at the Democratic National Convention about his sister's death from smoking— House Democratic Leader Richard Gephardt collected thirty-three checks, totaling $17,000, from employees of Philip Morris Companies, Inc.

bers of Congress and thirty-four for congressional staff members. And these were hardly disinterested parties along for a free ride; nineteen of the lawmakers and aides served on committees with direct oversight of tobacco or FDA issues.

Because congressional aides often help the industry get access to their bosses or promote ideas in drafting legislation, they too receive tokens of appreciation. In a 1990 memo entitled "Monthly Cigarette Distribution List—Additions," Philip Morris executives asked Ellen Wright, in the company's customer-service department, to add Ellen Hollis, a legislative assistant to Representative W. J. (Billy) Tauzin, then a Louisiana Democrat (he is now a Republican), to its list of congressional aides receiving complimentary cartons of cigarettes. Hollis was to receive "1 carton of Marlboro 100s (regular, soft pack)." Susan Butler, the appointment secretary to Representative Jimmy Duncan, got a carton of Virginia Slims Lights.

What has the tobacco industry gotten in return for the largesse it has showered on Capitol Hill? Almost anything it wants. And even when the tobacco industry loses, it wins.

In 1965, with the passage of the Federal Cigarette Labeling and Advertising Act, the tobacco industry suffered its first defeat since the turn of the century. The new law required manufacturers to put warning labels ("Smoking May Be Hazardous to Your Health") on packs of cigarettes. But even that legislation had been watered down by the tobacco industry.

The labeling law also had an unintended side effect: It gave the tobacco companies an almost ironclad defense in lawsuits brought against them. With the warnings, the companies could claim that people were aware of the dangers, had made an informed judgment, and therefore had taken responsibility for the risks imposed by smoking.

Congress forced additional label changes in 1984, placing sterner notices—including a list of diseases attributed to smoking and a warning of birth defects—on cigarette packs. At that time, negotiations among the industry, the public-health community, and Congress were arduous, often focusing on particular phrasing. Late one evening, Peter Knight, an aide to then-Representative Albert Gore, Jr., was meeting with Howard Liebengood, the Tobacco Institute's top lobbyist, to discuss, yet again, the warning-label issue. In an interview with author Michael Pertschuk, Knight later recalled how Liebengood finally got fed up with the endless bickering over semantics:

"[Liebengood] said, 'Listen, I don't think we can go with this. I think we should just change the label. We should just have one label, and it should say, "This shit'll kill you." ' "

As the tobacco companies have promoted one of life's two proverbial inevitabilities—death—it has, with Congress's help, avoided the other: taxes.

From 1951 to 1983, Congress did not raise the federal excise tax on tobacco. Today the federal and state taxes on a pack of cigarettes are the lowest of those of all Western industrialized countries. From 1987 to 1996, Members of Congress introduced at least thirty-three bills aimed specifically at raising the federal excise tax. None passed.

In 1990, lobbyists for Philip Morris heard that—despite George Bush's "Read my lips" pledge two years earlier—a tax increase, including a hike in tobacco taxes, was on the way. One of the lobbyists, Kathleen Linehan, grew concerned. "We should activate every tool at our disposal immediately," Linehan told her colleagues in an internal memo. "I have a feeling this is not a test; this is the real thing."

In March 1990, Jim Dyer, a former Philip Morris lobbyist who is now the staff director of the House Appropriations Committee, helped get Philip Morris executives invited to the White House. According to internal memoranda released by Doctors Ought to Care, a Houston-based antitobacco organization, Ehud

Houminer, then the president and chief executive officer of Philip Morris USA—one of Philip Morris Companies, Inc.'s many subsidiaries—accepted an invitation to the Chairman's Foundation Dinner at the White House.

"The Chairman's Foundation Dinner is sponsored by the National Republican Senatorial Campaign Committee to allow executives of the nation's business community to meet with Bush Administration officials and Republican Senators in an informal atmosphere," Dyer's memo to Houminer reads. Hosted by President Bush and with at least eight Senators in attendance, the dinner would give Houminer, in Dyer's words, "the opportunity to meet not only the President, but the members of the Committee that will be writing the version of the 1991 budget." Other tobacco-industry bigwigs were also invited to the dinner.

When President Bush finally signed the tax increase into law in November 1990, the tobacco industry could breathe a sigh of relief—and without even choking. Instead of the sixteen-cent increase that Senator Pete Domenici, a Republican from New Mexico, had originally proposed, the legislation contained only an eight-cent increase, to twenty-four cents a pack.

How did the tobacco industry pull it off? Senator Wendell Ford, a Democrat from Kentucky, agreed to support higher airport landing fees, which Democrat Dan Rostenkowski, the chairman of the House Ways and Means Committee, wanted (because his Chicago district stood to gain from them). In return, Rostenkowski agreed to back the smaller tobacco-tax increase. Deal done.

"I think compared with what could have happened," one lawmaker observed, "[they're] walking away from this feeling that they have dodged a bullet."

In 1991, a powerful congressional aide left Capitol Hill to seek his fortune in the private sector. He had made many enemies in his day, but he had powerful friends as well and had gained a wealth of experience and knowledge of issues and how Congress works. After several years of a modest practice, he was approached by representatives of Philip Morris. Would the former aide help the company with its problems—Waxman chief among them—on Capitol Hill?

The former aide, who told the Center his story on the condition that his name not be used, said no. He did not want to help the industry—"you merchants of death," he called them—in any way. And, he added, he certainly did not want to press their case with his old colleagues on Capitol Hill.

But Philip Morris did not give up. The company approached him with a new offer: His job would not be to lobby, but merely to monitor and advise the company on congressional activities. Philip Morris was prepared to give him a five-year, multimillion-dollar contract. The former aide said yes and soon went to work for the "death merchants."

The tobacco industry employs an army of at least 150 Washington lobbyists who deal with tax, farm, trade, and other issues on Capitol Hill. That number, large as it is, doesn't include such hired guns as former Senate Majority Leader George Mitchell of Maine, who represented the industry for part of the tobacco settlement talks through the Washington law firm of Verner, Liipfert, Bernard, McPherson & Hand. The industry has more than 200 other lobbyists spread out across the country to weaken or kill antitobacco legislation at the state and local levels. At least forty of the tobacco industry's Washington lobbyists are former Capitol Hill lawmakers and top congressional aides.

In October 1997, Howard Baker, Jr., the former Senate Republican leader, registered with Congress to represent Philip Morris, R. J. Reynolds Tobacco Company, Brown and Williamson Tobacco Corporation, Loews Corporation, and UST. A week later, Baker resigned his post as the chairman of the board of trustees of the Mayo Foundation, which oversees the world-renowned Mayo Clinic, following a storm of protest from Mayo physicians. Over the years, the Mayo Clinic has been in the forefront of research into nicotine addiction and antismoking public education.

This is not the first time that Baker—who lost his first wife, Joy, and his father-in-law, the lengendary Senator Everett Dirksen of Illinois, to lung cancer—has worked for the tobacco industry in Washington. In 1989, as he completed his one-year ban on lobbying the White House (he'd been White House chief of staff in President Reagan's second term), Philip Morris lobbyist Jim Dyer wrote in an internal memo that Baker was in a "special position" to accomplish four goals for the company in Washington. Dyer variously described Baker as "a unique intelligence source," "a high-level advocate," "a master strategist," and "a goodwill ambassador."

||||||||||||||||||||||.|||||||||||||||||||

The tobacco industry employs an army of at least 150 Washington lobbyists who deal with tax, farm, trade, and other issues on Capitol Hill. At least forty of them are former Capitol Hill lawmakers and congressional aides.

||||||||||||||||||||||||||||||||||||||

"Senator Baker enjoys special access that few Washingtonians can ever hope to achieve," Dyer wrote in the memo. "From President Bush thru Messrs. [Secretary of State James] Baker, [Treasury Secretary Nicholas] Brady, [Office of Management and Budget director Richard] Darman and to the congressional leadership, the Senator is regarded as a wise counselor."

Why does the tobacco industry work so hard to recruit the movers and shakers of Capitol Hill? Walter Huddleston, who signed on as a lobbyist for Brown and Williamson after losing his Senate seat, is among those who know that former membership has its privileges. "We have access that a non-Member would not have," he told a reporter for the *Dallas-Morning News* in 1997. "We do have floor privileges. We can go into the private dining rooms. We can go to the cloakrooms. Just walking down the hall, you can spot a former colleague, and he'll stop and chat with you, and you can make a lobbying point with him."

Baker and Huddleston are just two of the players on the tobacco industry's all-star team of lobbyists in the nation's capital. Here are some of the others in its starting lineup:

- Haley Barbour went to work as a lobbyist for five of the six biggest tobacco companies after he stepped down as the chairman of the Republican National Committee in early 1997.
- Ed Gillespie, one of Barbour's partners in Barbour, Griffith & Rogers, was a top aide to Republican House Majority Leader Dick Armey of Texas. He now walks the halls of Congress as a lobbyist for Brown and Williamson and Philip

Morris. He told the Center he was interested in promoting legislation that would be "good for kids and good for Republicans."

- Tom Spulak, as general counsel to the House, success-fully defended Representatives Waxman and Ron Wyden, a Democrat from Oregon, in 1994 against a lawsuit filed by Brown and Williamson that sought to prevent them from releasing secret company documents. Now he's a lobbyist for R. J. Reynolds at Shaw, Pittman, Potts & Trowbridge.
- Michael Barrett led investigations against defense contractors, the securities industry, and Citibank as the chief counsel of the House of Energy and Commerce Subcommittee on Oversight. At the end of his twenty-five-year career on Capitol Hill, Barrett became a lobbyist for all three of his former adversaries—and for Philip Morris, which paid him $500,000 in 1996 alone, more than five and a half times what he earned at the peak of his previous career as a public servant.
- Former Democratic Representatives Ray Kogovsek of Colorado and Roy Rowland of Georgia represented Philip Morris as associates in the Washington firm of Black Kelly Scruggs and Healey.
- Former Republican Representative Stanford Parris of Virginia, now with the Washington law firm of Dickstein Shapiro Morin & Oskinsky, is a registered lobbyist for Lorillard Tobacco company, a subsidiary of Loews Corporation.
- Former Democratic Representative James Stanton of Ohio is a registered lobbyist for Philip Morris.
- Former Democratic Representatives Ed Jenkins of Georgia and Alan Wheat of Missouri, who are both name partners in the Washington firm of Winburn Jenkins & Wheat, were registered lobbyists for Philip Morris in 1996. Jenkins told the Center that everyone in the firm is registered to lobby for Philip Morris—"to be on the safe side"—but that he doesn't specifically lobby for tobacco.

Congressional aides who have passed through the revolving door include Jeff Schlagenhauf, formerly Bliley's top aide, who's now employed as the president of the Smokeless Tobacco Council; Jayne Fitzgerald, formerly counsel to the House Ways and Means Committee, who's now a registered lobbyist for Lorillard Tobacco and R. J. Reynolds; and Darryl Nirenberg, formerly chief of staff to Republican Senator Jesse Helms of North Carolina, who's now a registered lobbyist for Liggett Group, Inc., and the Smokeless Tobacco Council.

When the Occupational Safety and Health Administration (OSHA) proposed a ban on smoking in the workplace in 1994, the National Smokers Alliance swung into action, alerting its members to OSHA's alarming proposal. In short order, the agency received some 20,000 pieces of mail on the issue, according to William Thomas Humber, the organization's president. It was an apparent groundswell of grassroots opposition. Or was it?

The National Smokers Alliance was set up in 1993 with $1 million in seed money from Philip Morris. It describes itself as "a not-for-profit grassroots membership organization, dedicated to promoting policies of accommodation for both smokers and non-smokers" and claims, in its promotional literature and on its Web site, to have 3 million members. The alliance's tax return says that it is "committed to fighting excessive regulation and taxation of tobacco products at all levels of government, and opposing discrimination of [sic] smokers in public places and the work-place." News stories have variously described the organization as "a grassroots, pro-smoking organization" and "a support group for tobacco users."

In truth, the National Smokers Alliance is nothing but a support group for the tobacco industry. Gary Auxier, its senior vice president, told the Center that members pay annual dues of $10. But according to tax records obtained by the Center, membership dues and assessments accounted for only $73,596 of its $9 million in revenue in 1996.

Victor Crawford, a lobbyist for the Tobacco Institute who became an antismoking advocate after he found out he had lung cancer, explained the industry's deployment of sham organizations before he died in 1996. "You [as a tobacco lobbyist] often work for front groups," Crawford told the *Journal of the American Medi-*

cal Association. "For example, if we wanted to get rid of [FDA Commissioner David] Kessler . . . I would have funded AIDS groups and got them fired up that he's not approving anti-AIDS drugs fast enough. Raise all kinds of hell and go to Bill Clinton and get him to fire Kessler. And who would benefit? Tobacco, of course. But the AIDS people would do the dirty work because they're so involved, and that's how it's done. You never leave your fingerprints at the scene of the crime."

And if fingerprints are found, it is usually too late—long after the industry has finished its work. The tobacco companies have set up a battery of "junk science" organizations—among them the Council for Tobacco Research U.S.A., Inc.; Healthy Buildings International, Inc.; and the Center for Indoor Air Research, to name just a few—to offer up made-to-order research on smoking. They have also established a dizzying array of antitax organizations—Enough Is Enough, No More Taxes, Citizens Against Tax Abuse and Government Waste, and Californians for Uniform Statewide Restrictions—to fight proposed increases in state tobacco taxes.

The tobacco companies have also set up a collection of front organizations to take lawmakers on vacations disguised as "fact-finding" missions. Andrew Whist, Philip Morris's senior vice president for external affairs, runs one such group, the New York Society for International Affairs. Established in 1982, the "society" is financed almost entirely by Philip Morris and, according to *The Wall Street Journal,* is headquartered in Whist's Manhattan apartment. It has taken governors and state legislators on all-expenses-paid trips to such places as Australia and Costa Rica to promote foreign trade.

> **Victor Crawford, a lobbyist for the Tobacco Institute who became an antismoking advocate after he found out he had lung cancer, explained the industry's deployment of front groups to the *Journal of the American Medical Association* before he died in 1996. "You never," he said, "leave your fingerprints at the scene of the crime."**

Whist is also the chairman of the America-European Community Association, another front organization financed by Philip Morris and whose board of directors counts among its members former Republican Senator Charles Mathias of Maryland. (Mathias is also chairman of the board of the New York Society for International Affairs.) "We will continue to ensure that when important issues are debated," Whist wrote in the association's 1996 annual report, "the voice of commerce is heard."

One of those who heard the voice was Senator William Roth, a Republican from Delaware who currently chairs the Finance Committee. In 1991, before he took the helm of the panel, the association gave Roth an all-expenses-paid trip to Berlin, and it also gave then-Senator Rudy Boschwitz, a Republican from Minnesota, a free trip to England with his wife.

Among other Capitol Hill lawmakers who have participated in various events sponsored by the America-European Community Association over the years: Democratic Senator Charles Robb of Virginia; John Dingell of Michigan, the ranking Democrat on the House Commerce Committee; former Democratic Senator Sam Nunn of Georgia; Representative Doug Bereuter, a Republican from Nebraska; Democratic Senator Christopher Dodd of Connecticut; and the late Senator John Heinz, a Republican from Pennsylvania.

Amazingly, the organization managed to operate from its inception in 1980 through much of 1997 without anyone publicly identifying it as one of Philip Morris's many front groups.

Then there is the Ramhurst Corporation, of Winston-Salem, North Carolina, a consulting firm that specializes in stomping out antitobacco initiatives around the country. In New Jersey in 1996, the firm—whose primary client and source of income is R. J. Reynolds—helped beat back a proposed increase in the state's excise tax that was earmarked for the state's schools. Karl Gallant, a Ramhurst operative, also runs ARMPAC, Representative Tom DeLay's leadership PAC, and helped raise money for Representative John Shadegg, a Republican from Arizona who succeeded Newt Gingrich as the general chairman of GOPAC. Another Ramhurst employee is David Armey, the son of Republican House Majority Leader Richard Armey.

The tobacco companies have also helped finance the rising tide of libertarian organizations such as the Cato Institute, Citizens for a Sound Economy, and the Progress and Freedom Foundation. In most cases, the issue papers and studies these groups generate do not specifically single out tobacco; rather, they take aim at the FDA, which has been seeking to regulate tobacco.

Citizens for a Sound Economy was established in 1984 by David Koch, the executive vice president of the Chemical Tech Group of Koch Industries, Inc., a privately held petroleum company. Its chairman is C. Boyden Gray, a former White House counsel under President Bush and heir to the Reynolds tobacco fortune. "The FDA cannot now keep up with its current regulatory duties," Lydia Verheggen, Citizens for a Sound Economy's director of health-care policy, told the Center. "Why on earth should we expect them to be able to deal with tobacco?"

Citizens for a Sound Economy has never attacked the issue of tobacco head on at the national level, although it has joined the tobacco industry in advocating an overhaul of the nation's product-liability laws. But in Oregon the organization aired radio ads attacking antitobacco legislation, and in New Jersey it helped kill a proposal by Governor Christine Todd Whitman to finance improvements in the state's educational system through an increase in excise taxes on tobacco products.

Citizens for a Sound Economy does not disclose where its money comes from and did not respond to the Center's inquiries. But in 1991, the organization and its sister foundation reportedly received nearly $200,000 from Philip Morris.

Such is the hold of the tobacco industry on Congress that in 1994, when the FDA began to assert that it could regulate tobacco and tobacco advertising, thirty-four Senators and 124 Representatives signed a letter to FDA Commissioner Kessler in which they asserted that such a move by the agency would jeopardize 10,000 jobs and "trample First Amendment rights to advertise legal products to adults." According to Common Cause, the lawmakers who signed the letter had, on average, received three times as much money from tobacco interests as those who did not sign it.

"That was the industry flexing its muscle," former FDA Commissioner Kessler told the Center. What was most surprising to Kessler during his tenure was the stunning contrast between the tobacco industry's trustworthiness as perceived by the public and its inordinate clout in Washington. "It was out of sync. Their public credibility was nonexistent. But the money was so powerful, and it was money all over Washington. They literally could buy anything, they could hire anyone. . . . The financial influence clouds everything."

The strategy has reaped billions of dollars for the industry throughout this century. "Every major piece of federal legislation passed since the first Surgeon General's report that protects health and safety has specifically excluded the cigarette—Consumer Product Safety Act, Controlled Substances Act, Federal Hazardous Substances Act," Greg Connolly, who directs a project established by the Massachusetts Department of Public Health to curtail smoking, told television producer Martin Koughan in 1994. "Why? Because the tobacco industry has bought off Congress. Rather than doing something about the problem since 1964, Congress has turned its back on the problem. And the reason is, the tobacco industry has money."

Each year Big Tobacco spends $5 billion to $6 billion to push its products. And despite more than thirty years of public-health campaigns in the nation's schools, 28 percent of American kids aged twelve to seventeen continue to light up.

Each year Big Tobacco also spends untold millions to keep lawmakers in Washington and in state legislatures right where it wants them: in its pocket. Despite the media spotlight on the industry since the seven tobacco executives stood before Congress in April 1994, despite the litigation, despite revelations about the industry's decades of lying to the American people, Congress's addiction to money continues. Despite what some have observed as a sea change in both public opinion and congressional pronouncements, actions still speak louder than words. In 1997, congressional leaders included a provision in the budget bill—rejected by both chambers of Congress after it became public—that would have saved the industry $50 billion. Newt Gingrich, who was one of those believed responsible for inserting the provision, denied it in typical Washington fashion. "We did not cut a break for the tobacco folks," he said.

We should all not get a break like that.

7

|||||●|||||

The Gun Club

I T WASN'T UNTIL AFTER HE WAS SHOT AND KILLED THAT RUSSELL COLE-man got mixed up in politics.

Coleman worked at Thrifty Liquor in Shreveport, Louisiana. One night in August 1995 near closing time, three men entered the store and started browsing. One of them walked up behind Coleman, who was standing near the door waiting to lock up. The man, Bobby Lee Hampton, pulled a .380 semiautomatic pistol and shot three times into Coleman's back. Only after Coleman was dead did Hampton and his two friends announce to the remaining employees that they were robbing the store.

By autumn, Coleman's name had become familiar to readers of *American Hunter* and *Firearms Business* magazines and to visitors to the National Rifle Association's Web site. Tanya Metaksa, the executive director of the Institute for Legislative Action, the NRA's lobbying arm, made the story of Coleman's murder a staple in her speeches.

What made Coleman such a celebrity in pro-gun circles was that, at the time of his shooting, he had been waiting for approval of his application to buy a handgun, which he wanted for self-defense. For the NRA, Coleman was proof that the new Brady Handgun Violence Prevention Act, commonly known as the Brady law, which required a delay before Coleman could buy the gun, was counterproductive. Coleman's death seemed such a useful anecdote for the organization that Representative Steve Stockman, a Republican from Texas, decided to mention the liquor-store clerk's name in the introduction of his bill to repeal the Brady law.

At that point, Coleman's family was still reeling from his death and unaware of his new fame. Then one day a coworker of Coleman's told them that a man named John Velleco had called him asking about Russell and mentioned that a politician was planning to use Coleman's name in a piece of legislation. It turned out that Velleco was a lobbyist for Gun Owners of America, a pro-gun group with ties to Stockman.

Barbara Coleman, Russell's mother, was furious. She believed that a gun would not have helped her son. "Even if he had a gun in his hand at the time, the guy just walked up without any notice and just started shooting," Coleman told the Center for Public Integrity. Shreveport Police Lieutenant Charlie Owens was blunter. "He could have been armed with a grenade and it wouldn't have helped him," he told *The Times,* a local newspaper.

Barbara Coleman had never been active in the gun debate before, but now she wanted her son's name out of it. She called up Stockman, wrote letters to the gun publications—did everything she could. She sought help from the Washington-based Violence Policy Center. As Coleman told the Center, "It was important to set the record straight."

Whether or not Russell Coleman could have saved himself with a gun, there is no dispute that it was a gun—wielded by a convicted felon—that killed him. Coleman is one of more

• • • • • • • • • • • • • • • • • •

There are more federal laws governing safety in the manufacture of teddy bears than of guns.

• • • • • • • • • • • • • • • • • •

than 590,000 Americans who have died from gunshot wounds—including suicide and accident fatalities—since 1979. That is more than the population of Denver, Cleveland, or Washington, D.C. In addition, an estimated 100,000 people are treated for gun injuries every year in the nation's emergency rooms.

There are guns in nearly half of all American homes, and

according to a 1993 study published in the *New England Journal of Medicine,* the presence of a firearm in the home increases the chance of a suicide or murder there, often committed by a family member or friend. Only one other widely available consumer product kills more Americans: cars.

Nearly 90 percent of Americans believe that people should have to obtain a license to own a gun, according to the University of Chicago's National Opinion Research Center. An overwhelming majority also approve of such ideas as allowing an individual to buy no more than one gun a month and requiring every gun buyer to have safety training. Even gun owners favor some government oversight—72 percent support criminal background checks before a person can buy a gun, and two-thirds of households with handguns support mandatory registration. Yet there are more federal laws governing safety in the manufacture of teddy bears than of guns.

The Bureau of Alcohol, Tobacco, and Firearms, commonly known as the ATF, does not have the authority to set safety or design standards for guns. It cannot require manufacturers to recall guns with dangerous defects; all it can do is require that dealers and manufacturers register and pay taxes, and it can enforce what laws there are on the books.

The problem is, there are not many federal gun laws on the books. Anyone twenty-one or older can walk into a gun store or up to a table at a gun show and buy a twenty-four-ounce Glock G-20 pistol that can "easily slip into a waist, shoulder, or ankle holster," as the description on the American Firearms Industry's Web site puts it; or a 9mm Smith & Wesson SIGMA pistol, with its "patented three-dot sight system that allows the shooter to quickly bring the pistol on target"; or an Interarms Walther P-99, whose "truly interesting feature is the ease of changing from single action to double action"; or any other of the countless handguns and rifles advertised in speciality magazines and on the Internet. There is no need to pass a safety test or to get a license. Even the five-day waiting period required under the Brady law, the one that kept Russell Coleman from buying a gun right away, is set to expire in 1998 because of a provision that was added just before its passage. Now gun dealers need only run an "instant check" on government records to find out if their prospective

|||||||||||||||||||||||||||||||||||||||||||||||||||||||||||||||||||||||||

There are not many federal gun laws on the books. Anyone twenty-one or older can walk into a gun store or up to a table at a gun show and buy a 24-ounce Glock G-20 pistol that can "easily slip into a waist, shoulder, or ankle holster," as the description on the American Firearms Industry's Web site puts it.

buyer is a convicted felon. If the search comes up with nothing, the customer walks out of the store with a gun.

The dearth of laws on gun safety and ownership in the United States is far from an oversight. It is the direct result of decades of pressure politics by the National Rifle Association and a host of other advocacy groups such as Gun Owners of America, whose executive director, Larry Pratt, learned the art of hot-button fund-raising under the tutelage of Richard Viguerie, the right-wing direct-mail wizard. Not that the NRA lacks radical credentials— "revolution" is definitely part of its political vocabulary.

"People recognize that a government by and for the people is predicated on people having the ability of overthrowing the duly constituted authorities when they become injurious to the rights of the individual," Joe Phillips, an NRA lobbyist, told the Center. "I don't think we're at the point of revolution right now, but I think there are a lot of people who would like to push in that direction." Two of the books he offers for background reading are about the federal government's raids on the Branch Davidian compound near Waco, Texas, and the Weaver family's cabin on Ruby Ridge in Idaho.

With the revolution still not at hand, though, the NRA uses every conventional trick in the lobbying trade—indeed, the group invented many of them—to fight proposals to regulate guns. The NRA's leaders dip into their PAC, one of the biggest in politics, to reward supporters handsomely and to attack detractors ruthlessly. They use their Web site and fax machines to mobilize members to call and write their lawmakers. They feed money to front groups, such as the Law Enforcement Alliance of America, a group of police officers opposed to gun control; track down favorable witnesses for Capitol Hill hearings; and latch on to victim stories, such as Russell Coleman's, without checking with the family.

Over the past two decades, the gun lobby has opposed every attempt to regulate guns: The NRA has fought off proposals to ban new generations of "cop-killer" bullets, so-named because they are capable of piercing body armor. It has stalled proposals to require chemical "tags" on explosives that would make them easier to trace, a strategy proposed by law-enforcement officials as a way to track down terrorists. In 1996, at the NRA's urging, Congress forbade the National Center for Injury Prevention, a division of the federal Centers for Disease Control and Prevention (CDC) that had been underwriting research on the relationship between guns and violence, from "engaging in any activities to advocate or promote gun control." Congress also required the CDC to transfer $2.6 million, the exact amount that had been allocated to gun research, to research on traumatic brain injury. "There is no room in good government for bad practices like recklessly biased research and blatant political advocacy—especially at taxpayers' expense," Metaksa said at the time.

Among the many items on the NRA's long legislative wish list are staving off environmental regulations on lead; reversing a law that prohibits police officers with domestic-violence misdemeanor records from possessing a gun, on or off the job; making it simpler to import military surplus weapons; and making it more difficult for people injured by defective guns to sue their manufacturers.

Congress is completely cowed by the gun lobby. Even gun-control advocates on Capitol Hill admit, off the record, that they have given up on comprehensive gun-control legislation. Instead, they play defense, and when they try to advance a gun-safety initiative, they do it piece by piece: a bill to limit gun sales to an individual to one per month, another to ban cheap "junk guns," another to prohibit "cop-killer" bullets—none of which have passed.

For many longtime gun-control advocates, the explanation for Congress's inertia comes down to simple fright. "Part of the issue revolved around the question: Were you fearful?" former Democratic Senator Howard Metzenbaum of Ohio, who spent years fighting for gun control, told the Center. "Because the gun lobby is a very powerful one." Several miles beyond the Capitol dome, not far from St. Elizabeth's Hospital, the psychiatric institution where John Hinckley, President Reagan's would-be assassin, is confined, is D.C. General Hospital. Some of Hinckley's bullets hit Reagan's press secretary, James Brady, who suffered brain damage. Brady's wife Sarah, inspired to lead a crusade for new gun laws, became the director of Handgun Control, Inc. The 1993 law that required the five-day waiting period and instant check for felonies is named for the Bradys.

The cluster of brick buildings that make up D.C. General look more like an aging factory than a hospital, and inside them the tile floors and dull walls are grimy. Prisoners from a nearby penitentiary, dressed in bright orange coveralls and shackled at hands and feet, are a common sight. The police officers who accompany them are on a first-name basis with the doctors. In 1996, the trauma surgeons here treated more than eighty kids aged eighteen or younger for gunshot wounds; for many of them, Dr. Paul Oriaifo, the director of the trauma unit, told the Center, it wasn't their first time. "You will be looking at them and they'll say, 'See this scar here, and that's another gunshot wound,'" Oriaifo said. "They're always scared. They pull at you. They say, 'Save me.'"

Among the many items on the NRA's long legislative wish list are reversing a law that prohibits police officers with domestic-violence misdemeanor records from possessing a gun, on or off the job; and making it more difficult for people injured by defective guns to sue their manufacturers.

While doctors are extracting bullets and sewing up wounds, over on Capitol Hill the politicians who write the laws are getting their pictures taken with gun manufacturers. One classic clutch-and-grin photograph, displayed in an industry newsletter, shows Senator Orrin Hatch, a Republican from Utah, holding a plaque that commends him for his "defense of our heritage, our industry, and our way of life." Surrounding him are a woman and four men, smiling stiffly for the camera.

One of them is an executive of Fabrique National, the French conglomerate that supplies M249 assault weapons and M240 grenade launchers to the U.S. military. Another is the president of O. F. Mossberg & Sons, Inc., one of several companies that got their start in an area of Connecticut known as "Gun Valley." Two others work for North American Arms, Inc., and Browning Arms Company, both based in Hatch's home state of Utah. A visit to the Web page of North American Arms shows another photo of Hatch, this time reading the company's catalog. According to the caption, he carries "several of the firm's firearm products."

Paul Smith, Hatch's press secretary, confirmed to the Center that the Senator owns guns and probably has one from North American Arms. Hatch is also close to the NRA. "It's a welcome change while here inside the Beltway to be surrounded by so many like-minded men and women," he told an NRA conference on the Second Amendment in 1995. "Efforts such as this conference and the unprecedented display of America's growing concern for the preservation of our liberty provide us with substantial opportunities to make inroads into the despotism of gun control." Hatch is a good friend to have: In 1994, he became the chairman of the Senate Judiciary Committee, which has jurisdiction over all gun laws.

Richard Feldman, the director of the American Shooting Sports Council, which published the photograph of Hatch and the gun-industry executives in its newsletter, told the Center: "So many times, people say, 'How do you feel when your people are selling this gun that was used in a horrible crime?' No different, I'm sure, than a car dealer feels when he sold a car to some family whose teenage son or daughter got drunk and innocently destroyed a family. Does the automobile dealership feel responsibility? I don't think so."

Hatch is hardly the only proud gun owner in Congress. In Senator Phil Gramm's office, guns are part of the decor. A Winchester rifle is displayed over the Texas Republican's desk, according to a report in *The Washington Post,* and on a table near the door is a Civil War pistol. "I own more shotguns than I need, but not as many as I want," Gramm told NRA conventiongoers in 1995, when he was seeking support for his presidential bid. Gramm also gave the NRA his name for use in a fund-raising letter that same year. Gramm is able to display the Winchester and the pistol in his office, even though a local ordinance bans guns in Washington, D.C. The reason? Rules issued by the Capitol Police Board say that "nothing . . . shall prohibit any Member of Congress from maintaining firearms within the confines of his office."

The gun culture on Capitol Hill stretches back to Congress's beginnings, and there have been occasions when a Member actually drew a gun during debate. In the 1850s, for example, Senator Henry Foote of Mississippi pulled out a gun during a fight with Senator Thomas Hart Benton of Missouri. And from its own earliest days, the NRA turned to Congress for support. Having opened its doors in New York City in 1871, with a shooting range on Long Island, the NRA started promoting sharpshooting contests. The two Union soldiers who founded the group had been dismayed by the quality of shooting among Army recruits and thought that turning it into a sport would improve the quality of fighting men. In 1903, succumbing to the NRA's lobbying on the subject, Congress established the National Board for the Promotion of Rifle Practice.

It was a bit difficult to tell where the NRA ended and the board began—a third of the board's officers were also members of the NRA. For more than ninety years, the federal government supplied the sharpshooting groups sponsored by the board with surplus military firearms and ammunition. In 1995, the program, by then known as the Corporation for the Promotion of Rifle Practice and Firearms Safety, was "privatized" and was supposed to find its own funds. But in 1996, Congress gave it $76 million worth of old rifles, ammunition, and other goods to get it started. Senator Frank Lautenberg, a Democrat from New Jersey, tried to strip the funding, but his amendment lost twenty-nine to seventy-one.

> **"I own more shotguns than I need, but not as many as I want,"** Republican Senator Phil Gramm told NRA conventiongoers in 1995, when he was seeking support for his presidential bid.

Lawmakers are no longer allowed to take firearms onto the floor, but they're allowed to shoot them outside for sport, as they do at the annual Great Congressional Shootout at the Prince George's County Trap and Shoot Center in Glenn Dale, Maryland. Some 250 Members of Congress belong to the Sportsmen's Caucus, which weighs in on environmental laws, such as wetlands, endangered-species protection, and other legislation affecting hunters. Its members, though, can also be relied upon to vote against any gun-control proposals. In 1996, some two dozen lawmakers and lobbyists, many decked out in cowboy hats and hunting vests, competed in the caucus's first shootout, in which Representative Bill Brewster, a Democrat from Oklahoma, took home the "Top Gun" trophy for outshooting his colleagues. The NRA and gun manufacturers sponsored the event. The following year Brewster took home the top prize again. The fund-raising arm of the caucus, the Sportsmen's Caucus Foundation, shares office space in Washington with Olin Corporation, the company that makes Winchester ammunition.

Even though Congress's relationship with the NRA stretches back nearly 100 years, the 1960s marked the true beginning of modern gun politics. First John F. Kennedy was shot, then Martin Luther King, Jr., and Robert F. Kennedy. The NRA was right there in the thick of the controversy. Lee Harvey Oswald, President Kennedy's assassin, had bought his Italian-made Mannlicher-Carcano by mail for $19.95 from an advertisement in the back of *American Rifleman,* the NRA's flagship magazine. Over the next few years, public outrage against guns was enough to force Congress to do something in response. The Gun Control Act of 1968 banned such mail-order sales and required firearms dealers to obtain federal licenses, among other requirements. But the law contained plenty of loopholes and omissions. It did not require gun registration, for instance, and while it banned imports of cheap "Saturday-night specials," it did not ban those made in the United States.

Nevertheless, some NRA members were upset about the new law. This faction found a leader in Harlon Carter, a hard-liner who hated the very idea of gun control. When the NRA formed a lobbying arm, the Institute for Legislative Action, in 1975, Carter was placed in charge. Infighting between Carter's supporters and the "old guard"—who believed the organization should focus less on lobbying and more on programs for sportsmen and hunters—led to a showdown the following year. Carter organized his supporters, who used parliamentary procedures to foil the "old guard's" plans to move the NRA's headquarters to Colorado Springs, far from Washington and Congress. Carter not only won, he took over as the chief executive officer of the NRA in 1977.

These were the years that made the NRA one of the most powerful lobbies in Washington. In addition to stopping any further regulation of guns, it managed to win a new law in 1986 that weakened many of the provisions of the 1968 Gun Control Act. For example, the new law allowed people without federal licenses to sell guns, as long as they did so as a "hobby." This provision included selling them at gun shows in the person's own state. The number of these shows multiplied, and they soon became the site of many illegal gun sales.

By the mid-1990s, the NRA had become an empire—an interlocking network of groups—with an annual budget running in the hundreds of millions of dollars and 3 million members. There was the lobbying arm, the Institute for Legislative Action; a firearms museum; a Firearms Civil Rights Legal Defense Fund; and a foundation. The NRA even provided funding for the U.S. Olympic Sports Shooting Team (although it stopped doing so in March 1994). It published books, sold clothes, and ran a successful direct-mail operation. Several Members of Congress served on the NRA's board of directors: Republican Senators Larry Craig of Idaho and Ted Stevens of Alaska and Democratic Representatives Bill K. Brewster of Oklahoma and John Dingell of Michigan. James McClure, a Republican from Idaho, led many of the NRA's battles when he was in the Senate and signed up the gun group as a client for his lobbying firm after he left.

The NRA's methods of persuasion were as effective as they were crude. It used its PAC to support lawmakers who voted the way the organization wanted and to punish those who didn't. The PAC gave direct contributions to candidates but spent far more on "independent expenditures," which aren't limited under federal law. That way the NRA could spend hundreds of thousands of dollars on mailings and advertisements to support or oppose a candidate in a single race, beyond the $10,000 that it could legally give directly to the candidate.

A glimpse into how this strategy worked was provided in former Oregon Senator Bob Packwood's diaries, released when he was being investigated for sexual harassment. "Met with [blank] from the National Rifle Association," reads the entry dated October 6, 1992. "He showed me the piece the National Rifle Association is going to send out hitting [blank]. God, is it tough. . . . I cannot tell you how tough it is! They are going to send it to 90,000 members. And, he said if he has enough money he's going to send it out to 100,000 Oregon gun owners, or something like that." When Packwood's diaries were first released, he was nervous enough about the entry to rewrite it. The sanitized version did not mention the NRA's mailing. Instead, Packwood said, "I kind of like the guy, but he is a bit of a braggart about how many races he sees the NRA winning. . . . My intuition tells me the tide is turning against the NRA."

Since 1987, the gun lobby has managed to pump more than $12.7 million into congressional campaigns. In the early 1990s, however, it suffered a few legislative defeats. In 1993, Congress passed the Brady bill, and Congress enacted a ban on guns defined as "assault weapons" in 1994. Even then, though, these losses hardly spelled the end for the gun lobby. The Brady law was weaker than many state gun-control laws, and although the assault-weapon ban was popular with the public, only a small percentage of crimes are committed with this type of firearm. To avoid the ban on assault weapons, some manufacturers have simply redesigned certain models so that they do not fall under the definition.

Still, the gun group's response was vintage NRA. After Congress passed the assault-weapon ban just months before the 1994 elections, the NRA went on a rampage. One of the TV ads it ran featured actor Charlton Heston, a longtime NRA ally who would later win a seat on the organization's board of directors. "You said you wouldn't vote for a waiting period," Heston said, addressing the targeted lawmaker, "but . . . you voted for the first federal gun ban in American history."

The NRA spent nearly $3.7 million in the 1994 elections and claimed credit for winning 211 of the 276 races in which it endorsed candidates. One of those it helped elect was Representative Bob Barr, a Republican from Georgia, who got $4,950 from the

NRA's PAC. The NRA's Tanya Metaksa traveled to Georgia and spent more than sixteen hours riding around with the candidate on a bus, making campaign stops. "[Metaksa's effort] made a tremendous difference in that race, and that personified the tremendous grassroots support and grassroots ability" of the NRA, Barr told an NRA conference in 1995. Barr quickly proved his mettle as the most ferocious opponent of gun-control laws in Congress. He cajoled House Speaker Newt Gingrich, whose Atlanta district adjoined his, to get tough against gun control. Gingrich appointed Barr to be the chairman of a special seven-member Firearms Legislative Task Force, which met weekly to develop a pro-gun agenda. Barr also secured a seat on the House Judiciary Committee, which has jurisdiction over gun issues.

There, working closely with the NRA, Barr helped plan a series of hearings on guns, concentrating on such topics as the Second Amendment and the use of the weapons for self-defense. "We have received input from this organization that has been a tremendous help to us," he told an NRA gathering in April. Later that summer, some Democrats on the committee found out—and told reporters—that NRA-paid consultants were helping to organize an upcoming hearing on Ruby Ridge and Waco by contacting potential witnesses. Barr also spearheaded fights against proposals to require chemical markers in explosives, meant

> "**M**et with [blank] from the National Rifle Association," reads the entry dated October 6, 1992, in the diaries of former Oregon Senator Bob Packwood. "He showed me the piece the National Rifle Association is going to send out hitting [blank]. God, is it tough . . . I cannot tell you how tough it is!"

to make it easier for law-enforcement authorities to track down terrorists. In the spring of 1996, Barr achieved his biggest success yet: a 239-to-173 vote to repeal the ban on assault weapons that had been passed by the previous Congress. The ban still stands, since the Senate did not vote to repeal it. Indeed, Barr's agenda is so close to the NRA's that no one was surprised when he hired Chip Walker, the NRA's media-relations manager, as his new press secretary. In his next race, Barr got even more support from the NRA, whose PAC spent more than $68,000 to help reelect him.

Despite its swagger, the NRA has continued to suffer some blows into the mid-1990s. In the months leading up to its 1997 annual conference, a series of leaks by warring factions claimed that the NRA was more than $57 million in the red. The IRS is reportedly doing an extensive audit to see whether the NRA has violated its nonprofit status. The gun group also was publicly bruised when its ties to radical militia groups came to light—especially after the April 1995 bombing of the Alfred P. Murrah Federal Building in Oklahoma City. The Violence Policy Center found and circulated a fund-raising letter from the NRA that referred to federal agents as "jack-booted government thugs, wearing black, armed to the teeth." The letter was signed by Wayne LaPierre, the NRA's chief executive officer. In the resulting furor, former President George Bush resigned his lifetime membership in the organization.

That was not all, though. There were reports that Tanya Metaksa had had a secret meeting with members of the Michigan militia and that her computer bulletin board featured instructions on how to make a bomb. Rather than denying the allegations, the NRA tried to explain them away. In April, Knox told a reporter for *The Washington Post* that perhaps the NRA bulletin boards should be monitored more carefully, but he also pointed out that such bomb recipes were widely available on the Internet.

The NRA is not the only gun group with radical ties. In 1996, the Center reported that Larry Pratt, the executive director of Gun Owners of America, had attended several meetings organized by members of militias. He spoke at the Dallas Preparedness Expo—a gathering that featured survivalists and other right-wing groups—in 1995, alongside people such as Bo Gritz, who was white supremacist David Duke's vice-presidential running mate in 1988. "We don't prioritize allies, we prioritize positions," Pratt told the Center at the time. "And we're willing to go anywhere and work with anyone for our issue." He subsequently was forced to resign as a cochairman of Republican Pat Buchanan's 1996 presidential campaign.

None of this information played well with the American public. It also inspired the gun industry itself, long content to let the NRA do the lobbying in Washington, to step forward and try to differentiate itself from its radical image. "Businesspeople are businesspeople," Robert Ricker, the American Shooting Sports Council's director of government affairs, told the Center. "Why would a company like a Ruger or a Beretta pay thousands of dollars to form a trade association when they could sit back and let the consumers [the NRA] carry the water for them?"

In fact, the NRA has always carried water for the gun industry, although both NRA officials and gun-industry representatives fiercely deny that the NRA gets substantial industry funding. "More than zero and less than minuscule," Richard Feldman, the director of the ASSC, told the Center when asked whether the gun industry gave money to the NRA.

But that depends on your definition of "minuscule." An examination of the NRA's tax returns shows that from 1992 to 1995, it earned more than $26 million from selling advertising in its publications, most of it from industry—gun manufacturers, dealers, accessory makers, and the like. NRA lobbyist Joe Phillips told the Center that the bucks stopped there: "We do not take industry money other than advertising in our magazine." However, when the Center analyzed a list of donors in annual reports published by the NRA Foundation, it found dozens of donors with ties to industry who collectively gave the NRA at least $147,000 and perhaps as much as $399,962 in 1995 and 1996 (contributions are listed in ranges).

There is William Ruger, of the Connecticut-based gun manufacturer Sturm, Ruger & Company, who is listed as giving $25,000 to $50,000 in 1995. Petersen Publishing Company, which publishes *Guns & Ammo* magazine, gave $35,000 to $75,000 over both years. In 1994, Philip Morris Companies, Inc. gave $10,000 to $25,000, and the Smokeless Tobacco Council gave $1,000 to $4,999.

Several NRA board members have business interests themselves. Robert Hogdon, for instance, owns a company that manufactures gunpowder. Steve Hornady's company manufactures ammunition and reloading equipment. Kenneth Oehler is the president of a firm that makes devices that measure bullet velocity.

Despite these connections, as the NRA's radical reputation has grown, so has the desire of the gun industry to provide another voice on gun issues in Washington. The idea is to present gun manufacturers as a business like any other, a source of employment and tax revenue. Every year the ASSC, whose membership includes some 400 gun manufacturers, gun shops, and sporting-goods stores, flies fifty or so gun-industry executives to Washington to meet with lawmakers.

Still, the gun industry has drawn much of its lobbying staff from the ranks of the NRA. Richard Feldman once served as the NRA's political director for Northeastern states. Another ASSC staffer was assistant general counsel to the NRA and a third worked there in public affairs. James Baker, who was the director of the NRA's lobbying arm until 1994, remains on contract with the gun group. As a lobbyist-for-hire, he also represents another trade association, the Sporting Arms and Manufacturers Institute. Mark Barnes spent years as a top aide to Senator Ted Stevens, a Republican from Alaska and an NRA board member. Barnes's client list includes both the NRA and firearms importers. The Center for Public Integrity's analysis of federal lobbying disclosure forms shows that in 1996, gun companies and trade associations hired at least forty Washington lobbyists. These include such companies as Colt Manufacturing Company; Beretta U.S.A. Corporation; Sturm, Ruger & Company, Inc.; and Smith & Wesson Corporation.

Although these companies have thus far not contributed huge amounts of campaign money, they're starting to give more. When E. I. du Pont de Nemours & Company sold Remington Arms Company, Inc., in 1993, the new president, Thomas L. Millner, a North Carolina furniture-manufacturing executive, was quick to say that it would not be the same old behind-the-scenes strategy. "The industry hasn't done a good job of selling itself," he told Gannett News Service. "It has let the NRA do it for it." In the 1995–96 election cycle, Remington's PAC raised $25,464. Millner has made personal lobbying visits to Washington. William Ruger has always been a generous donor, giving more than $140,000 to congressional campaigns since 1987.

Feldman told the Center that he is not interested in starting a PAC. "We all know each other," he said. "Nothing stops me from calling them up and saying, 'Would you write a $1,000 check to Congressman Barr's reelection campaign?' "

They did not use Russell Coleman's name, but the message was the same. In 1997, the NRA spent more than $2 million on advertisements to defeat a Washington state initiative that would have required licenses and training for handgun purchasers. If the initiative passed, said some of the ads, it would put "stalking victims at even greater risk by making them wait for permission to protect themselves." The ads worked. Seventy-one percent of voters rejected the initiative.

Meanwhile, in Washington, D.C., lawmakers were not going anywhere regarding gun-control proposals. "They won't because the Congress is not interested in taking up this issue," Richard Feldman told National Public Radio. "I think the Congress would like to see the gun issue go away."

8

IIIII●IIIII

Prescription for Disasters

IN JULY 1993, DOROTHY WILSON OF PHILADELPHIA TRAVELED TO THE
nation's capital to testify before a congressional subcommittee
that was considering legislation to reduce the powers of the
Food and Drug Administration. As Wilson later explained, the
trip was not easy. Confined to a wheelchair because of muscle
weakness, spasms, and pain that felt as sharp as electric shocks,
she needed morphine and other powerful painkillers to get
through the day.

Wilson had once been a vigorous woman—a manager for
Unisys Corporation who worked sixty-to-seventy-hour weeks and
still had enough energy to swim regularly and walk several miles
a day. That all changed in May 1988, when her physician recommended L-tryptophan, a nonprescription nutritional supplement,
to help with a bout of insomnia. Wilson had been apprehensive
about taking sleep medications because of their side effects, but
she was told that L-tryptophan was different. An amino acid that
occurs naturally in such foods as turkey and milk, it was supposedly nonaddictive and safe.

After using L-tryptophan for four months, however, Wilson
began to feel a strange pain in her legs during her daily walk.
Soon the sensation spread to her arms, torso, neck, and scalp. Her
menstrual cycle stopped, and her appetite vanished. She began to

experience excruciating muscle spasms and had to struggle just to get out of a chair.

Wilson's physician tested her blood and was puzzled by the results: elevated liver enzymes and an extremely high count of eosinophils, a type of white blood cell. The symptoms were like nothing he had ever seen.

Wilson was subsequently diagnosed with breast cancer and in April 1989 had a mastectomy. She had stopped taking L-tryptophan during her cancer treatment, but after her surgery the insomnia returned and she resumed taking it. After all, she testified, she had been led to believe that "it was as good for me as vitamin C." Ten months later, a severe rash appeared on her skin and she became so weak that she developed bedsores from her inability to move at night. The once-energetic woman had to rely on her elderly mother and a friend to feed and bathe her.

Then, in November 1989, Wilson heard a TV news report about an illness called eosinophilia-myalgia syndrome, or EMS, which physicians had linked to the use of L-tryptophan. Soon afterward, she was contacted by the specialists who had treated her at the University of Pennsylvania. They now suspected that EMS was the cause of her agony. "How could this happen?" she recalled asking. L-tryptophan, she had believed, "was a pure product which the FDA controlled. Wasn't I taking something like milk and turkey? Where was my government?"

As Wilson sat before the congressional subcommittee, it was too late for the legislators to do anything to protect her or to alleviate her pain. Instead, she was there to ask that they not further weaken the FDA, which she felt already had a tough time protecting the public. "Please understand," she warned, "that there are many more accidents waiting to happen."

Unfortunately, Congress didn't listen.

L-tryptophan—a substance with potentially harmful side effects that was marketed in the United States for more than two decades with virtually no regulation—is just one example of how the federal regulatory system does not always work.

L-tryptophan—a substance with potentially harmful side effects that was marketed in the United States for more than two decades with virtually no regulation—is just one example of how the federal regulatory system, which is supposed to protect the American public from unsafe medications and food additives, does not always work. And Congress, rather than strengthening the safeguards, has in recent years repeatedly put corporate profits and special interests above the public good.

|||||||||||||||||||||||||||||||||||||||||||

An estimated 80 percent of the prescription drugs given to children are not tested to see whether they are safe for young users. Instead, pediatricians are forced essentially to guess the correct doses.

|||||||||||||||||||||||||||||||||||||||||||

It was not always this way. Back in 1906, with the passage of the Pure Food and Drug Act, Congress promised to ensure the safety of drugs. In the decades that followed, the public was protected by government regulators such as FDA medical officer Frances Kelsey, who in 1962 succeeded in keeping the drug thalidomide—developed in Germany and marketed in Europe and other parts of the world—from being sold in the United States, in the process probably preventing tens of thousands of birth defects here. That year, as a result of the scare, Congress passed the Kefauver-Harris amendment, which required that drugs be demonstrated through well-controlled studies to be safe and effective for their intended uses. The immediate outcome was that half of the prescription drugs on the market had to be withdrawn because they could not meet even that basic standard.

Since then, Americans have come to rely on the federal government to protect them from hazardous drugs and other products. But the FDA's first chief, Harvey Wiley, issued an ominous warning in 1930 that seems to have gone mostly unheeded: "There is a distinct tendency to put regulations and rules for the enforcement of the law into the hands of the industries engaged in food and drug activities. I consider this one of the most pernicious threats to pure food and drugs."

More than 100 million Americans take medicines that were not intended for their ailments, even though the drugs have never been approved by the FDA for those "off-label" purposes. Drug manufacturers aggressively promote such off-label uses, easily circumventing FDA regulations that are meant to bar them from doing so.

An estimated 80 percent of the prescription drugs given to children are not tested to see whether they are safe for young users. Instead, pediatricians are forced essentially to guess the correct doses, even though children metabolize drugs at a different rate and sometimes react to them differently than adults.

Untested—and sometimes unsafe—products such as L-tryptophan are put on the market because they are classified as nutritional supplements rather than drugs. Although companies are legally required to inform the FDA within fifteen days of dangerous side effects, they routinely fail to do so. As a result, drugs can remain on the market for years without government action.

Every year manufacturers spend hundreds of millions of dollars on advertising that encourages people to "ask your doctor" to prescribe certain medications. Consumer advocates warn that the drug ads sometimes contain misleading information and that consumers lack the expertise to evaluate the ads, which gloss over such facts as whether an alternative treatment is cheaper or more effective. Moreover, thanks to a recent FDA rule change, manufacturers can now advertise prescription medications on television without having to include detailed data about side effects and other important concerns.

Who suffers? The public. It has been estimated that 10 to 20 percent of all drug therapies cause adverse reactions, ranging from nausea and skin rashes to life-threatening ailments. Such ill effects may kill as many as 160,000 Americans a year and hospitalize ten times that many. Some estimates have set the national cost, in terms of both medical treatment and lost productivity, in the billions of dollars.

With all of these threats to the health of Americans, you would think that Congress would be holding hearings or writing legislation to protect the public. Instead, in recent years Congress has actually sought to weaken regulations intended to protect the nation's health by reducing the oversight authority of the FDA and allowing manufacturers wider latitude to claim that their products provide health benefits—whether or not there is supportive scien-

tific evidence. In 1997, Congress passed legislation that reduces
the amount of testing that drugs undergo and that allows companies to tout uses for which the drugs have not been approved by
federal regulators. Under the new rules, companies can promote
such untested uses first and then later do the research to determine whether their products are safe and effective.

Some Members of Congress argue that weakening the FDA
will actually benefit the public. They contend that less regulation
will speed the development of lifesaving drugs and make it easier
for doctors to get information about new cures. They proclaim
that the public should not be denied the possible benefits of
substances like L-tryptophan, even if those products have not
been tested for safety.

But behind Congress's "helpful" veneer, it is hard not to suspect another motivation. According to an analysis by the Center
for Public Integrity, the pharmaceutical industry gave more than
$9.3 million in PAC and "soft money" during the 1995–96 elec-
tion cycle, and employees chipped in at least another $1.2 million.
Over the last decade, the industry has filled Congress's prescription for campaign contributions to the tune of nearly $28 million.
The U.S. subsidiary of the British firm Glaxo Wellcome, Inc., the
world's largest pharmaceutical company, gave $411,454 in PAC
contributions and another $610,000 in "soft money" to congres-
sional candidates and party committees in the 1996 elections. Eli
Lilly and Company, the Indiana-based pharmaceutical giant, was
another big "soft-money" donor, giving $746,835 in 1995–96.

Many of the Capitol Hill lawmakers who have been the most
critical of the FDA have raked in plenty of campaign money from
pharmaceutical companies. Republican Representative Richard
Burr of North Carolina, for example, has championed legislation
that would allow pharmaceutical companies greater leeway in dis-
seminating information on off-label uses of drugs; he got $5,000
from Glaxo Wellcome's PAC in 1996. The industry gave more
than $193,000 to the sixteen Republicans on the House Com-
merce Subcommittee on Health and Environment and more than
$57,000 to the thirteen Democrats.

But campaign contributions represent only a fraction of the
drug-industry money that influences that political process. When
House Speaker Newt Gingrich and seven other Members of Con-

gress went to Michigan in November 1996 for a meeting with Republican governors, they flew in an Eli Lilly corporate jet. When Senate Majority Leader Trent Lott flew to San Diego to attend the 1996 Republican National Convention, he went on a Glaxo Wellcome airplane. Republican Jesse Helms of North Carolina flew in a Glaxo Wellcome plane three times during his 1996 Senate reelection campaign. When Haley Barbour, the chairman of the Republican National Committee, hosted a party for the news media at his party's 1996 convention, Eli Lilly picked up the tab. Legislators sometimes also go on trips underwritten by the industry, and from 1987 to 1996, drug companies paid nearly $430,000 in speaking fees to Capitol Hill lawmakers.

All told, drug companies and organizations representing the pharmaceutical industry spent more than $41 million to influence Congress in 1996, according to public filings. The Pharmaceutical Research and Manufacturers of America (PhRMA), the industry's chief trade group, spent nearly $5.4 million to influence Congress in 1996 (the fifth-highest total), according to federal lobbying records. Former Republican Senator Paul Laxalt of Nevada was paid $45,000 in the first half of 1996 as a lobbyist for the Generic Pharmaceutical Industry Association.

Individual companies also spend lavishly on lobbying efforts. New Jersey-based Merck & Company, Inc., for example, spent $4.8 million in 1996 to lobby for legislation that made it easier for the pharmaceutical giant to export

> **In recent years Congress has sought to reduce the oversight authority of the Food and Drug Administration and to allow manufacturers wider latitude to claim that their products provide health benefits—whether or not there is supportive scientific evidence.**

its products. In 1996, with FDA-revamping legislation and lucrative tax breaks at stake, Glaxo Wellcome augmented its five full-time lobbyists in Washington by hiring fifty freelancers, including several former Capitol Hill lawmakers.

Glaxo Wellcome, in particular, has cultivated some valuable friendships on Capitol Hill. In 1994, Congress extended the patents on drugs from seventeen to twenty years, in order to make them uniform with those of other countries. Although Congress did not intend the law to be used in such a way, big pharmaceutical manufacturers soon discovered a legal loophole allowing them to block the sale of generic versions of drugs that had been on the market for years. The slipup enabled Glaxo Wellcome to compel Americans suffering from ulcers to use Zantac, its brand-name ulcer drug, rather than cheaper generics. That move gave Glaxo Wellcome a windfall estimated at $6 million a day, all of which came out of the public's pockets. For ulcer patients, relief cost $100 more each month, prompting Democratic Senator David Pryor of Arkansas to lament, "Can we look our people in the face when we go back home and say, 'No, we decided not to give you that break—we decided to give that break to the drug companies?' "

In the end, Congress chose to side with Glaxo Wellcome. A move to close the loophole was blocked in the Senate Judiciary Committee in 1995 with the help of its chairman, Republican Senator Orrin Hatch of Utah, a recipient of $20,000 in Glaxo Wellcome political contributions from 1990 to 1995. Another supporter of Glaxo Wellcome's patent extension was Republican Senator Lauch Faircloth of North Carolina, a Glaxo Wellcome shareholder who had also received $15,000 in political contributions from 1990 to 1995. Democrat Edward Kennedy of Massachusetts, in a speech on the Senate floor, pointed to Glaxo Wellcome's clout as an example of how corporate greed influenced politics. "What has happened since discovery of the loophole is a lesson in greed," Kennedy said. "Glaxo and the other brand-name manufacturers began an intense lobbying campaign to prevent this inadvertent mistake from being corrected. Corporate profits, not research and development, will be the prime beneficiary."

("We were disappointed to be the target of such attacks," Rick Sluder, a spokesman for Glaxo Wellcome, told the Center. "In our view, all we were seeking was equal treatment with all other American industries that got the patent extension.")

Additionally, the pharmaceutical industry helps define the debate in Congress by underwriting patient organizations, whose representatives sometimes testify on behalf of bills that benefit the industry. One group that has advocated revamping the FDA and loosening regulation is the National Coalition for Cancer Survivorship, an organization that, according to a report in *The New York Times,* received a third of its $730,000 annual budget from drug and biotechnology companies.

Drug companies have also pumped money into conservative think tanks and foundations, which in turn have produced op-ed articles and newspaper and television ads calling for Congress to "reform" the FDA by reducing the agency's authority over drug companies. From 1992 through 1995, Eli Lilly alone invested $623,000 in such efforts. In 1994 and 1995, $400,000 in industry money—including a $25,000 contribution from PhRMA—went to the Progress and Freedom Foundation, a think tank with ties to House Speaker Newt Gingrich. (The foundation was started by Jeffrey Eisenbach, who previously headed GOPAC, Gingrich's political fund-raising organization.) The foundation benefited greatly from Gingrich's sympathetic attitude toward the drug industry. In 1994, for example, it received a $30,000 donation from the U.S. subsidiary of Solvay, a Belgian pharmaceutical and chemical company, on whose behalf Gingrich had interceded with the FDA and introduced tariff-lifting legislation.

With the Republican takeover of Congress in the 1994 elections, the industry finally had a chance to rid itself of the burdensome federal regulators altogether. The industry's chief ally, Gingrich, had denounced the FDA as "the leading job killer in America" and its commissioner at the time, David Kessler, as "a thug and a bully." The Progress and Freedom Foundation produced a study that derided the FDA as a "government monopoly" and called its safety precautions on new drugs "excessive." The foundation drew up a blueprint in which government-licensed private-sector firms, rather than the FDA, would assume direct authority over the drug testing and approval process. In addition, the foundation wanted to make it more difficult for patients who alleged that they had been harmed by those drugs to sue the manufacturers. The study was financed largely by the drug industry, although Tom Lenard, a senior fellow at the foundation, told the Center that it was not an industry proposal. "I think most people could read the output," he said, "and see that it's an independent study."

In 1996, Republican lawmakers in both chambers launched a

coordinated attack to "reform" the FDA. In the House, Republican Representatives Richard Burr of North Carolina, James Greenwood of Pennsylvania, and Joe Barton of Texas introduced legislation; Thomas Bliley, a Republican from Virginia who chairs the Commerce Committee, appointed Greenwood to guide the bills on a "fast track" toward early passage. Meanwhile, Republican Nancy Kassebaum of Kansas, who chaired the Senate Committee on Labor and Human Resources, put together a sweeping proposal written with extensive input from the pharmaceutical industry. One of Kassebaum's key advisers was Peter Barton Hutt, a former chief counsel of the FDA who had gone on to work for Covington & Burling, a Washington law firm whose clients included drug companies. "If you're a drug lawyer in Washington and have not had some input into this bill, you should consider some other line of work," Patrick Korten, a deputy vice president of PhRMA, told a reporter for *The New York Times*. "At least sixty or seventy lawyers have dipped a pinkie finger into it."

> **The pharmaceutical industry's chief ally, House Speaker Newt Gingrich, had denounced the FDA as "the leading job killer in America" and its commissioner at the time, David Kessler, as "a thug and a bully."**

The resulting bills in the Senate and the House would have forced the FDA to relinquish much of its power to evaluate drugs, food additives, and medical devices to private contractors paid by the drug companies. The bills also would have reduced the number of clinical trials and the amount of data that companies are required to supply as proof that drugs are safe. Both bills contained provisions that would have allowed companies to advertise and promote drugs for uses that the FDA had not approved.

FDA Commissioner Kessler warned that the legislation would "end up rolling back fifty years of public protection." He was not the only one who was alarmed.

At a Senate hearing in February, Thomas Moore, a senior fellow at George Washington University's Center for Health Policy Research and an expert on drug regulation, held up two bottles. One contained Coumadin, a brand of the blood-thinning medication Warfarin, used by millions of hypertension patients. The other contained rat poison. As Moore explained to the Senators, the poison and the medicine were the same chemical. The only difference between health and death was how much of it someone took. Moore explained that it had taken years of research to find a safe dosage for Coumadin and that it was vital to continue to require drug makers to do such spadework before advertising a product. "We abandon that policy at our peril," he warned.

The 1996 FDA "reform" effort stalled, in part because of differences that arose between the congressional advocates and their industry patrons and in part because of vigorous opposition by groups such as the consumer-advocacy organization Public Citizen and lawmakers such as Kennedy, who recalled for legislators his worries when his son's cancer was treated with an experimental drug. "This was something I wanted for my son, to make sure that drug studies were done and done effectively," he said. "Families need assurance that a drug is safe and effective."

In 1997, however, the proponents of weakening the FDA's authority regrouped and tried once again. This time they had a new strategy. The Prescription Drug User Fee Act, which had enabled the FDA to cut approval times for new drugs by collecting fees from companies to subsidize faster testing, was up for renewal. In late June, Senator James Jeffords, a Republican from Vermont and the chairman of the Labor and Human Resources Committee, introduced the FDA Modernization and Accountability Act of 1997, which tied renewal of the user-fees program to an overhaul of the FDA. The new bill—drafted with the help of Jeffords's aide James Hawkins, a former lobbyist for the medical device industry—was a slightly softened version of the previous year's proposal. ("We were working basically with the same document for three years, and it seemed like a sound way to proceed," Hawkins told the Center.) Like the 1996 Kassebaum bill, the 1997 Jeffords bill allowed drug companies to send physicians literature providing information on untested uses of drugs and allowed companies to get by with just a single clinical trial on a new drug, as opposed to the two or more required in the past. The bill weakened the FDA's authority in other ways as well. It allowed food manufacturers, for instance, to make health claims for their products without first having to seek approval from the FDA.

The Senate Labor Committee approved the bill in June, readying it for a vote by the full Senate. More than a month later, a few days before Senators were scheduled to leave Washington for their August break, Jeffords suddenly brought a revised bill to the Senate floor and lobbied his fellow lawmakers to approve it quickly before the recess. In the end, the Senate decided to wait. But former Senator Howard Metzenbaum, now president of the Consumer Federation of America, a nonprofit advocacy group, criticized Jeffords for attempting to rush the bill through Congress. "I served nineteen years in the United States Senate," Metzenbaum told the *Los Angeles Times,* "and I don't know of . . . any other instance . . . where you bring a bill to the floor of this major impact without knowing what's in the bill."

With FDA "modernization" now intertwined with renewal of the user-fee program, however, few in Congress cared to oppose the bill and possibly take the blame for shutting down testing on new drugs for which seriously ill patients were clamoring. In September 1997, despite a last-minute effort by Kennedy to oppose a portion reducing restrictions on untested uses of medical devices, the Jeffords bill passed the Senate ninety-eight to two; a similar bill passed the House two weeks later by a voice vote. In a ceremony at which he signed the legislation on November 21, 1997, President Clinton said: "The FDA has always set the gold standard for protecting the public safety. Today it wins the gold medal for leading the way into the future."

But while the pharmaceutical industry and its congressional patrons hailed the "modernization" of the FDA, another event that fall provided an unsettling omen of what perils might come from weakening the FDA's powers. Two popular off-label diet drugs—dexfenfluramine, known by its brand name Redux, and fenfluramine, combined with phentermine in the "Fen-Phen" regimen—were withdrawn from the market after studies revealed that they

What many Americans may not realize is that often the medicines they are taking have never been approved by the FDA—at least not for the uses for which their physicians have prescribed them.

caused heart damage in as many as a third of users. In a written statement distributed by Public Citizen in September, Lewis Rubin, the head of pulmonary and critical care at the University of Maryland Medical School, warned that other disasters like "Fen-Phen" now might lie down the road. "Imagine what the impact on the health of America would have been," he said, "had we allowed those pharmaceutical companies to promote these drugs for off-label use."

What many Americans may not realize is that often the medicines they are taking have never been approved by the FDA—at least not for the uses for which their physicians have prescribed them. The FDA has no authority over physicians, who are allowed to prescribe medications for any purpose. Thus, an estimated 40 percent of the drugs prescribed in the United States are for off-label uses that physicians have learned about from medical journals and other sources. The antidepressant Prozac, for example, is also used to treat obsessive-compulsive disorder and to aid in weight loss. Rogaine, originally a blood-pressure medication, was used off-label for years as a baldness remedy before its maker obtained FDA approval to market it for that purpose. As recently as the mid-1980s, a University of Washington study found that off-label use was relatively rare, but since then off-label uses of drugs are growing. *AMA Drug Evaluations,* one of the three compendiums that list both labeled and unlabeled uses for drugs, now contains upward of 5,000 off-label uses.

The ability to prescribe off-label drug uses is undeniably practical for physicians, particularly those who must treat new or rare diseases or confront tough adversaries such as cancer and AIDS. Both physicians and the pharmaceutical industry also complain that off-label use is necessary because the FDA moves too slowly in approving uses—although in recent years the agency has taken steps to speed the process, reducing the amount of documentation necessary for permission to list a new use on a drug label. But it is not always the FDA bureaucratic logjam that keeps a promising drug use off-label. By not applying for approval, companies do not have to spend millions on clinical trials or safety research— and they can keep more of the profits from an old drug.

But because off-label drug uses are not tested as thoroughly as approved uses are, sometimes they turn out to be dangerous. In the 1980s, small-scale studies showed that two drugs designed to control severely irregular heartbeats—Enkaid and Tambocor— could be effective in treating patients with milder heart problems. Physicians began prescribing them off-label, and sales soared. Then, in 1989, the National Institutes of Health conducted a broader trial, which showed that the drugs actually caused cardiac arrest in some patients. The off-label prescriptions were stopped. But by that time, according to one estimate, 50,000 patients had already died after taking the drugs.

The death toll from the off-label heart drugs might have been even higher had the companies that made them been allowed to promote their use. At the time, FDA rules barred companies from publicizing anything but approved uses of their drugs—a restriction that repeatedly came under attack from the drug industry and antiregulatory conservative forces. In 1994, the Washington Legal Foundation, a conservative antiregulatory group, sued the FDA, charging, among other things, that the no-promotion rule violated the First Amendment. (That suit is still pending.) In 1996, pharmaceutical-industry allies in Congress tried and failed to legalize the promotion of drugs for untested purposes. The following year, as part of 1997's so-called FDA "reform" package, they at last succeeded in weakening the rule; drug companies can now distribute FDA-approved articles on off-label uses to doctors.

The FDA long resisted such a loosening of the rules because it feared that drug manufacturers "might promote uses that do not work or are dangerous," Michael Friedman, the FDA's deputy commissioner for operations, told the House Government Reform and Oversight Subcommittee on Human Resources and Intergovernmental Relations in 1996. "Also, [manufacturers] would have no incentive to conduct the necessary scientific research and present data to the FDA to verify the safety and effectiveness of those off-label uses. In fact, because the agency might determine that the new use is not supported by evidence, there would be an incentive to avoid FDA review."

But if adults are endangered by unapproved uses for drugs, the situation is far worse for the young—and unfortunately, it is nothing new. Back in the 1950s, the antibiotic chloramphenicol drew accolades for its seemingly miraculous ability to kill bacteria that were resistant to penicillin, and it was given to thousands of infants. If the drug had been subjected to child-safety studies beforehand, researchers might have discovered that it is metabolized relatively slowly by infants and that too-large doses can cause a toxic buildup. Instead, physicians learned this fact only after several hundred children had died. Similarly, in the 1960s, the antibiotic tetracycline was prescribed to children, based on research that showed it to be safe for adults. As a result, a generation of kids grew up with discolored smiles and, in the most severe cases, suffered decay and loss of their teeth.

Those examples should have inspired caution, but they did not. Although the FDA has offered incentives to drug companies to seek pediatric labeling approval for their drugs, few bother to do so. Only 20 percent of the drugs licensed by the FDA since 1962 have received approval for children.

"Off-label use of medications has, by default, become an established standard of care for children," Sanford Cohen, M.D., representing the American Academy of Pediatrics, testified to Congress in 1997. "Infants and children frequently are exposed to medications without the benefit of adequate studies to document safety and efficacy or to establish doses appropriate for their age."

The FDA compiled a list of the ten most frequently prescribed off-label medications, of which 5 million prescriptions are written for children each year. At the top of the list is Albuterol in inhalant form, an asthma treatment. The drug is prescribed more than 1.6 million times annually to patients under twelve, even though the Web site for the U.S. Pharmacopoeia—a nonprofit organization that provides information on prescription drugs—notes only that the proper dose for children that age "must be determined by your doctor" and that the possible side effects are presumed to be similar to those in adults—namely, anxiety, dizziness, headaches, elevated blood pressure, and nausea.

Prozac, a drug originally approved for adults, is prescribed nearly 350,000 times a year to patients under sixteen. Prozac prescriptions for teenagers increased by 47 percent from 1995 to 1996. The drug is used not only to treat depression, but also increasingly for attention-deficit hyperactivity disorder (ADHD). This is happening even though there has been relatively little research on whether Prozac does children any good or what risks it might pose. (The side effects of Prozac in adults can include sleeplessness, abnormal dreams, anxiety, and other effects; in addition, critics say, it may induce violent or suicidal behavior.) It was not until November 1997 that University of Texas researchers published the first large-scale study of children and Prozac, which observed the effects of the drug and a placebo on ninety-six depressed patients aged seven to seventeen. They found that after eight weeks, 50 percent of those on Prozac improved, compared with one-third who took the placebo.

● ● ● ● ● ● ● ● ● ● ● ● ● ● ● ● ● ●

Drug companies often do not want to bear the cost of pediatric trials, which can run as much as $30,000 per participant.

● ● ● ● ● ● ● ● ● ● ● ● ● ● ● ● ● ●

Why won't drug companies test more drugs for pediatric safety and submit them for FDA approval for use by children? Setting up studies involving children is more complicated than it is for adults, because federal regulations require that children not be exposed to anything greater than minimal risk unless there is a strong chance that they will directly benefit. Still, researchers say it is possible to design studies that meet those requirements. But there is another problem: Drug companies often do not want to bear the cost of pediatric trials, which can run as much as $30,000 per participant.

In August 1997, the Clinton Administration moved to require companies to test new drugs for child safety and to determine the proper doses for children if they expect that a new drug will be taken by more than 100,000 young patients a year. "The rule I announce today will put an end to this guesswork," Clinton proclaimed in August. "It will require manufacturers of all medicines needed by children to study the drug's effects on children. The results will then be displayed on drug labels to help pediatricians and other health-care professionals make good decisions about how to treat their young patients." Enforcement would be relatively mild; the FDA could sue companies and seek fines for noncompliance, but it would not have the power to keep the drugs off pharmacy shelves. The Administration estimates that the new requirements would cost the industry $13.5 million to $21 million a year—a modest amount for an industry that generates more than $60 billion a year in U.S. sales.

Even FDA labeling approval, however, does not always guarantee that a drug will be safe, critics say. Psychiatrist Peter Breggin notes that drugs are approved on the basis of trials that last just a few weeks. "People assume that FDA approval and the widespread distribution of a drug—with many patients taking it for months or years—means that long-term studies have found it safe in regard to side effects, drug interactions, dependency, addiction, and withdrawal," he writes in his book *Toxic Psychiatry*. "Thus, FDA approval grossly misleads the public, lulling it into an unfounded sense of security."

Indeed, approved drugs sometimes carry significant risks. And 3 to 5 percent of American school-age children—including 10 to 12 percent of boys between six and fourteen—are being given Ritalin, a powerful stimulant used to treat ADHD. But the drug is not always effective—25 to 40 percent of young patients don't improve while taking it—and the drug has dangerous potential side effects. It can slow growth; cause insomnia, joint pain, and mood disturbances; and elevate blood pressure. Most frighteningly, in rare cases the drug can induce the uncontrolled vocal outbursts and tics of Tourette's syndrome, which may not be reversible. The mechanism by which the drug works is not yet understood, and its long-term effects are not known. Critics note that ADHD children often are given Ritalin as a cure-all, while the nonchemical part of treatment—such as behavioral therapy and changes in the classroom—are neglected. They attribute Ritalin's popularity at least in part to the fact that Ciba-Geigy Corporation (now called Novartis Corporation), the drug's Swiss manufacturer, donated nearly $1 million from 1991 to 1994 to Children and Adults with Attention Deficit Disorders (CHADD), a parents' lobby. Todd Forte, a spokesman for Novartis, told the Center that the money the company gave to CHADD paid for informational pamphlets that described attention deficit disorder and the drugs commonly used to treat it.

For the 30 percent of children who did not respond to Ritalin or could not tolerate its side effects, physicians began to prescribe Desipramine, a drug used to treat depression in adults. Although the drug had not been approved by the FDA for children, studies indicated that it helped curb hyperactivity. From 1986 to 1990, the number of Desipramine prescriptions for children under fourteen rose from 22,000 to 150,000. But Desipramine carried risks. In particular, overdoses—a greater danger in hyperactive children, who have a tendency toward impulsive behavior—could interfere with heart function. From 1986 to 1992, thirty-one children died from overdoses.

Some in Congress ponder weakening the FDA's oversight authority, even though experience shows that it is already too easy for dangerous products to get on the market. In the early 1970s, researchers discovered that L-tryptophan—the drug that caused Dorothy Wilson's illness—controlled the production of serotonin, a brain chemical that regulates sleep, mood, and appetite. Richard Wurtman, a neuroscience professor at Harvard Medical School and the Massachusetts Institute of Technology, who led the work, thought L-tryptophan offered great promise; he envisioned its use as a drug to treat sleep, mood, and eating disorders. As he testified to a House subcommittee in 1991, "I had assumed that pharmaceutical companies might take this discovery and invest the $10 million or $20 million—whatever it took then—to do appropriate safety and efficacy studies."

But that did not happen. Instead, companies saved millions by simply putting L-tryptophan on the market as a nutritional supplement—even though, as Wurtman noted in his testimony, it clearly was not the kind of substance that people might need to take to make up for a deficiency in their diets. (Giving an isolated amino acid to a protein-deficient person, for instance, would be harmful.) In reality, L-tryptophan was a drug, and the millions of people who bought it used it as such—for depression, premenstrual syndrome, insomnia. So as not to incur government regulation, companies simply did not put any information about L-tryptophan's effectiveness—which could be touted by word of mouth—on the label. Nor did they list recommended dosages or possible harmful effects. Thus, as Wurtman put it, "L-tryptophan was, in every sense, an accident waiting to happen."

Initially, the FDA went along. But after research showed that large doses of isolated amino acids could be toxic, the agency reconsidered and tried to take L-tryptophan off the market until companies submitted it for approval. After L-tryptophan makers brought suit, however, the agency backed down. One reason, FDA regulators told the House subcommittee years later, was that the agency figured Congress was not on its side. In 1976, Congress had limited the FDA's power to regulate vitamin doses. Although amino acids were not vitamins, the agency took the law as a sign that legislators wanted the FDA to keep its hands off supplements unless they were clearly dangerous. Emboldened, companies began making claims for L-tryptophan in product inserts and advertisements—claims the FDA later analyzed and determined were illegal. Physicians even recommended what essentially was an unapproved drug to their patients. The FDA, inhibited by what it saw as Congress's support of health foods, took no action.

By 1989, U.S. consumers were buying $300 million worth of L-tryptophan a year. But around the country, growing numbers of people were developing eosinophilia-myalgia syndrome, or EMS, a mysterious illness characterized by muscular pain, fatigue, and swelling of the extremities; some also developed polyneuropathy, a gradual weakening that led to paralysis. In the worst cases, EMS was fatal. In October 1989, physicians investigating three cases in New Mexico noticed a common thread: All three patients had taken L-tryptophan. Tamar Stieber, a reporter for the *Albuquerque Journal* who won a Pulitzer Prize for her articles on the subject, focused the news media's attention on the connection, and other cases began to surface. In November, after the FDA had received reports of 291 cases of EMS and four deaths among L-tryptophan users, it announced a recall of the supplement. Four months later, it banned the drug outright. In the end, L-tryptophan-related illnesses numbered more than 1,500, including twenty-one deaths.

Although researchers have not pinpointed exactly what causes EMS, a team of health authorities who investigated the 1989 outbreak traced those illnesses back to L-tryptophan produced by a single maker, the Japanese pharmaceutical and chemical company Showa Denko, as the most likely cause. In 1988, they learned that the company had changed its production process, reducing the amount of filtering for impurities in the vats where a genetically engineered microorganism fermented L-tryptophan. The manufacturer ended up paying 200 billion yen—roughly equivalent to $1.6 billion in today's dollars—to settle lawsuits by victims in the United States.

That explanation for the disaster gave other L-tryptophan makers an out, and soon they were lobbying the FDA to allow them to start selling their products again. But others, including then-FDA commissioner David Kessler, were not convinced that L-tryptophan, even in a purified form, was safe. The first documented case of an L-tryptophan user developing EMS, after all, had occurred in 1978 in Montreal. Another case studied by Mayo Clinic researchers dated to 1986, and at least forty-five instances of EMS occurred in the United States before Showa Denko had reduced its filtering in 1988. In a 1992 article, Victor Herbert, M.D., the chief of the Hematology and Nutrition Research Laboratory at the Bronx Veterans Administration Medical Center, detailed additional health risks posed by L-tryptophan, including osteoporosis. In the 1960s and 1970s, researchers such as George Washington University pathologist Herschel Sidransky discovered evidence linking the substance to bladder and liver cancer in laboratory animals. Others noted that in Canada, where L-tryptophan is regulated as a prescription drug, only ten to twelve cases of EMS were reported—compared with more than 1,500 in the United States.

|||||||||||||||||||||||||||||||||||||||||||

In 1996, the FDA accused the pharmaceutical manufacturer Pfizer, Inc., of being forty-four to 514 days late in reporting serious reactions to eight of its drugs, including the popular antidepressant Zoloft.

|||||||||||||||||||||||||||||||||||||||||||

After the L-tryptophan deaths, one might have expected Congress to act to prevent future tragedies. Instead, Congress, at the behest of the supplement manufacturers' lobby, did the opposite. It passed the Dietary Supplement Health and Education Act of 1994, under which any new food supplement is presumed safe unless the FDA can prove that it is dangerous. The result is that regulators essentially have to wait until a product such as L-tryptophan injures consumers before they can take action. In addition, manufacturers of supplements can make virtually any claims on labels that they wish, as long as the labels include the disclaimer that the products have not been evaluated by the FDA and that they are "not intended to treat, cure, or prevent any disease."

Some Members of Congress have wanted to cut the FDA's authority over supplements even further. In 1995, Representative Frank Pallone, a Democrat from New Jersey, introduced the Food and Dietary Supplement Consumer Information Act, which would have prevented regulators from classifying supplements such as L-tryptophan as drugs. He claimed that weakening the FDA was necessary to ensure the public's access to "low-cost medicine."

In 1990, the General Accounting Office found that more than half of the 198 drugs approved from 1976 to 1985 produced reactions serious enough to warrant significant labeling changes, such as blindness and birth defects. Six had sufficiently serious side effects that FDA approval was withdrawn.

But getting unsafe products off the market can be difficult. FDA regulations require drug manufacturers to report dangerous side effects during clinical testing; following a drug's approval, an adverse reaction must be reported within fifteen days after the manufacturer learns of the problem. For decades, however, drug companies have often failed to comply. In 1979, SmithKline Beecham Corporation learned that Selacryn, a hypertension drug developed in France that it had licensed and was about to market in the United States, had caused numerous cases of liver damage. SmithKline neglected to inform the FDA for eight months. In that period, the drug was linked to at least thirty-six deaths and more than 500 serious illnesses in the United States.

In 1985, another big manufacturer, Eli Lilly, pleaded guilty to criminal charges after it failed to notify the FDA of numerous deaths overseas from use of the arthritis drug Oraflex. In January 1982, three months before the drug was approved by the FDA for sale in the United States, Eli Lilly had neglected to share with FDA regulators a British government report detailing two deaths from liver complications among Oraflex users, as well as twenty-three people who had died from other causes after using the drug. Following the drug's approval, Eli Lilly spent $12 million on promotion, but then hastily withdrew Oraflex four months later— the day after the drug's product license was suspended in the United Kingdom. During that brief period, at least twenty-six U.S.

patients died from liver or kidney failure after using Oraflex, and 200 others suffered nonfatal liver and kidney failure.

In 1996, the FDA accused the pharmaceutical manufacturer Pfizer, Inc., of being forty-four to 514 days late in reporting serious reactions to eight of its drugs, including the popular antidepressant Zoloft. That same year, the FDA recommended an investigation to determine whether Pharmacia & Upjohn, Inc., had concealed safety concerns about the company's sleeping pill Halcion, which some users alleged caused depression and suicidal urges. A federal grand jury in Michigan questioned employees about the possible destruction of "clinical data and analyses" of the drug. Although the grand jury's findings were not made public, a spokesperson for the company told the Center that acting FDA Commissioner Michael A. Friedman determined that "criminal or civil enforcement proceedings were not warranted."

When companies do get caught, they seldom receive more than a monetary slap on the wrist. In the Selacryn case, Smith-Kline pleaded guilty to criminal charges and was fined $34,000— the maximum that the weak federal statute enacted by Congress allowed. In the Oraflex case, a judge ultimately fined Eli Lilly and one of its executives a total of $40,000, which came to about $1,538 per death.

Who is to blame? John Abraham, the author of a report on Halcion for Britain's Economic and Social Research Council, concluded that the FDA is less likely to take dangerous drugs off the market than are European drug regulators. (Halcion, for example, was banned in the United Kingdom in 1991 after reports of side effects surfaced. In the United States, it remained on the market, despite a 1992 FDA review that showed the manufacturer had engaged in "an ongoing pattern of misconduct" in its Halcion studies.) One reason, Abraham theorized, is that congressional moves to deregulate the drug industry have blunted the FDA's enthusiasm for taking on drug companies.

The FDA's regulatory powers are weakening at a time when drug companies are marketing their products more aggressively than ever. In March 1996 at the American Pharmaceutical Association's annual convention in Nashville, one of the scheduled events was a symposium called "Business Opportunities in Pharmaceutical Care: Focus on Bedwetting." The pharmacists in attendance learned that 10 percent of the parents and grandparents who came into their drugstores had children or grandchildren who were bed-wetters, and that the adults were often anxious and desperate about the situation. One speaker, Quentin Srnka, a pharmacist and an associate professor at the University of Tennessee at Memphis, described a bed-wetting consultation service, which charged drugstore customers for advice about drugs and other treatments. "The bottom line is that if you charge thirty dollars per person," he explained, "you can make sixty dollars an hour."

The symposium was sponsored by Rhône-Poulenc Rohrer, Inc., the maker of Desmopressin nasal spray. In 1995, the company had embarked on an $800,000 public-relations campaign to publicize bed-wetting as a problem and to persuade families to seek treatment, including a public-service announcement featuring Michael Landon, Jr., the late actor's son, relating his youthful bed-wetting experience. Although the campaign did not overtly promote Desmopressin, as Doug Arbesfeld, Rhône-Poulenc Rohrer's director of corporate marketing communications, noted, "the object is to raise awareness of the product." He explained that "we're interested in people seeing physicians . . . and if the product is right for that person, it gets prescribed." Another executive of Rhône-Poulenc Rohrer credited the campaign with stimulating a 25 percent increase in U.S. sales of the nine-year-old prescription drug.

That jump occurred even though Desmopressin is expensive—it can cost as much as $100 a month—and only a third of children who wet their beds produce deficient levels of antidiuretic hormone (the theory upon which Desmopressin treatment is based). The cause of bed-wetting is unknown and may result from multiple factors, but most children who wet their beds are otherwise healthy and generally outgrow the condition. For those who do not, a 1995 study by Mayo Clinic researcher Jeffrey Monda showed that behavioral treatment—the use of an inexpensive moisture-sensitive alarm—was far more effective than drugs.

Desmopressin is just one of the numerous drugs that pharmaceutical companies are now pitching directly to the public, under the guise of suggesting that patients "ask your doctor." Increasingly, the aggressive marketing of drugs benefits corporate bottom lines, but it may not be an equally good deal for the public. Pharmaceutical companies spent nearly $600 million in 1996 on newspaper, magazine, and television commercials to promote prescription drugs. Such direct-to-consumer advertising now exceeds the amount that the companies spend buying advertising space in medical journals to inform physicians about their drugs.

Some experts predict that the amount spent on direct advertising of drugs will soon top $1 billion per year, now that the FDA has loosened restrictions on television advertising. For years, the FDA required that all ads touting a drug for a particular medical condition contain a detailed explanation of possible risks, side effects, and situations in which the drug should not be taken—the same sort of information provided on package inserts and in medical journals. That requirement discouraged drug companies from pushing their products on TV. In August 1997, however, the FDA decided to allow companies to get by with a quick mention—in both voice-over and on-screen type—of what they perceive to be the drug's major risks as well as a telephone number or Web site address where more information can be obtained.

By appealing directly to consumers, drug companies strive to build brand loyalty, the same way soft-drink or toothpaste manufacturers do. But the television ads do not give consumers complete information about the drugs and their possible side effects. Even the print ads, which contain more detailed information, do not mention alternative drugs or treatments that may be more effective, less costly, or both. And consumers do not have the scientific or medical training to fill in the gaps.

Nevertheless, drug companies may find that consumers are not so easily led. An opinion poll commissioned in 1997 by the Patients' Coalition, a group of more than 100 organizations representing people with serious illnesses, showed overwhelming support for continued FDA regulation of drugs. Sixty-seven percent of respondents stated that they trusted the FDA more than they did the pharmaceutical industry to make sure that medicines and drugs were safe; just 13 percent of the public trusted drug companies more than the FDA.

Clearly, the public wants a strong watchdog in Washington to look out for its health and safety. If only Congress could get the message.

9

||||||●|||||

The Grim Reapers

H OMER STULL WAS ON THE GRAVEYARD SHIFT. HE WORKED UNTIL THE predawn hours before hauling his tired, sore body into his maroon Cutlass Supreme and driving home, the new sun rising in his rearview mirror over the meatpacking plant on the Midwest flatlands. Another grueling shift was over.

The blond twenty-year-old could take the punishment and the dirtiest jobs the foreman dished out—he knew it came with the territory of being young and new on the job. Besides, unlike so many others in Liberal, Kansas, he did not intend for meatpacking to be his life's work. He dreamed of becoming a law-enforcement officer and was studying criminal justice at a community college in his time off. He even had taken a few rides in a squad car for the police department in Tyrone, Oklahoma, just over the state line, and his roommate was a cop. The meatpacking job was just for the summer—although, he had never told his boss that.

It was hard, messy work, the kind you do not talk about much at the supper table. But it allowed Stull to care for his infant son during the day while the baby's mother worked. Things were rough between Stull and his girlfriend, but the baby, the new job at the plant, and his plans to become a policeman brought new hope. Soon the three of them would be moving in together, like a regular family. Life was starting to look up.

At the plant, one of Stull's jobs was to clean out the bloody debris stuck to a huge metal screen near the top of a thirty-foot-high tank. The tank collected the blood from more than 4,000 cattle slaughtered each day at the National Beef Packing Company. He was supposed to use a long-handled tool to do the job, but the handle, his brother said later, was broken.

No one knows for sure what happened, because no one who was there survived. The company says that Stull crawled onto a ladder leading to the tank's screen early one Sunday morning in June 1991 to clean it by hand—a common enough practice. But he did not know that a power shortage had prevented the cattle blood from draining out and that, as a result, the tank was a deadly gas chamber of hydrogen sulfide. The poisonous fumes from the stagnating blood caused his knees to buckle and quickly sapped his strength. He choked to death, retching in a tank that holds 27,000 gallons of bovine blood. Two shift buddies came to his rescue, but they too were overcome by the fumes and died. Workers on the next shift found three men lying on the screen like crumpled laundry.

This was not the first time that such an accident had happened at the plant. In 1983, the tank had claimed the lives of two men in the same way. At the time, the Occupational Safety and Health Administration (OSHA), the federal agency responsible for protecting American workers, fined the National Beef Packing Company $960 and asked it to improve its cleaning routines. OSHA checked on the company once, okayed its safety procedures, and never came back.

At the time of Stull's accident, OSHA had for sixteen years been developing and trying to implement a nationwide safety standard for enclosed spaces, but business interests, Republican Administrations, and Congress had fought their efforts tooth-and-nail.

"How many more workers must die before the government finally lives up to its responsibility to protect workers?" Diann Clodfelter, Stull's sister, asked the Senate Labor and Human Resources Committee a year after her brother's death. "Why is it taking so long?"

It is taking so long because powerful business interests repeatedly challenge new safety standards, delay their implementation, misinform the public, lobby to slash OSHA's budget, and use campaign contributions to influence lawmakers on important committees.

OSHA published a final confined-space rule in January 1993. But after all that time studying and trying to pass the standard, it expressly excluded construction, agriculture, and shipyard employers—industries that traditionally receive special treatment from OSHA and Congress, yet that had high numbers of injuries and deaths in confined spaces. Although organized labor generally supported the confined-space rule, leaders of the United Steelworkers of America expressed outrage that three industries had been excluded. The union went to court in an attempt to force OSHA to revise the standard. Lynn Williams, then the president of the union, wrote a letter to Labor Secretary Robert Reich that the exemptions "may account for at least as many confined-space accidents as those which are covered."

Every day in the United States millions of employees leave their homes for work unaware that their health and lives are at risk. Consider the following incidents:

- In July 1990, seventeen workers were killed in an explosion at an Atlantic Richfield Chemical Company plant in Channelview, Texas, while doing maintenance on a compressor unit located near tanks containing petrochemical residues and waste water. Two of the workers who died had previously complained to family members about safety at the plant.
- In September 1991, twenty-five workers were killed and fifty-six others injured when hydraulic fluid from a conveyor belt sprayed over a gas-fired chicken fryer at the Imperial Food Products Company's chicken-processing plant in Hamlet, North Carolina. Workers tried to claw their way out of locked exit doors. The plant had no fire alarm or sprinkler system. Emmett Roe, the owner, served less than five years—or sixty-five days for each person killed—at a minimum-security prison.
- In the early 1990s, more than 100 young Mexican-American and Mexican workers were exposed to lethal doses of

silica while working in the sandblasting trade in Midland and Odessa, Texas. Workers were not informed about or required to use respirators to protect themselves against silica dust from sand, which can cause silicosis, a disabling and fatal lung disease. More than 1 million workers across the country are exposed to silica dust on the job, and 100,000 are at high risk for developing silicosis, according to the Labor Department.

- In April 1996, more than 5,000 federal office workers, many of whom had complained about headaches and nausea, were moved because the U.S. Transportation Department headquarters in Washington, D.C., was declared a "sick building." Indoor air pollution, or sick-building syndrome, affects millions of workers and forces many to leave their jobs. Workers can become ill when harmful chemicals and bacteria are trapped in buildings with poor ventilation.
- In July 1997, 100 workers in the Brewster Heights Packing Company plant became ill in Seattle, when they were exposed to poisonous carbon-monoxide fumes after vents in a dryer and water heater on the apple-packing line were covered, preventing propane fumes from escaping.

In 1995, there were more than 2 million nonfatal workplace injuries in the United States, according to the Bureau of Labor Statistics. A total of 11,308 nonfatal amputations occurred—10,693 fingers, 101 hands, and 306 feet or toes. There were more than 120,000 fractures of the head, neck, back, shoulders, fingers, hands, feet, and toes. More than 50,000 people suffered burns on the job; of this total, 13,861 were the victims of chemical burns, and of that number, 7,756 received burns to the eyes. The most common injuries—876,792 in all—were muscle and tendon sprains, strains, and tears.

As traumatic as such injuries are, these workers lived. There were 6,210 people, on the other hand, who never saw their next paychecks. Highway traffic incidents accounted for the highest portion—21 percent—of all work fatalities in 1995; slightly more than half of the victims were truck drivers or passengers. Homicide is the second-leading cause of job-related deaths.

Despite the chilling statistics, work-related injuries and deaths have declined since the creation of OSHA in 1970. Few would dispute that an agency like OSHA was desperately needed. The number of Americans killed or injured on the job before the birth of the controversial agency is staggering. For example, during World War II, 292,000 U.S. servicemen were killed in battle— but 300,000 workers were killed in factory accidents. While some 17,000 fighting men lost an arm or a leg, nearly 53,000 workers suffered major amputations.

> During World War II, 292,000 U.S. servicemen were killed in battle—but 300,000 workers were killed in factory accidents. While some 17,000 fighting men lost an arm or a leg, nearly 53,000 workers suffered major amputations.

Yet OSHA has always been hampered when it comes to developing, passing, and enforcing regulations and safety standards to protect American workers. And the entity that has constricted it has been Congress. Treating it as the federal government's favorite whipping boy, Congress and big business have spent twenty-eight years emasculating the agency rather than helping it create a better working environment for all. Together they have shaped the agency's image from one of protector of American working men and women to one of meddler in company business.

Take, for instance, the "tooth-fairy story." Representative David McIntosh, a Republican from Indiana, told his colleagues in February 1995 that an OSHA safety standard would "require that all baby teeth [extracted at a dentist's office] be disposed of as hazardous waste material rather than be given back to the parents to allow the tooth fairy to come. . . ." Representative Charles Norwood, a Republican from Georgia, added to the tale a month later by saying to his colleagues, "Having practiced dentistry for twenty-five years, I was one of the people under the gun when I would try to give back my children their baby teeth."

The story was about as real as the tooth fairy itself—a fantasy concocted by Republican lawmakers to paint OSHA as the Wicked Witch of the East in order to try to gut the agency's budget or eliminate it altogether. OSHA officials explained that the safety standard does not bar a dentist or dental assistant wearing gloves from putting the tooth in a container and giving it to the parents.

"I spent time in front of a congressional committee actually debating had we or had we not banned the tooth fairy," Joseph Dear, the Assistant Labor Secretary who runs OSHA, reportedly told a group of industrial hygienists in May 1995. Norwood himself later acknowledged that the standard didn't specifically bar giving an extracted tooth to a child, but he pointed out that it did prohibit the release of tissues or organs contaminated by body fluids, including "saliva in dental procedures."

Demonizing OSHA is not the only tactic that business interests and their supporters in Congress use. With a small budget and a tiny proportion of inspectors to businesses, the agency can barely keep up, so when it has managed to implement standards or safety programs, it has often been punched where it hurts the most: below the budget belt.

In March 1997, for example, OSHA launched a program to reduce the number of amputations in ten targeted manufacturing industries. In 1994, these industries had more than 650 amputations—nearly a tenth of all amputations in manufacturing. "It is unconscionable for workers to be losing their fingers and suffering other disabling injuries simply because mechanic power presses are not properly guarded or maintained," Greg Watchman, then the acting Assistant Labor Secretary for occupational safety and health, said.

Mechanical power presses punch out parts for cars, metal doors and windows, and a wide variety of other products. Workers' fingers and hands are at risk at the point of contact where metal is inserted and withdrawn. OSHA estimates that nearly 300,000 power presses are in use nationwide and that employers are paying anywhere from $5,500 to $47,000 in workers' compensation and indirect costs for each of the injuries. The agency began inspecting and fining violators in July 1997.

Treating OSHA as the federal government's favorite whipping boy, Congress and big business have spent twenty-eight years emasculating the agency rather than helping it create a better working environment for all.

"We have a couple of problems with [OSHA's program]," Laura Nukoneczny, the top lobbyist of the Precision Metal Forming Association (PMA), told the Center for Public Integrity. "The program seems to have been born from somebody's hunch. The Bureau of Labor Statistics has reported that those kinds of amputations have been on the decline for some years." Nukoneczny added that many of the companies using the machines are family businesses with fewer than 100 employees. "These are companies that don't have a lot of resources to deal with this kind of nonsense," she said.

PMA is confronting this problem by lobbying Members of Congress who sit on important committees that oversee OSHA's budget to get the agency to stop the enforcement program and the investigations.

The Center for Public Integrity obtained a letter from a confidential source to PMA's membership outlining the association's strategy for handling the program. "You can assist PMA's efforts to 'educate' Congress about this [power-press program] by contacting your congressional representatives directly," the letter said. "While every Member counts, PMA is concentrating, in particular, on several Members of the Senate subcommittee which decides OSHA's funding, the Public Health and Safety Subcommittee. The above Senators have received funding in the past from PMA's Voice of the Industry Committee and should be encouraged to examine OSHA's justification for this program."

Yet where would Americans be without one of Congress's favorite political footballs? If there were no OSHA, workers would continue to die from asbestosis, a lung disease caused by asbestos inhalation. Without OSHA, workers would have no protection from dangerous confined spaces. Without OSHA, textile workers would still get brown-lung disease, a condition resulting from inhalation of cotton, flax, or hemp dust. Without OSHA, dangerous chemicals would keep making workers sick.

Today a weakened OSHA translates into injury and death for countless American workers. And Congress deserves most of the blame for being the champion of business rather than the guardian of the American employee.

When Republicans won control of Congress in 1994, big business finally got a chance to enact legislation that would take care of some nagging problems and stave off future troubles. Chief in its sight has been OSHA and an ergonomics standard that would create safety regulations on repetitive-strain injuries such as carpal tunnel syndrome or back injuries from repeated lifting.

The Republican victory had the business community licking its chops over how it could carve up and devour OSHA. In January 1995, nearly fifty of the GOP's most powerful allies, calling themselves the Coalition on Occupational Safety and Health (COSH), gathered in the boardroom of the National Association of Manufacturers. The coalition now had allies in powerful positions in Congress: Majority Leader Richard Armey of Texas and House Republican Conference chairman John A. Boehner of Ohio were both former members of the House labor committees and were now top dogs. Republican T. Cass Ballenger, a plastics manufacturer from North Carolina with no love for OSHA, was now the chairman of the House Workforce Protections Subcommittee overseeing OSHA. Ballenger could hardly contain his glee when describing to a reporter how he had raised money from business during the 1994 campaign.

"I'd say, 'Guess who might be chairman of the committee who'd be in charge of OSHA.'

"And they'd say, 'Who?'

"And I'd say, 'Me!'

"And I'd say, 'I need some money.' And—*whoosh!*—I got it. This was my sales pitch: 'Businessmen, wouldn't you like to have a friend overseeing OSHA?'"

The fact that Ballenger was a manufacturer and chairing a workplace-safety subcommittee that has control over the regulatory agency overseeing his own business did not raise too many eyebrows in Washington. In the first year of chairing the subcommittee, Ballenger looked around at his fellow Republicans and

Representative David McIntosh, a Republican from Indiana, told his colleagues in February 1995 that an OSHA safety standard would "require that all baby teeth [extracted at a dentist's office] be disposed of as hazardous waste material rather than be given back to the parents to allow the tooth fairy to come."

said: "My subcommittee is so conservative it makes me look liberal. We could kill motherhood tomorrow if it was necessary."

According to a report in *The Washington Post*, the coalition put together a list of issues and presented them to Ballenger, who wrote a bill curtailing OSHA's regulatory enforcement powers. "We had several groups that came up with finished bills they wanted," Ballenger said. "The North Carolina Citizens for Business and Industry—of which I've been a member for thirty years—came up with a complete bill. COSH had ideas. We had ex-heads of OSHA come in here and give advice. They all knew exactly what I should do."

Ballenger did as he was told. His bill would have turned OSHA from a regulatory agency into a consulting agency for employers, channeling half of OSHA's budget into training programs and incentives for voluntary action. It would have exempted large numbers of employers from random inspections and reduced the rights of workers to file complaints with OSHA. It also would have slowed down any new safety standards from being proposed by requiring OSHA to undertake a lengthy review process, including cost-benefit analysis, risk analysis, and peer review by panels whose members included business groups affected by the standard. It would have abolished the National Institute of Occupational Safety and Health (NIOSH)—the workplace research entity—and the Mine Safety and Health Administration, transferring some of the latter's authority to OSHA.

"They're effectively repealing what this [agency] is supposed to be about, which is to protect workers and provide a federal role of regulation and oversight," Margaret Seminario, the AFL-CIO's director of occupational safety, told a reporter for *National Journal.*

Some lawmakers thought that Ballenger's bill didn't go far enough. According to an account in *The Washington Post*, Charles Norwood wanted to abolish OSHA altogether but was talked out of it by Boehner. Norwood wanted to prevent OSHA from entering a workplace where there had been a serious accident or death if the employer's work-loss ratio was below average. He got a provision in the bill that would have prohibited OSHA from issuing fines other than those specifically related to the serious incident. Employees also would have been required to take a workplace violation to management first before reporting it to OSHA. If there was no action by management, the employee would have to wait thirty days before calling OSHA.

"They need to do what the hell they're told," Norwood told a reporter for *The Washington Post*. "They've been sitting in their cubicle for twenty-five years thinking they knew what was best for every industry in this country. They don't. And they don't want to know. All they want to know is what they can get away with to collect money from us."

Ballenger's bill was not the only one to take aim at OSHA's powers. Representative Joel Hefly, a Republican from Colorado, sought to repeal OSHA's authority to inspect, investigate, and issue citations, relying instead on complaints and lawsuits for enforcement. But Ballenger's, along with others, was seen as too extreme and never made it out of committee.

Although the Republicans were not successful in gutting or eliminating OSHA completely, they did prevent the agency from enacting an ergonomics standard that it had been working on since 1990 and that could help millions of workers avoid crippling disabilities, such as repetitive-strain injury from performing the same task over and over. The standard would limit the time that workers could be forced to perform one specific task—unassisted or frequent heavy lifting, for example—that might lead to a repetitive-strain injury or a cumulative-trauma disorder.

Representative Henry Bonilla, a Republican from Texas, has led the charge against OSHA's ergonomics standard through restrictive appropriation riders. In March 1995, Republicans cut $16 million from OSHA's budget and ordered it to stop work on the standard. OSHA pulled back and narrowed the standard to apply only to workplaces in which at least two workers had been diagnosed with similar injuries. In 1996, Bonilla drafted another rider to block the standard again and to prevent OSHA from collecting any data from employers on repetitive injuries. But House Democrats were able to defeat the rider.

In 1997, Bonilla tried again, drafting an appropriations rider that would delay the standard by requiring the National Academy of Sciences to study and gather other research on repetitive injuries. Bonilla's rider didn't make it, but both the House and the Senate appropriations committees passed legislation prohibiting OSHA from issuing a proposed or final rule on ergonomics until October 1, 1998.

Behind the scenes of the ergonomic struggles are powerful groups—specifically, United Parcel Service of America, Inc.; the American Trucking Association; the National Association of Manufacturers; and their front groups, COSH, the National Coalition on Ergonomics, and the Coalition for Ergonomics Research.

Leading the pack is UPS, the giant worldwide delivery company. According to a report in *The Washington Post,* UPS pays, on average, nearly $1 million a day in workers' compensation. UPS's injury rate in 1996 was 33.8 per 100 workers, double the average for the transportation industry, according to the Bureau of Labor Statistics. That figure is not surprising, given that UPS delivers more and heavier packages than any other company, including Federal Express Corporation. On a typical day, according to an article in *The New York Times,* UPS has 55,000 delivery trucks on the road and sorts and delivers 11.5 million packages.

In the early 1990s, OSHA increased its scrutiny of UPS after workers complained about on-the-job safety, and it issued more than 1,300 citations nationwide for safety violations. OSHA even fined UPS $3 million for failing to protect its workers from hazardous materials that spilled out of damaged packages.

The fight for an ergonomics standard was on. It would be played out behind closed doors on Capitol Hill, at town house parties with lobbyists and lawmakers, and at party conventions. The weapons of choice from both sides of the ergonomics debate would be contributions in both "hard" and "soft money" donations to congressional campaigns.

Although there are many opponents of OSHA and ergonomics, none are as large as UPS or have the big guns that it has in its arsenal. From 1991 to 1996, UPS contributed more than $7.6 million to lawmakers or their committees. The majority of that money, $7.3 million, went for direct contributions to congressional campaigns, and $317,675 was for "soft money" contributions to the national party committees from 1991 to 1996. The largest recipient of UPS "soft money" was the Republican National Committee, which received $143,425 from 1991 to 1996.

In 1994 alone, the year the Republicans won the House and Senate, UPS contributed $2.6 million. In 1995, a nonelection year, the company gave $210,000 to Republican House campaigns, with about 9 percent of that going to members of the labor committees, including $5,000 to Ballenger. From 1991 to 1996, Ballenger received $24,500 from UPS. House Speaker Newt Gingrich tops the list of lawmakers who have received money from UPS, with $25,000 in contributions over the same period. Senator Tim Hutchinson, a Republican from Arkansas who sits on the Senate Committee on Labor and Human Resources, received $24,000. Before being elected to the Senate in 1996, Hutchinson sat on the Subcommittee on Workforce Protections of the House Committee on Economic and Educational Opportunities. Bonilla, who has gone after the ergonomics standard with a vengeance, received $14,250 from UPS in the same period. Norwood, who wanted to see OSHA eliminated, received $11,000 from UPS.

The American Trucking Association contributed more than $1.6 million to congressional candidates from 1987 to 1996. Ballenger received $2,000 from the association from 1991 to 1996, and Bonilla got $3,000. Hutchinson received $7,000.

Other opponents of the ergonomics standard include the American Insurance Association, which represents more than 300 property and casualty insurance companies, and Associated General Contractors of America, which represents more than 33,000 construction firms. The insurance association contributed nearly $1.2 million to congressional candidates from 1987 to 1996, and the contractors' association gave $2.8 million during the same period.

But money is not the sole weapon the antiergonomics camp has deployed against OSHA and its proposed standard. High-paid lobbyists serve as their foot soldiers before Congress, lobbying against the need for such a standard. And UPS has hired a special-forces commando to take the lead against ergonomics and OSHA.

Dorothy Strunk, whose lobbying efforts helped kill the ergonomics standard, was for twenty-three years a top Republican aide on the House Education and Labor Committee. In 1987, President Reagan picked her to run the Mine Safety and Health Administration, but her nomination was thwarted by the United Mine Workers Union. In 1992, she became the acting Assistant

Labor Secretary for occupational safety and health. Strunk even inaugurated work on the ergonomics standard at OSHA.

Strunk advised Ballenger on an early draft of his legislation to weaken OSHA. She brings to the table more than just her understanding of OSHA and how it works; she also brings long relationships with Republican lawmakers who are now in positions of authority. According to a report in *The Washington Post,* the first draft of the Ballenger bill, in fact, was referred to as "Dottie's draft"—an account disputed by Ballenger's chief of staff, who told the Center, "All OSHA bills introduced by Representative Ballenger were drafted by subcommittee staff and staffers from Mr. Ballenger's personal office."

||||||||||||||||||||||||||||||||||||||||

United Parcel Service of America, Inc., even keeps a town house three blocks from Capitol Hill to host meet-and-greets where it can wine and dine lawmakers and make contributions.

||||||||||||||||||||||||||||||||||||||||

UPS and Federal Express are members of the ATA, which in turn is a member of the National Coalition on Ergonomics, a lobbying group, and Strunk is on the NAM's Ergonomics Steering Committee. The U.S. Chamber of Commerce is also a member of the coalition. Then there is the Coalition for Ergonomic Research, which also opposes an ergonomic standard. Its spokesperson is Laurie Baulig, the American Trucking Association's vice president for labor and human-resources policy. She is also the cochairperson of the National Coalition on Ergonomics. And there is the National Federation of Independent Business, which gave $1.1 million in PAC and "soft money" contributions in the 1996 elections, 93 percent of which went to Republican candidates, according to the Center for Responsive Politics. The NFIB is a member of the coalition as well.

Not to be outdone by big business, the labor unions spent $2.3 million lobbying on their issues, including support for the ergonomics standard. The AFL-CIO gave $14.8 million to congressional candidates from 1987 to 1996, of which $638,360 was in "soft money" contributions. From early 1996 to July 1997, the organization paid $16,206 to fly ten Democratic Members of Congress and five staffers to speaking engagements in places like Los Angeles, New York City, and Atlanta. It spent $4,062 to send

Democratic Senator John D. Rockefeller of West Virginia and one aide on three trips, and $3,968 on four trips for House Minority Leader Richard Gephardt and two of his aides during the same period.

When companies are not attacking the ergonomics standard and OSHA through campaign contributions, "soft money" donations, and high-priced inside lobbyists, they use stealth tactics such as paying members to deliver speeches, sponsoring fact-finding trips or events at conventions, or hosting Washington parties for lawmakers.

From 1986 to 1996, for example, the ATA paid lawmakers $501,100 to deliver speeches. The National Association of Manufacturers (NAM) spent $82,164 on speeches by lawmakers during the same period. More recently, NAM spent $2,760 on trips for lawmakers, executive appointees, or their aides to Boca Raton, Florida, and New Orleans in 1996 and 1997, according to an analysis by the Center for Public Integrity. The trucking association spent $13,217 during the same period to shuttle lawmakers or aides to Phoenix, Arizona, and Orlando, Florida.

At a UPS-sponsored beach reception during the 1996 Republican National Convention in San Diego, House Speaker Newt Gingrich, standing next to a personalized surfboard, posed with a UPS official who sported his own board bearing the company logo.

UPS even keeps a town house three blocks from Capitol Hill to host meet-and-greets where it can wine and dine lawmakers and make contributions, according to the Center for Responsive Politics. Lawmakers have used the town house for their own events as an in-kind contribution from UPS.

But the fight has also left a landscape of casualties like Henry Gallet of Kansas City, Kansas, who injured his back when UPS increased its weight limit from seventy to 150 pounds in 1994. On the very day the new limit went into effect, Gallet's back was pierced with a sharp pain and later required surgery. Like an old soldier, Gallet keeps a small plastic cup containing the two-and-a-half-inch screws and steel clamps used to fuse his slipped vertebra back into place—a grim souvenir of the war on repetitive-strain injuries.

*   *   *

The delivery industry is not the only industry with a high incidence of repetitive-strain injuries among its workers. The meatpacking industry has a long history of such injuries crippling its workers and ruining their lives. But in the late 1980s, OSHA enforced ergonomic workplace safety violations with heavy fines, and the meatpacking industry responded by improving conditions and safety in America's slaughterhouses. The industry in effect said: If you can't beat OSHA, join 'em.

Instead of fighting OSHA on ergonomics, the industry decided to apply ergonomic solutions to repetitive motions, and it has since seen some success in reducing the number of injured workers. But even though the industry has responded with more ergonomic-friendly workstations, it has addressed only half of the problem. The other half, the speed of the conveyor belt, is the reason that so many motions are performed over and over in the first place, and little has been done to address this problem, making the meatpacking industry the most dangerous in the country.

In the late 1980s, OSHA went on the offensive against crippling cumulative-trauma disorders in the meatpacking industry. The agency found that several companies were intentionally hiding injuries that occurred at their plants.

In April 1987, OSHA cited John Morrell & Company in Sioux Falls, South Dakota, for sixty-nine cases of willfully not reporting injuries and illnesses that occurred there and assessed a $690,000 fine. Three months later, OSHA cited Iowa Beef Processors, Inc., the nation's largest meatpacker, $2.59 million for the same violation. In May 1988, OSHA cited IBP's flagships plant in Dakota City, Nebraska, for $3.1 million, and in November, the agency cited Morrell again for $4.33 million. OSHA said that both plants had widespread problems with cumulative-trauma disorders.

Instead of just citing the companies and going away, however, OSHA decided to put together ergonomics guidelines for the industry. After consulting with the American Meat Institute, the United Food and Commercial Workers International Union (UFCW), and NIOSH, OSHA published its ergonomics guidelines in August 1990.

As part of an enforcement program, OSHA offered the meatpacking industry the chance to enter into agreements with the agency to abate the industry's cumulative-trauma disorders with ergonomic measures. If companies participated, they would be subject to visits by OSHA to monitor conditions and respond to complaints, but would not be cited or penalized on ergonomic safety.

After several years, the cooperative effort now seems to be working.

"In those industries where significant OSHA enforcement action has occurred and where ergonomics programs have been implemented throughout the industry—meatpacking and automotive manufacturing, for example—the [cumulative-trauma disorder] rates are actually declining," said Joseph Dear, the Assistant Labor Secretary for occupational safety and health, in 1995.

"We're still one of the highest industries, but we've seen greater awareness of ergonomics and cumulative-trauma disorders," Sara Lilygren, the American Meat Institute's senior vice president for legislation and public affairs, told the Center. "Before, cumulative-trauma disorders were regarded as just part of the job. That's changed now."

Even the unions agree that the program has helped reduce repetitive-strain injuries. "The numbers went down in a lot of the industries where OSHA has hit them over the head," said Debbie Berkowitz, the director of health and safety for the UFCW. "And the numbers have not gone down where OSHA has not hit them."

But while being hit over the head got the meat industry's attention about cumulative-trauma disorders and safety, it still has not convinced the industry to support an OSHA ergonomics standard. "We're more comfortable with guidelines than standards," Lilygren said. "The guidelines have been successful in bringing down some of the numbers. We prefer not to see a standard."

> **According to the Bureau of Labor Statistics, meatpacking has a nonfatal injury and illness rate of 36.4 per 100 full-time workers and the highest rate for repeated-trauma disorders, at 1,257 per 10,000 full-time workers.**

Little wonder. According to the Bureau of Labor Statistics, meatpacking has a nonfatal injury and illness rate of 36.4 per

100 full-time workers and the highest rate for repeated-trauma disorders, at 1,257 per 10,000 full-time workers.

The American Meat Institute, for example, spent $266,246 lobbying Congress on a variety of issues including the Labor Department's budget. Its president is Patrick Boyle, from 1986 to 1989 administrator of agricultural marketing services at the Agriculture Department and a former aide to former Senator Pete Wilson, the current Republican governor of California. ConAgra, Inc., spent $286,000 in 1996 lobbying Congress; Cargill, Inc., spent $255,000; and IBP spent $40,000 on lobbying.

And they have amassed powerful friends in Congress through lobbying, campaign contributions, and paying Congress Members for speaking engagements. Some Members of Congress even own large shares of meatpacking plants. For example, Senator Lauch Faircloth, a Republican from North Carolina, owns more than $1 million of stock in Lundy Packing Company of Clinton, North Carolina. It was in the Lundy plant that eighteen-year-old Solomon Velásquez, a sanitation worker who had not been properly trained, was killed in an industrial meat blender. The state Labor Department fined the plant $64,000 in February 1997 and found that the blender and other pieces of equipment in the plant lacked guards required to protect workers from entangling themselves. In April 1997, the plant was also fined $2,388 by the state Department of Environment and Natural Resources for not controlling odors.

Faircloth is also a 75 percent owner of Coharie Hog Farm in Clinton, North Carolina, and his assets are valued at more than $5 million. Faircloth sits on the Senate Appropriations Committee and on its Subcommittee on Labor, Health and Human Services, and Education, which oversees work-related issues such as safety.

Several other Capitol Hill lawmakers have ties to the meatpacking industry. Representative Christopher Cannon, a Republican from Utah, owns stock in Premium Beef of Nebraska in Gordon, Nebraska. Senator Michael DeWine, a Republican from Ohio, owns stock in Hudson Foods, Inc.; and IBP. DeWine sits on the Committee on Labor and Human Resources and is the chairman of the Subcommittee on Employment and Training.

In July 1993, IBP appointed Wendy Lee Gramm, the wife of Senator Phil Gramm of Texas, to its board of directors. From 1991 to 1994, IBP's PAC gave $31,000 to the National Republican

Senatorial Committee, which Gramm chaired at the time. It also gave $5,000, the legal limit, to Gramm's campaign for the 1996 GOP presidential nomination.

Alec Cortelis, who was the finance chairman of Gramm's presidential campaign, is also on IBP's board of directors. In 1995, IBP helped Gramm's presidential campaign by encouraging its managers to attend a "straw poll" in Ames, Iowa, through a memo that read, in part: "IBP is encouraging its management employees to attend and participate in this grand event. Tickets and bus transportation will be provided by the Phil Gramm for President Campaign."

Over the years, some Capitol Hill lawmakers have held sizable investments in ConAgra, Inc., the nation's second-largest meatpacking company. Norman Sisisky, a Democrat from Virginia, reported owning $100,000 to $250,000 in ConAgra stock in 1991. Claiborne Pell, a Democrat from Rhode Island who retired from the Senate in 1997, reported $50,000 to $100,000 in ConAgra stock in 1995. And Representative Greg Ganske, a Republican from Iowa, valued his ConAgra shares at $15,000 to $50,000 in 1995. Five other lawmakers had ConAgra holdings in the $1,000-to-$15,000 range, including Republican Nick Smith of Michigan, a member of the House Agriculture Committee.

And some lawmakers have received campaign contributions from the companies that they own stock in, such as Ganske, who received $7,000 from ConAgra from 1991 to 1996, according to an analysis by the Center. Ganske also received $3,000 from the AMI and $8,000 from Cargill.

Faircloth received money from a variety of meat- and poultry-producing companies and interests, including $9,964 from the National Pork Producers Council, for a total of $34,964 since 1991.

Overall, meat and poultry processing interests contributed more than $6 million to congressional campaigns from 1987 to 1996. They gave another $703,992 in "soft money" to the national party committees during this time.

Then there is the annual lunch on Capitol Hill, courtesy of the American Meat Institute and the National Hot Dog and Sausage Council, to commemorate "National Hot Dog Month." Here again, lawmakers and their aides can defy the rules that apply to the rest of us—namely, that there is no such thing as a free lunch.

10

||||||•||||||

Fear of Flying

"THERE WAS NO WARNING," SAID CHRISTINE PETERS, RECALLING the terrors of USAir Flight 1016. Peters, an administrator at the University of South Carolina in Columbia, was heading to Pittsburgh to visit her mother, who was to undergo surgery for cancer later that week. She bought a discount ticket at the last minute, to take advantage of the long Fourth of July weekend.

The big DC-9 on which Peters was a passenger on July 2, 1994, was five minutes from touchdown in Charlotte, North Carolina—a stopover on its way to Pittsburgh—after a thirty-five-minute hop from Columbia, South Carolina. She was not distracted by the turbulent descent. She was accustomed to flying, having traveled often as part of her job, and this seemed like any normal trip. She was engrossed in a magazine article, racing to complete it before the plane reached its gate.

Then Peters heard what sounded like the jet reversing its engines to brake. But the plane was not even on the runway. Next she felt the rapid deceleration of the plane, followed by the thrust of the pilot gunning the engines, and she was pitched back into her seat. "I glanced out the window to my right and saw [the tops of] trees," Peters later wrote in testimony to the National Transportation Safety Board (NTSB), which investigates all major transportation accidents in the United States. Before she could prepare herself for the impact, the plane slammed to earth. More violent impacts followed. "I was basically at the mercy of the plane . . . sort of like a rag doll," she wrote.

After it hit the ground, the DC-9 split into four sections and skidded wildly. The tail section came to rest against the carport of a house. After the screaming of passengers and the whining of twisted metal, there was silence.

Peters, still in her seat, was covered with tree branches and debris from the crash. Slowly passengers began calling for help.

A fireball flared in Peters's face. "I thought, 'I'm engulfed in flames and I'm going to die,'" she told the *Pittsburgh Post-Gazette* after the crash. She began crawling through the wreckage, looking for a way out. She heard the man in the next seat plead for help. "Only the top of a head and the cowboy boot on his foot were visible," Peters recalled in an interview with the Center for Public Integrity. She saw a flight attendant, and the two of them opened one of the plane's emergency exits. Flames shot toward them, blocking the passage.

"It's so incredible, when you listen to the stewardesses giving the speech of 'Here's your two exit doors.' When you crash the way we crashed, there *are* no exit doors," Peters told the *Post-Gazette*. "Definitely, none. My main thought was to look where there was light, see if it was outside, and try to head for that."

Peters was one of twenty survivors of Flight 1016. Thirty-seven died in the crash. It was not the impact alone that killed those thirty-seven

When the Federal Aviation Administration announces that a passenger can fly round-the-clock for 438 years before being involved in a fatal accident, it is doing the job Congress gave it: selling plane tickets.

passengers. Zebb Strawn, a Charlotte sheriff's deputy, told the *Post-Gazette* that he heard someone banging on the tail section of the plane. "There was nothing I could do," he said. "I couldn't get to him. There were flames between him and me."

Keith Herrin, a friend of Strawn's, was also at the scene. "They were screaming and banging," Strawn said of the passengers trapped in the tail section, "but we couldn't get them out."

Flying, as anyone who has ever tried to reason with a nervous fellow passenger has intoned, is the safest form of travel. The Federal Aviation Administration, the agency that regulates the airline industry, can cite reams of statistics to back up that assertion. In theory, given the accident rate of American carriers, a passenger would have to fly 24 hours a day for 438 years before being involved in a fatal accident, according to the FAA.

Of course, there was nothing theoretical about the fifty-seven passengers on USAir Flight 1016. They trusted the FAA to put their interests above the airlines. And they were betrayed. But not by the FAA alone. They were betrayed by Congress.

Congress compromised the FAA, giving it two missions that created an indisputable conflict of interest. The first was to regulate the airlines. The second was to promote them. So when the FAA announces that a passenger can fly round-the-clock for 438 years before being involved in a fatal accident, its purpose is not to inform the public about the safety of flying. The FAA is doing the job Congress gave it: selling plane tickets.

And like any other travel agent, Congress is collecting a commission on those sales. The airline industry, which pleads poverty whenever the subject of safety is raised, has pumped at least $7.5 million into congressional campaigns in the past ten years. From 1987 to 1996, the industry also paid 137 Members of Congress $312,750 in speaking fees. The airlines have rewarded their congressional agents with ribbons of free tickets; United Airlines alone gave Republicans 300 vouchers for free flights in the first six months of 1996, according to the Center for Responsive Politics. The airline's largesse was bipartisan; United gave Democrats 490 discounted tickets for travel to the Democratic National Convention in Chicago, as well as thirty-three free fares. United spokesman Joe Hopkins told the Center that providing free and discounted fares to Members of Congress is "a business decision, not a political decision."

The airline industry is also happy to serve as an employment service for ex-Members of Congress and their staff. At least forty-seven lawmakers and congressional aides have gone from the payroll to lobby for the industry. Ann Eppard, the former chief of staff for Republican Bud Shuster of Pennsylvania, who now chairs the House Transportation and Infrastructure Committee, has lobbied for United Airlines. Jim Courter, a former Republican Representative from New Jersey, lobbied Congress, the FAA, and the Transportation Department to get ValuJet recertified after the May 11, 1996, Florida Everglades crash that killed 110 people shut the airline down. Courter's firm, Verner, Liipfert, Bernhard, McPherson & Hand, was paid $390,000 for Courter's efforts on the no-frills airline's behalf.

In return for the generosity of the airline industry, Congress has put the safety of its profits ahead of the safety of the flying public.

For nearly four decades, technology that would save lives has been available to airlines. For years, safety experts—both in the government and in the private sector—have called on the airlines to adopt this technology. And year after year, the airlines and the FAA have insisted that the cost of this technology is too high. Despite the evidence that horrific deaths could be prevented, that crippling injuries could be avoided, that air crashes need not be fatal, Congress has endorsed the view of the industry and the FAA: Saving lives is not cost-effective.

Congress changed the FAA's dual mandate only in the wake of the ValuJet crash, when it became clear that the FAA was more concerned with promoting that airline than regulating it, despite its numerous safety violations. Although the FAA is officially no longer in the industry's pocket, Congress is still clearing the industry's agenda for takeoff while leaving safety issues in an endless holding pattern. Perhaps nothing demonstrates this state of affairs better than the ordinary airline seat.

In 1987, Congress passed the Airport and Airway Safety and Capacity Expansion Act. Buried in the minutiae of the bill was a directive ordering the FAA, in the words of Democrat Norman

Former Republican Representative Jim Courter of New Jersey lobbied Congress, the FAA, and the Transportation Department to get ValuJet recertified after the May 11, 1996, Florida Everglades crash that killed 110 people shut the airline down. Courter's firm was paid $390,000 for his efforts.

Mineta of California, then the chairman of the House aviation subcommittee, "to go forward with important safety-related rule-making, including rulemaking to require higher standards for the strength of airline seats."

Six years earlier, the NTSB had issued a report that studied the effects of seventy-seven large-force crashes on airline seats and the people riding in them.

"The limiting factor for survival in these crashes is not human tolerance limits; instead, it is the lethal nature of the environment inside the fuselage," the NTSB stated. "Occupants are being injured, trapped, and killed in survivable accidents." Or, as James Oberstar of Minnesota, the ranking Democrat on the House Transportation and Infrastructure Committee, said in an interview with the Center, "What happens, of course, in the crash is that the seats shear and more people are killed by being crushed than by the force of the crash."

Among the report's gruesome findings:

- In 1976, an Allegheny Airlines DC-9 crashed 6,000 feet from a runway at Philadelphia International Airport. Of the thirty-six passengers who suffered severe injury, the majority had their spines snapped when their seats failed.

- In 1972, a United Airlines Boeing 737 crashed in a residential area near Chicago's Midway Airport. Of the sixty-one people on board, sixteen died on impact, while twenty-seven others became tangled in wreckage, immobilized by limbs that shattered when their seats failed. They survived just long enough to perish from the fire, smoke, and toxic fumes that filled the fuselage.

- The NTSB reported that seats failed in 84.4 percent of the crashes it studied, "allowing the occupant to become a missile traveling at essentially the same velocity as the aircraft just before impact."

When the NTSB issued its report in 1981, an airline seat had to be able to withstand nine g's of force. That means the seat was designed to withstand the forward momentum of a head-on crash that placed nine times the force of gravity on a person weighing an average 170 pounds, or a total of 1,530 pounds. By way of comparison, the seats in a tiny Chevy Metro—or any other car, for that matter—will survive twenty g's, or 3,400 pounds of force.

The nine-g standard was set by the Federal Aviation Agency, the FAA's predecessor, in 1952—when the commercial jet was still on the drawing board and propeller planes had the skies to themselves. In 1987—when Congress finally told the FAA to set a higher standard for seat strength—an airline seat was required to withstand that same nine g's of force.

Yet seven years later, when USAir Flight 1016 crashed, killing thirty-seven passengers, the seats on the plane were still required to withstand no more than nine g's. According to the NTSB accident report, the crash damaged, dislodged, or destroyed ninety-one of the 103 seats on the DC-9. Christine Peters was lucky enough to have been sitting in one of only twelve seats that survived the crash intact.

What happened to the better seat standard that Congress had mandated?

Nothing. "There are a number of factors about the cost-benefit analysis," Oberstar told the Center, "about the complexity of the rule-making process, of the signoffs and the levels they have to go through."

The rule-making process in Washington is indeed complex, but in the case of airline seats, there is a very simple reason nothing has been done. Among "the signoffs and the levels" the FAA must go through are the very companies the rule would affect: the airlines.

Why hasn't the FAA required the airlines to use stronger seats?

"Plain and simple—dollars," Thomas McSweeny—who, as director of the Aircraft Certification Service, is one of the FAA's top safety officials—told *The Washington Post* in a 1989 interview.

||||||||||||||||||||||||||||||||||||||||||

After a rule-making process that has dragged on for over a decade, the FAA requires only the Boeing 777 to use stronger seats. Those seats can withstand sixteen g's, or 20 percent less force than a seat in the family car can.

||||||||||||||||||||||||||||||||||||||||||

In 1988, the FAA calculated that installing new seats would cost the airlines $33 million but would save them $62 million in claims made by the families and estates of passengers killed in air crashes. The Air Transport Association of America, the lobbying arm of some twenty-one airlines and air cargo companies, waged a war of numbers to kill the rule. Its cost estimate: $215 million a year.

The FAA chose to accept the industry's estimate. "The number of lives saved does not equate to that kind of cash," McSweeny told the *Post*. By 1996, the Air Transport Association had upped its estimate of the cost of replacing seats to well over $3 billion.

To date, after a rule-making process that has dragged on for over a decade, the FAA requires only the Boeing 777 to use stronger seats. Those seats can withstand sixteen g's, or 20 percent less force than a seat in the family car can. All other aircraft, even those rolling off the assembly line today, need only meet the nine-g standard.

As for Oberstar, the House's number-one recipient of campaign money from aviation interests, he is content to bide his time on the issue of seats. "I feel that as a committee with two or three staffpeople and a dozen issues to draw your attention to, you can spend only so much time on a subject and repeatedly come back and revisit and push," he told the Center.

Congress's record on those other issues that demand its attention is not particularly better than its success with seats. Consider the following:

- For forty years, the FAA has falsely claimed that "bogus" parts—replacement parts that do not meet the FAA's safety standards—have never resulted in an air crash. When the NTSB proved the FAA wrong, the FAA forced the NTSB's inspectors to classify these accidents as "maintenance" problems. An internal Transportation Department investigation in December 1994 found that 43 percent of aircraft parts were bogus. The FAA's own record was not much better: Thirty-nine percent of the parts used on its own aircraft were bogus as well. There were even two bogus parts used on Marine One, the presidential helicopter. Of those bad parts in commercial use, fully a third could have catastrophic consequences.

- In 1993, the FAA abandoned its "zero tolerance" program aimed at keeping guns, bombs, and terrorists off aircraft after the airlines opposed fines levied by the FAA for security breaches identified in spot checks. That same year the agency failed to meet its deadline to have explosives-detection systems in place. In the wake of the July 1996 crash of TWA Flight 800 off Long Island, a presidential commission called for airlines to match bags to passengers boarding airlines. This measure would have reduced the chances of a bomb being placed on board aircraft. Airlines were to comply by November 1996, but with a presidential election in the wings, the Clinton Administration backed down. A week later, American Airlines delivered $250,000 in "soft money" to the Democratic National Committee.

• Terrorism is not the only cause of explosions in the skies. Some airplanes manage to blow up on their own. As early as 1965, the FAA's own investigators urged the agency to require airlines to fill unusued fuel tanks with inert gases to prevent accidental explosions caused by lightning, heat, or electrical failures—a precaution that is taken on all military aircraft. No such precautions are taken by the commercial airlines, and the failure to do so may have led to the tragic explosion of TWA Flight 800.

Seldom is the relationship between Congress and the FAA clear. The conventional wisdom has it that Congress ignores aviation issues until there is an air disaster, and then it calls hearings and waits for the dust to settle. In the meantime, the FAA functions most often as the creature of industry—or it does not function at all, as the nation's air-traffic-control system makes clear.

Outmoded, temperamental, and prone to outages, the air-traffic-control system has been the victim of repeated failures on the part of Congress to reform it. Since 1981, when the FAA announced it would overhaul the system, Congress has spent $20 billion on a modernization program that will come on-line, at the earliest, in 2003.

In the meantime, the FAA is importing vacuum tubes from Eastern Europe to keep the thirty-year-old computers that monitor air traffic running. Stanley Rivers, the deputy director of the Airways Facilities Service of the FAA, which maintains the air-traffic-control system, described the system's condition to the *Austin American-Statesman* in 1995. "Cables are brittle, vacuum tubes do not stand too much handling, circuit boards can break when flexed, and transistors can fail under the strain of testing," he said.

Some of the machines—notably, the IBM 9020e—are so old and outmoded that no one makes or sells replacement parts for them. The FAA used to have two extra 9020e's for training purposes; now they have one. The other had to be cannibalized for spare parts.

> Some of the machines that monitor air traffic—notably, the IBM 9029e—are so old and outmoded that no one makes or sells replacement parts for them.

The National Air Traffic Controllers Association, the organization that represents controllers, provided the Center with data on computer outages—malfunctions that leave controllers without radar contact with the aircraft in their area—in the system in the eight months between April 30 and December 30, 1996. There were a total of 599 outages, including twenty-nine in Chicago, thirty-six in Cleveland, thirty-nine in New York City, and fifty-eight in Washington. Not all failures are total. Sometimes controllers can still see jets on their screens but lose the background maps that provide the planes' location. Other times, the planes themselves disappear from the scopes. And sometimes the screens go completely blank.

"The majority, if not all, of us have lost confidence in the equipment, and that says enough in itself," Andy Acres, who heads the traffic controllers' group in Washington, D.C., told *The Washington Post* in 1997.

The air-traffic-control equipment isn't the only part of the nation's air-transportation infrastructure that the FAA has allowed to lag dangerously behind the times. On December 22, 1995, Charlotte-Douglas International Airport got an early Christmas present: Terminal Doppler Weather Radar, a highly precise early-warning system that can pinpoint the location of hazards like wind shear and microbursts.

The FAA had scheduled Charlotte to receive the radar in October 1993. But, like the new generation of air-traffic-control computers, installation was delayed. The first Doppler radar installation came on-line in Houston in July 1994—the same month that USAir Flight 1016 went down in Charlotte.

In its accident report, the NTSB found that a severe microburst drove the plane to the ground. The board noted that Doppler radar could have given the crew members on Flight 1016 enough warning about the severe weather conditions before they began their approach to the runway, when planes are most vulnerable to the effects of wind shear. While the NTSB found that a combination of pilot error and poor communication between the flight crew and the air-traffic controllers ultimately caused the crash, the lack of comprehensive information about the severity of the storm as the DC-9 approached was a key factor in the accident.

In reviewing an accident, the NTSB reconstructs the sequence of events that led to the crash, not just to understand why a particular disaster occurred, but also to prevent future tragedies. The board makes recommendations to the FAA based on its findings. The FAA, as often as not, ignores them, and Congress turns a blind eye to the agency's disregard for the public's safety. In its report on the crash of Flight 1016, for example, the NTSB urged the FAA to require infants and small children to be restrained "in a manner appropriate to their size"—a requirement that has yet to be made.

Two infants rode aboard Flight 1016. One survived the crash; the other didn't.

Tywonda Brown's nine-month-old daughter was flung from her arms when the plane slammed into the ground. "I tried to hold on to her," she told NTSB investigators after the crash. "I tried to hold her, and I couldn't."

Danasia Brown died of severe head injuries and blunt-force trauma after the force of the crash hurled her through the cabin at a speed of 120 miles an hour. Perhaps the only thing more tragic than her death itself was its utter avoidability. In October 1993, the House of Representatives considered a measure that would have required infants to be restrained in safety seats when they flew. Congress heard testimony from survivors of a horrific 1989 crash in Sioux City, Iowa. A United Airlines DC-9 slammed into the ground and exploded after losing complete control of its hydraulic system. Lori Michaelson, a survivor of the disaster that killed 112 of the 296 passengers on board, was traveling with her eleven-month-old daughter, Sabrina.

"I can still remember the look in the flight attendant's eyes as we both knew this baby had a slim chance of surviving the crash landing," Michaelson testified to Congress. "Picture me—a person only five feet, three inches tall—trying to bend over to reach the floor to hold on to my baby, a task that was almost physically impossible. Imagine the sickening feeling of realizing our baby was being sucked out of my grasp as the plane flipped over. There has never been such a feeling of helplessness and terror in my life."

Michaelson's daughter miraculously survived the crash. She was flung into an overhead luggage rack fifteen feet away; another passenger heard her cries and rescued her from the burning wreckage.

Twenty-three-month-old Evan Tso wasn't so lucky. His mother, Sylvia Tso, who survived the crash, was unable to hold on to him. The force of the impact carried him down the aisle. He was among the 112 who did not survive.

Tragedies such as the death of Evan Tso led to recommendations from the NTSB that infants ride in safety seats. Groups as diverse as the Air Line Pilots Association; the Aviation Consumer Action Project, a passenger advocacy group; the Association of Flight Attendants; and even the Air Transport Association backed the NTSB. In October 1993, Republican Representative Jim Lightfoot of Iowa, an amateur pilot, and Democratic Representative Jolene Unsoeld of Washington introduced an amendment to the Aviation Infrastructure and Investment Act that would have made the NTSB's proposal law.

In the floor debate, Unsoeld noted that FAA regulations "require that you, the other passengers, the flight attendants, the pilot, the bags in the overhead compartment, and even the soda cans in the kitchen be secured, but not your infant."

Unsoeld closed her remarks with an eloquent plea. "All we are asking is that children under the age of two be given the same protections as you or I. Please support the youngest and most vulnerable of your constituents. Please think of their future."

Her plea fell on deaf ears.

James Oberstar rose to the floor immediately following Unsoeld's remarks. He argued that if airlines required infants to fly in child-safety seats, more parents would travel by automobile than by airplane. He argued further that very few infants died in plane crashes relative to those killed in automobile crashes. Finally he said, "far more significant for safety of passengers aboard aircraft in the event of a tragedy has been the subcommittee's insistence that the FAA proceed with its seat-strengthening requirement for airlines, to strengthen from nine g's to sixteen g's the force resistance of airline seats."

Of course, those are the same stronger seats that the FAA has yet to require. Oberstar then offered a measure that would force airlines to provide child restraints for parents who bought tickets for their children, but would provide no protection for the estimated 10,000 infants and toddlers who fly for free each day. "I think this substitute amendment reinstitutes in the equation the element of choice and puts the choice on the passenger, on the parent, rather than forcing or imposing a requirement on the airline and upon all the traveling public at great cost, with rather minimal benefit," Oberstar said.

His measure passed by a vote of 270 to 155. Those great costs to the airlines and the public clearly outweighed the minimal benefits, among them the life of nine-month-old Danasia Brown, who died just nine months after the Lightfoot-Unsoeld amendment was defeated.

YOUR MONEY

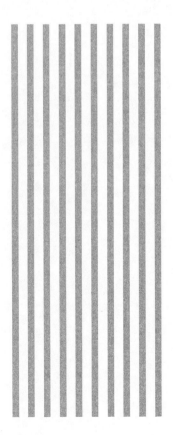

11

||||||●|||||

Your Money or Your Life

A T EIGHTY-FIVE YEARS OF AGE, MERLE DAVIS COULD NOT DEFEND HER-self against the unremitting abuse meted out by the staff of the Cogburn Health Center in Mobile, Alabama. "Mimaw," as her family affectionately called her, had been admitted to the nursing home for what was to be a brief stay—a postoperative regimen of physical therapy designed to help her regain the ability to walk. But, according to family members, the frail octogenarian's three weeks of convalescence became a terrifying seven-month ordeal that left her physically and psychologically battered—her ribs broken, her face bloodied, her pride destroyed, and the mental clarity she had always enjoyed replaced by hallucinations and incoherent babbling.

As her daughter later recounted, attendants at the nursing home saved themselves the trouble of walking Davis to the toilet by outfitting her in diapers. She was sometimes shackled in a chair. She was prescribed medication that made her so confused that she began wandering around the facility. Nurses who were upset about having to track down their itinerant patient insisted that doctors prescribe additional drugs, which left Davis even more confused. When she refused to take yet another round of new medications, the staff either hid the drugs in her food or, against her will—(and in violation of federal law)—administered them by injection. The combination of potent pharmaceuticals left her weak and increasingly befuddled, and on her drug-induced wanderings she fell repeatedly. One incident left her with a gash across her head, but the staff apparently was not overly concerned: They let her sleep in her soiled clothes on bloodstained sheets. The last time Davis stumbled the force of the impact was so great that one of her eyes literally popped out of its socket.

Ironically, it was that fourteenth fall—a trauma that left Merle Davis half-blind—that ultimately saved her. It was only then that she was moved to a hospital, where she was taken off the debilitating drug cocktail and nursed back to her normal lucidity and health. She later settled a lawsuit with the Cogburn Health Center for $690,000, although the nursing home did not admit any wrongdoing.

Unfortunately, Davis's harrowing experience was by no means unusual. Two of every five Americans will spend time in a nursing home, and if recent history is any guide, many will be subjected to forced isolation, malnutrition, physical abuse, and the indiscriminate administration of psychiatric drugs. The same goes for those committed to psychiatric institutions and substance-abuse facilities, where unscrupulous operators have routinely paid bribes for bogus referrals, held patients against their will, and administered rounds of electroconvulsive therapy for the sole purpose of bilking insurance companies.

In short, the United States has a health-delivery system that, at its worst, has literally incarcerated, even enslaved, the elderly and infirm—all while publicly claiming to have their best interests at heart. And ironically, in many cases it is Medicare and Medicaid, the government-funded health-care programs, that foot the bill for these atrocities.

But the ironies do not end there. Just consider: It is Congress, the nation's most powerful caretaker institution, that bears much responsibility for this neglect of one of America's most vulnerable groups of citizens. Although Congress passed legislation in 1987 that was intended to penalize nursing-home operators who violated specific standards of care and rights of residents, accounts of the wholesale flouting of the law have brought little congressional response. In fact, in 1995 Congress actually tried to repeal this safeguard against wanton abuse of the nation's elderly.

There is, however, at least one constituency that has welcomed such indifference from lawmakers: the nation's nursing homes, which from 1987 to 1996 made their gratitude known with campaign contributions totaling more than $2.8 million. The giving was hardly random: In 1995 and 1996, for example, with the nursing-home law facing repeal, the operators of these businesses plied members of the Senate Finance Committee with at least $49,750, members of the House Commerce Committee with at least $136,253, and members of the House Ways and Means Committee with at least $82,369. Among the largest donors was the nursing-home industry's lobbying arm, euphemistically known as the American Health Care Association.

By all accounts, the law that Congress sought to dismantle was a good one. Conceived as a nursing-home resident's bill of rights, and bolstered with stiff penalties for noncompliance, the 1987 measure was designed to address the violence and dehumanization that at the time was rampant in these facilities.

But once the law was on the books, Congress turned its back on the elderly.

"We did good when we got the law enacted, but since then it's been all downhill," Howard Bedlin, a former lobbyist for the American Association of Retired Persons, told the Center for Public Integrity. "Enforcement is the key. You can have the most stringent standards possible, but if you don't enforce them, it means diddly-squat."

The standards indeed were not enforced, thereby rendering them all but meaningless. Blame that inattention on the Health Care Financing Administration (HCFA), the arm of the Department of Health and Human Services that is charged with enforcing the law. Although Congress directed HCFA to write and implement regulations by 1988, the agency somehow missed its deadlines by seven years—a lapse that caused lawmakers on Capitol Hill no apparent concern. As a result of the foot-dragging, HCFA's only remedy for substandard nursing homes was to shut them down—an existing regulatory option that the agency was loath to exercise.

Undercover agents discovered that a California podiatrist was visiting nursing homes and submitting bills to Medicare of up to $6,000 for surgeries, when in fact he was merely clipping residents' toenails.

As finally implemented, the regulations that HCFA crafted generally reflect the concerns of nursing-home operators rather than of their patients—the very constituency that Congress intended the law to protect. Nursing homes cited for violations, for example, are given a second chance to correct the infractions before penalties are levied. But advocates for nursing-home patients argue that, because follow-up inspections are the exception rather than the rule, the threat of fines is ultimately hollow. Despite repeated requests for clarification about this reluctance to impose sanctions, HCFA officials declined comment.

"HCFA has created the environment whereby patient abuse has escalated," a Senate investigator told the Center. "They've created an environment where practically anything can get reimbursed." He described a recent investigation by the Office of the Inspector General at the Health and Human Services Department, in which undercover agents discovered that a California podiatrist had falsely billed Medicare for hundreds of thousands of dollars over a three-year period. The podiatrist was visiting nursing homes and submitting bills of up to $6,000 for surgeries, when in fact he was merely clipping residents' toenails.

The Senate investigator noted that the doctor was often abusive to the nursing-home residents, behavior that he claimed is common. "As soon as the fraudulent billings go up," he said, "the quality of care goes down."

The nursing-home industry decided to go for broke in 1995, aiming for nothing less than the total elimination of federal regulation. But when the industry came up short in its effort to kill the nursing home reforms that Congress passed in 1987, it regrouped and set out instead to prevent the law from being enforced. The point man in this effort was Alan Solomont, who at the time was the chief executive officer and founder of ADS Group, the largest nursing-home company in Massachusetts. Solomont was both politically well connected and well versed in the ways of Washington. He chaired the Democratic Business Council, which raised nearly $20 million for the Democratic Party in 1996. What's more, Solomont, members of his family, and employees of ADS Group gave at least $256,760 to the Democrats in 1995 and 1996, and he had his nursing-home buddies kick in another $1.1 million. For all this, Solomon spent the night in the White

House's Lincoln Bedroom and was even an occasional jogging partner of President Clinton.

But the nursing-home industry had more connections to bank on than just Alan Solomont. Paul Willging, the executive vice president of the industry's lobbying organization, for example, was the deputy chief of HCFA during the Reagan Administration. Arkansas-based Beverly Enterprises, Inc., the nation's largest nursing-home company (and one whose pitiful track record has resulted in government sanctions and multimillion-dollar lawsuits across the country, according to a report by the Food and Allied Service Trades union), was able to parlay its $70,000 contribution to the Democrats in 1996 into some meaningful benefits for one of its directors, Risa Lavizzo-Mourey: an invitation to a Clinton "coffee" and, more important, an appointment to the President's Advisory Commission on Consumer Protection and Quality in the Health Care Industry. Congress even has its own nursing-home owner, Representative Dan Miller, a Republican from Florida. Miller's Suncoast Manor Nursing Center was cited by Florida officials in 1994 and 1995 for a number of violations, including leaving residents unattended for long periods and such unsanitary conditions as rusting appliances and dried food on walls. Miller serves on the appropriations subcommittee that has jurisdiction over the Health and Human Services Department, the very agency that oversees nursing homes, and his congressional campaign accepted $18,850 in 1993 from PACs representing health professionals, hospitals, nursing homes, and health services. Miller apparently sees no conflict of interest in taking the money or sitting on the committee: His chief aide, Marty Reiser, flatly denied that Miller uses his position on the committee to benefit his own business. "We studiously avoid doing anything for the nursing-home industry," Reiser told the Center.

With such allies on his side, Solomont aimed to weaken the pro-consumer regulations forced on his industry. And he capitalized admirably on his Clinton Administration connections: He and a team of lobbyists met with Donna Shalala, the Secretary of Health and Human Services. He twice met and corresponded extensively with Bruce Vladeck, the administrator of HCFA. Solomont penned specific suggestions on how Vladeck should loosen nursing-home regulations, according to *Time* magazine. And Vla-

||||||||||||||||||||||||||||||||||||||||||||||||||||||||||||||||||||||||||

Congress even has its own nursing home owner, Representative Dan Miller, a Republican from Florida. Miller's Suncoast Nursing Center was cited by Florida officials in 1994 and 1995 for various violations.

deck obviously thought highly of the Democratic insider's useful recommendations: In January 1997, he announced that fines on nursing homes should be used only as a last resort.

When asked whether his campaign contributions had influenced Vladeck's decision, Solomont told the Center that, while his donations and his longtime activism in the Democratic Party may have given him access, the reason he was listened to was his expertise in the nursing-home industry. "I think that the line gets blurred—appropriately," he said. "I don't check my politics at the door when I go to work." Solomont will have plenty of opportunity to continue blurring the line: After selling ADS, he became the Democratic Party's national finance chairman and now works as a consultant, helping nursing-home operators deal with their "regulatory trouble."

The last-resort rule should serve to ensure yet more abuses heaped on an already betrayed public. After all, the evidence reveals that even the opportunity to correct violations in advance of sanctions has not decreased the number of infractions. Consider what Toby Edelman, a staff attorney for the National Senior Citizens Law Center, said of nursing homes in an interview with the Center for Public Integrity: "They are given a chance to correct, they come into compliance, and the next year they have the same problems."

Now, with the threat of fines no longer looming very large, the "come into compliance" part of the equation may go the way of Merle Davis's trust in nursing-home operators.

On Capitol Hill, the story of the Golden Rule is a sorry tale of quid pro quo.

In this legislative version of the well-known Biblical edict, Golden Rule Insurance Company learned that lawmakers are inclined to do favors unto those with checkbooks at the ready. Specifically, this Indianapolis-based health-insurance company—which for years has been a leading proponent of medical savings accounts—cozied up to key lawmakers via the power of its purse. From 1987 to 1996, Patrick Rooney, the company's chairman of the board, and John Whelan, its president and Chief Executive Officer, contributed at least $157,100 to House Speaker Newt Gingrich and to GOPAC, the political action committee he chaired, and from 1991 to 1996 Golden Rule poured at least $495,875 in "soft money" into the coffers of the Republican Party.

Gingrich in turn lauded Golden Rule in remarks entered into *The Congressional Record,* although his praise was lost on the Democratically controlled House Energy and Commerce Subcommittee on Oversight and Investigations, which forged ahead with its investigation of the company's alleged practice of failing to pay off health-insurance claims and canceling policyholders who had the gall to actually get sick. But when the Republicans took control of the House following the 1994 elections, the chairmanship of the subcommittee was passed to Representative Joe Barton, a Gingrich foot soldier who raised money for GOPAC. Early in 1995, Barton quietly administered the last rites to the Golden Rule investigation. A few months later, his efforts were rewarded with a $1,000 campaign contribution from Golden Rule's PAC—the first time the company had ever included the Texas Republican on its gift list.

And so it goes. While the public obsesses about the quality of health care, the loss of insurance benefits, and the ability to afford treatment, Congress is instead concerned about the well-being of physicians, hospitals, insurance companies, and other benevolent special interests.

In 1980, 54 percent of workers at large and medium-size U.S. firms had the full cost of their families' health insurance paid by their employers; by 1993, the figure had plummeted to 20 percent.

Ironically, this indifference to the health of the citizenry comes at a time when the trends are increasingly foreboding. An estimated 40 million Americans, for example, are without health insurance—an increase of more than 6 million in just four years—

and another 11 million have problems both getting and paying for medical care. One of every seven children in the United States goes without health insurance. In 1980, 54 percent of workers at large and medium-size U.S. firms had the full cost of their families' health insurance paid by their employers; by 1993, the figure had plummeted to 20 percent. What is more, the National Coalition on Health Care projects that the number of uninsured Americans will reach 47 million by 2005.

But while the health-care crisis escalates, Congress has taken on a sort of bystander role—refereeing the battles waged among members of the medical establishment, who are determined to guarantee for themselves increasingly large fees and government reimbursements.

The behind-the-scenes tale of Congress's failed attempt to craft a national health-care program in 1994 illustrates how the industry plays puppeteer with legislators. Health-care interests dumped nearly $2.7 million in campaign contributions into the laps of members of the powerful House Ways and Means Committee, which was at the center of the legislation. In the years leading up to the legislation, more than eighty-five Members of Congress were treated to 181 trips sponsored by this industry—"fact-finding" missions to such vital health-care-related outposts as Montego Bay and Paris. And the party favors were handed out by familiar faces, including twelve lawmakers-turned-lobbyists. With such ready access to their onetime colleagues, meaningful health-care reform never had a chance.

In the aftermath of the national health-care debacle, Congress tried to pacify voters with what became known as the Kassebaum-Kennedy bill—a measure promoted by politicians as giving workers the ability to move their health care with them from one job to another. This concept, which garnered enthusiastic public support, had already undergone successful test-marketing by Congress itself. For example, Representative Bill Gradison of Ohio, the former ranking Republican on the Ways and Means Subcommittee on Health, was able to take along his generous congressional medical benefits when he suddenly resigned his job and assumed the presidency of the Health Insurance Association of America, a $666,000-a-year job. And the "portability" benefit undoubtedly proved meaningful to Dan Rostenkowski, the once powerful chairman of the House Ways and Means Committee, and other lawmakers whose congressional tenures were followed by time behind bars. Although they are required to use Bureau of Prisons medical care while incarcerated, they retain their former health insurance upon release.

As originally conceived, the Kassebaum-Kennedy bill offered valuable relief to those changing jobs. But lawmakers saw to it that the benefits for the working poor and middle class would be accompanied by generous payoffs for special interests. As a result, the law ultimately included large loopholes for insurers and the American Medical Association, according to an investigation by Ramon Castellblanch, a researcher at the Johns Hopkins School of Public Health. For example, the American Family Life Assurance Company, a huge cancer-insurance peddler that has made nearly $2 million in political contributions over the past decade, received a startling gift from Congress: The new law axed existing consumer protections that forced the company to warn the elderly when they were buying insurance that duplicated what they already received under Medicare.

The AMA got its charity in the form of a provision that loosened antikickback statutes for physicians. Under the new law, the Department of Health and Human Services is directed to guide physicians through the antitrust statutes to help them avoid prosecution. This was done courtesy of Republican Henry Hyde of Illinois, the chairman of the House Judiciary Committee, who received $10,000 from the AMA in 1996. All told, the AMA gave congressional candidates $3.2 million in 1995 and 1996, as Kassebaum-Kennedy was being considered. In the first six months of 1996 alone, the AMA spent $8.56 million on lobbying—an investment that earned physicians regulatory changes that are expected to cost the government nearly $400 million over the next five years.

But when it comes to health care, Congress seems unconcerned by such losses. And that is no surprise, since it is estimated that $100 billion of the $1 trillion spent each year on health care is lost to fraud, waste, and abuse. So what's a mere few hundred million of taxpayer money?

Congress started paying serious attention to health-care fraud only when Members figured out that Medicare was heading for bankruptcy—that the warnings of those concerned about the long-term viability of the program not only were based in fact, but actually required lawmakers to take remedial action. Even Donna Shalala couldn't seem to convince lawmakers that the war against fraud was winnable. "When I first went to the Hill with ideas about going after health-care fraud four years ago, Congress literally laughed," Shalala told reporters in 1997. "They said, 'Well, we've heard that before from every Administration.' "

Since then, Shalala's office has been involved in a number of fraud prosecutions. But these proceedings have hardly left the industry in a collective sweat. "Physicians go so far as to joke at the government's ineptness to investigate and prosecute fraud," an anonymous witness—himself an executive at a major medical institution—told a Senate committee that was investigating Medicare abuse in February 1996. "The general feeling in the industry is that [the government] will prosecute the small fish, but it's too connected to the medical industry to prosecute the major abusers.

"The bigger the crime," he said, "the easier it is to get away with it."

By way of example, this whistle-blower told the Senate committee how physicians subcontracted by the government to test new medical devices frequently owned stock in the companies that manufacture the devices. This relationship created a perverse incentive for them not only to recommend government approval of the devices, but also to use them as much as possible. Hospitals colluded with them, he added, so that they could attract patients seeking the latest surgical technology. Because Medicare would not pay for operations using these experimental devices, physicians subjected patients to a second, unnecessary operation using more traditional devices. That may have put patients at risk, but it got surgeons their coveted government reimbursements. And for good measure, the physicians sometimes earned millions from stock options when—as a result of their endorsements—the devices were approved by the government for widespread use. This probably did not raise the eyebrows of Senate committee members, since potential conflicts of interest involving companies in the health-care business are as common on Capitol Hill as head colds: According to the Center's analysis, 148 Capitol Hill lawmakers and aides owned stock in health-care companies in 1996.

The operators of psychiatric facilities have also had their

hands in the government till. Across the nation, they have been abusing emergency involuntary-commitment laws to keep patients against their will—a sinister ploy to drain their Medicare, Medicaid, and insurance money.

In Massachusetts, for example, a patient can be held in a psychiatric facility without a court review for ten days, but that detainment sometimes stretches into three weeks, according to an investigation by *The Boston Globe*. The number of patients placed in psychiatric wards against their will in Massachusetts increased by more than 50 percent since 1990, the *Globe* found—the result of a growing trend in which psychiatric hospitals make their money by preying on vulnerable Medicare and Medicaid patients.

In Louisiana, psychiatric facilities virtually sprang up out of the ground to cash in on this government-sponsored bonanza. Lax enforcement and political shenanigans in bayou country resulted in Medicaid-paid private psychiatric hospitalization increasing by nearly 100 times, *The New Orleans Times-Picayune* reported. The newspaper's investigation revealed that millions of taxpayer dollars were funneled to psychiatric hospitals owned by current and former state government officials. Some of the facilities provided only cursory care while reaping massive profits.

In nearby Texas, National Medical Enterprises, Inc. (NME), earned the distinction of committing the biggest mental-health scam ever. NME's modus operandi was simple: It paid an estimated $40 million in kickbacks to psychiatrists and public officials to secure patient referrals. (For good measure, the company cultivated friendships on Capitol Hill by heaping $10,000 in speaking fees on lawmakers from 1986 to 1990.) Once at NME facilities, patients reportedly suffered an array of tortures, including months of forced confinement. Mail was censored, strip searches were performed, communication with families was prohibited. John David Deaton, who was just seventeen

> **On Capitol Hill, potential conflicts of interest involving companies in the health-care business are as common as head colds: The Center found that at least 148 lawmakers and congressional aides owned stock in health-care companies in 1996.**

when bouts with depression landed him in an NME hospital, was bound to his bed for 300 days. "For eleven months, I ate, slept, bathed, attended to personal hygiene, changed clothes, endured therapy, and eliminated waste [while] shackled to my bed," Deaton told the House Judiciary Subcommittee on Crime and Criminal Justice in 1994. "I was held in bondage for insurance money, an abuse which should not be allowed to happen in America." In the end, Deaton was freed not because police officers or social workers came to his rescue, but because his insurance company stopped paying his bills.

For its indiscretions, NME was slapped with a record $379 million in fines by the federal government and agreed to sell off its chain of psychiatric hospitals. But this being the land of opportunity, NME simply regrouped: In the 1994 election cycle, the company bestowed at least $27,679 on Members of Congress. A year later, NME hired the powerhouse firm of Akin, Gump, Strauss, Hauer & Feld to lobby on Medicaid, Medicare, and other hospital-related issues. The company merged with American Medical International, Inc., and changed its name to Tenet Healthcare Corporation, and all was forgiven. Today it is the second-largest investor-owned hospital chain in the country.

"When I spoke before a congressional subcommittee, they said they were appalled," John David Deaton told reporters. "They said this would not happen again. But I haven't seen anything done about it."

If your orthopedist in Bend, Oregon, says that back surgery is in order, head south for San Francisco and consult with a doctor there. The reason: A doctor in Bend is almost three times more likely to operate on your back than is his Northern California counterpart, whose prescription for the same condition may well be something less drastic, such as rest and physical therapy.

Similarly, you don't want to be in Ogden, Utah, if the diagnosis is breast cancer, because surgeons there are fifteen times more likely to perform a mastectomy than are physicians on Long Island. Never mind that studies in the last decade have shown that in the early stages of breast cancer, surgery that spares the breast is just as effective as its removal.

But Bend and Ogden are not anomalies. According to *The Dartmouth Atlas of Health Care in the United States,* the same kind of surgery is performed at dramatically different rates across the country. In fact, the Dartmouth study found that surgical rates often differ widely among neighboring cities.

These findings speak to an alarming trend: an epidemic of unnecessary surgery in the United States. By one estimate, 37 percent of the most common "surgical interventions" are inappropriate. An example is removal of the prostate as a treatment for prostate cancer, an operation that has not been proven to prolong life, according to John Birkmeyer, an assistant professor of surgery at Dartmouth Medical School, who worked on the atlas. Although the surgery can have such drastic consequences as incontinence and impotence, 239,000 were performed in 1995.

Women have also been regular victims of unnecessary surgery. Studies dating back more than a half-century, for example, demonstrate that hysterectomies have been overperformed. Congress held hearings on this matter in 1978, and guidelines for performing the procedure were finally crafted in 1989. But a 1993 study in the *Journal of the American Medical Association* still found that 41 percent of hysterectomies were of dubious value.

Or consider cesarean-section deliveries, for which obstetricians are paid more than they are for regular births. The number of cesareans has increased fivefold since 1970, and today one of every four babies in the United States is delivered via this procedure. But studies have shown that when obstetricians are paid the same for C-sections as for natural births, the number of C-sections drops.

"There is no question that economic incentives influence almost every elective procedure, medical or surgical," Dr. Arnold Relman, the former editor of *The New England Journal of Medicine,* told the Center.

Perhaps the biggest cash cow is coronary-bypass surgery. Although it is one of this country's most common major surgeries, studies both here and in Europe have found that 45 percent of bypass operations are either unnecessary or questionable. Despite physicians' assurances of safety, recent studies reveal that six of every 100 patients undergoing this surgery suffer strokes or brain damage. But as Dr. Relman noted, the risk is worthwhile—at least for one party involved: "Doctors," he says, "can become wealthy by doing a large number of bypasses."

They can increase their fortunes by performing other operations as well—an incentive that many believe influences their decisions. "If you get paid for each discrete activity, it is human nature to want to do as many of those activities as you can," Arthur Levin, the director of the Center for Medical Consumers, a patient-advocacy group, told the Center. "I don't think there's any question that the desire to earn money is one of the motivating factors."

• • • • • • • • • • • • • • • • • • •

A doctor in Bend, Oregon, is almost three times more likely to operate on your back than is his Northern California counterpart, whose prescription for the same condition may well be something less drastic, such as rest and physical therapy.

• • • • • • • • • • • • • • • • • •

In Southern California, for instance, when an HMO stopped paying its cardiologists for each surgical procedure they performed, the number of angioplasties dropped by 80 percent. Studies examining other surgeries showed 20 to 30 percent drops.

In 1989, Congress created the Agency for Health Care Policy and Research to set guidelines for the medical profession. This move rankled the medical establishment, which took particular issue with the agency's 1995 guidelines declaring that spinal surgery for the treatment of back pain was largely unnecessary. Spine surgeons, using the front group the Center for Patient Advocacy, lobbied Congress to gut the agency. It survived, but the victory was Pyrrhic: The agency was directed to stop issuing guidelines and to remake itself to serve the needs of the medical industry.

The medical profession has a long history of getting its way—a testament to its abilities to distribute cash and to marshal a lobbying juggernaut. From 1986 to 1996, for example, the medical industry plied Capitol Hill lawmakers with more than $1.8 million in speaking fees—the AMA taking the gold medal for its $178,500 largesse, followed by the American Hospital Association at $142,750. Meanwhile, Members of Congress can hardly avoid the onslaught of medical-industry lobbyists, whose ranks in 1996 totaled more than 1,200, according to an analysis by the Center for Public Integrity—more than one of every ten registered lobbyists in Washington. This presence on Capitol Hill has served the industry well. The political power of physicians, for instance, is such that they have created the means of virtually exempting themselves from both government oversight and outside scrutiny. It is almost impossible, for example, to find information about how many times a particular surgeon has performed a given operation and whether he or she has encountered any problems, according to Arthur Levin of the Center for Medical Consumers. With a few exceptions, surgery is not subject to controlled studies or to effectiveness research.

Physicians dismiss federal regulation on the grounds that the AMA and other professional organizations have their own guidelines. But these guidelines serve the physicians better than they do their patients. "If a specialty society wants to protect its turf, it goes out and establishes guidelines," Robert Brook, a professor of medicine at UCLA and a specialist in medical guidelines, told *Medical Economics* magazine. "All efforts by single specialists to produce guidelines should cease."

While new medical technology is tested by the Food and Drug Administration, nobody regulates the physicians using it—a system that sometimes produces tragic, even fatal, results. In the early 1990s, for instance, gallbladder surgery using new microscopic instruments and video displays became the rage among surgeons. With hardly any training, physicians across the country began performing laparoscopic cholecystectomy until it became the preferred method for gallbladder removal. In fact, so eager were they to try out the surgery that gallbladder removal increased by 40 percent in some areas of the nation.

But while the new technique may have seemed no more complicated than playing a video game, the results were sometimes catastrophic. In New York State, at least six people died and more than 180 others sustained serious injuries from August 1990 to June 1992 as physicians mistakenly hacked away at bile ducts, bladders, bowels, and aortas. Nationwide, it has been estimated that injury rates for various laparoscopic surgeries are two to four times those for traditional operations.

"The surgeons would train in this technique rather minimally—often at a weekend conference at a resort hotel," Peter Slocum, the director of public affairs for the New York State Department of

Health, told the Center for Medical Consumers. "They'd operate on a couple of pigs, and then they did it on their patients."

This might seem cause for concern, but letting doctors be doctors and letting the market do its work is all well and good with Congress. With their love of quick fixes, lawmakers have lately embraced managed care as a market solution to such medical abuses as unnecessary surgery. But managed care is a blunt instrument. When health plans put a cap on fees, for instance, surgeons may want to operate more to make up for lost income.

Managed care may achieve reductions, Levin said, but "the question is, have you reduced [surgery] rationally? Have you reduced it where it should be reduced and increased it where it should be increased?"

The market solution is likely to perpetuate the problem rather than fix it. People without enough money will not be able to get the operations they need, while people with too much money will get operations they do not need. As for physicians, they will get the money. And Congress, as always, will get its cut.

The last mistake Adolpho Anguiano ever made was going to the Columbia Sunrise Hospital in Las Vegas, Nevada, for his chest pains. He was uninsured and homeless, so the hospital gave him a glass of juice and sent him on his way. Marc Gardner, who was the hospital's administrator at the time, later told a reporter that Anguiano began to plead: "I am really ill. I apologize. I'm filthy. I'm sorry. I'm homeless. But you really need to treat me." The hospital's staff ignored Anguiano's pleas and summoned armed guards to escort him from the emergency room. Gardner recalled that Anguiano walked about thirty feet onto the hospital lawn, where he slumped to the ground. Within an hour, he was dead of pneumonia. It was Gardner's job to keep the incident quiet.

At the time, Sunrise Hospital was pulling in $1 billion a year—a total unmatched by other hospitals in the Columbia/HCA Healthcare Corporation chain. But that still was not good enough for management, which had charged Gardner with making the bottom line grow by 50 percent. One way of accomplishing that was to severely cut costs, which meant turning away uninsured patients like Adolpho Anguiano.

But the first place Gardner found to pinch pennies was in the hospital's vaunted neonatal unit, where newborns received intensive care. "Babies don't complain too much," he told a reporter in describing the hospital's attitude. "A baby doesn't know if they are getting bad care."

This is the new face of health care. Columbia/HCA was founded only a decade ago and quickly grew to be a $20 billion giant. It is the nation's ninth-largest employer, with 350 hospitals, home health-care facilities, and laboratories in thirty-eight states.

"Do we have an obligation to provide health care for everybody?" Richard Scott, the hard-driving former chairman of Columbia/HCA, once asked a reporter. "Is any fast-food restaurant obligated to feed everyone who shows up?"

Hospitals were traditionally public trusts. Most were operated on a not-for-profit basis, which made them eligible for federal grants and loans. In exchange, they agreed to dedicate their assets to charitable purposes and were expected to provide care to the poor. But in the past few years, for-profit companies such as Columbia/HCA—which by definition must be concerned more about investors than they are about the indigent—have snatched up hundreds of community hospitals. Although only about 15 percent of the nation's 5,200 hospitals are currently run on a for-profit basis, this figure is projected to reach 25 percent within the next few years.

Columbia/HCA, which controls about half of the for-profit market, has its modus operandi figured out: The company buys several hospitals in an area, closes some down, and consolidates services in fewer locations—a strategy designed to increase both the patient count and the profitability of those hospitals that remain open. The fallout from this strategy is that basic services such as twenty-four-hour emergency rooms are cut in some locations. What is more, residents in many locations are left entirely without care and large numbers of workers are left unemployed.

Columbia/HCA's explosive growth was built on exploiting the greed of its physicians. It urges them to become "shareholders" in the Columbia/HCA health network, which may include hospitals, home-care services, and rehabilitation centers. Physicians who lure patients to Columbia/HCA-owned affiliates are rewarded with large bonuses. At the same time, these healers are urged to turn away uninsured patients.

Columbia/HCA ranks all of its hospitals by their profitability, and hospital managers are pressured to bring home a 20 percent rate of return. This ethos has encouraged ruthless cost-cutting, with Columbia/HCA facilities often short-staffed as nurses are laid off to cut costs. It has also turned medicine into something resembling an assembly line. Gardner, for example, told how an obstetrician-gynecologist at another Columbia/HCA hospital earned a $155,000 "production bonus" for performing a large number of surgical procedures. How many were unnecessary is impossible to determine.

Gardner eventually quit Columbia/HCA and told his story to the press. He admitted that during his years with Columbia/HCA, "I committed felonies every day."

In 1997, the FBI, the Internal Revenue Service, and the Department of Health and Human Services launched an investigation of Columbia/HCA involving more than 700 agents across the country. In California, Indiana, and Kentucky, investigators found numerous errors in medication and a dangerous lack of nurses. The investigation is still ongoing, but some analysts predict that Columbia/HCA may face fines of up to $1.5 billion.

With the exception of Democratic Representative Fortney (Pete) Stark of California, who repeatedly called for Columbia/HCA to be held accountable for its misdeeds, Congress remained passive as the for-profit Goliath rewrote the rules of health care in America. By contrast, Columbia/HCA was quite active on Capitol Hill, stuffing Members' pockets with substantial political contributions. In 1995 and 1996, the company and its executives ponied up more than $489,000 in contributions to congressional candidates and party committees. The biggest single chunk— $100,000 in "soft money" for the Tennessee Unity '96 Committee—came from Patricia Frist, the wife of Columbia/HCA chairman and chief executive officer, Thomas Frist.

Columbia/HCA spends hundreds of thousands of dollars a year to influence federal policy. In 1996, the hospital giant employed thirteen lobbyists, eight of whom formerly worked in the executive or legislative branches. The Federation of American Health Systems—the Little Rock, Arkansas-based association of for-profit hospitals, whose largest member is Columbia/HCA—employs twenty-one lobbyists, including a former aide to Gingrich and a former top official in the Bush Administration. Columbia/HCA also lobbies aggressively at the state level, especially in the Southeast, where it expanded the most rapidly. The company has thirty-three lobbyists on the payroll in Florida alone, where it owns one-quarter of the acute-care hospital beds in the state. (Its PAC is the largest contributor in the state, making $216,000 in donations in 1994.) Vernon Peeples, a former state representative in Florida, has said, "What you're running into is the possibility, if not the probability, that Columbia is so big now you can't successfully fight them."

With the investigation in full force, Frist, then Columbia/ HCA's vice chairman, stepped up to take over the company. "We need to have the perception out there that we care," the new chairman said at a news conference in July 1997.

Frist is very much a creature of Columbia/HCA. In fact, as the chairman and chief executive officer of Hospital Corporation of America, which he founded with his father and which was eventually absorbed by Columbia/HCA, he made $127 million in stock options in 1992. As he flew around the country in his plane looking for hospitals to buy, Frist invented the technique used so successfully by Columbia/HCA: negotiating behind closed doors with local hospital boards and offering them such inducements as the establishment of local charitable foundations.

Columbia/HCA's staunchest ally in Congress is undoubtedly its CEO's brother, Senator Bill Frist, a Republican from Tennessee, who owns up to $25 million worth of the health-care company's stock. The holdings are in a trust, which, according to Frist's office, were placed there of his own accord, since the Senate Ethics Committee saw no conflict of interest.

Bill Frist has repeatedly denied that he works for the interests of his family's firm, although others take issue with his claims. "The economic welfare of Columbia is tied directly to the economic welfare of the Frist family," said Dr. Arnold Relman, who, in addition to being the former editor of *The New England Journal of Medicine*,

Columbia/HCA Healthcare Corporation's staunchest ally in Congress is undoubtedly its CEO's brother, Senator Bill Frist, a Republican from Tennessee, who owns about $20 million worth of the company's stock.

is professor emeritus at Harvard Medical School and a longtime critic of Columbia/HCA. "Senator Frist can clearly influence policy in small ways that don't necessarily make the headlines."

Frist, who is a member of the Senate Republican Task Force on Health Care, has indeed used his Senate perch to advance the family business. In 1996, he held up a bill requiring forty-eight-hour hospital stays for new mothers, even though he was listed as a sponsor. The bill passed after Frist inserted a loophole that could still result in hospitals pressuring mothers out after only one day. Frist also plays a key role in influencing legislation on Medicare, from which Columbia/HCA derives more than a third of its profits.

There have been other health-care-related bills that posed obvious conflicts of interest, but Frist has never recused himself from a vote. He has even been the driving force behind at least one: As an add-on to the 1997 budget legislation, Frist cosponsored a bill that would allow Medicare to make payments to physician-hospital joint ventures and not just to insurance companies. As *The Commercial Appeal* of Memphis—the largest newspaper in Frist's home state—pointed out, the bill would also benefit Columbia/HCA, which has joint ventures with its physicians.

The Senator also placed a call to the Federal Trade Commission's top antitrust official in reference to antitrust laws for physician-hospital partnerships, an issue for which Columbia/HCA has come under scrutiny. (Senator Frist did not respond to the Center's requests for an interview.)

But sometimes the company's CEO can get along just fine without the help of his brother. For example, Columbia/HCA spent $200,000 on hiring politically connected lobbyists in 1996, including Tom Loeffler of Arter & Hadden, a Republican Representative from Texas from 1979 to 1986 and the former chief deputy whip. The company hired Bill Brack, formerly the chief of staff for Republican Senator Hank Brown of Colorado, and Michael Levy, who served as Assistant Secretary for Legislative Affairs in the Treasury Department. And four former congressional and Executive Branch employees from the firm Whitten & Diamond were hired to get permission for Columbia/HCA to bid on managing hospitals in Saudi Arabia.

Seems like that might be a case of exporting hazardous materials overseas.

12

|||||●|||||

The Price Isn't Right

SHELLY McPHAIL AND JEFFREY KINNAMON KNOW THAT THEIR HOUSE-hold income of $71,800 a year means that they are far from poor. Members of America's vaunted middle class, they have a TV, a microwave, a washing machine. But because they live in Cambridge, Massachusetts, outside Boston—the third-most-expensive metropolitan area in the nation—their paychecks do not seem to stretch much beyond the basics.

There is the '88 Chevy Nova—finally paid off, but still needing gasoline, repairs, maintenance, and insurance. There is day care for baby Ruby—$585 a month, and that is just for a half-day. Jeffrey, thirty-two, still pays around $167 a month on his student loans. The couple recently took out a home-equity loan of about $3,000 to redo the wiring and plumbing in their kitchen and to put in new cabinets and floors. The linoleum tiles had been peeling so badly that they were afraid Ruby would hurt herself crawling on them.

And then there is food. The $400 or so that the couple spends monthly at Star Market, a supermarket chain with dozens of stores in the Boston area, is approximately what Shelly paid for rent before she married Jeffrey. It is nearly half the $897 monthly mortgage payment on their two-bedroom condominium—"almost enough," Shelly says, "for two airplane tickets to Illinois," where her parents live.

That grocery bill is not Shelly and Jeffrey's biggest monthly expense, but it is higher than it should be because of policies set 450 miles away in Washington, D.C. An analysis of their grocery receipts for one month—July 1997—shows that they bought dozens of items that cost as much as they did because Congress has been unable or unwilling to take action that would lower prices.

The agribusinesses that provide an increasing share of the nation's fruit, vegetables, grain, and meat pour millions of dollars into political and lobbying campaigns, both to protect the subsidies they get from the federal government and to prevent Congress from restraining their anticompetitive behavior. So do the agricultural insurance firms, the multinational pharmaceutical concerns, and every other special interest that has a role in stocking the nation's grocery shelves. And what is true for Shelly and Jeffrey at Star Market is also true for shoppers at Food Lion and Piggly Wiggly, at Pathmark and Food 4 Less—at every supermarket in every state.

Much of the reason why sugar, fruit, milk, and nearly every food item on Shelly and Jeffrey's shopping list costs so much has to do with decades of muddled farm policy. Most farm laws have their roots in the 1930s, a good thirty years before Ruby's parents were born. Driven by the high demand for American grain during World War I, farmers planted more and more, knowing little about proper soil conservation. When the market collapsed and the soil turned to dust, thousands of families lost their land. Congress reacted by passing a series of laws meant to save the nation's farmers. There was a price-support program; there was the framework for marketing orders for milk, fruit, and vegetables; and there was government-subsidized crop insurance.

As the decades went by, however, the people who received most of the federal farm benefits looked less and less like the farmers the laws were originally intended to help. The support programs proved a boon for large agribusinesses and absentee landlords who learned how to work the system, while the number of small family farms declined rapidly. Millions of dollars went to those whose return addresses were nowhere near Kansas, Nebraska, or the Dakotas. From 1985 to 1994, for instance, some 6,200 people who listed their residence as Houston took nearly $70 million in farm subsidies from the federal government, according to the Environmental Working Group, a Washington-based advocacy organization. Residents of Los Angeles got $10.8 million, and residents of New York City took $7 million. The organization calculated that the top 2 percent of farm-subsidy recipients received 27 percent of all farm subsidies over the same period, a total of $29.2 billion.

Congress has not fared better in managing the crop-insurance program, which was designed to insure farmers against such natural disasters as hail and drought. But few farmers participated in the program, passed in 1938, for the simple reason that whenever disaster struck, Congress would vote for relief payments to farmers. In 1980, Congress expanded the insurance program and introduced private insurers into the mix, with the idea that disaster payments could be phased out as the free-enterprise system took over. By 1994, however, only a third of the nation's farmers had signed up for insurance, which nevertheless cost taxpayers some $900 million a year. Meanwhile, Congress was voting an average of $1.5 billion a year in disaster payments.

In 1994, Congress finally seemed to crack down, requiring farmers to take out crop-insurance policies before they could get subsidy payments. But the lawmakers also expanded the definition of who could qualify for the program. The list included not just wheat, corn, and other grain farmers but also those who raised Christmas trees, tropical fish, and turf grass. By 1996, the program had doubled, with more than 200 million acres of cropland insured. In 1996, Congress again changed the rules. Farmers could forgo insurance—but only if they waived all rights to any disaster aid.

Enter a new cash crop: government handouts to private insurance companies. About twenty private insurance companies are in the game, including Rain and Hail Insurance Services, Inc.; IGF Insurance Company; Producers Lloyds Insurance Company; and American Agrisurance, Inc. The Agriculture Department pays them to sell insurance policies to farmers; in 1994 and 1995, these companies collected about $665 million in "administrative payments," which were fixed at 31 percent of the premiums they sold. When the General Accounting Office (GAO) took a close look at how the nine largest companies used the tax dollars they collected for administrative expenses, it found that the companies spent $38 million less than what they received for administrative expenses. They also found $43 million in expenses for such items as stadium sky boxes, fishing trips, and corporate aircraft, as well as unusually high agent commissions. One company spent $44,000 on a Canadian fishing trip. Other "expenses" included a $928 bill from a cruise-ship line, $364 from a book-and-record shop, and $17,514 worth of chocolates to reward employees. Amazingly, the law does not forbid such expenditures.

The insurance companies cannot use the government money to lobby. But they do. The GAO found $418,400 reported as lobbying and related expenses. Most of the money went to various crop-insurance trade associations, which push the companies' agenda on Capitol Hill. From 1991 to 1996, crop-insurance companies, trade associations, and farm bureaus, which offer insurance, paid Members of Congress at least $122,050 in speaking fees, and from 1988 to 1996 they gave $6.6 million in PAC contributions to congressional campaigns and "soft money" to the national party committees.

All the lobbying came in handy in 1997. In the wake of the GAO's exposé, the Agriculture Department cut the rate at which insurance companies get "administrative payments"—from 31 percent of premiums sold to 24.5 percent or $156 million. That is when the insurance-company lobbyists went to work. They got Republican Joe Skeen of New Mexico, the chairman of the House Appropriations Subcommittee on Agriculture, to push the rate up to 27 percent of premiums, or $188.6 million. Skeen's biggest source of reelection money in the 1996 race, according to the Center for Responsive Politics, was agriculture interests, with $111,150 in PAC and individual contributions. Of that amount, $27,450 came from crop-insurance companies such as Rain & Hail, the American Association of Crop Insurers, and the Farm Credit Council. When the House voted on the appropriations bill, lawmakers rejected two amendments. One would have slashed funds from the crop insurers and given it to the nutrition program for poor women and children; the other would have devoted funds to an antismoking program for youth.

The insurance lobbyists had won. The votes were a "fulfillment of a commitment to American farmers and taxpayers," Paul Equale, the executive vice president of public affairs for the Independent Insurance Agents of America, said. Robert Robinson, the author of the critical GAO report, told the Center: "It was a classic case where lobbying really works, where a relatively small number of people dramatically affected the outcome."

Ruby arrived in the world on December 2, 1996, and, like most healthy infants, quickly exhibited a tremendous talent for eating. By the summer of 1997, when she was seven months old, Ruby was gaining weight fast. Shelly wanted to breast-feed her but wasn't able to, so Ruby was getting her pounds primarily through a diet of Similac, made by Ross Laboratories, a division of Abbott Laboratories.

Ruby's Similac costs her parents roughly $88 a month. Shelly chose Similac because her physician's office offered free samples, it was one of the oldest brands around, and Ruby seemed to do well on it. In truth, though, Shelly didn't have much of a choice. Two companies, Ross Laboratories and Mead Johnson & Company, part of Bristol-Myers Squibb Company, control 90 percent of the infant-formula market. A third manufacturer, Wyeth-Ayerst Laboratories, dropped out of the business in 1996. A fourth, Carnation, Inc., a subsidiary of Nestlè USA, Inc., sells formula but has not made much of a dent in the market.

||||||||||||||||||||||||||||||||||||||||||||

Since the early 1980s, infant-formula manufacturers have raised wholesale prices by more than 12 percent a year. By comparison, over the same period the wholesale price of milk, the main ingredient in infant formula, rose by just 2.1 percent a year.

||||||||||||||||||||||||||||||||||||||||||||

Abbott, at least, is not shy about how aggressively it markets its formula. "Abbott's traditionally close relationship with pediatricians and other health-care providers serves as the foundation for the company's solid market position in the United States," reads one of the company's filings with the Securities and Exchange Commission. "Pediatricians are also key to the success of consumer education programs, such as the Welcome Addition Club. The Welcome Addition Club is a program that provides new and expectant parents with a broad range of information, from nutrition and breast-feeding tips to basic parenting skills."

"I feel very manipulated by the infant-formula companies," Shelly told the Center. "I have only two choices of what to buy."

Millions of kids old enough to babysit Ruby by 1997 had spent their own infancies drinking formula made by one of the same two companies. Since the early 1980s, infant-formula manufacturers have raised wholesale prices by more than 12 percent a year. By comparison, over the same period the wholesale price of milk, the main ingredient in infant formula, rose by just 2.1 percent a year. What is more, the infant-formula manufacturers raised their prices in lock step, within weeks—often days—of each other, never varying by more than a couple of cents. "The pricing strategies of the two companies," a report by the Washington-based Center on Budget and Policy Priorities concluded in 1996, "suggest a market strategy designed to maximize profits rather than to compete aggressively with each other for market share."

The companies have refused to disclose information on how much it costs them to manufacture formula, even when challenged by their own retailers. "Dominick's [a supermarket chain] refused to accept our last price increase until I mailed a personal letter," a Bristol-Myers Squibb sales official wrote in an interoffice memorandum in 1990. "We need to tell him . . . that we do not disclose specific cost information, as it is confidential in nature. . . . I also plan to discontinue shipping the first time a price deduction is made." Internal documents that were made public during a trial in Kansas, however, showed the total costs of manufacturing and distributing infant formula to be about 25 percent of the wholesale price.

"If you're physically unable to nurse your child, to me it's like saying this is a prescription you have to give your child," Shelly told the Center. Infant formula, after all, is not a discretionary purchase. Consumers must pay whatever the companies charge.

The high price of formula came to the attention of Congress in the late 1980s, not because of middle-class families like Shelly and Jeffrey's but because of poor ones. Indirectly, through the Special Supplemental Food Program for Women, Infants, and Children, commonly known as WIC, the federal government was—and is—the largest buyer of infant formula nationwide. Back in 1988, according to the Center on Budget and Policy Priorities, the WIC program reached 3.6 million women and children, just half of those who qualified for it. The higher the infant-formula prices, the fewer infants the government can afford to feed.

In an attempt to rein in costs, in the mid-1980s several states experimented with competitive bidding for WIC contracts. Abbott and Bristol-Myers Squibb resisted at first, but when a third company, Wyeth-Ayerst, jumped in with bids, they were forced to follow suit. The savings realized by the new system allowed the states to feed more children. By 1989, forty-four states had some sort of program designed to increase competition for the WIC contracts. It is often said in Washington that states are the laboratories for change, and that was the case here. In 1988 and 1989, Congress passed new laws requiring all states to start competitive bidding systems.

But infant-formula prices continued to rise. In 1990 and again in 1991, the Senate Judiciary Committee and the Senate Agriculture, Nutrition, and Forestry Committee held hearings on the price of infant formula. These inspired the Federal Trade Commission to launch an investigation of antitrust behavior among the three companies. Soon some twenty lawsuits across the nation were filed by state attorneys general, in class actions, and, in some cases, by Nestlè. The lawsuits charged Abbott and Bristol-Myers Squibb with fixing prices and also alleged that the companies kept out competitors by agreeing not to advertise directly to consumers; instead, they marketed their products to physicians, who in turn promoted them to patients.

"We cannot tolerate price-fixing that puts corporate profits ahead of hungry infants, children, and pregnant women," Senator Patrick Leahy, a Democrat from Vermont, told his colleagues in 1992. That year Congress passed a law mandating penalties of up to $100 million for infant-formula companies attempting to influence bids by others. By all appearances, Congress seemed to be cracking down on the infant-formula industry.

Or was it? By the time Ruby was born, most of the big infant-formula manufacturers had settled the lawsuits out of court without admitting wrongdoing. The FTC's investigation resulted in a settlement with two companies; the agency lost its case against

Abbott Laboratories. In 1996, Abbott Laboratories settled twenty lawsuits in seventeen states by agreeing to pay $25 million in cash and $7.5 million in formula. That amounted to just 1.7 percent of the company's $1.9 billion in profits that year.

Abbott Laboratories and Bristol-Myers Squibb are generous campaign contributors. From 1987 to 1996, the two companies and their executives gave more than $2.7 million to congressional candidates and the national party committee. Abbott Laboratories gave at least $100,000 to underwrite the costs of both the Democratic and the Republican National Conventions in 1996. Over the years, the two companies have paid Capitol Hill lawmakers $30,000 in speaking fees. And between them they retained thirteen Washington lobbying firms in 1996.

> **The nation's milk farmers have been subsidized all the way back to the Depression in a system so complicated "there aren't four people in the United States of America who understand [it]," a former director of the USDA's Agricultural Marketing Service told the Center.**

Duane Burnham, Abbott's chairman and chief executive officer, who pulled in more than $3.7 million in salary, bonuses, and other compensation in 1996, also gave $45,000 to a group advocating the relocation of a statue honoring suffragists from the Capitol basement to the Rotunda. The public-relations firm of Burson-Marsteller, hired partially with Burnham's funds, tried to pitch the rededication ceremony as an opportunity for donors to mingle with powerful Capitol Hill lawmakers. "The June 26 ceremony in the U.S. Capitol Rotunda to rededicate the group portrait monument . . . provides an opportunity to spotlight your client before leadership and grassroots members of eighty-nine national women's organizations; Members of Congress (including the leadership in the House and Senate); and the House and Senate press and radio and television corps," read an internal memo obtained by *Roll Call*, a biweekly newspaper that covers Capitol Hill. The Senate Rules Committee nixed the idea of honoring corporate sponsors at the ceremony.

A number of Members of Congress also have a personal interest in the well-being of Abbott Laboratories and Bristol-Myers Squibb. Fifty-eight owned stock in one or both companies from 1991 to 1996, according to their financial disclosure forms; of that number, nine held shares worth at least $50,000. Representative Porter J. Goss, a Republican from Florida, had at least $100,000 worth of stock in both companies.

In July 1997, Ruby did not drink milk yet, but her mother did. Shelly and Jeffrey spent a bit more than $6 to buy two and a half gallons of skim milk—fifty cents more than they would have paid for the same amount just a few weeks earlier. On June 29, Star Market raised its milk prices by twenty cents a gallon. Along with other stores in the area, Star Market blamed the increase on new price supports for New England dairy farmers that went into effect on July 1. Milk processors were required to pay dairy farmers about twenty-six cents more per gallon of milk, and executives of the supermarket chain explained that Star Market was merely passing along this expense to consumers. The total cost to consumers in New England could be as high as $70 million a year, according to an estimate by Public Voice for Food and Health Policy, a Washington-based advocacy organization.

The nation's milk farmers have been subsidized all the way back to the Depression in a system so complicated "there aren't four people in the United States of America who understand [it]," Dan Haley, a former director of the USDA's Agriculture Marketing Service and now a lobbyist, told the Center. More than twenty-five years ago, President Nixon hinted that he planned to cut price supports for milk. Then the money started to pour in—$2 million from the dairy lobby for his 1972 reelection campaign. Nixon dropped the idea.

In March 1996, Congress passed the Federal Agriculture Improvement and Reform Act, which was widely hailed for dismantling the complex system of farm-support programs, particularly milk. Yet buried in the fine print of the farm bill was a provision giving the Secretary of Agriculture the authority to approve the Northeast Interstate Dairy Compact. This new bureaucratic entity would have the power to set milk prices in six Northeastern states: Connecticut, Maine, Massachusetts, New Hampshire,

Rhode Island, and Vermont. It was clearly a handout to the region's dairy farmers, who already were beginning to look like an endangered species—Vermont alone had lost nearly half of its dairy farms in the previous decade.

Flashback to December 1995. In a standoff with the Republican Congress, President Clinton had just vetoed the budget bill. One of the dozens of items Congress had stuck into the mammoth piece of legislation was the farm bill.

Republican Richard Lugar of Indiana, the chairman of the Senate Agriculture Committee, was eager to revive the farm bill but afraid that he did not have enough votes to pass it. He was running for President and had made farm reform a major theme of his campaign. It was then, apparently, that Senator Leahy approached Lugar. "[Leahy] indicated that if certain accommodations could be made, he would certainly be prepared to vote for a very close relative of the farm bill that had been part of the budget bill the President had vetoed," Charles Connor, the staff director of the Senate Agriculture Committee, later told *Milling & Baking News,* a trade publication. If Leahy got his way, he would bring other votes with him. Lugar agreed.

One of the "accommodations" that Leahy insisted on was the Northeast Interstate Dairy Compact, which he had been trying for eight years to push through Congress. In February, when the Senate started its formal debate on the farm bill, the compact was in it. Leahy stood up to defend it. "This is not a case where it is farmers against consumers, as though the two are different, or consumers against farmers," he told his colleagues. "This is a case where producers and users come together to make it work."

Leahy had political enemies, though, in the Senators from Wisconsin, the nation's second-largest dairy state. "If we allow this kind of a price-fixing scheme to make its way through Congress, then there will be no way to prevent in a logical way any other group of states setting up similar price-fixing mechanisms under the same justification, not only in dairy but in any other industry," Senator Herbert Kohl, a Democrat, said. Kohl and Russell Feingold, Wisconsin's other Senator, had sponsored an amendment to eliminate the compact. On February 7, 1996, the Senate passed their amendment by a vote of fifty to forty-six.

According to the textbook version of how laws are made, that should have been the end of the Northeast Interstate Dairy Compact. But it was not. As the ranking Democrat on the Agriculture Committee, Leahy became one of the negotiators charged with ironing out the differences between the House and Senate versions of the bill.

Meanwhile, Lugar's presidential campaign was failing fast. He was doing so poorly in the primaries that his campaign was in danger of losing federal matching funds. He needed to win at least 20 percent of the vote by March 23 to reestablish his eligibility for future funds. Vermont's primary was March 5. Lugar campaigned hard and decided to attend a large dairy convention in Vermont the weekend before the primary. When the votes were counted the following Tuesday, Lugar got 14 percent, the highest he had collected yet, but not enough to reestablish his eligibility for matching funds. The next day he dropped out of the presidential race.

A few weeks later, in the meetings where House and Senate negotiators hammered out the final version of the farm bill, Lugar stuck up for Leahy—and the Northeast Interstate Dairy Compact. In a vote at 1 A.M. one night in late March, all fourteen House Members participating in the discussions voted against the compact. After a few hours' sleep, Leahy decided to try again, this time warning the Members that the Senate wouldn't approve a bill without the compact in it. "I just told everybody, 'You want to finish this today, you have to revisit [the compact],' " Leahy told Gannett News Service.

> Over the years, various "specialty crop" groups—from the Florida Fruit and Vegetable Association to the Michigan Red Tart Cherry Advisory Board to the National Peach Council to the Popcorn Institute—have poured more than $4.6 million into congressional campaigns.

"And Dick Lugar, God bless him, stayed very strong and committed. He said, 'If Leahy doesn't get this, we'll probably not get the farm bill.' " Although the Senate had voted against it and the House didn't want it, the dairy compact was put back into the farm bill and became law.

"It's not that we're unsympathetic with the plight of dairy farmers—we just think the solution of the problem is not to raise the price of milk to consumers," Arthur Yeagher, the director of Public Voice for Food and Health Policy, told the Center.

And what goes up does not necessarily come down. Retail prices for milk in Massachusetts remained steady from October 1996 to July 1997, even though the prices paid to farmers had declined by 32 cents, according to the Massachusetts Department of Food and Agriculture. Indeed, Leahy's response to criticism of the compact was to call for an investigation into price-fixing by the stores.

It is not just a deal among Senators that inflates the price of the milk that Shelly and Jeffrey buy. Somebody has to pay for those seemingly ubiquitous "Got Milk?" and "milk mustache" ads. The advertising bucks come from two federal programs that require the nation's dairy farmers and processors to pay fifteen cents and twenty cents, respectively, per 100 pounds of milk produced. The Agriculture Department supervises the whole thing. Consumers pay two ways: They absorb the cost of the advertisements, and if the ads are successful, public demand for the product increases and so, sometimes, does the price.

You know these types of programs through their slogans: "the other white meat" (pork), "real food for real people" (beef), "the incredible edible egg." There are similar promotional programs for honey, potatoes, watermelon, and mushrooms, and in the 1996 farm bill Congress added new ones for popcorn, kiwi, and canola oil.

"At a time when health authorities agree that Americans should be eating less meat, dairy products, and eggs," a 1995 report by the Center for Science in the Public Interest concluded, "it simply doesn't make sense for the federal government to be overseeing multimillion-dollar campaigns that encourage consumers to increase consumption of these foods."

The federally sanctioned advertising programs are just one small corner of the benefits heaped on agricultural interests as part of the Agricultural Marketing Agreement Act of 1937. The same law that sanctions milk mustaches also allows growers to band together and set conditions on how their goods are sent to market. Some of these are relatively benign, such as labeling requirements for different sizes or quality of fruit, or researching new uses for the product. But depending on how they are written and implemented, the rules can also be used to keep food off the market to maintain artificially high prices.

At present, there are thirty-three federal marketing orders, and each one has different rules. What is more, nearly all of them have a trade association that looks after their interests—from the Florida Fruit and Vegetable Association to the Michigan Red Tart Cherry Advisory Board to the National Peach Council to the Popcorn Institute. Over the years, these "specialty crop" groups have poured more than $4.6 million into congressional campaigns and paid at least $163,550 in speaking fees to Members of Congress.

When President Reagan took office in 1981, his staff at the Office of Management and Budget (OMB) launched a war on all government regulations, and marketing orders were on the hit list. The worst of the lot was a California marketing order on oranges and lemons. Sunkist, a giant citrus cooperative, all but controlled the committee that met weekly to decide how many oranges could be shipped to market. This strategy kept supply down and the price for consumers up. Growers left heaps of perfectly edible oranges on the side of the road to rot.

The co-ops' clout with Congress was enormous. In 1980, the Federal Trade Commission launched investigations into Sunkist and two other co-ops for alleged antitrust violations. In 1980, Republican Representatives Mark Andrews of North Dakota and Charles Pashayan of California pushed an amendment through the House that forbade the agency from investigating agriculture marketing orders at all. Sunkist's fingerprints were all over it. "The attempted FTC usurpation of authority in these . . . areas not only results in the harassment of farmers and cooperatives but also is a waste of public funds," William Quarles, Jr., a vice president of Sunkist, wrote in a letter to selected Members of Congress.

James Moody, a Washington lawyer who has made a career of fighting marketing orders, told the Center that, throughout the 1980s, every attempt to get rid of the citrus rules ran up against the powerful political machine of Sunkist. The company's main lobbyist in Washington was James Lake—an Agriculture Department official under Nixon and later press secretary for Ronald Reagan's 1980 race—who, more than ten years later, would plead guilty to funneling illegal campaign contributions to Henry Espy's congressional campaign. Espy's brother, Mike Espy, was at the time Agriculture Secretary in the Clinton Administration. "Facts determine about half a decision. . . . The other half is whose ear you can get," Lake told a reporter for *National Journal* in 1983. Lake used his clout within the Reagan Administration to defend the citrus growers within the Reagan Administration. Congress forbade OMB from examining marketing orders, a prohibition that, like the one forbidding FTC investigations, exists to this day.

The same strategy worked yet again. Moody and his client, Carl Pescosolido, filed lawsuits against Sunkist under the False Claims Act, a law that dates back to 1863. In 1992, when Congress amended the law, it included a section that specifically prohibited any lawsuits charging violations with the Agricultural Adjustment Act—in other words, marketing orders.

Congress did its best to fend off attacks on the marketing orders. Only in 1994, after more than a decade of controversy, was the marketing order for California and Arizona citrus terminated. And it was the U.S. Agriculture Department that put an end to the program, not Congress.

Meanwhile, dozens of marketing orders remain on the books, covering everything from apricots and avocados to papayas and pears. The ones for hazelnuts, walnuts, spearmint oil, dates, and raisins include some sort of supply limits—the feature that critics found most objectionable about the citrus order. And new ones are being created all the time. In 1997, for instance, the Agriculture Department announced one for Midwestern tart cherries, championed by Senator Carl Levin, a Democrat from Michigan. It also added new supply controls for Florida small red seedless grapefruit, requested by growers who were upset that overproduction was driving prices down. Moody is kept busy trying to fight them all. "When you keep edible food off the market, that's morally unjust," Moody told the Center. "I call it nutritional genocide."

Shelly bought two packs of M&Ms in July 1997. Not much else on Shelly and Jeffrey's grocery list contained sugar. In this way, they are not like most of us; the average American consumes

Dwayne Andreas, the chairman of Archer-Daniels-Midland Company, the high-powered agribusiness giant, has put the ADM jet at the disposal of Capitol Hill lawmakers and presidential candidates; then–Senator Robert Dole of Kansas used the plane at least twenty-four times from 1993 to mid-1995.

sixty-five pounds of sugar a year. Of course, there is sugar on your grocery list even when you might think there is not. There is sugar in Gerber baby food, in Kraft fat-free Thousand Island dressing. There is sugar in Spam, frozen waffles, Doritos, and Special K. There is sugar in Green Giant Corn Niblets, Del Monte carrots, even dog biscuits. And if there is no sugar, there is that omnipresent sugar substitute—corn syrup. It is in Kraft barbecue sauce, Rice-A-Roni, Manischewitz instant soup, Chef Boyardee spaghetti and meatballs, and Wheat Thins. When you total it up, people eat even more corn syrup, on average, than refined sugar—some eighty-one pounds' worth a year.

Americans pay an inflated price for sugar because of a U.S. loan and price-support program that, like most farm programs, dates to the Depression. A five-pound bag of sugar costs fifty cents more than it would if the federal government did not help sugar farmers, according to an estimate by Public Voice for Food and Health Policy. A 1993 GAO estimate puts the program's total cost to consumers at $1.4 billion a year.

That does not even count the inflated prices for corn syrup. Because corn sweeteners are a substitute for sugar in many foods, high sugar prices allow the syrup manufacturers to charge elevated prices themselves. Archer-Daniels-Midland Company (ADM), the high-powered agribusiness giant, profits by some $200 million a year from its corn-syrup business. The company and its chairman, Dwayne Andreas, have given approximately $5 million to politicians of both political parties and to the parties themselves and millions more in contributions to foundations and other nonprofit organizations operated by Capitol Hill lawmakers. Andreas has also put the ADM jet at the disposal of Capitol Hill lawmakers and presidential candidates; then-Senator Robert Dole of Kansas used the plane at least twenty-four times from 1993 to mid-1995. In 1982, Andreas sold Dole's wife and brother-in-law an oceanfront condominium in Bal Harbour, Florida, for just $150,000, well below the market price.

Other lawmakers have a financial stake themselves in ADM. From 1991 to 1996, six Members of Congress reported owning stock in the company, and three of them—Senator Michael De-Wine, a Republican from Ohio; Representative Norman Sisisky, a Democrat from Virginia; and Representative Jim Leach, a Republican from Iowa—own $50,000 or more of the stock.

A very small group of farmers reaps most of the benefits of the sugar program. One percent of sugarcane growers get nearly 50 percent of all the price-support benefits. The Fanjuls—a family who fled Cuba after Castro's takeover—have sugar holdings in Florida and the Dominican Republic totaling more than 400,000 acres. They benefit by about $65 million every year, profiting from the program both as domestic producers and as importers. When the Fanjuls import sugar from their Dominican fields, they can sell it at inflated U.S. prices. The United States limits imports, but the Fanjuls own a third of the quota.

For decades, sugar growers have had their way with Congress, using the most practical—and cynical—methods on the lobbyists' play sheet to protect their lucrative subsidy. For starters, the industry has more than 100 lobbyists working the halls of Congress on its behalf. Sugar growers have lavished millions in contributions to the campaigns of candidates to federal office and to political parties—$11.9 million from 1979 to 1994, according to the Center for Responsive Politics. The industry also paid Members of Congress at least $157,932 in speaking fees from 1986 to 1990. It spent at least $55,187 on trips for Capitol Hill lawmakers and their aides in 1996 and 1997.

The Fanjul family alone gave at least $2.6 million to political candidates and committees since 1979, if you tally their individual contributions, their employees' contributions, and PAC contributions. They are not partial to a particular political party, either. One brother, José, was the vice chairman of Dole's finance committee during the 1996 GOP primaries, while the other, Alfonso, served on President Clinton's finance committee.

The sugar forces followed a simple—and successful—lobbying strategy: They kept any and all discussion of sugar subsidies bottled up in the Senate and House Agriculture Committees. By woo-ing members of those committees, most of whom came from farm states, the sugar lobby could be sure that it would do well every time the farm bill was rewritten, a ritual that occurred once every five years. It was rare for any lawmaker outside the committee to challenge what had been done there behind closed doors. What-ever the committee did became law.

When Congress started rewriting the farm bill in 1995, though, the sugar lobby faced some formidable opposition. After the Republicans took over Congress, Representative Richard Armey, a Republican from Texas and a longtime critic of the program, stepped up to become Majority Leader. Representative Dan Miller vowed to eliminate the subsidy. Although he hailed from Florida, the sugar lobby's stronghold, Miller's district did not include sugar farmers. Sugar foes had some industrial clout behind them—Coca-Cola, M&M/Mars, ice-cream manufacturers, and other sugar users—all of them tired of paying high prices for sugar and generous campaign contributors in their own right.

Environmental activists also rallied against the sugar program. Decades of sugarcane farming have devastated Florida's Ever-glades, leaving the egrets, manatees, and panthers that live in these wetlands with fewer acres every year. Some, like the pan-ther, are on the nation's en-dangered-species list. As sugar farmers have drained and dammed these lands, they have interrupted water flow. Phosphorus runoff from the farming also harms the plants and animals, according to en-vironmentalists. Tens of thou-sands of acres of wetlands

||||||||||||||||||||||||||||||||||||||||||||

A very small group of farmers reaps most of the benefits of the sugar program. One percent of sugarcane growers get nearly 50 percent of all the price-support benefits.

||||||||||||||||||||||||||||||||||||||||||||

have simply vanished, and cleaning up will cost more than $1 billion. Environmental activists were outraged that the U.S. gov-ernment was subsidizing an industry that was causing so much damage.

On February 7, 1996, the Senate voted, thirty-five to sixty-one, against an amendment by Senator Judd Gregg, a Republican from New Hampshire, to eliminate the sugar subsidy program.

Senators who voted the way the sugar industry wanted had received an average of $13,473 over the previous six years from sugar-industry PACs. Those who voted to eliminate the subsidy received an average of just $1,461, according to an analysis by the Center for Responsive Politics. The Senators decided to devote some money to cleaning up the Everglades—$200 million—but instead of forcing the sugar industry to pay, they docked the taxpayers. The cleanup money came straight from the U.S. Treasury.

A week later, nineteen congressional aides spent a few days in Clewiston, Florida—"America's Sweetest Town," according to the sign near the city limits. Clewiston is home to U.S. Sugar Corporation, which operates Florida's second-largest sugarcane farm on more than 120,000 acres. (It is so large that the company maintains its own private railroad.) The trip was paid for by the Florida Sugar Cane League, which reported spending at least $14,541 on the affair. "If all the people who have to make decisions on policy in the United States only sit in their windowless offices and never see what the real world is about and never see what people have to do to make a living, make a crop, and comply with regulations, they will never have an appreciation for what you do," Dalton Yancey, the league's vice president, told Gannett News Service in 1997.

Later that month, when the House debated the farm bill, Miller had his chance. "As I have said before, it is the 'sugar' daddy of all corporate welfare," he told his colleagues, urging them to vote for his amendment that would phase out the sugar program. "[If] we want to target corporate welfare, this is one program we should target. In my home state of Florida, seventy-five percent of the sugar is controlled by two plantations, seventy-five percent by two companies. That is corporate welfare. It is not the small farmer we are talking about, as some people want to make you think." The two biggest sugar companies in Florida are the Fanjuls' Flo-Sun and U.S. Sugar Corporation.

The vote was close: The House rejected Miller's amendment 217 to 208. Five lawmakers who had originally cosponsored it ended up voting against it. Not one of them had gotten a single contribution from a sugar-industry PAC during the session. After the vote, however, sugar-industry PACs rewarded four of five lawmakers; the fifth, Patricia Schroeder, a Democrat from Colorado, had decided to leave Congress and so was not collecting any campaign money. And sixteen of the seventeen lawmakers whose aides had traveled to Clewiston that month voted to keep the sugar subsidy program.

"It's harder to say no face-to-face," Richard Cathy, one of the congressional aides who went on the trip to Clewiston and who found it "educational," told the Center. His former boss, Representative Mac Collins, a Republican from Georgia, was the one lawmaker on the trip who did say no, voting against the sugar program. But Collins, who had a seat on the Ways and Means Committee, which writes tax laws, did agree to oppose any new tax on the sugar industry to pay for cleaning up the Everglades. "There were parts we could help them with," Cathy said, "and parts we couldn't."

The sugar industry had already set its sights on getting rid of the opposition. In an interview with the Center, Miller recalled: "They came into my area and approached several people and said, 'We want to get Dan Miller.'"

Miller won his reelection bid, but the Florida sugar industry won a bigger fight. After spending at least $22.7 million, it defeated a Florida state ballot initiative that would have taxed sugar growers a penny a pound toward Everglades cleanup. The environmental group Save Our Everglades had spent at least $13 million.

Infant formula, milk, and sugar are not the only items on Jeffrey and Shelly's grocery list—or any typical American's list—that cost more than they should because of what Congress does or does not do. The advocacy group Public Voice for Food and Health Policy estimates that consumers pay about thirty-three cents extra per eighteen-ounce jar of peanut butter, thanks to a peanut subsidy program that, like sugar, survived the farm debate of 1996. In his 1994 race, Republican Representative Thomas Ewing of Illinois did not receive a penny from peanut PACs. After he rose to the chairmanship of the agriculture subcommittee overseeing the peanut program, however, he ranked second among his House colleagues, with $21,000 in contributions from peanut PACs.

Breakfast cereal also costs much more than it might. As in the infant-formula market, a small group of producers dominates. Although Representative Charles Schumer, a Democrat from New York, has yelled about it and called for studies—"The high price of cereal is my pet peeve. . . . Cold-cereal prices of five dollars a box make my blood boil when I shop"—Congress has taken no meaningful action. Ditto for numerous other items where a small number of companies control the market—diapers, tampons, and laundry detergent among them.

For people like Shelly and Jeffrey, the high prices are a source of frustration. They are conscientious voters, and Shelly even made a $25 contribution to Bill Clinton's 1992 presidential campaign. But they cannot possibly match the clout and lobbying power of multinational drug companies, huge dairy cooperatives, and sugar barons.

"I understand logically why they [contribute], but I think it corrupts the system," Shelly told the Center. "The market is supposed to be regulated by supply and demand, and all this seems completely contrary to that."

13

|||||●|||||

Department of Highway Robbery

N O ISSUE TENDS TO MAKE AMERICANS ANGRIER THAN TAXES. MIL-
lions of Americans feel they are working harder and harder
but keeping less and less of what they earn.

If you are a middle-class taxpayer, you have good reason to
be angry. Back in 1956, a family of four in Wichita, Kansas,
earning $4,780 a year (the median income nationwide), paid state
and federal income and Social Security taxes of $414, about 8.7
percent of their annual income. Forty years later, a family in
Wichita earning $42,300 a year (the median family income in
1996), paid combined taxes of $8,076, or 19.1 percent of their
annual income. That is an increase of 120 percent.

But not everyone has gotten socked by the tax system. At the
same time Congress has squeezed the nation's middle class harder
and harder, it has made April 15 a relatively painless experience
for the rich. In 1967, Treasury Secretary Joseph Barr triggered a
huge public outcry when he disclosed that 155 households with
annual incomes of more than $200,000 in 1967 had paid no
taxes. By 1993, some 1,000 American households with annual
incomes of more than $200,000 paid no taxes.

The Internal Revenue Service (IRS) has encouraged big-time tax
avoidance by cutting back audits of the rich while stepping up audits
of taxpayers who earn $25,000 per year or less. Jennifer Long, an

IRS agent from Houston, told members of the Senate Finance Committee in 1997 that she was told to target people who did not have the resources to fight back. "The IRS," she said, "will often pursue a taxpayer who is viewed to be vulnerable, has limited formal education, has suffered a financial tragedy, is having financial crisis, or may not necessarily have a solid grasp of their legal rights."

Along with the rich, corporate America has been paying a smaller and smaller share of the federal tax burden. In 1993, about half of the 4 million corporations in the United States did not pay a penny in federal income taxes. Only about a third of the 1,085 coal companies across the nation paid any federal income taxes, and only one or two of the fifty-six corporations that manufacture tobacco products paid any, either.

These tax evaders are not necessarily cheating the system. Thanks to Congress, they do not need to. For decades, Capitol Hill lawmakers have been quietly larding the tax code with loopholes for corporations and wealthy individuals. To make up for the lost revenue, they have plundered the middle class. As a result, the Internal Revenue Code has become a cruelly efficient system for transferring wealth from those at the bottom of the social pyramid to those at the top.

Take a look at the pie chart in the back of your IRS 1040 instruction booklet that details the sources of federal revenues. The chart shows that corporate income taxes provided just 11 percent of the federal government's total revenues in 1996, while personal income taxes provided 42 percent. Most remarkable still is something that the chart does not show: The slice of the pie attributable to corporate income taxes shrank from 28 percent in 1956, while the individual slice decreased only a little from 47 percent the same year. After factoring in Social Security and Medicare taxes, individuals were footing almost 80 percent of the federal tax burden in 1996—up from 57 percent forty years before.

Here is another way to look at it: If today's corporate taxpay-

> In 1993, about half of the 4 million corporations in the United States did not pay a penny in federal income taxes.

ers were paying the same share of federal revenues that they did back in 1956, they would have sent another $270 billion or so into the U.S. Treasury in 1996. That is enough to eliminate the employee portion of the payroll (FICA) tax.

Just about every lawmaker on Capitol Hill claims to want to make the nation's tax system fairer and easier to understand. Each call for reform, though, ends with a tax system that is ever more convoluted and confused. The original income-tax code of 1913 was twenty-six pages long. Today it has ballooned to 4,760 pages.

It is no accident that the tax code is so complex. Every impenetrable clause inserted into the tax code means more billable hours for the Washington tax lawyers and lobbyists who are among the richest sources of reelection revenue for congressional incumbents. Every new corporate tax loophole that is proposed provides employment for a herd of $500-an-hour K Street lobbyists. Every new tax break that lawmakers maneuver through Congress translates into more campaign contributions from grateful deep pockets.

The maddening complexity of the tax code also helps mask the fact that a system championed as "progressive" has become a feeding trough for the nation's privileged classes. As *Forbes* magazine once observed, the tax code "has become a cookie jar, full of good things for everybody but the general public, a profit center for politicians and tax professionals."

In theory, the nation's tax system could not be simpler. For corporations, the statutory federal income tax rate is 35 percent, or $350,000 for every $1 million in profits. In 1997, for instance, Goodyear Tire and Rubber Company reported profits of $844.6 million. Therefore, the company paid $295.6 million in federal income taxes, right?

Wrong. In 1997, Goodyear paid just $22.8 million in federal income taxes—an effective tax rate of just 3 percent. To achieve this advantageous result, the company exploited a number of loopholes, including one that allows corporations to deduct taxes paid to foreign governments from their payments to the U.S. Treasury. By exploiting a similar array of loopholes, Mobil Corporation paid zero taxes in 1994 on reported income of $241 million. In

1995, McDonnell Douglas Corporation—which then ranked among the nation's 100 biggest companies—received a tax rebate of $257 million. That's roughly equal to the average tax paid in 1995 by 74,450 of the tax filers with adjusted gross incomes of $30,000 to $39,999 a year.

Citizens for Tax Justice, a Washington-based nonpartisan research and advocacy group, has catalogued more than 120 separate tax breaks that Congress has bestowed on corporate America. There is a handout for everybody, from a provision that allows for oil, gas, and energy tax breaks worth more than $3 billion a year to a hodge-podge of tax breaks for timber, agriculture, and mineral companies, which are collectively worth about $1.4 billion a year.

The seemingly benign phrase "accelerated depreciation" sits atop a rule that allows businesses to write off the cost of equipment faster than it actually wears out. Valued at more than $28 billion a year, accelerated depreciation is corporate America's single biggest tax loophole. Then there is the net-operating-loss deduction, under which corporations that lose money one year can deduct the amount of the loss from their tax obligations in future years. (Congress does not offer the same relief to families that suffer through a bad year and have to dip into savings to meet expenses; it abolished income-averaging as part of the Tax Reform Act of 1986.) Congress passed the net-operating-loss provision in 1919, describing it as a one-year emergency measure that would stimulate economic growth as the United States emerged from World War I. Eight decades later, the law is still on the books; it cost the Treasury an average of $10 billion a year in the 1980s.

Even despoiling the environment or bilking the government can net a company some lucrative tax breaks. That is because the "corporate income tax" is actually a tax on profits; the IRS allows corporations to write off all their expenses, ranging from workers' wages and rent to legal fees and fines. This provision allowed Exxon Corporation to turn one of the worst environmental catastrophes in U.S. history—the 1989 Exxon *Valdez* affair, in which an oil tanker ran aground in Alaska and spilled millions of gallons of crude into Prince William Sound—into a gargantuan tax break, with the company writing off all expenses related to the disaster, including its legal bills and cleanup costs. Unisys Corporation saved a bundle in 1991 by writing off nearly all of the $190 million in penalties it agreed to pay to settle charges of contracting fraud with the federal government.

You have probably never heard of Section 936 of the Internal Revenue Code, but like other such loopholes and windfalls, you pay for it. This one represents a tax break worth billions every year to U.S. corporations that have operations in Puerto Rico. The prime beneficiaries of the provision are pharmaceutical companies, which make up the most profitable legal industry in the United States, with profit margins four times the average among Fortune 500 firms. In 1993, Senator David Pryor, a Democrat from Arkansas, proposed legislation that would have reduced the Section 936 giveaway to about $600 million per year. The corporate drug lords fought back, arguing that Section 936 had turned Puerto Rico into "a showcase of free enterprise" and created good jobs for workers. What the pharmaceutical industry liked to leave unmentioned was the fact that the companies with operations in Puerto Rico netted three times more in tax breaks than they paid out in wages.

Many big pharmaceutical companies are headquartered in New Jersey, and it was Democrat Bill Bradley, then a Senator from that state, who led the opposition to Pryor's legislation. During backroom negotiations, Bradley managed to preserve most of 936's tax breaks.

Two years later, Representative John Kasich, a Republican from Ohio, led another attempt to kill Section 936. But soon Haley Barbour, then the chairman of the Republican National Committee (RNC), swung into action, personally lobbying against Kasich's proposal in meetings with congressional leaders. At the same time, his law firm—Barbour, despite public promises to the contrary, didn't sever his financial ties to the firm when he as-

Capitol Hill lawmakers generally slip new loopholes into the law as quietly as possible. Consider a clause buried in the Internal Revenue Code, which gives a tax break to two companies that are identified only as being owned by "a Texas resident whose birthdate is May 16, 1931, and a Michigan resident whose birthday is November 16, 1941."

sumed the chairmanship of the RNC—was representing the Pharmaceutical Research and Manufacturers of America. In the end, Congress eliminated the Section 936 tax break for new investments but allowed companies already operating in Puerto Rico to retain their golden goose egg for another decade.

Not wanting to be seen handing out big tax breaks to corporations, Capitol Hill lawmakers generally slip new loopholes into the law as quietly as possible. Consider a clause buried in paragraph two of Section 621(f) of the Internal Revenue Code, which gives a tax break to two companies that are identified only as being owned by "a Texas resident whose birthdate is May 16, 1931, and a Michigan resident whose birthday is November 16, 1941." Journalists have long attempted to crack the mystery, but thus far no one has determined the names of the companies or their owners, how much the loophole costs the government, or who inserted the clause into the tax code. James Jaffe, a former House Ways and Means Committee staffer, described the prevailing attitude on Capitol Hill to *The Philadelphia Inquirer*: "We don't talk. We have people who clearly know but who have yet to talk to a reporter—ever."

On a broader scale, Congress turned a 1996 bill to raise the minimum wage—to $5.15 per hour, or $10,712 per year, based on a forty-hour week—into a porkfest of tax cuts for the privileged. The biggest winner was the National Federation of Independent Business, which gave more than $1.3 million to congressional candidates in the 1995–96 election cycle—chump change, considering that its members won about $11 billion in tax breaks during the minimum-wage sweepstakes.

But plenty of other fat cats were feeding at the congressional trough. In a billion-dollar giveaway to corporate raiders, the minimum-wage bill allowed leveraged-buyout specialists to take a tax deduction for the fees they pay to investment banks and advisers. It also permitted newspaper publishers to treat their distributors and carriers as independent contractors instead of as employees, sparing the companies the burden of having to pay Social Security benefits. "This is probably the best thing that has happened to the industry, from a legislative standpoint, in anyone's memory," John Sturm, the president of the Newspaper Association of America, told *Editor and Publisher* magazine at the time. The minimum-wage bill did away with a surtax on diesel fuel for yachts and on luxury-car purchases and allowed Alaska seafood processors to deduct the cost of workers' meals, a provision that was maneuvered into the law by Senator Frank Murkowski, a Republican from—surprise—Alaska.

Passage of the minimum-wage bill cost taxpayers $21 billion in corporate freebies. But this giveaway was but a warmup for 1997's far more extravagant and costly Taxpayer Relief Act, a thinly disguised package of $275 billion in tax cuts aimed mostly at corporations and wealthy individuals. One opaque provision promised to "simplify foreign tax-credit limitation for dividends from 1,050 companies to provide look-throughs starting in 2003." Translation: Some 1,050 corporations with overseas operations will be allowed to take bigger deductions on their foreign earnings. Cost to the Treasury: at least $1 billion per year, according to Representative Peter DeFazio, a Democrat from Oregon, who opposed the measure.

Another impenetrable provision doubles the deduction that computer manufacturers are allowed for donating outdated computer equipment to schools. The Taxpayer Relief Act also reduced the excise tax on hard cider from $1.07 a gallon to 22.6 cents a gallon. This goodie was pushed through by Senators Daniel Patrick Moynihan, a Democrat from New York, and James Jeffords, a Republican from Vermont, at the urging of apple growers and distillers in their states. Yet another provision handed Amway Corporation a $280 million tax break for two Asian affiliates. It could not have hurt that, from 1994 to 1996, Amway gave $366,000 to Republican Party causes and candidates and that it employs Roger Mentz, who was the Assistant Treasury Secretary for Tax Policy in the Reagan Administration, as its tax lobbyist.

When the personal income tax was introduced back in 1913, there was a broad national consensus that the wealthy should pay the lion's share of taxes. Newspaper ads paid for by automaker Henry Ford a few years later earnestly declared that the fiscal burden should not fall "too heavily on the backs of the poor." And during the 1920s, Treasury Secretary Andrew Mellon declared, "The fairness of taxing more lightly income from wages, salaries, than from investment is beyond question."

The nation's tax system reflected those sentiments. At the start of the 1920s, the richest 1 percent of all Americans accounted for more than three-fourths of all personal income taxes collected. More than eight out of ten households in the United States paid no federal income taxes at all. Citizens could easily monitor the system, because tax returns were considered public records and were made available to any interested parties with a "material interest." Although Congress's affinity for drilling loopholes in the Internal Revenue Code soon began eroding the progressivity of the tax system, even as late as 1939 a tiny fraction of the nation's population—700,000 people— paid 90 percent of all income taxes.

Over the past half-century, however, the income tax has become a mass tax, with three-quarters of Americans now paying. Almost everyone else, including the working poor, contributes to the Treasury via Social Security taxes, self-employment taxes, and other assessments.

Meanwhile, wealthy Americans—aided by tax lawyers and friends in high places in Washington—have been reducing their own tax payments. In 1995, it was disclosed that dozens of the superrich had renounced their U.S. citizenship as a means of evading federal income and inheritance taxes. Among these "runaway billionaires" are Kenneth Dart of Dart Container Corporation, a foam-cup manufacturer, who is now a citizen of Belize; Ted Arison, the founder of Carnival Cruise Lines, whose stock is worth $3 billion and who is now a citizen of Israel; and John Dorrance III, the billionaire heir to the Campbell Soup fortune who renounced his U.S. citizenship for Irish citizenship. Because Ireland imposes minuscule taxes on the rich, Dorrance's move will save his heirs nearly $700 million in estate taxes alone. "Every time you buy a jar of soup," then-Representative Patricia Schroeder, a Democrat from Colorado, told her colleagues, "think of that can of soup and the guy living in Ireland, thumbing his nose at American taxpayers."

In 1995 it was disclosed that dozens of the super-rich had renounced their U.S. citizenship as a means of evading federal income and inheritance taxes. Among these is billionaire John Dorrance III, the heir to the Campbell Soup fortune, who renounced his U.S. citizenship for Irish citizenship.

The Treasury Department declared war against Dorrance and other "economic Benedict Arnolds," and President Clinton proposed that they be slapped with a huge capital-gains tax before being allowed to renounce their citizenship. Republicans called for a compromise, saying that expatriates should be required to pay taxes on money earned in the United States for ten years after changing their nationality. After the public furor died down, however, the politicians quietly dropped the matter; to date, the loophole remains wide open.

Congress showered so many tax breaks on rich Americans in 1997 that some of the runaways might now be ready to return home. Lawmakers slashed the tax on capital gains—the profits from the sale of such assets as real estate, stocks, and bonds—to 20 percent, just about half of what it was in 1978 and less than the income-tax rate for all taxpayers except those in the lowest bracket. In other words, earned income soon will be taxed more harshly than unearned income.

The Capitol Hill lawmakers who pushed for cutting the capital-gains tax said that it would boost investment and hence economic growth, a theory that most economists dismiss. They also insisted that cutting the capital-gains tax would mostly benefit the average middle-class taxpayer, a claim at variance with statistics maintained by the IRS. In 1993, for example, of the 1.7 million tax returns with capital gains subject to the 28 percent rate, none were filed by taxpayers with less than $50,000 in adjusted gross income. Filers with incomes of $100,000 a year or more had 86 percent of the capital gains reported to the IRS. A study by Citizens for Tax Justice showed that the measure would provide an average annual tax break of $21,850 to the richest 1.4 percent of the population. For those making $30,000 to $50,000, the tax break amounted to just $38 a year.

In another bequest to the wealthy, Congress—led by Republican Senator Jon Kyl of Arizona and Republican Representative Christopher Cox of California—attempted to raise the exemption on estate taxes from $600,000 to $1 million. Cox and Kyl named their measure the Family Heritage Preservation Act and, as in the case of the capital-gains tax, portrayed it as a boon to the average taxpayer. They also argued that the law was necessary to save "land-rich, cash-poor" farmers, who have been unfairly hit by estate taxes as the value of their land has appreciated. To drive home this point, conservatives wheeled out Chester Thigpen, an elderly Mississippi farmer whose heirs fear they will be forced to sell off their inheritance simply to pay estate taxes.

All the theatrics obscured a few simple facts: Roughly 99 percent of inheritances are exempt from estate taxes. Only 4 percent of farms are subject to estate taxes, and cases such as Thigpen's could have been eased by simply raising the exemption on farms. Instead, farmers were used as a cover to push through a measure that will bring an average tax cut of $16,000 to the richest 1 percent of the population. (The measure did not pass.)

As Congress lets the rich off the tax hook, it has steadily increased the tax that falls hardest on the middle class and the working poor: the payroll tax for Social Security and Medicare. When imposed by President Franklin Roosevelt during the New Deal, the payroll, or FICA, tax—whose cost is split between employer and employee—was only 2 percent. But it has been climbing steadily since 1950 and now stands at 15.3 percent. The payroll tax brings in $535 billion a year, almost as much as the $670 million raised by the personal income tax and 36 percent of total federal revenues. The Institute for Policy Innovation estimates that 40 percent of workers now pay more in payroll taxes than they do in income taxes.

The income tax, with all its flaws, at least retains some aspects of progressivity. The payroll tax, on the other hand, is brutally regressive. A factory worker who earns $30,000 a year pays FICA taxes totaling $2,295—7.65 percent of his or her income. What about a corporate executive who is paid $1 million per year? Because the FICA tax is not charged on earnings above $65,400, the executive pays $5,003 a year, or 0.5 percent of his or her salary.

Every few years, some brave soul calls for reducing the burden of payroll taxes. Former Representative Jack Kemp, who was Republican Robert Dole's running mate in 1996, has proposed making them tax-deductible, a move that would eliminate the double taxation. Alan Krueger, a professor of economics at Princeton University, has proposed exempting the first $10,000 of earnings.

But Capitol Hill lawmakers invariably reject such proposals, saying that they do not want to tinker with the Social Security system. It is more likely, though, that they realize that reducing the payroll tax would require closing some of the loopholes they have inserted into the tax code.

* * *

In recent years, corporate salaries have soared so high that even *BusinessWeek* complained in a headline in 1997 that executive pay is "out of control." The magazine reported that the average salary and bonus for a chief executive officer rose by 39 percent in 1996, to $2.3 million. Average total compensation, which includes retirement benefits, incentive plans, and other bonuses, went up by 54 percent, to $5.8 million.

The rewards have been far smaller for those at the other end of the pay pyramid. The earnings of factory workers rose by about 3 percent in 1996, leaving average compensation for corporate CEOs 209 times higher.

Lawrence Coss, the chairman and chief executive officer of Green Tree Financial Corporation, is the nation's highest-paid chief executive, raking in $102.4 million in 1996. In the number-two spot, with a paltry $97.6 million pay package, is Andrew Grove of Intel Corporation. Coss and Grove both run highly profitable companies, but for many corporate executives, even failure can be rewarding. Michael Ovitz, who was fired by the board of directors of Walt Disney Company after fourteen months as its chief executive officer, left with a package worth $90 million. John Walter resigned under pressure after less than a year at the top of AT&T and walked off with a severance package worth nearly $26 million. In 1996, the year before Walter's resignation, AT&T had announced 40,000 layoffs. Downsized workers who had been on the job less than a year received severance of one week's pay—$673.07.

||||||||||||||||||||||||||||||||||||||||||||||

As Congress lets the rich off the tax hook, it has steadily increased the tax that falls hardest on the middle class and the working poor: the payroll tax for Social Security and Medicare.

||||||||||||||||||||||||||||||||||||||||||||||

The tax system encourages such outrages by allowing corporations to write off all executive compensation, no matter how high. In 1993, President Clinton proposed capping the write-off at $1 million a year. Corporations, he said, had a choice: reduce salaries or pay more taxes.

Then Washington's army of corporate lobbyists went to work.

First, they persuaded President Clinton to limit his proposal to publicly held companies. Clinton also agreed to exempt executives at subsidiaries, so that the $1 million cap applies only to executives of the parent corporations. To skirt the proposal's application to the latter group, many companies began deferring pay above $1 million until after retirement. Hence, on the day that a corporate executive rides off into the sunset, he or she can receive a mountain of deferred compensation, all of which the company can use as a tax write-off.

Further undermining the compensation cap is the increasing use of stock options to supplement executive pay. Stock options give executives the right, but not the obligation, to buy shares in their company at a fixed price. A survey by *Executive Compensation Reports* found that stock options account for 45 percent of executive pay at fifty-five of the nation's biggest corporations. For example, Steve Case, the chairman and chief executive officer of America Online, Inc., was paid a salary of $200,000 in 1996. But from June 1995 to June 1996, Case made $27.4 million on stock options. (He was offered shares at $2.92 and sold them at prices between $38.45 and $55.00 each.)

In 1996, hugely profitable companies such as Microsoft Corporation, Intel, and Disney used the stock-option loophole to great effect, reducing their tax load by $352 million, $196 million, and $44 million, respectively. The Disney stock-option deduction alone cost the U.S. Treasury about $160 million that year.

Capital Hill lawmakers huff and puff endlessly about the unfairness of the tax system, and they promise that corrective action is just around the corner. In fact, they spend a great deal of time conniving to lower taxes that fall on a tiny minority—the wealthy—and dreaming up new loopholes for corporations. Restoring progressivity to the tax system and helping out the middle class are tasks that Congress never manages to get around to.

It is not hard to see why. Corporations and the rich pay the bills for Members of Congress, and lawmakers with oversight of the tax system always receive special attention from the deep-pocket crowd. Contributions to members of the tax-writing House Ways and Means Committee grew from a total of $4.4 million during the 1977–78 election cycle to nearly $16.7 million in 1995–96.

Big-name tax lobbyists win further favor for their corporate clients by snuggling up to Members of Congress during junkets, campaign fund-raisers, and social affairs. Washington superlobbyist J. D. (Jerry Don) Williams—whose biggest coup came in 1982, when he is said to have saved his client Cigna Corporation and the insurance industry $2.3 billion—regularly invites lawmakers to hunt at the duck blind he owns on Maryland's Eastern Shore. Williams, the chairman of the Washington firm of Williams & Jensen, has a client list longer than you can shake a stick at: American Home Products Corporation; American Savings Bank; Anschutz Corporation; Bass Enterprises Production Company; the Church Alliance; Cigna Corporation; Continental Airlines Holding, Inc.; Everglades Trust; Fieldale Farms Corporation; Foster Farms, Inc.; Hudson Foods; Keystone, Inc.; Estee Lauder, Inc.; Norfolk Southern Corporation; Oklahoma Gas and Electric Company; Owens-Illinois, Inc.; Perdue Farms, Inc.; Pharmaceutical Research and Manufacturers of America; Pilgrim's Pride Corporation; the Pittston Company; Southern Pacific Transportation Company; Southwest Airlines; Terranext, Inc.; Texaco, Inc.; Texas Pacific Group; TTX Company; Turner Broadcasting System, Inc.; Tyson Foods, Inc. And that is not even counting the clients the firm's thirty or so other lobbyists prowl the halls of Congress for.

But the most revealing glimpse into the U.S. tax system may come to us courtesy of the Packwood diaries, the treasure left to the public by Republican Bob Packwood of Oregon, the chairman of the Senate Finance Committee, who was forced to resign from the Senate in 1995 in the wake of charges that he had sexually harassed female aides, colleagues, and reporters. As recorded in his fatal diary entries, Packwood was thrown into a panic when his wife Georgie—fed up with the Senator's philandering and drinking—asked for a divorce. To lighten the burden of alimony payments—which he feared would be large because Georgie was unemployed—Packwood set out to show his wife had marketable skills by finding her a high-paying job.

That Georgie had few marketable skills proved to be only a minor obstacle. To accomplish this, Packwood simply "hit up," as he put it in his diary, lobbyists and business executives who owed him favors for the good deeds he had performed, at their behest, from the Finance Committee. In an interview with the Center, Packwood acknowledged approaching several targets, including Steven Saunders, a Washington lobbyist for Mitsubishi Electric Corporation. Packwood wrote in his diary that when he asked if Saunders could put Georgie on a $7,500-a-year retainer, the lobbyist replied, "Consider it done." Just days later, at a Finance Committee hearing, Packwood sharply questioned an American executive about Japanese patent practices. He asked virtually the same questions that Saunders had submitted to a committee aide.

Packwood next turned to one of his former fund-raisers, businessman Timothy Lee, who offered to set Georgie up as an antiques dealer. Lee approached several people to finance the business, including William Furman, an Oregon businessman who had cosponsored fund-raisers for the Senator. Packwood was pleased—though not surprised—by the offer, writing in his diary that Furman was "eternally appreciative to me" as a result of a tax break Packwood had inserted in the 1986 Tax Reform Act. "He says that but for what I did for him in '86 . . . he'd be out of business. Now he's prosperous beyond imagination." Furman admits that he talked to Lee about the proposal but insists that Lee never followed up.

Packwood also called on Ron Crawford, a lobbyist for Shell Oil Company, General Motors Corporation, and the American Iron and Steel Institute. Packwood, who had once employed the lobbyist's wife as an aide, had frequently done favors for Crawford's clients. As Packwood gratefully remarked in his diary about Crawford's financial support for his campaigns, "the advantage Ron brings me is that much of his income is dependent upon his relationship with me."

And so Crawford too readily agreed to help out when Packwood came calling. "He'll put up $7,500 a year for Georgie," the Senator reported in his diary. "That's three out of three."

Packwood confided to his diaries that he regarded the U.S. Senate, where he served for twenty-seven years, as but a stepping-stone to a more lucrative career as an influence peddler. Perhaps someday, he mused, "I can become a lobbyist at five or six or four hundred thousand" dollars a year. Less than two years after he resigned in disgrace, Packwood started his own lobbying firm, Sunrise Research Corporation. His first big job: representing wealthy taxpayers seeking a reduction in the inheritance tax.

14

||||| ● |||||

El Dorado on the Potomac

E̲VERY MONTH E̲LLEN H̲EISNER, A WORKING MOTHER OF TWO TEENAGE girls in Watertown, South Dakota, writes a check for $26.65 to Tele-Communications, Inc., a cable television company based in Englewood, Colorado. She is not happy about what she gets for her money or the fact that the company keeps raising its rates. But she feels as if she does not have much of a choice.

In fact, she does not. As is the rule in thousands of communities from coast to coast, a single company—in this case TCI, the nation's largest cable company—owns the local franchise. There is no competition.

Heisner could give up the Lifetime channel and the animal shows she likes so much, tell the kids there will be no more MTV, and stick to watching the local network affiliates. Or could she? In Watertown, as in much of South Dakota, broadcast television reception is poor. "Without [cable]," Heisner told the Center, "we get maybe two channels."

Or Heisner could take the plunge and switch from cable to satellite TV. But after buying or leasing a satellite dish, she would still have to pay a monthly subscription fee. The satellite service Primestar, for example, would charge her $149 to install a dish and $35 a month for a basic set of seventy-five channels. And because TCI is a part owner of Primestar, a portion of Heisner's checks would still end up in Colorado. Plus, she would be missing the local broadcast stations, which satellite services do not carry.

What Heisner does not know is that, regardless of whether she chooses cable or satellite, some of her money ends up getting recirculated in the form of political contributions to Capitol Hill lawmakers, including Republican Senator Larry Pressler of South Dakota. Over an eight-day period in the summer of 1996, TCI gave $15,000 to Pressler, who was then in charge of the most sweeping rewrite of the nation's telecommunications laws in sixty years. The company's executives, in fact, took a personal interest in filling Pressler's political war chest. In May 1995, for example, Peter Barton, the president

Fifty-four of the Senators who voted in favor of the telecommunications overhaul in 1995 had supported regulating cable just three years earlier. Money apparently got the job done.

and chief executive officer of Liberty Media Corporation, a TCI subsidiary, arranged a fund-raiser for Pressler when he was passing through Denver.

Unlike Heisner, TCI had every reason to be happy with what it got in exchange for its checks.

Back in 1992, Pressler had slammed TCI by name during a debate on the Senate floor and had gone on to vote for regulating cable rates. "The point is wherever they want to control, they can exercise their monopoly power," Pressler had told his colleagues. "They can, and they do."

But things changed in a big way on November 8, 1994, when the Republican Party won control of both chambers of Congress. Pressler became the chairman of the Senate Commerce, Science, and Transportation Committee (and, later, of its Subcommittee on Communications). Then, in the name of deregulation, Pressler ordered up and pushed through legislation that did exactly what TCI wanted. The Telecommunications Act of 1996 reversed the popular Cable Television Consumer Protection and Competition Act of 1992 that had brought more than $3 billion in savings to cable subscribers nationwide.

Pressler was not the only Senator to flip-flop on the issue of cable-TV rates. Fifty-four of the Senators who voted in favor of the telecommunications overhaul in 1995 had supported regulating cable just three years earlier. Money apparently got the job done: The cable-TV industry gave at least $15.9 million in political contributions to congressional candidates from 1987 to 1996. The cable industry did not restrict its generosity to campaign contributions, however. The National Cable Television Association doled out nearly $350,000 in speaking fees to Members of Congress from 1986 to 1996. The trade association had fifty-seven lobbyists on its payroll, both in-house and from eleven outside firms, and it underwrote twenty-six trips for Members of Congress and their staffers in 1996 alone. Half of those were to the association's annual convention in Los Angeles, where several staffers from the House and Senate Commerce Committees were invited to speak.

"The cable industry actually got more than what it wanted," Jeffrey Hopps, a lobbyist who represents educational and public-access stations, told the Center. "There was no quid pro quo for what the industry got. It did not have to live up to higher standards in exchange for the regulation rollback."

Soon after the new law took effect in 1996, cable companies across the nation took advantage of their newfound freedom to jack up rates. TCI raised its rates by an average of 13 percent, and in some cases as high as 28 percent, according to the trade publication *Multichannel News*. The cable industry as a whole raised rates by an average of 8.5 percent over an eleven-month period.

When asked what she thought of TCI's contributions to Pressler, Ellen Heisner hesitated for a moment before saying, "That's kind of like buying votes."

The communications industry has a stake in what you do with nearly every waking moment. A conglomerate owns the station to which your clock radio is set. Another—or maybe the same one—owns the newspaper you read on the bus to work. When you make a phone call at your office, that is money for a communications mogul somewhere, and if it is a conference call, that is even more. Ditto when you log on to the Internet to read your e-mail, when your boss pages you at a meeting, or when you use a cellular phone on the street. If you buy a greeting card for your mother, a video for your kids, or a magazine to read at the beach—that is money, too. Going to the movies or turning on cable to catch the latest stock quotes? That is right—more money for the communications industry.

But if the industry has a special interest in what you do all day, it has an even bigger one in what Members of Congress do. It is Congress, after all, that sets the rules that the complex communications industry runs by. In order to get to you, the industry must get to Congress first. And get to Congress it does. Between the phone companies and Hollywood, Microsoft and news factories, there is plenty to keep Members of Congress plugged in.

At the Motion Picture Association of America (MPAA), Jack Valenti, a lobbying fixture in the nation's capital, presides over thirty-two lobbyists—some on the association's staff, others for hire. When the movie *Rob Roy* came out, lawmakers and top Administration officials were among the first to see Liam Neeson in a kilt at the MPAA's plush—and private—seventy-seat theater. Private screenings are a regular perk the association offers to Members of Congress. The Cellular Telecommunications Industry Association flew twenty lawmakers and congressional aides to San Francisco and Dallas in 1996 and 1997 to discuss congressional views on telecommunications policy. Miami, Key Biscayne, and Atlanta were the locales of choice for the U.S. Telephone Association to discuss weighty matters affecting the regional "Baby Bells."

The industry usually gets its way, too. Consider the clout of ABC, CBS, and NBC. The broadcast networks cashed in big when, in 1997, Congress gave them their government-owned spectrum for the next generation of technology: digital TV. Broadcasters get the spectrum free of charge, courtesy of the taxpayers—and they do not even have to give back their old "analog" spectrum. From 1987 to 1996, broadcasters poured more than $14 million into congressional campaigns, and they paid for more than sixty trips by Members of Congress and their staff.

In 1996 and 1997, the National Association of Broadcasters alone paid for at least twenty-one trips for lawmakers and congressional aides, including an annual convention in Las Vegas.

There, attendees—such as Catherine Reid, the senior counsel of the House Commerce Committee, chaired by Republican Thomas Bliley of Virginia—"participate[d] on a panel regarding issues related to communications policies, including spectrum management issues." One legislative assistant, Tamara Somerville, even took part in a panel discussion on campaign finance reform. Her boss, Senator Mitch McConnell, a Republican from Kentucky, is a longtime foe of campaign finance rules.

Overall, communications interests gave more than $60.6 million in campaign contributions to congressional candidates from 1987 to 1996. They spent more than $1.5 million on honoraria for Members of Congress and paid for 167 trips by Members and their staffs.

Of course, many lawmakers have a selfish reason to cater to communications interests: They own big blocks of stock in the companies. Democratic Senator John Kerry of Massachusetts, Republican Senator Judd Gregg of New Hampshire, and Republican Representative Porter Goss of Florida are among the nine Members of Congress who have had a $50,000 or larger stake in Motorola, Inc., since 1991. Democratic Representative Norman Sisisky of Virginia and Republican Representative Martin Hoke of Ohio are among six Members who have owned $50,000 or more in Walt Disney Company; Democratic Senator Bob Graham of Florida and Republican Representative Rodney Frelinghuysen of New Jersey are among eight who have that large a stake in Microsoft Corporation; Democratic Representative Nita Lowey of New York and Republican Senator John Warner of Virginia have owned $50,000 or more in Bell Atlantic Corporation. Former Democratic Senator Claiborne Pell of Rhode Island and Democratic Representative W. G. Hefner of North Carolina are among four with $50,000 or more in Time Warner, Inc. Bliley, who okayed more trips sponsored by telecommunications companies than any other lawmaker, moved his investments into a blind trust in 1995 only

The broadcast networks cashed in big when, in 1997, Congress gave them their government-owned spectrum for the next generation of technology: digital TV. Broadcasters get the spectrum free of charge, courtesy of the taxpayers.

Many lawmakers have a selfish reason to cater to communications interests: They own big blocks of stock in the companies.

after he had been criticized for chairing the most important committee overseeing telecommunications issues while he also held stocks in such companies as GTE Corporation, a telephone company. Overall, forty-two Members of Congress have owned stock in Motorola; eighty-one in AT&T; forty in US West Communications, Inc.; thirty in Bell Atlantic; thirty-six in Walt Disney; twenty-nine in Microsoft; and sixteen in Time Warner, to name some of the companies.

Little wonder, then, that the massive law that Congress passed in 1996 was a deregulatory dream come true for the $500 billion telecommunications industry. Pressler and other Capitol Hill lawmakers who had pushed for the law pledged that it would bring widespread economic benefits—including huge savings to consumers—by allowing the cable-television and long-distance and local telephone companies to compete head-to-head.

But John McCain, a Republican from Arizona who in 1997 succeeded Pressler as the chairman of the Senate Commerce, Science, and Transportation Committee, brands the Telecommunications Act a failure and ridicules those who contend that it is working. "To believe that," he told reporters at a press briefing in November 1997, "you have to believe that the way to lower rates is to raise them, the way to achieve competition is through consolidation, and the way to achieve deregulation is through overregulation."

More than $100 billion in mergers swept through Wall Street in the first year after Congress passed the new law and made the universe of telecommunications companies look like the Big Bang in reverse. Buyouts of radio companies alone went from $69 million in 1991 to $13.4 billion in 1996.

Time Warner, Inc. bought Turner Broadcasting System, Inc., adding CNN to an empire that already encompassed HBO, *People* magazine, the Book-of-the-Month Club, and dozens of news and entertainment properties. The largest radio network nationwide, Westinghouse Electric Corporation/CBS, Inc., gobbled up the second largest, Infinity Broadcasting Corporation. News Corp swallowed New World Communications Group; Bell Atlantic Corporation merged with Nynex Corporation; and U.S. West, Inc. acquired Continental Cablevision, Inc.

Mark Crispin Miller, a professor of film and media studies at Johns Hopkins University, told the Center, "In the name of competition, Congress and its corporate backers have done everything to suppress competition, to make competition a thing of the past."

They kept calling, writing, or dropping by, day after day after day, like the most annoyingly persistent suitors. "It was constant," a congressional aide told the Center. "There would be six or seven different lobbying visits a day."

It was 1995, and the fight between the "Baby Bells" and the long-distance telephone companies had erupted into a full-blown war. And just like a war, the conflagration had drawn in combatants who were not originally involved. It was no longer just a telephone fight. Cable, broadcasting, motion-picture, publishing, newspaper, even security-alarm companies had all jumped into the lobbying fray. They had millions to spend, and they all wanted something from Congress.

This was the best of all possible news for Washington lobbyists, and the telecommunications bill was soon dubbed a "full-employment bill" for lobbyists. Companies in the telecommunications industry hired more than 800 lobbyists to work Capitol Hill for them, according to the Center's analysis of lobbying disclosure forms. The revolving door seemed to spin out of control.

Former Democratic Representative Tom Downey of New York, a close friend of Vice President Albert Gore, Jr., signed up Time Warner as a client. Former Republican Representative Thomas Tauke of Iowa, who had sponsored several bills favoring local telephone companies while in Congress, was already on Nynex's payroll. Former Republican Senator Howard Baker, Jr., of Tennessee took the job of directing the Competitive Long Distance Coalition, a group of long-distance telephone companies. Former

Democratic Representative Dennis Eckart of Ohio signed on as a lobbyist for TCI and SBC Communications, Inc., among others. Former Republican Representative Vin Weber of Minnesota signed up AT&T. Former Republican Senator Paul Laxalt of Nevada signed up SBC Communications and the Competitive Long Distance Coalition. Roy Neel, a longtime aide to Gore, left the White House in 1995 to direct the U.S. Telephone Association, which represents local phone companies. Peter Knight, another former Gore aide who had been a key fund-raiser for the 1996 Clinton-Gore campaign, signed up Bell Atlantic and Pacific Telesis Group.

"Members of Congress don't think there are any good guys or bad guys in this," Neel told a reporter for *The New York Times*. "This is not about right or wrong—it's ultimately about money." Neel might just as well have been talking about his own bank account. As a White House aide, he made $125,000 a year. In his first year at the U.S. Telephone Association, Neel's salary and benefits package came to $566,572. (Neel declined the Center's request for an interview.)

For these companies, an unintelligible sentence or paragraph inserted in the telecommunications bill could be worth millions of dollars. Consider this one: "Paragraph (1) does not prohibit or limit the provision, directly or through an affiliate, of alarm monitoring services by a Bell operating company that was engaged in providing alarm monitoring services as of November 30, 1995, directly or through an affiliate."

The sentence represents the handiwork of the lobbying team for a single company: Ameritech Corporation, the Chicago-based "Baby Bell." Congress allowed Ameritech to keep its alarm business, which generated $250 million in revenues in 1994, while all the other regional Bell operating companies had to wait until 2001 to get into the security business. Ameritech's PAC and the company's top executives gave $2 million to congressional candidates from 1987 to 1996. It also gave $100,000 to underwrite the cost of the 1996 Democratic National Convention.

Special-interest deals survived even when exposed to the supposedly powerful disinfectant of sunlight. Days before the Senate first voted on the telecommunications legislation in June 1995, a letter from Timothy Boggs, a lobbyist for Time Warner, which owns HBO, started circulating on the House floor.

"Dear Chairman Pressler," Boggs's letter began. "As you requested . . . Home Box Office has reached an agreement with the National Cable Television Cooperative, Inc., for HBO programming. As discussed with you and your staff, this agreement is entirely contingent on the removal of the program access provisions at Section 204(b) of S. 652, prior to Senate action on the legislation."

Although no other letters surfaced, *Broadcasting & Cable* magazine reported that Viacom had struck a similar deal with Pressler. Just what was it about Section 204(b) that Time Warner and Viacom hated so much? That section of the bill would have prohibited them from offering volume discounts on their channels to large cable-system operators. Richard Cutler, the president of Satellite Cable Services, Inc., a small cable operator in South Dakota, had complained that large companies forced small ones to pay prohibitive amounts for these channels, making it difficult for them to give their customers what they wanted. "A typical small-system operator pays fifty-four percent more per subscriber than the largest cable companies pay for identical programming," Cutler told Pressler's committee.

As soon as the letter was exposed to public scrutiny, Pressler backed away from it, denying that he had cut a deal with Boggs. "Nothing I said during our short meeting could be construed as suggesting some sort of quid pro quo, which would be wrong, if not illegal," Pressler wrote in a letter to Boggs. In the same letter, however, Pressler admitted that he had met with Boggs and other Time Warner executives and suggested that they try to strike a deal with Cutler.

Time Warner executives had given Pressler more than $39,000 in contributions in the 1995–96 election cycle alone—$27,500 of it on a single day in March 1995, when the company held a fund-raiser for him. Boggs himself had given Pressler the maximum an individual is allowed under federal law, $2,000 ($1,000 each for the primary and general elections).

Despite the very public embarrassment, Time Warner and Viacom got exactly what they wanted. On June 15, 1995, the

> The telecommunications bill was dubbed a "full-employment bill" for lobbyists. Companies in the telecommunications industry hired more than 800 lobbyists to work Capitol Hill for them.

Senate voted fifty-nine to thirty-nine to strike the volume-discount provision from the bill.

They were shaping legislation affecting a $500 billion industry that commands a sizable chunk of every American household's budget, but for the hundreds of lobbyists who earned a livelihood from it, the telecommunications debate was like an elaborate game of strategy rather than one of substance. They had to know how to court a Senator, how to "spin" the news media, how to convert polling data into television advertisements. They had to know how to raise campaign money, how to distribute it, who was friends with whom, and how to use those relationships to advantage. They had to know how a law was made.

Nobody followed the rules. During the summer of 1995, the regional Bell operating companies got the House leadership to insert a series of changes in the legislation after the House Commerce Committee had already voted on it. The bill that went to the House floor for a vote in August looked little like what the committee had approved.

John Bryant, a Democrat from Texas, was furious. "Mr. Chairman, the impact is that the Bell companies could enter long distance without facing real local competition," he railed before his colleagues on the House floor. "This is complicated, it is arcane, it is tedious, but it is the work of this committee, and, unfortunately, the work of this committee has been thrown out." In its place, he concluded, was the work of lobbyists in the back room.

The House passed the bill anyway, 305 to 117, on August 4, 1995. That fall the long-distance companies rallied with a massive lobbying blitz. MCI paid for a massive television advertising campaign featuring an old woman confronted by Washington bureaucrats on her front lawn.

"We're from Washington—we're here to fix your phone," they tell the woman.

"But it's not broken," she replies.

The long-distance companies also worked all their inside contacts, getting help from Bliley, who has an AT&T facility in his district.

In the end, the long-distance companies won concessions, just as their foes, the "Baby Bells," had—with the hard work of "lobbyists in the back room."

"I would like to say that Members carefully weighed [the issues] and decided on good policy, but my tongue would be stuck inside of my cheek," Brian Moir, a lobbyist for the International Communications Association, which represents 500 large corporate users of telecommunications equipment and services, told the Center.

On December 21, 1995, the day after the lawmakers struck a deal on the telecommunications bill, AT&T gave $190,000 in "soft money" to the Democratic National Committee (DNC), and its PAC distributed $166,000 to congressional candidates. On December 29, MCI gave $100,000 in "soft money" to the DNC and $20,000 in "soft money" to the National Republican Congressional Committee.

"The Members must have had fund-raisers," Tom Berkelman, an AT&T lobbyist, told the Center when asked why his company had distributed so much money in December 1995. In any case, he added, money did not really affect the debate. "There was so much on all sides, they kind of canceled each other out."

There is nothing extraordinary about the two rows of chairs. With their rigid wooden backs, they are not even particularly comfortable. But if you were a Member of Congress, you would leap at the opportunity to sit in one of them.

The chairs are in the House Commerce Committee's hearing room in the Rayburn Office Building. A seat there is worth tens of thousands of dollars of cold, hard campaign cash.

"Everybody jumped for the Telecommunications Subcommittee first," Peter Kostmayer, a former Democratic Representative from Pennsylvania, told the Center for Responsive Politics in 1994. "There was a Member sitting next to me, and every time another Member bid for that subcommittee, he went, 'Ding!'—as if a cash register was going off."

Pressler, facing a tough reelection fight in 1996, needed campaign money badly. So did Republican Jack Fields of Texas, the chairman of the House Commerce Subcommittee on Telecommunications and Finance.

Pressler had never been known for his fund-raising prowess. In fact, he had once railed against PACs and the money game in an op-ed piece. As soon as he rose to the chairmanship of the committee, though, Pressler started shaking the money tree. In early 1995, he went on a cross-country fund-raising trip. Time Warner hosted an event at the '21' Club in New York City, News Corp sponsored another one, and the Motion Picture Association of America rolled out the green carpet for Pressler in Hollywood.

By November 1996, Pressler had collected $352,625 from the telecommunications industry. He lost by just 9,087 votes to Democratic challenger Tim Johnson, who had been critical of Pressler's handling of telecommunications issues.

Fields needed cash, too, but for a different reason: He was carrying a $670,000 debt from a failed Senate campaign. He wasted little time in placing a collect call to the telecommunications industry. Just a few months after he had taken over the chairmanship of the Subcommittee on Telecommunications and Finance, Fields hosted a $625-a-plate fund-raising dinner at the Grand Hyatt in Washington. The event was "crawling with telecommunications lobbyists," according to an account in an industry trade publication.

An analysis of Fields's campaign-finance reports shows that he collected more than $80,000 that week alone, most of it from executives of—and lobbyists for—such companies as Nynex, Southwestern Bell Telephone Company, Time Warner, and U.S. Long Distance Corporation.

By December 1995, when Congress had nearly completed its work on the telecommunications legislation, Fields had had ample time to pay off his campaign debts. It was then that he announced his intention to retire.

Pressler and Fields still work on Capitol Hill, but not as Members of Congress. Both started their own lobbying firms. "I have formed the Twenty First Century Group," Fields wrote in a mailing to prospective clients, "a company which will focus on issues before the Commerce Committee, particularly in the areas of telecommunications."

In 1995, as the telecommunications debate raged red-hot on Capitol Hill, the average American spent $1,800 on televisions, radios, sound equipment, videos, computers, and on-line services. That is more than the average amount spent on gasoline ($1,005) or electricity ($870).

The decisions that Capitol Hill lawmakers were making would affect how much Americans would pay in the future for cable and phone service. Yet if they relied on television and the newspapers to tell them what was going on, they were likely to find reports that portrayed the debate as a fight between corporate titans rather than one that affected people's pocketbooks.

One evening in late January 1995, as the new Republican Congress was just starting its work, some thirty telecommunications-industry CEOs dined with Newt Gingrich and Republican members of the House Commerce Committee. The dinner, sponsored by the Heritage Foundation, a conservative think tank, followed two days of closed-door meetings between the CEOs and lawmakers.

All the major networks were represented—ABC, CBS, NBC, Fox. But their employees in the newsrooms were not. They were not invited. Still, attendees told Mike Mills, a reporter for *The Washington Post,* that Gingrich had taken the opportunity to bash the news media. Gingrich had been taking lots of heat for his $4.5 million book deal with Rupert Murdoch. Gingrich eventually declined the advance but made a deal to accept royalties. Gerald Levin, Time Warner's chairman and chief executive officer, reportedly asked Gingrich what media companies could do to make coverage more "fair."

Broadcasters had reason to curry favor on Capitol Hill. They are dependent on government in numerous ways: It is the government that grants broadcast licenses. It is the government that owns the spectrum they use to broadcast their signals. It is the government that can decide whether to ban certain types of advertising, such as liquor or tobacco.

Furthermore, the large corporations that own broadcasting networks in the age of the mega-merger have interests before Congress that go far beyond broadcasting. Westinghouse, which owns CBS, also generates nuclear power and manufactures air conditioners. General Electric, which owns NBC, has been known for decades as an appliance manufacturer.

The built-in conflict did not escape the notice of everyone in the broadcast media. In a June 1995 show on the debate, Ted Koppel, the host of ABC News's *Nightline,* remarked, "Because I've seen so little coverage of this on television, it suggests to me that if the interest of one of these very powerful groups is even threatened, the people who are not going to be covering it are the people on television, precisely because they're working for the very folks who are in charge here."

Broadcasters did a particularly poor job of covering the parts of the telecommunications debate worth the most to them. "They get their airwaves for free," Gene Kimmelman, a lobbyist for Consumers Union of the United States, remarked on a radio show in December 1995. "They don't pay anything. There was a proposal here to start making them pay. Not one television station I know of has covered that issue."

In October 1995, Ted Turner's CNN refused to air the "old lady" advertisements paid for by long-distance companies that were critical of the telecommunications bill. CNN officials said that airing the advertisements would produce a conflict of interest. Turner Broadcasting supported the bill, and Ted Turner had been an active force on Capitol Hill, lobbying to reduce limits on how many stations a broadcasting company can own.

Once the new telecommunications law was in place, Turner Broadcasting merged with Time Warner in a deal worth $7.5 billion. It is virtually impossible for an American to get through a single day without exposure to some part of that empire, whether it is a glance through *People* magazine, going to the theater for the latest *Batman* movie, or hearing a Hootie and the Blowfish song on the radio. Now called Time Warner Turner, the company owns roller coasters, cookbooks, Daffy Duck, CNN, and the Book-of-the-Month Club.

Time Warner even has joint ventures with TCI, the largest cable provider in the country. That is the same company that Ellen Heisner and other residents of Watertown, South Dakota, must use for cable television. And just like TCI, Time Warner has raised its cable rates around the country.

But the residents of Watertown do not have the access to Capitol Hill lawmakers that Turner and other telecommunications-industry executives have. The day after Clinton signed the new law Turner was mingling with Gingrich; then-Senator Sam Nunn, a Democrat from Georgia; and Democrat Edward Markey of Massachusetts, a member of the House Commerce Committee. The occasion was his network's premiere of a made-for-TV Civil War epic.

"Glad we got the bill through," Turner told a journalist covering the premiere.

15

||||||●|||||

Future Shock

Rose Holzsager is eighty-six years old. She is petite, with white pixie hair, and her speech is brisk and energetic. She lives in a retirement community in Silver Spring, Maryland, and on a clear day she can see the Washington Monument from her balcony. "Social Security isn't everything," she said. "I invested well when I was working. But Social Security still means a lot."

Holzsager first went to work in 1923, when she was twelve years old. "My father took sick and couldn't work," she explained. Because there was no Social Security—which provides disability protection—back then, Holzsager and her older sisters were forced to quit school and take jobs to support the family. "My school had a morning session and afternoon session," she remembered. She skipped the afternoon sessions to work for $12 a week. Eventually, she managed an office where she worked as an accountant and a paralegal secretary. "They used to call me the not-so-silent partner."

Holzsager has suffered health problems. She has had a heart attack, a mastectomy, and knee-replacement surgery, and her hands are crippled by rheumatoid arthritis. Yet she is an essential member of her community: She is the president of her seniors group, chairs her ladies' club, and keeps the cash at bingo games. On her coffee table is displayed a large orange button. One word is printed across the front: "Medicare." "I worry about it," Holzsager told the Center for Public Integrity.

Valeri Vanourek lives halfway across the country from Rose Holzsager. She is twenty-six years old and works in the marketing department of Sotheby's auction house in Chicago. Just before she turned twenty-five, she decided to set up a 401(k) retirement account for herself. "It's a necessary evil," she said of the money that she is setting aside. "Of course I miss the money, but it's something that you just have to do."

Vanourek is still paying back her student loans. She does not own a car. She would like to save for a home but has not been able to. The subject of Social Security raises her ire. "I just think it's mismanaged," she told the Center. "I don't think there's going to be anything left for me." She looks at her paycheck stub, at the line showing the deductions made for the Federal Insurance Contributions Act, or FICA, which finances the Social Security system. "If I could get that back right now, I'd have about a month's extra salary. Why don't they just take that money and put it somewhere else and don't touch it for forty years until I need it?"

Valeri Vanourek and Rose Holzsager have never met, but thanks to the Social Security system, their lives are inextricably linked. Most of the FICA taxes that Vanourek and other workers have deducted from their earnings go to pay the benefits of retirees like Holzsager. It was not easy for Holzsager to save for her retirement, through the Great Depression, a World War, and the Cold War, but she managed. Vanourek knows it will not be easy to save for her own retirement in an age of high taxes and economic uncertainty, but she thinks she will manage, too.

Congress, by contrast, has not managed to set aside any money for anyone's retirement. It has not even bothered to try.

Since 1980, the tax that pays for all of the benefits paid out under the various Social Security programs has been increased seven times. Each time Congress promised that the extra money raised would be used to keep the Social Security system solvent and to provide for benefits to future generations. Each time Congress has instead used the money to pay for current spending.

In the same period that Congress was repeatedly raising FICA, it was slashing federal income taxes for the wealthy and for corporations, putting more and more of the burden of paying for government programs on the middle class.

The result: a three-decade-long string of budget deficits, a smoke-and-mirrors Social Security system, and an uncertain future for all Americans.

Every year since 1984, the retirement portion of FICA has brought in more money than was paid out in benefits. In 1987, for example, Congress collected an extra $20.7 billion in payroll taxes. In 1989 it collected an extra $51.4 billion, in 1991 an extra $52 billion, in 1993 an extra $49.4 billion, and in 1995 an extra $31.6 billion. This money is sometimes referred to as the "trust fund" of Social Security.

It might shock most Americans to know that all of this money has been spent. Those glowing news accounts about Congress and President Clinton balancing the budget, about the shrinking federal deficit, often ignore a simple fact: According to the best estimate of Congress and the White House, the federal budget is being balanced in part with an extra $422.5 billion taken from Social Security over the course of the five-year budget-balancing plan passed in 1997.

In return for that $422.5 billion, Congress has given you its own brand of IOU—a promise that when you need that money for your retirement, lawmakers will have no choice but to raise taxes.

> **Every year since 1984, the retirement portion of the payroll tax has brought in more money than was paid out in benefits. It might shock most Americans to know that all of this money has been spent.**

Every year the House Ways and Means Committee publishes something called the *Green Book,* which provides background material and statistical data on the programs over which the committee has jurisdiction. Consider these passages from the *1996 Green Book:*

- "When more Social Security taxes are received than are spent, the money does not sit idle in the Treasury, but is used to finance other operations of the government. The surplus is then reflected in a higher balance of securities being posted to the trust funds. Simply put, these balances, like those of a bank account, represent a promise that, if needed to pay Social Security benefits, the government will obtain resources in the future equal to the value of the securities."

- "The building up of federal securities in a federal trust fund—like that of Social Security—is not a means in and of itself for the government to accumulate assets. It certainly has established claims against the government for the Social Security system, but the Social Security system is part of the government. Those claims are not resources the government has at its disposal to pay future Social Security benefits."

In other words, all of the payroll taxes of young workers like Valeri Vanourek are being spent as soon as they are collected. Consequently, raising her payroll taxes now would not make any more money available for her retirement. By the same token, cutting the benefits of older Americans like Rose Holzsager would only mean that Congress would have even more money to spend on other programs.

Of course, the house of cards remains standing as long as the government takes in more in Social Security taxes than it spends in benefits. As things now stand, that will be the case for another fourteen years. Then, in 2012, one year into the retirements of the Baby Boomers, benefits paid out will start to exceed taxes coming in, according to the Trustees of Social Security and Medicare. The retirement of the Baby Boom generation will nearly double the number of retirees receiving Social Security benefits, yet the number of workers paying for those benefits will increase by only 16 percent. By 2019, Congress—which, according to the 1996 Green Book, has no "resources . . . at its disposal to pay future Social Security benefits"—will have to "obtain resources . . . equal to the value of the securities." And at that point, where will the $2.9 trillion in "resources" come from?

That is what scares young workers like Valeri Vanourek.

Vanourek's annual FICA taxes already equal about a month's worth of take-home pay. Each week the government takes 7.65 percent of her earnings just for Social Security and Medicare, and Valeri's employer must send an equal amount to the federal government. Compare that with the average rate that Rose Holz-sager paid over her working years. From 1937 to 1949, the tax was 1 percent of income. Through the 1950s, it averaged less than 2 percent; through the 1960s, 3.8 percent; and through the 1970s, 5.7 percent. History tells us that FICA taxes have only one way to go: up.

And benefits, relative to those taxes paid, have only one way to go: down.

A typical wage earner who retired in 1980—around the time Rose became eligible for retirement—got back everything she and her employer had paid in FICA taxes during her lifetime in just under four years. People who retired in 1996 will, on average, have to wait twenty-one years. By 2005 the break-even point will have stretched to thirty years, and by 2015 to more than thirty-four years. As for Valeri Vanourek, due to retire in 2037, there is little point in estimating how many years she will have to wait for her benefits. Under current law, Social Security will be able to pay only about three-fourths of the benefits of those retiring after 2031.

Congress recognizes as much. The *1996 Green Book* states that, "although Social Security tax rates and benefit formulas are set by law, they are not immutable. . . . Congress has modified taxes and benefits many times since the beginning of the program . . . There is little doubt they eventually will be altered, as it is projected that demographic phenomena will cause the program's projected outgo to outstrip its resources significantly in thirty-three years. Higher taxes or benefit cuts would be necessary, at that point or before. . . ."

> The retirement of the Baby Boom generation will nearly double the number of retirees receiving Social Security benefits, yet the number of workers paying for those benefits will increase by only 16 percent.

Someday, in other words, Congress will have to change the system. It will either cut benefits or raise taxes, or perhaps both. Congress simply will not honor the promises it has made to workers like Valeri Vanourek, who pay into the system for their entire working lives. In the meantime, Congress seems to prefer changing the subject.

*　　*　　*

"I think it is a nutty idea," then-Vice President George Bush said on October 28, 1987, as he stood on a Houston stage with Robert Dole, Jack Kemp, Alexander Haig, Pat Robertson, and Pierre (Pete) du Pont. The scene was the first debate of the presidential primary campaign, where the candidates had gathered to debate the issues. "It may be a new idea," Bush went on, "but it's a dumb one, too."

Bush was ridiculing a proposal that du Pont had just aired for the first time in a national forum. Like many a dark horse in a presidential primary, du Pont was betting that the audacity of his idea might garner him attention and set him apart from the rest of the field. He had proposed eliminating farm subsidies in one fell swoop and slowing down the historic arms agreements with the Soviet Union that had led to the end of the Cold War. But his biggest attention-grabber concerned a plan to change Social Security.

"Frankly, Pete," Jack Kemp said with some derision, "we don't know exactly which libertarian or market-oriented solution you're going to come up with next."

The idea du Pont put forth that evening was the privatization of the Social Security system: to invest FICA taxes in the stock market. Less than ten years later, a desperate gambit by a long shot in a presidential primary had become the subject of thousands of newspaper, magazine, and television news stories; two versions of it were formally proposed to the Trustees of Social Security by a commission appointed by Health and Human Services Secretary Donna Shalala; it was lavishly praised by experts testifying before congressional committees; and bills were introduced to begin changing the system. In short, the nutty idea had become respectable.

Just ask Jack Kemp. Speaking in 1996 at a conference sponsored by the Investment Company Institute, the lobbying arm of the mutual-fund industry, Kemp supported funneling the Social Security taxes of Americans into the stock market. "If everybody in America owned stocks and bonds and mutual funds," he said, "we'd be a nation of millionaires."

In Washington, the wisdom of any proposal is directly proportional to the amount of money behind it. Make no mistake:

Privatizing Social Security *would* create lots of millionaires. But they would be those who trade stocks and bonds and mutual funds for a living—not average Americans. Privatization schemes would change Social Security from a defined benefit plan to a defined contribution plan. In a defined benefit plan, participants are guaranteed a monthly benefit based on their lifetime earnings. In a defined contribution plan, the ultimate benefit is unknown and participants bear all the risk.

The retirement system that Members of Congress have given themselves and other federal employees is a defined benefit plan—the payments are guaranteed. According to the General Accounting Office, it is the seventh-largest mandatory spending program in the federal budget. In 1996, federal retirees and their dependents (there are 2.3 million of them) received $40 billion in benefits. Congress indexed its own benefits for inflation way back in 1962 (the average congressional pension is $47,000 and rising); it did not bother to adjust Social Security benefits for inflation until 1975. When Democrat Thomas Foley, the former Speaker of the House, left office in 1995, he began collecting a pension of $124,000 a year. The average retiree collected $10,307 in annual Social Security benefits.

The unfunded liability for the federal pensions—how much red ink in promised benefits flows through the government's books—was $915 billion in 1997. Representative John Mica, a Republican from Florida, laid out the problem in testimony before the House Budget Committee in March 1996. "We inherited a retirement trust fund full of paper IOUs that are called 'nonmarketable Treasury securities,'" Mica told his colleagues. "These IOUs are euphemistically referred to as 'trust-fund assets.' No wonder the federal retirement system is in a constant state of crisis."

If the problems of the federal pension system sound eerily like those of the Social Security system, it is for the simple reason that both systems face the same crisis. Yet Congress is not insisting that its own pension plan be changed to a defined contribution system; it is not suggesting that the Federal Employee Retirement System is bankrupting the country, or that the system be privatized; it is not holding hearings with a parade of witnesses from Wall Street investment firms and Washington think tanks, offering testimony that if every Member of Congress owned stocks and bonds and mutual funds, there would be a Congress of millionaires.

That is because Capitol Hill lawmakers are willing to find the money in the budget to pay for what they have promised themselves. But they are more than content to suggest that, when it comes to your own retirement, you bear the entire risk.

Turning Social Security into a defined contribution plan would not be risky for everyone. Those managing the investments would do well, even if the investments themselves lost money. If $63 billion a year were put into the stock market—as Senator Robert Kerrey, a Democrat from Nebraska, has proposed—the 1 percent fee that the managers of most mutual funds charge would amount to $630 million. If the system were completely privatized, so that the entire half-trillion dollars that FICA taxes raise each year would go into the market, Wall Street's cut would amount to at least $5 billion a year. And, of course, those fees are charged every year, meaning that Wall Street would get cut after cut of that half-trillion.

Your cut, though, would not be guaranteed.

It is little wonder, then, that some of the biggest firms on Wall Street have been pushing proposals like Kerrey's.

Take what has become one of the most famous lines of those who want to take the Social Security system private: More young Americans believe that UFOs exist than that Social Security will be around when they retire. A group known as Third Millennium, which advocates the privatization of the Social Security system, commissioned the poll from which the UFO line is drawn. Its pollster was Frank Luntz, who helped craft the GOP's "Contract with America."

In 1996, Third Millennium made public some of the sources of its funding; included was the Merrill Lynch & Company Foundation, Inc., the philanthropic arm of one of the nation's largest brokerages, which would stand to earn billions under virtually any privatization scheme. Another contributor was Peter Peterson, the president of the Concord Coalition, a privatization advocate in his own right and the chairman of the Blackstone Group, a billion-dollar private investment firm.

Third Millennium is one of a handful of front groups pushing for the privatization of the Social Security system. There is also the Cato Institute, a nonprofit organization that bills itself as a promoter of "individual liberty, limited government, and free markets." The cochairman of the Cato Institute's Project on Social Security Privatization is one José Piñera, a native of Chile who served in the government of brutal dictator Augusto Ugarte Pinochet. Piñera and other representatives of the Cato Institute have gone before congressional committees to extol the benefits of privatizing Social Security on at least a dozen occasions since 1994.

Michael Tanner, the director of Cato's Project on Social Security Privatization, said that the organization intends to raise and spend $3 million drumming up support for privatization. Tanner told the Center for Public Integrity that about a third of the money has come from Wall Street firms, including American International Group, Inc., Citibank, and State Street Corporation. William Shipman, a principal of State Street Global Advisors, is another cochairman of Cato's privatization project. Shipman has appeared with representatives of Cato to testify before Congress.

Tanner rejects suggestions that Wall Street is the driving force behind Cato's support for privatization, noting that it first pushed the idea in 1979. "It's an ideological cause for us," Tanner told the Center. "It doesn't stem from donations."

Indeed, Tanner laments a lack of support on the part of investment firms. "Wall Street has been very timid about getting involved in this," Tanner said. "There's a concern over what happens to their private funds if Social Security funds are invested in the market."

Tanner's view of the benefits of privatization echoes those of others who have pushed various schemes before Congress: "The stock market's really got to tank for you to do worse than you would under Social Security."

Lost in all the rhetoric of UFOs and a nation of millionaires

> To go from a "pay as you go" system to a system of personal investments means that today's workers would get hit with a double whammy: being forced to set aside money for their own retirements at the same time they are paying for the Social Security benefits of current retirees.

is a simple fact about privatization: To go from a "pay as you go" system, with today's workers paying for the retirement of today's retirees, to a system of personal investments means that today's workers would get hit with a double whammy: being forced to set aside money for their own retirements at the same time they are paying for the Social Security benefits of current retirees. And that means one thing: Privatization will require an even higher payroll tax.

Two privatization proposals advanced by the 1994–1996 Advisory Council on Social Security, a study group mandated by Congress and appointed by the Health and Human Services Secretary, called for increases in the retirement (non-Medicare) portion of the payroll tax of up to 26 percent—rising from 6.2 percent for an individual to 7.8 percent.

Then there is Kerrey's plan to divert 16 percent of the payroll tax—or about $63 billion a year—to private individual retirement accounts (IRAs). Without an increase in the payroll tax, such a plan would merely accelerate the day of reckoning, when the cost of benefits would exceed the revenues from FICA.

Kerrey's proposal does not mention who would manage the private IRAs, and at what price. But to get a sense of how scrupulous Congress has been in managing your money, you need look no further than recent instances of Medicare fraud. Consider a few cases from the Office of Inspector General of the Health and Human Services Department:

- In 1996, ABC Home Health Services, Inc., was found guilty of committing seventy-two counts of Medicare fraud by a jury in Savannah, Georgia. ABC Home Health Services and its chairman and chief executive officer, Robert J. (Jack) Mills, were convicted of charging Medicare for such items as golf-course memberships; personal trips by Mills, his friends, and family to Cozumel, Mexico; utility costs for luxury beach condominiums; rental on a BMW driven by Mills's son while at college; and $84,000 for a panoply of promotional items, including gourmet popcorn, golf tees, earrings, cuff links, combs, and sewing kits. The total charged to Medicare for these and other items: more than $1 million.

- A 1996 audit of Blue Cross and Blue Shield of Michigan found that, from 1990 to 1993, the company charged at least $15.6 million in unallowable costs to Medicare, including $8.1 million in overcharges, $1.3 million for investments, and $600,000 for "various items which were unreasonable, not in accordance with federal regulation, or did not benefit the Medicare program."

- In 1997, SmithKline Beecham Clinical Laboratories paid $325 million in settlements of civil claims. Among other things, SmithKline had billed for tests not performed; inserted false diagnosis codes to obtain reimbursements; paid kickbacks to physicians for patient referrals; double-billed for laboratory tests for patients with end-stage renal disease; and billed for services that were neither ordered nor medically necessary. Medicare, Medicaid, and other federal health programs picked up the tab.

A 1995 report by the General Accounting Office found that while the number of Medicare claims had increased to 700 million from 450 million five years earlier, the budget to check those claims for fraud had been cut by a fifth. GAO officials have testified that at least 10 percent of Medicare payments are lost to "fraud, waste, and abuse."

Congress took quick action. It expanded Operation: Restore Trust—which audits physicians, hospitals, insurers, and other health-care providers that do business with Medicare—by 140 percent. Sounds good—except for one thing. Operation: Restore Trust was expanded from five states to twelve. Providers in the other thirty-eight states are still on the honor system. That is one of the reasons that the Trustees of Social Security reported in 1997 that the Hospital Insurance Fund of Medicare was due to go broke in 2001.

Efforts to overhaul Medicare have largely been efforts to shift the profits of treating senior citizens from one group of providers to another. In 1996, the Coalition to Save Medicare backed a Republican plan to push senior citizens into managed-care plans. Among the coalition's members: the U.S. Chamber of Commerce, the National Association of Manufacturers, and, more to the point, the Alliance for Managed Care—which represented Aetna Life and Casualty Company, Cigna Corporation, MetraHealth Insurance Company, and Prudential Insurance Company of America, four of the nation's largest managed-care companies—and the Council for Affordable Health Insurance. The council represents two dozen medium-sized insurance companies, including Golden Rule Insurance Company, a top donor to House Speaker Newt Gingrich and his political action committee, GOPAC. (From 1987 to 1996, the company and its employees contributed more than $213,000.)

Because the Republican proposal would have capped payments to hospitals, the American Hospital Association lobbied to kill the plan. On July 10, 1995, Democratic Senator Edward Kennedy of Massachusetts attacked the GOP plot to benefit the managed-care industry at the expense of hospitals. "Cuts in Medicare will also damage the overall health-care system," he complained. "The system as a whole will suffer because these deep Republican cuts will hurt hospitals and other providers, especially rural hospitals, public hospitals, and academic health centers."

The hospital industry's Washington lobbyists clearly had an easy ally in Kennedy. From 1993 to 1996, the Senator received $84,775 in campaign contributions from hospital employees and their family members.

Because of the imminence of the Medicare bankruptcy, Congress has had to act. Seventy Senators voted in 1997 for a plan to raise premiums for the program on senior citizens with incomes of more than $50,000 a year for individuals, or $75,000 a year for couples. Benefits under Medicare would be means-tested, meaning that wealthier seniors would pay more for their coverage. Threatened opposition from senior-citizen groups scuttled the plan.

"We jumped before they told us to jump," an aide to Republican House Whip Tom DeLay told a reporter for *The Washington Post* shortly after the House killed the plan. When one considers that those who identified themselves as retired gave at least $130 million to congressional candidates from 1987 to 1996, it is easy to understand why the House balked at touching benefits for seniors.

Instead of addressing Medicare's impending bankruptcy, Congress mandated another "blue-ribbon commission," like the Advisory Council on Social Security, to study the crisis. The panel will issue its report in 1999, and Congress will take no action until then.

While 40 million Americans go without any health insurance, all senior citizens—even those with annual incomes of more than $1 million—are covered by Medicare. Those same millionaires also receive Social Security benefits.

In 1993, the Internal Revenue Service reported that 9,616 tax returns had been filed by individuals or couples with adjusted gross incomes of more than $1 million who reported receiving payments from Social Security. The average annual benefit paid was $17,590. Social Security payments to millionaires in 1993 totaled $169 million.

Additionally, there were 444,217 tax returns filed by individuals or couples with adjusted gross incomes of $100,000 to $1 million who reported receiving payments from Social Security. The average annual benefit paid was $14,508. The total Social Security payments to this affluent group was $6.6 billion.

For the record, the IRS reported that the average benefit for all tax filers—individuals and couples—with adjusted gross incomes of less than $100,000 a year who reported receiving payments from Social Security was $10,760—or $897 a month.

> While 40 million Americans go without any health insurance, all senior citizens—even those with annual incomes of more than $1 million—are covered by Medicare.

Although the benefits paid by Social Security are not means-tested, the tax that pays for them is. If your income is large, you will pay a tiny percentage of it for the retirement portion of Social Security. If you are in the middle class, you will pay a larger percentage of your income.

Unlike the federal income tax, which taxes profits made from speculating on the stock market or rental income from an apartment building, FICA is strictly a tax on money earned by a worker at his or her job. But not all income is treated equally. In 1997, all income over $65,400 was exempt from Social Security withholding. In other words, a married couple with a combined income of $65,400 would have $4,054.80 withheld from their paychecks in the course of a year—or 6.2 percent. An individual earning $6,540,000 a year would have the same $4,054.80 withheld—or less than one-hundredth of 1 percent of income.

For better or worse, FICA is truly a middle-class tax—which is perhaps the biggest reason the future of Social Security is so uncertain.

In 1995, a technical panel of the Advisory Council on Social Security issued a report on trends in retirement saving. The panel, a group of academics and economists, studied data on savings rates, the labor market, retirement patterns, and private pensions. "Traditional manufacturing employment is declining, and service jobs are on the rise," its report said. "Some evidence suggests that the quality of jobs is becoming more bimodal, with job growth among low-skilled, low-paid service workers and high-skilled, high-paid technical and professional employees. This pattern of job growth is reflected in the changing American income distribution, which is becoming more unequal."

In other words, the America of the future will have at the top an increasing number of people who have much, if not most, of their earnings exempted from Social Security taxes and an even larger number of people at the bottom who are paying a much higher percentage of their earnings in Social Security taxes.

From 1973 to 1993, the incomes of the wealthiest one-fifth of Americans increased by 25 percent. The income of the poorest one-fifth of Americans decreased by 15 percent. Those in the middle barely kept even with inflation.

And the middle is shrinking.

The Bureau of Labor Statistics projects that, of the 17.7 million new jobs that will be added by 2005, service and retail industries will account for 16.2 million of them, or 92 percent. The three occupations with the largest job growth will be cashiers, janitors, and retail salespersons.

Low-wage service-industry jobs are far less likely to offer pension coverage to workers, and they are also far less likely to offer wages that allow an individual to save for his or her own retirement.

Some of the consequences of the declining incomes of the

middle class are already evident. Consider that cornerstone of the American Dream—buying a home. A house is also the primary asset of most Americans when they retire. In 1976, for the average homeowner, mortgage payments represented 24 percent of income. In 1995, they averaged 33 percent.

The report of the technical panel concludes that "the increase in earnings and income inequality is a concern . . . because it bodes ill for retirement-income adequacy in the future."

Social Security, which will be needed more than ever, will be running out of money. The wages of workers who support the system will be declining. The number of retirees who depend on the system will be increasing.

Troy Jordan works for Nest Egg Consulting, Inc., a retirement-planning service in Wichita, Kansas, where he advises factory workers and professionals, young workers and workers near retirement, on how to plan for their futures. "Our main theme is that there's only one thing you can totally count on, and that's yourself, and you have to prepare yourself for any and all outcomes," he told the Center. "If somebody has a moderate lifestyle and they have twenty-five years to retirement, they can get it done. It's much more difficult now; you don't have the supports of Social Security and pensions.

"We're finding more and more people saving earlier. It's a strain for them on the things they need today. The general feeling is that people are expecting that Social Security is going to be dramatically reduced. People are frustrated, but they feel they can't have any impact."

Who can blame them?

YOUR FREEDOMS

16

||||||●|||||

The Return of the Trusts

FOR 129 YEARS AFTER WILLIAM BREYER MIXED HIS FIRST BATCH OF ICE cream in 1866, the dessert bearing his name was made in his hometown of Philadelphia. Beginning in 1924, it was produced in a West Philly neighborhood—an aging industrial section of the city whose most notable landmark was the green neon "Breyers" sign atop the famous ice-cream factory. This was the largest ice cream plant in the world, with an annual capacity of 1 million gallons, and it operated through three ownership changes over more than seven decades.

For the last seventeen of those years, Ben Makarewicz faithfully sterilized the machines that mixed the ice cream's trademark all-natural ingredients. Makarewicz figured he would work at Breyers until retirement. After all, the Philadelphia native was earning close to $40,000 a year, he was provided health insurance and other benefits, and he had good friends at the plant, whose payroll counted 240 employees. "I loved it," Makarewicz said of his job. "I enjoyed going to work."

But Makarewicz's enthusiasm about his workplace was apparently of no interest to Unilever, an Anglo-Dutch firm that bought Breyers in 1993 and two years later padlocked the company's flagship locale. Makarewicz and every one of his coworkers were terminated.

Makarewicz was fifty-nine when the factory was closed. He began his job search the very next morning and continued it every subsequent day for a year and a half—but to no avail. "I put applications in but didn't find anything," he said. "I tried dairies, Dietz and Watson [a meat-processing company]—it didn't make any difference. I was open for anything." In the end, his only option—taken grudgingly—was early retirement.

"I didn't get any offers," he added, "because when you get to be a certain age, nobody wants you."

Surviving without the Breyers paycheck has been an unending struggle. "My wife does work part-time, so that helps out a lot," said Makarewkicz. "We spent all our savings, but now I'm sixty-two, so I can start taking my Social Security."

In 1997, that government pension earned Makarewicz $669 a month—or $8,028 for the year. For 1995, the company that unceremoniously axed him and his 239 cohorts reported profits of $2.3 billion.

Unilever is a global economic powerhouse—a conglomerate whose 500 companies spread across ninety countries command a workforce of more than 300,000. In the United States, where Unilever employs 21,000 workers at eighty-five offices and factories, it is anything but a household name. But its products are certainly well known: Lux, Dove, and Lifebuoy carry the Unilever label, so do Wisk and All, Aim and Pepsodent, Promise, Country Crock, and I Can't Believe It's Not Butter. Unilever owns Igloo and Bird's Eye frozen foods. Ditto Calvin Klein's Obsession and Elizabeth Taylor's Passion. It even owns Vaseline and Lipton Tea, along with a long list of other brand-name consumer goods.

Unilever purchased Breyers Ice Cream Company from Kraft Foods, Inc. It was a deal that fit nicely with Unilever's business strategy: gain market share through acquisitions rather than build companies from the ground up. Breyers, the top-selling brand of ice cream, became one of many product segments for a company that already owned the Gold Seal, Good Humor, Klondike, and Popsicle brands. The estimated $300 million purchase catapulted Unilever into the top spot among U.S. ice cream makers, giving it a hefty 20 percent of the market. It also gave the company five factories, from Massachusetts to California, to go with the plant whose beginnings could be traced to William Breyer's kitchen.

That plant had been a particularly valued asset. In 1989, Kraft had named it its "Factory of the Year." In the winter of '94, employees voluntarily toiled seven days straight for weeks as Unilever, seeking to capitalize on its new acquisition, flooded the market with the venerable Breyers brand. The following August, at a six-minute meeting, Unilever executives matter-of-factly announced that the Philadelphia workers were no longer needed.

"Unilever, they just wanted the name," Makarewicz said. "Instead of fighting the competition, they just bought it."

There was a time when Congress, the courts, the Justice Department, and the Federal Trade Commission (FTC) frowned on buying the competition. In 1969, after International Telephone & Telegraph embarked on a massive acquisition spree, snatching up the world's largest hotel chain (Sheraton), the second-largest car rental agency (Avis), and one of the nation's largest insurers (Hartford Fire Insurance Company), Attorney General John Mitchell attacked the giant, saying that "the danger that super-concentration poses to our economic and political-social structure cannot be overestimated." The Federal Trade Commission warned that conglomerates like ITT "pose a serious threat to America's democratic and social institutions by creating a degree of centralized private decision-making that is incompatible with a free-enterprise system." And Democratic Senator Philip Hart of Michigan, the chairman of the Judiciary Committee's Antitrust and Monopoly Subcommittee from 1963 to 1976, crusaded against the threat posed by such massive concentrations of economic power by constantly summoning auto, steel, and pharmaceutical executives before his committee and publicly grilling them.

Congress's attention to the merger mania of the 1960s was not without good reason. Just as the Founding Fathers devised a system of checks and balances to prevent a concentration of political power in the hands of a few, Congress crafted the antitrust laws to prevent the concentration of economic power. The great trusts that arose in the latter part of the nineteenth century—John D. Rockefeller's Standard Oil, the Armour and Swift meatpackers, U.S. Steel, the whiskey trust, the railroad trust—defied laws; corrupted public officials; chewed up and spit out workers; bilked, cheated, and poisoned consumers; ruined small investors; and, through their wealth and power, set themselves above the law.

The Age of the Robber Barons has returned.

Bill Gates's Microsoft Corporation has a near-monopoly on computer operating systems. Four meatpackers control 82 percent of the beef market. Anheuser-Busch, Inc., and Miller Brewing Company control two-thirds of the beer market. Procter & Gamble and Unilever sell 73 percent of all laundry detergent. Whirlpool and General Electric sell nearly two of every three home appliances. Nike and Reebok hold 59 percent of the athletic-shoe market.

> Anheuser Busch and Miller control two-thirds of the beer market. Procter & Gamble and Unilever sell 73 percent of laundry detergent. Whirlpool and General Electric sell nearly two of every three home appliances.

All of these industries are, by the government's own definition, highly concentrated. Economists estimate that well over a third of the U.S. economy is affected by monopoly power and that the total cost to consumers of overcharges stemming from this concentration is roughly 10 percent of the gross domestic product—the nation's broadest measure of economic activity. That is a staggering $725 billion annually—about $2,760 for every one of the nation's residents—which is directly traceable to Congress's willful neglect of the antitrust laws it wrote.

More mergers mean not only higher prices but also fewer employees. Scott Paper Ltd. laid off 11,000 workers before its 1995 merger with Kimberly-Clark Corporation; the day after the companies merged Kimberly-Clark announced it would send another 6,000 workers to the unemployment line. While seeking government approval of their merger, Bell Atlantic Corporation and Nynex Corporation crowed that the consolidation would not result in a loss of union jobs; instead, the telecommunications giants told managerial workers to find jobs elsewhere. When life-insurance giant Aetna Life and Casualty Company merged with U.S. Healthcare, Inc., in 1996, the firm announced 9,373 job cuts—2,600 of them in Connecticut, whose economy is in large part tied to the insurance industry.

The wave of mergers that started in the go-go 1980s picked up speed in the 1990s. According to Mergerstat Review, a California firm that tracks corporate acquisitions, there was a record $266.5 billion worth of deals in 1995—far outstripping the previous high of $177 billion in 1988. In 1996, the volume of deals skyrocketed to $492.9 billion.

That same year the Justice Department's antitrust division received 3,094 premerger notifications. This government unit, which, along with the Federal Trade Commission, is charged with protecting Americans from consolidations of corporate power, investigated 186 of these proposed deals and ultimately brought court challenges against nine—a scant three-tenths of 1 percent of the year's total mergers.

But 1996 was hardly an anomaly. In the ten years beginning in 1987, the Justice Department investigated 790 of the roughly 23,600 mergers it was called on to approve, and just fifty-two— a mere two-tenths of 1 percent—were challenged in court. It is little wonder, then, that Unilever's 1993 purchase of Breyers Ice Cream Company—which made the foreign conglomerate the country's number-one ice cream producer—sailed through Justice unchallenged.

Former Democratic Senator Paul Simon of Illinois, who served on the antitrust subcommittee, is among those who believe that the current state of antitrust enforcement is pitiful. "We just have done nothing," he said of Congress's oversight role. "In fact, during the Reagan years, the antitrust division was all but dead. Congress has done very, very little in the antitrust area."

Why has Congress shirked its responsibility to the American people? "Those who are involved in these big takeovers seem to be big contributors," Simon said. "And we are not in the business of offending big contributors."

In 1995, the chairmanship of the Senate antitrust subcommittee was passed to Strom Thurmond, the South Carolina Republican whose congressional tenure is unmatched in length. Like Phil Hart, who a quarter-century earlier had used the committee to scrutinize the consolidation of American industry, Thurmond also sought to have an effect on the Justice Department and the FTC—albeit one of an entirely different nature. "I am pleased that the federal antitrust agencies are taking steps to reduce unnecessary burdens on business mergers," Thurmond said in a March 1995 statement. "Easing the regulatory hurdles facing lawful transactions has been one of my top priorities for the antitrust subcommittee this year, a fact known by the antitrust agencies in Washington." Should these agencies fail to cooperate, Thurmond added, he was prepared to get his way via the introduction of new legislation.

Thurmond's predecessor as subcommittee chairman was Democrat Howard Metzenbaum of Ohio. Generally viewed as a critic of Big Business, Metzenbaum was nevertheless not above being a featured speaker at the 1986 Predators' Ball—the lavish party thrown by junk-bond king Michael Milken and his firm, Drexel Burnham Lambert, Inc., at the height of the hostile-takeover spree. In late 1988, with Drexel the target of both Securities and Exchange Commission probes and civil-racketeering charges, Metzenbaum sponsored legislation that would have wiped out hundreds of millions of dollars' worth of damages facing the disgraced brokerage firm. At Metzenbaum's urging, the measure sailed through his subcommittee. It later died, however, making it to the floor of neither the House nor the Senate.

Of course, it may be unfair to pick on individual Senators. Sometimes, it is the overwhelming majority who become the cheerleaders of consolidation. In July 1997, for example, no fewer than seventy-five Senators signed a letter to President Clinton, authored by Democrat John (Jay) Rockefeller IV of West Virginia, demanding a trade war if the European Commission (EC) raised objections to the Boeing-McDonnell Douglas merger.

The letter urged Clinton to "consider stern retaliatory measures commensurate with the Europeans' action" if the EC tried to block the merger. In case there was any misunderstanding of the Senate's intent, Rockefeller clarified: "We all know the costs of a trade war, but we also understand the dangers of letting the European Commission interfere with our national economic security."

Ordinarily, the Senate will not risk a trade war, certainly not when the issue is protecting American jobs, prying open markets closed to American goods, or protesting human-rights violations in China. But then, political prisoners in China or unemployed factory workers in Wichita, Kansas, don't own the Senate. Boeing does.

*   *   *

In 1945, there were twenty-two commercial aircraft companies scattered across the United States. In 1996, there were two: Boeing Company and McDonnell Douglas Corporation. Today just one remains.

Boeing's 1997 merger with McDonnell Douglas, one of the largest corporate consolidations in history, created a company with annual sales of $45.8 billion. Traditionally, the FTC deemed a company a monopoly if it controlled more than 60 percent of an industry. By swallowing McDonnell Douglas, Boeing emerged as the only domestic manufacturer of commercial aircraft, with a 70 percent share of the international market. (The rest is held by Airbus, the four-nation European consortium.)

To get a sense of the size and importance of Boeing, consider the U.S. trade deficit. Every month the Commerce Department adds up the hundreds of billions of dollars' worth of U.S. exports and the hundreds of billions of dollars' worth of imports, then calculates the difference between them. Commerce releases these figures on the nation's trade balance, which are duly reported in newspapers:

- "America's deficit with Western Europe climbed to an all-time high of $4.3 billion in July as U.S. exports dropped $2 billion, led by a big decline in civilian aircraft sales" (Associated Press, September 18, 1996).

> Traditionally, the FTC deemed a company a monopoly if it controlled more than 60 percent of an industry. By swallowing McDonnell Douglas, Boeing emerged as the only domestic manufacturer of commercial aircraft, with a 70 percent share of the international market.

- "The U.S. trade deficit narrowed dramatically in October, falling to $7.99 billion, the smallest in seven months. American exports hit an all-time high, boosted by a big rise in sales of commercial jetliners" (Associated Press, December 19, 1996).
- "The Commerce Department said today the deficit in goods and services totaled $8.4 billion, up from a revised $7.8 billion in March. The March imbalance, initially estimated at $8.5

|||||||||||||||||||||||||||||||||||||||||||||||||||||||||||||||||||||||

In 1995, Boeing not only wriggled its way out of paying any federal income taxes, but actually received a $33 million rebate, making its effective tax rate minus 9 percent.

billion, narrowed with the help of surging sales of commercial aircraft to China" (Associated Press, June 19, 1997).

All those mentions of commercial jetliners or civilian aircraft refer only to Boeing. When Boeing has a good month, the nation's trade deficit decreases significantly. When Boeing stumbles, the trade deficit soars. No other single U.S. company has the same impact on the nation's trade balance.

Just as daunting as Boeing's economic force is the company's political might. From 1991 to 1996, Boeing and McDonnell Douglas, along with employees and their family members, contributed $2.9 million to congressional campaigns and the national party committees. Boeing's top official in Washington, Chris Hansen, attended one of the Clinton Administration's infamous 1996 "coffees." Franklin Raines left Boeing's board of directors to become Clinton's budget director.

Boeing employs an army of about a hundred lobbyists, who work vigorously to bend federal policy—including provisions related to tax law, the budget, telecommunications, health care, land use, utilities deregulation, environmental policy, labor law, international trade—to the company's agenda. In 1996, Boeing spent roughly $5.2 million for its Washington lobbying operation as the company's minions pressed its cause before virtually every important governmental institution, including Congress, the White House, the office of the U.S. Trade Representative, the Pentagon, the National Security Council, and the Departments of Commerce, Transportation, Agriculture, and Treasury.

A number of those lobbyists are accomplished in such specialties as "tax mitigation" and "tax avoidance"—skills that the average American would no doubt wish to master. After all, in 1995, Boeing not only wriggled its way out of paying any federal income taxes, but actually received a $33 million rebate from the U.S. Treasury, making its effective tax rate minus 9 percent. This feat was achieved by taking hefty deductions for research-and-development costs, as well as by judicious use of the Foreign Tax Credit—a strategy that earned the firm a cash refund from Uncle Sam for taxes it paid to China and other foreign governments.

But Boeing is a mere novice in the fine art of "tax mitigation" compared with its merger partner. McDonnell Douglas, using the same schemes, received a 1995 tax credit of $334 million from the IRS.

Before the merger, Boeing was the eighth-largest defense manufacturer, according to the Defense Department, with $1.7 billion in contracts with the Pentagon. By buying out McDonnell Douglas, Boeing vaulted into second place, with $11.6 billion. Number one was Lockheed Martin Corporation—another conglomerate created by mergers—with $12 billion in defense contracts. Pentagon planning documents obtained by *The Washington Post* reveal that Boeing or Lockheed will be the prime contractor on 60 percent of major new weapons-systems programs, which means the firms will split between them about $360 billion during the next few years alone.

And taxpayers will be paying more for less. When Alliant Techsystems, Inc., and Olin Corporation—the only two manufacturers of ammunition for the Army's main battle tank—tried merging in 1992, they calculated that the company's combined monopoly power would earn it an extra $100 million over five years. The FTC went to court to block the Alliant-Olin merger. However, no such concerns were raised by the FTC or Justice over the Boeing-McDonnell Douglas union—a seeming contradiction of FTC chairman Robert Pitofsky's philosophy. "When industries become more and more concentrated so only two or three players are left, then government has to step in," he told *Management Review* in a December 1995 interview.

But this time around, Pitofsky and his trust-busting cohorts apparently were unconcerned by the idea of a lone player left in the game. The merger was rubber-stamped by the FTC and the Justice Department, leaving only the European Commission—which oversees trade for the European Union—in its way. Although the EC had no legal authority to prevent the merger, it could authorize fines on Boeing up to 10 percent of its annual sales—which would have totaled a hefty $4.8 billion in 1996—to permit the company to do business in Europe. That move, in turn, led to Rockefeller's huffy letter to Clinton, which won the widespread endorsement of the Senator's colleagues. It is perhaps ironic that the Senate should threaten a trade war on Boeing's behalf, considering that Boeing has been the nation's biggest beneficiary of free-trade policies, especially China's most-favored-nation status.

Boeing is only one example of how Congress's abandonment of the antitrust laws has allowed corporate giants to write their own rules in Washington. Another comes from the banking industry, which has recently been transformed by a dizzying rash of mergers—a consolidation purportedly designed to benefit consumers, but one that has instead been a boon to the financial institutions themselves.

By making it easier for banks in different states to merge, the Riegle-Neal Interstate Banking and Branching Efficiency Act led to such "consumer benefits" as large numbers of layoffs and higher banking fees.

This consolidation has escalated at a furious pace. The Federal Deposit Insurance Corporation reports, for example, that 2,400 banks disappeared between 1993 and 1996—an astonishing 17 percent of the total. At the end of 1984, the forty-two largest banking organizations held 25 percent of domestic deposits. By early 1996, the thirteen largest banking organizations held those 25 percent of deposits.

These, however, are merely national trends. The real story behind this sea change in the nation's banking business is better told via the effects of mergers on local communities—on towns such as Santa Fe, New Mexico.

The picturesque state capital is served by only ten banks. Of those, Bank of Santa Fe, First National Bank of Santa Fe, Wells Fargo Bank, and NationsBank collectively control 79 percent of the market, according to the FDIC. The leader, NationsBank, entered the Santa Fe market only in 1996, with the purchase of Boatmen's Bancshares, Inc., the parent company of Sunwest Bank.

After acquiring Sunwest, NationsBank laid off nearly eighty of its Santa Fe employees. It raised its monthly fees on checking accounts, making them some of the highest rates in town. The new number-one bank doubled the ATM charge to $1.50 for using a machine operated by a competitor. Wells Fargo Bank, which joined the Santa Fe landscape in 1996, following its merger with First Interstate Bancorp, charges the same inflated rate. Norwest Bank, which arrived in Santa Fe after its 1993 buyout of United New Mexico Bank, also charges $1.50 for transactions at machines it does not operate.

In its 1996 annual report, NationsBank proudly announced profits of $2.4 billion. Of that, $1.1 billion came from service charges on deposit accounts—ATM transaction fees, monthly fees on checking accounts, and the like. Nearly 46 percent of those profits were attributable to higher fees charged to customers like those in Santa Fe, Albuquerque, Dallas, Kansas City, Little Rock, St. Louis, and Wichita—all of whom saw NationsBank become the leader in local market share, thanks to the Boatmen's merger.

But consumers really have Congress to thank, because the groundwork for this and other such mergers was laid with the 1994 passage of the Riegle-Neal Interstate Banking and Branching Efficiency Act. The legislation garnered overwhelming bipartisan support, sailing through the Senate Banking Committee, for instance, by a vote of nineteen to zero. Members of Congress, who touted the act as decidedly pro-consumer, stressed that it would make banks more efficient and more competitive. No one bothered to mention that "more efficient" meant fewer employees and that the only competition would be for the shrinking number of bank jobs.

But that is precisely what this new law wrought. By making it easier for banks in different states to merge, the law intensified the consolidation in cities like Santa Fe, which in turn led to such "consumer benefits" as large numbers of layoffs and higher banking fees.

Perhaps the American Bankers Association (ABA) put it best when it called the bill " 'clean' pro-banking legislation." The cleanliness should not have come as a surprise, since the bankers paid for the law themselves: In the 1993–94 election cycle, the banking industry poured more than $17 million into congressional campaigns. Members of the Senate Banking, Housing, and Urban Affairs Committee received more than $1.1 million worth of campaign contributions from banking interests, while members of the House Banking, Finance, and Urban Affairs Committee got more than $1.8 million. For good measure, the bankers contributed $497,000 to those who sit on the Senate Finance Committee.

The bankers certainly got the attention of legislators, who

trumpeted their claims of competition and efficiency. Among those happy to spread the gospel was Senator Alfonse D'Amato, a Republican from New York, who proclaimed on the Senate floor: "Interstate branching will eliminate unnecessary overhead costs and make banking more efficient."

In D'Amato's own state, the 1996 merger of Chase Manhattan Bank and Chemical Bank created the country's largest bank—a financial behemoth with more than $300 billion in assets. As for D'Amato's predictions, the merger eliminated the unnecessary overhead costs of employing 12,000 expendable workers—4,000 of them in New York City alone. But if D'Amato was stung by the criticism of laid-off constituents, his uneasiness may have been mitigated by the $744,373 bestowed upon him by bankers from 1987 to 1996.

On August 4, 1994, Republican Representative Marge Roukema of New Jersey said in the House debate of the bill: "I supported this legislation because I have long felt that interstate banking and branching provided the best opportunity for banks to become more competitive." The competition that Roukema favored was not much of a boon for Garden State workers. In 1996, after Summit Bank and United Jersey Bank merged, 700 employees were laid off. But while her constituents may have lost out, pushing the bankers' agenda has nonetheless paid Roukema dividends: From 1987 to 1996, she's received more than $235,000 worth of contributions from banking interests.

Overall, between the end of 1994 and the end of 1996, 42,200 bank jobs disappeared, according to the Bureau of Labor Statistics. On the heels of the new law, Congress's predictions of increased bank "efficiency" had been quickly realized.

Many of the legislators who rewrote the rules on bank mergers are eager to do the same for banking deregulation. Among those leading the House charge is none other than New Jersey's Roukema, who in 1997 introduced a bill that would tear down the wall between banking and commerce. Roukema proudly admitted that the legislation had been drafted by the Alliance for Financial Modernization—whose members include commercial banks, savings and loans, investment banks, and trade groups such as the ABA.

Those searching for a lesson in the dangers of an unregulated banking industry need look back no further than the 1980s, when hundreds of savings and loans went bankrupt, costing taxpayers billions of dollars. The S&L scandal was greatly facilitated by Congress, which authorized thrifts to make all sorts of risky new loans. Then, after many of those loans turned bad, Congress helped cover up the impending debacle by permitting S&L managers to use a smoke-and-mirrors accounting system that allowed their financially ailing institutions to appear solvent.

Go back another half-century, and the Great Depression provides an even more alarming illustration. Congress passed the Glass-Steagall Act in the Depression's aftermath to prevent reckless stock-market speculation by banks. Now Congress, egged on by the bankers, is eager to remove those restrictions.

Financial companies have hired a battalion of former officials of the Federal Reserve Board and the Executive Branch, as well as former Members of Congress and their aides, to lobby for the industry's agenda. A 1996 article in *Institutional Investor* listed more than 125 of them. Until December 1996, for example, Joseph Seidel served as chief counsel to Republican Representative Jim Leach's House Banking Subcommittee. In that capacity, he wrote legislation that included several provisions favored by Wall Street, including a weakening of Glass-Steagall. In January of 1997, Seidel left Capitol Hill for Williams & Jensen, a lobbying firm that handles, among other things, banking and securities issues. Seidel himself now lobbies for such clients as CS First Boston Corporation and First Union Corporation.

The power of the bankers has left local communities with few options. The city of Albuquerque, New Mexico, decided to terminate its banking contract with NationsBank—which, as in nearby Santa Fe, became the top bank after its merger with Boatmen's—to protest layoffs there. Raymond Mariano, the mayor of Worcester, Massachusetts, blasted the executives of Fleet Bank, which merged with Shawmut Bank in 1995, in a memo to members of the city council. "They have gone back on their commitment to our community," he wrote. "They have planned massive job cuts and hid them until confronted with the facts."

But with Congress on the side of banks, the mergers—and the resultant layoffs—will no doubt continue. Or as Democratic Senator Don Riegle of Michigan put it after the banking committee unanimously approved the 1994 legislation facilitating interstate mergers: "That is the way we ought to try to make government work."

*   *   *

Robert Dole took to the Senate floor on June 19, 1995, to brand the Department of Justice (DOJ) overzealous in its use of antitrust statutes. The Senate Majority Leader was referring to an investigation into Microsoft's expansion into the Internet business. As is routine in such cases, Justice had subpoenaed thousands of pages of internal company memos, business plans, and other records from the Richmond, Washington-based software giant. "If this report is accurate," Dole said of an account of the document request, "DOJ is out of control."

At issue was the Microsoft Network, a service that was prepackaged with Microsoft's Windows 95—the operating system that is the central nervous system of most personal computers. In June, Justice announced it would investigate to determine whether the easy access to the network bundled with the new Windows upgrade would give Microsoft's Internet service an unfair advantage over Prodigy, America Online, CompuServe, and other providers. As an article in *The New Republic* put it, "It's flat-out impossible to compete when your competitor is preinstalled on every new computer."

A full-bore investigation of Microsoft might have interfered with the company's much-ballyhooed August 24 launch of Windows 95. Such a delay, of course, would have harmed Microsoft. But Microsoft is not an ordinary company; it is a monopolist. So delaying Windows 95 would have hurt the whole economy.

Consider these dire predictions:
- From *The Wall Street Journal*: "A bad stumble by Microsoft in launching the product would spill into the technology group and then ripple through the rest of the market with dismal effect."
- From a letter to the Justice Department by Michael Cowpland, the chairman and chief executive officer of Corel Corporation, a graphics-software company based in Ottawa, Ontario: "Any interference in the shipment of Windows 95 will not only adversely impact business in the United States, but also will have a worldwide adverse impact."
- Or, as Wall Street analyst Brian Oakes of J. P. Morgan Securities told *The San Francisco Examiner,* "People [on Wall Street] were saying, 'Windows 95 not go out? That's about 2 percent of the GDP right there.' "

For the record, 2 percent of the GDP (gross domestic product) in 1995 was \$144 billion, equivalent to the yearly earnings of 3.5 million families at median income. And all of it hinged on the introduction of one product by one company.

Rather than question how it was that Microsoft had come to dominate computer operating systems—and with it, a sizable chunk of the economy—Dole and Republican Senator Slade Gorton of Washington attacked Justice Department officials who had the temerity to ask that very question. "Let us understand what is going on here," Dole said. "A company develops a new product. A product that consumers want. But now the government steps in and is in effect attempting to dictate the terms on which that product can be marketed and sold. Pinch me, but I thought we were still in America."

"I . . . hope that this eleventh-hour investigation will not delay the introduction of Microsoft's much-anticipated software, an introduction that will increase both consumer choice and competition," Gorton said that same day.

But despite Gorton's defense of his constituent, Microsoft is not interested in competing; on the contrary, the empire that Bill Gates has built is dedicated to eliminating the competition. Consider an earlier antitrust investigation into the world's richest software company. In a blistering 1995 court decision, U.S. District Judge Stanley Sporkin spelled out some of Microsoft's anticompetitive practices:

- Microsoft manipulates its operating systems so that competitors' applications programs do not work properly—or at all.

> **If the minimum wage had increased at the same rate as Bill Gates's fortune, a full-time worker would earn no less than \$107.20 an hour, or \$223,000 a year.**

- Microsoft's clout has allowed it to force computer manufacturers to sign "per-processor licenses," meaning that they pay a royalty to Microsoft for every PC they sell, whether it contains a Microsoft operating system or not. If a computer manufacturer decided to install a different operating system—say, IBM's OS2—it would still owe a royalty to Microsoft.

- Microsoft has several times publicly announced the pending release of a new product well before it was ready for mar-

ket. The practice is designed to deter consumers from purchasing a competitor's product that is already available.

Sporkin was reviewing a consent decree that the Justice Department and Microsoft had negotiated in mid-1994; the case had
dragged on since 1990, when the FTC initiated an investigation
into Microsoft's business practices. After the FTC deadlocked on
whether to bring charges in 1993, Justice stepped in.

The facts before Sporkin were clear. Microsoft had gained a
monopoly in the computer-operating-system market through re-
straint of trade, violating Sections 1 and 2 of the Sherman Antitrust
Act. The consent decree with Microsoft, however, did nothing to
open this market to competition. As Sporkin wrote in his decision,
"Simply telling a defendant to go forth and sin no more does little
or nothing to address the unfair advantage it has already gained."

Ultimately, Sporkin rejected the consent decree, concluding that
Microsoft owned a monopolist position in a field central to this
country's long-term well-being. "The picture that emerges from these
proceedings is that the U.S. government is either incapable or unwilling to deal effectively with a potential threat to the nation's economic
well-being," Sporkin wrote. "It is clear to this court that if it signs
the decree presented to it, the message will be that Microsoft is so
powerful that neither the market nor the government is capable of
dealing with its monopolistic practices."

What followed confirmed Sporkin's worst fears. Both Microsoft and the Justice Department appealed the judge's ruling. Attorney Gary Reback, who filed a brief on behalf of software
manufacturers wary of Microsoft's domination, noted: "Someone
has to explain why the Department of Justice is treating Microsoft
like a client and not an adversary." In June, a federal appeals
court threw out Sporkin's decision in the case.

At Microsoft's request, the court also removed Sporkin from
the case—one of fewer than a dozen times in the history of the
Republic that a federal appeals court has yanked a trial judge off
a case. On August 21, after a seventeen-minute hearing, Judge
Thomas Penfield Jackson approved the Justice Department's deal
with Microsoft. Just two weeks before, on August 8, the government had dropped its probe of the Microsoft Network, allowing
Windows 95 to roll out as scheduled.

The message was sent. Microsoft is so powerful that no one is capable of dealing with its monopolistic practices. Those who try, beware.

Although Microsoft and its defenders say it has smashed the competition on the strength of superior technology and products, the company's success is in large measure based on the power it wields as market leader, not on performance. For example, Microsoft's bread-and-butter program, MS-DOS, was not developed in-house—rather, it was bought from a company called Seattle Computer Products. Microsoft made no attempt to improve its DOS 3.3 version until an upstart firm, Digital Research, Inc., issued a markedly better version called dr-dos. Microsoft swiftly issued two new versions of its DOS program to protect its market share from the upstart, then promptly stopped innovating after dr-dos had been killed off.

But operating systems are just one segment of the software industry; another is applications—such as word-processing programs and spreadsheets. Microsoft is among the top two or three companies in virtually every sector of the applications market. New versions of Windows, for example, will incorporate Web browsers—the programs that allow users to surf the Internet—into the operating system, rendering obsolete Netscape Navigator and other competitors' products. Jonathan Roberts, the director of marketing for Windows at Microsoft, told *The San Francisco Chronicle* in July of 1997, "I don't think the browser will be an independent application five years from now." Meaning, of course, that the Internet browser will be part of the operating system. Which will be made by Microsoft. Which will have a monopoly in yet another segment of the software industry.

In the spring of 1998, the Justice Department delayed the introduction of Windows 98. Once again the issue was Microsoft's Web browser, Internet Explorer, and whether the first screen that computer users see when they turn on their machines would carry Microsoft's logo. More substantive issues, like the company's dominance of the market for operating systems, weren't addressed.

Market dominance has been a consistent goal of Microsoft over the years. As early as 1991, Mike Maples, then senior vice president for the applications division, made it clear when he publicly announced, "My job is to get a fair share of the applications market, and to me that's one hundred percent."

Getting 100 percent of the market has been rewarding for

Microsoft and its founder, Bill Gates. The company had $8.6 billion in revenue and $2.2 billion in profits in 1996, for a margin of 26 percent. Compare that with the profit margins of such Fortune 500 stalwarts as General Motors Corporation (3.4 percent), Ford Motor Company (3 percent), Chrysler Corporation (5.7 percent), Eastman Kodak Company (8 percent), Xerox Corporation (3 percent), and General Electric Company (9 percent).

Much of that profit, of course, winds up in Bill Gates's pocket. Like the robber barons of old, Gates has amassed a fortune in the billions; he became the youngest billionaire in world history and has been named the wealthiest man in America by *Forbes* magazine. Between 1987 and 1997, his fortune increased thirty-two times, from an estimated $1.25 billion to an estimated $40 billion, according to *Forbes*. If the minimum wage had increased at the same rate, a full-time worker would earn no less than $107.20 an hour, or $223,000 a year.

Wealth of this sort is liable to get you more than front-row seats. In 1994, for example, shortly after Justice and Microsoft began negotiating on the consent decree that Judge Sporkin later overturned, Gates blew onto Martha's Vineyard—where President Clinton just happened to be vacationing—and, as luck would have it, was paired with Clinton for nine holes of golf. In 1997, Gates hosted the Microsoft Technology Summit, which attracted the likes of Vice President Albert Gore Jr., onetime Republican presidential candidate Malcolm (Steve) Forbes, Jr., and 100 corporate CEOs representing firms that make up a good chunk of the nation's economy. After the summit, guests reconvened for a private dinner at Gates's nearby $60 million estate.

Early in the twentieth century, when Theodore Roosevelt ordered his Attorney General to break up a railroad trust that J. P. Morgan had put together, Morgan raced off to Washington and told the President, "If we have done anything wrong, send your man to my man, and they can fix it up."

Roosevelt refused to send his man, and the Northern Securities Company trust was busted.

Late in the twentieth century, Bill Gates has amassed such extraordinary wealth and power that antitrust laws simply do not apply to him or his company. A bumper sticker offered by his critics sums it up: "We Are Microsoft. Resistance Is Futile. You Will All Be Assimilated."

17

|||||●|||||

Sold Out

DURING THE BITTER NATIONAL DEBATE OVER THE NORTH AMERICAN Free Trade Agreement (NAFTA) in 1993, advocates of the treaty argued that it would bring immense benefits to all Americans, not just the corporations that were lobbying furiously for its passage. In a speech on the House floor the day of the vote, Republican Stephen Buyer of Indiana called NAFTA "a job-creation engine" and promised that the treaty would produce a net gain of at least 200,000 new jobs for Americans within a year of its passage. Representative David Dreier, a Republican from California, scoffed at critics who said NAFTA would harm American workers, declaring emphatically, "The truth is that NAFTA is good for American workers, good for the world environment, and good for jobs in this country."

As it turned out, NAFTA did create plenty of jobs. Unfortunately for American workers, most of them were in Mexico. From 1993 to 1996, employment at *maquiladora* assembly plants, most of them owned by U.S. companies, soared by 48 percent while the average hourly wage of workers in these factories fell from $1.80 to $1.21.

The U.S. firms that were hiring most of the Mexican workers were simultaneously firing their higher-paid employees in the United States. Kathleen King of Philadelphia worked for the Frank H. Fleer

Corporation for eight years as a machine operator at a baseball-card plant, making about $10 an hour. In 1995, on the Monday after the Thanksgiving holiday, she and about 100 of her colleagues were summarily dismissed. The company offered no explanation, but they soon learned that Fleer was moving its operations to Mexico.

After being unemployed for more than a year, King finally landed a new job as a clerk at United Parcel Service, where she works the 11 P.M.–to–3 A.M. shift. She earns less than half of what she did at Fleer and rarely sees her husband, who runs a newsstand, or her teenage daughter. "The bottom line for these companies is to see how much money they can make and not worry about anybody else," King told the Center for Public Integrity. "That's what NAFTA was about."

One study found that forty large corporations that had lobbied for NAFTA and subsequently moved jobs to Mexico saw their profits rise by an average of 335 percent from 1992 to 1996.

King is one of the hundreds of thousands of U.S. workers who were "downsized" by companies that moved operations to Mexico following Congress's ratification of NAFTA. Hundreds of thousands more have been fired as a result of government trade policy—from the Caribbean Basin Initiative to expanding commercial ties with dictatorships such as China and Indonesia—that favors free trade above protecting jobs at home or promoting human rights abroad.

The Labor Department operates an employment training program for American workers who have lost their jobs because of low-wage foreign competition. It is awash in a mountain of paperwork from people seeking assistance, with each petition soberly reciting the tale of communities, families, and individuals abandoned by companies seeking cheap labor abroad: 600 workers laid off by Westinghouse Electric Corporation at a plant in Pensacola, Florida, when the company decided to build electric generators in Mexico and combustion turbines in Canada; 400 workers left jobless when Hasbro, Inc. moved its toy factory in Amsterdam, New York, to China; more than 400 workers fired at Zenith Electronics Corporation's factory in Springfield, Missouri, because of a "shift in production to Mexico."

The business community has lobbied long and hard to ensure

that Congress and the White House support its free-trade agenda. The price has not been cheap, especially because the public has been highly skeptical of the benefits of free trade. USA*NAFTA, the chief business coalition lobbying for the treaty, spent $5 million to $8 million on advertising alone. The Mexican government and Mexican business interests spent lavishly as well, unbuckling some $30 million to advance the treaty. That money paid for the services of sixty-three Washington lobbying and public-relations firms and thirty-three former U.S. government officials.

Corporate lobbying for expanded trade with China—one of the world's worst human-rights violators and a country whose workers make an average of less than $50 a month—has been equally pricey. In the year before a crucial 1996 congressional vote on commercial most-favored-nation (MFN) ties with China, big companies lobbying in favor shelled out at least $20 million in campaign donations.

Although the cost of lobbying is high, corporations get an excellent return on their investment. A study by the Institute for Policy Studies found that forty large corporations that had lobbied for NAFTA and subsequently moved jobs to Mexico saw their profits rise by an average of 335 percent from 1992 to 1996, a rate about five times higher than that among Fortune 500 companies.

Trade with China has been especially lucrative for big business. The Boeing Company, a leader of the corporate lobby for China, sells about one in ten of its planes to Beijing. In 1997, Boeing closed a $3 billion deal—its biggest commercial agreement ever—with China. Motorola, Inc., now racks up more than 10 percent of its worldwide sales in China and has been shifting huge numbers of jobs there as well. By 2000, the company expects to have 12,000 Chinese workers on its payroll.

American workers have gotten the short end of the trade stick. "Twenty years ago, you could find work that paid the bills,"

Nike workers in China earn an average wage of $1.80 a day and are forced to work up to twelve hours a day, often receiving only two days off per month, both in violation of Chinese law and Nike's touted code of conduct.

Kathleen King told the Center. "Today the good jobs have moved overseas. You can't make sneakers here anymore, you can't make clothing, you can't make a screw. We need global trade, but not so much that they take all the jobs away. Pretty soon we're not going to have much of a country left."

Corporations typically move factories overseas not to be closer to supplies of raw materials or to their customers, but to lower their labor costs and, hence, to increase their profits. Consider the geographic trajectory of Nike, Inc., the sportswear manufacturer that has repeatedly been cited for its abuse of workers' rights. After a brief stint employing U.S. workers to manufacture its footwear, Nike moved its shoe manufacturing abroad in 1967, contracting work out to factories in Japan. In the early 1970s, with Japanese wages on the rise, Nike began expanding its manufacturing base, shifting some of its production to the less expensive South Korean and Taiwanese markets. Within the last decade, Nike has signed on footwear operations in a half-dozen or more countries, including Indonesia, China, and Vietnam, watching its profits soar to record levels while seeking out the lowest wages possible. Nike workers in China, where more than a third of the company's footwear is produced, earn an average wage of $1.80 a day, and, according to a report issued by the Asia Monitor Resource Centre, are forced to work up to twelve hours a day, often receiving only two days off per month, in violation of both Chinese law and Nike's touted code of conduct. Meanwhile in Vietnam, where Nike has recently begun to shift more of its production, workers earn an average of twenty cents an hour laboring in conditions so deplorable that 75 percent of employees at one factory reported suffering from respiratory ailments. It costs Nike around $5 in Vietnam to produce a pair of shoes that retail for up to $150 in the United States.

Nike's chairman and chief executive officer, Philip Knight, is the seventeenth-richest man in America, according to *Forbes* magazine, with a net worth estimated at $5.4 billion. Knight's annual net income from dividends—$36.3 million in 1990—is more than his company's entire Vietnamese workforce of 35,000 would make in two years.

Economic globalization has been a gold mine for American corporate executives, but it has not been nearly so good for American workers. Because it is CEOs and their companies that fill campaign coffers, though, Congress and the White House have enthusiastically promoted free trade. In fact, one government agency not only encourages U.S. companies to relocate abroad but also helps pay their moving expenses.

The story involves the U.S. Agency for International Development (USAID), which during the early 1990s used taxpayer money to help finance the construction of textile factories in Latin America. It also used taxpayer money to help train workers at the foreign plants and to pay for advertisements that lured U.S. companies to Latin America.

A major recipient of USAID's largesse from 1984 to 1992—to the tune of more than $100 million—was the Salvadoran Foundation for Economic and Social Development (Fundacion Salvadoreña para el Dessarollo Economico y Social, or FUSADES). USAID urged FUSADES to conduct "a proactive, direct, and systematic sales effort involving direct contact with targeted U.S. firms to convince them to explore opportunities in El Salvador."

Advertisements touting cheap Salvadoran labor were a key part of the "proactive" campaign. One FUSADES ad, which ran in trade publications for the apparel industry, showed a woman hunched over a sewing machine. "Rosa Martinez produces apparel for U.S. markets on her sewing machine in El Salvador," read the accompanying text. "*You* can hire her for thirty-three cents an hour."

Numerous U.S. companies took the bait. Koret of California, Inc., a manufacturer of women's clothing, shut down its plant in San Francisco to move to Guatemala, thereby eliminating 300 jobs. Another manufacturer of women's clothing, Marcade Group, Inc. (now Aris Industries, Inc.), relocated to El Salvador after closing a Tennessee plant that employed 306 people.

Once in Latin America, these USAID-assisted firms tried to further reduce labor costs by keeping the factories union-free illegally. Business executives at a USAID-supported plant in Honduras told Charles Kernaghan of the workers'-rights organization the National Labor Committee—who investigated the USAID program by posing as a potential investor in a textile factory—that they used a blacklist to weed out union organizers. Kernaghan asked a USAID official if the USAID-sponsored corps could "deliver on their promise to keep unions out."

"Oh, yes," the official replied. "I think they can deliver on that."

With economic globalization having turned the entire world into one gigantic labor pool, U.S. companies no longer feel much loyalty to their American workers. When seeking to win public support for free trade, though, corporate executives routinely play the patriotism card.

||||||||||||||||||||||||||||||||||||||||

Before the vote on NAFTA, executives of General Electric Company said that increased business from NAFTA "could support 10,000 jobs for GE and its suppliers." After the vote, GE moved 2,254 U.S. jobs south of the border.

||||||||||||||||||||||||||||||||||||||||

Scores of executives wrapped themselves in the flag as the NAFTA debate raged on, mainly by vowing to protect their U.S. workers in the event that Congress approved the deal. When asked by CNN if NAFTA would result in job losses for his company's U.S. employees, Lawrence Bossidy, the chairman and chief executive officer of AlliedSignal, Inc., replied confidently: "I think quite the contrary. I think the jobs that were to move to Mexico have already moved there." In the first four years following Congress's ratification of NAFTA, AlliedSignal fired 1,125 U.S. workers to move more business to Mexico.

Other big companies were equally hypocritical. Before the vote, executives of General Electric Company said that increased business from NAFTA "could support 10,000 jobs for GE and its suppliers." After the vote, GE moved 2,254 U.S. jobs south of the border. Johnson & Johnson, in a company statement, said: "An estimated 800 more U.S. positions will be created as a result of trade with Mexico, should NAFTA be approved." As of 1996, the company had fired 512 workers in order to move some operations to Mexico and could point to no new jobs being created in the United States as a result of NAFTA. When Public Citizen called Johnson & Johnson to ask about the discrepancy between theory and practice, Jeffrey Leebau, a spokesman, replied, "The company does not want to engage in an interview on its experiences with NAFTA at this point."

Republican Cass Ballenger of North Carolina took to the House floor two days before the NAFTA vote to allay fears that businesses planned to move to Mexico to exploit cheap labor. "There is nothing to lose [with NAFTA] as far as the textile industry is concerned," Ballenger said. He cited a statement issued by the American Textile Manufacturers Institute that claimed its member firms "pledge not to move jobs, plants, or facilities from the United States to Mexico as a result of the North American Free Trade Agreement." Noting that textile and apparel manufacturing had increased by 900 percent and 500 percent, respectively, since Mexico had begun reducing its tariffs in 1987 as part of the General Agreement on Tariffs and Trade, Ballenger said, "There is no reason in the world this growth could not continue." Yet NAFTA decimated the U.S. textile and apparel industries, with at least 42,000 workers being fired as companies moved out of the country from 1994 to 1997.

Esperanza Amaya, for example, worked for twenty-three years at a jeans plant in El Paso, Texas, owned by Levi Strauss and Company—one of the textile companies that Ballenger promised would not move jobs to Mexico under NAFTA. Amaya started at Levi Strauss as a machine operator and worked her way up to the post of inspector, for which she was paid $10 an hour. After NAFTA passed, the company on several occasions sent Amaya to Mexico to train workers at one of its border factories.

Levi Strauss did not tell Amaya that she was training her replacements. In 1997, the company closed down its El Paso operations and fired 110 workers, including Amaya. Then Levi Strauss stepped up its hiring in Mexico, where workers get about $25 a week.

Five months after she was let go, Amaya was still looking for work. She was getting by, just barely, on a small unemployment check and a pension from Levi Strauss of $136 a month. "I've been looking for work, but there are no factories, no jobs," she told the Center. "I don't know how to look for another job because all I've ever done is work at Levi's. I thought I'd always be there."

In an interview with the Center for Public Integrity, David Weiskopf, the director of governmental affairs at Levi Strauss, denied that the jobs eliminated at the company's U.S. plants in the years since NAFTA had been moved overseas or to Mexico. Rather, he explained, Levi Strauss "simply couldn't maintain" its workforce levels and that the jobs had been lost because of "normal patterns of trade and competitive pressures."

It appears, however, that many of the companies moving to Mexico were not motivated to do so by a cash crunch. Allied-Signal's profits, for example, rose by 16.6 percent in 1996. Bossidy received a salary and other compensation of $12 million, more than his company's entire Mexican workforce—3,800 people—made in 1996. GE's Welch, another post-NAFTA job-killer, was also a winner. In 1996, he took home $27 million while his company's profits rose by 11 percent.

> Representative Edward Markey calls China "the Kmart for weapons of mass destruction" because of its transfer of nuclear technology to such countries as Iran, Pakistan, and Algeria. Yet U.S. firms have repeatedly turned over sensitive technology to Beijing in return for access to the Chinese market.

Congress has been miserly about helping employees who have lost their jobs (and in some cases their careers) because of NAFTA, allocating just $120 million for worker retraining from 1994 to 1996. Washington was far more generous when Wall Street—which holds billions of dollars' worth of Mexican government stocks and bonds—took a hit in the wake of Mexico's 1994 economic collapse. At that time, Congress and the Clinton Administration hastened to put together a $50 billion international bailout.

By enabling Mexico to make good on its commitments to foreign bondholders, the bailout amounted to a government-financed rescue of Wall Street investment houses. Indeed, at least $4 billion of the initial $20 billion in bailout money went to Wall Street investment houses and the richest of Mexico's rich.

The bailout also paid off for many of its architects. In early 1997, one day after Mexico paid off the final installment of the $13.5 billion that the U.S. Treasury had contributed to the bailout, Treasury Undersecretary Jeffrey Shafer announced that he was resigning his post. Shafer, who played a key role in putting together the bailout, quickly took up residence as vice chairman of Salomon Brothers International, which at the time of Mexico's economic crash held about $250 million in Mexican government securities.

In addition to killing off jobs in the United States, NAFTA has been a disappointment on many fronts. NAFTA's proponents promised that the U.S. trade surplus with Mexico would hit $9 billion by 1995. Instead, the $1 billion trade surplus of 1993 turned into an $18.3 billion trade deficit three years later. The U.S. trade deficit with Canada, the other NAFTA partner, grew from $12.2 billion in 1993 to $24 billion in 1996. NAFTA would protect the environment, its backers said, but four years after the deal was signed problems still abound as growth outstrips the poorly funded infrastructure of the border regions. Congress and President Clinton vowed to protect communities that had lost jobs because of NAFTA by creating the North American Development Bank, which would offer cheap loans to hard-hit areas. The bank was endowed with $3 billion, but it did not make a single loan during its first three and a half years in business.

Big business has devoted more time, money, and effort to its all-out lobbying campaign to maintain China's most-favored-nation trade status than it has to any other trade issue. It is also nowhere more apparent that the interests of the Fortune 500 do not necessarily coincide with the public interest.

Imports from China have ballooned the U.S. trade deficit. In 1995, the United States exported more to Taiwan's 21 million people ($19 billion) than it did to China's 1.2 billion people (less than $12 billion), but the United States runs an annual trade deficit of $45 billion with China.

Nor has freer trade with China enhanced international security. Representative Edward Markey, a Democrat from Massachusetts, calls China "the Kmart for weapons of mass destruction" because of its transfer of nuclear technology to such countries as Iran, Pakistan, and Algeria. Yet U.S. firms have repeatedly turned over sensitive technology to Beijing in return for access to the Chinese market. McDonnell Douglas Corporation once closed a deal to build jets in China by agreeing to include sensitive tooling technology on a promise that it would be used solely for civilian purposes. However, the machinery was subsequently diverted by Chinese authorities to a military aircraft and missile plant in Nanchang. On another occasion, McDonnell Douglas secured a joint-venture agreement with a state-owned aviation company by providing, in the words of *The Wall Street Journal,* "enough technical data to fill a library."

China has hardly advanced the cause of human rights, either. It still relies on torture, kangaroo courts, and police repression to stifle dissent, and it outlaws independent labor unions, forbids religious freedom, and employs prison labor on a vast scale. Experts agree that the situation has deteriorated markedly since 1994, when President Clinton announced that China's trade status would no longer be linked to its human-rights record.

U.S. corporations with major business interests in China argue that Beijing will simply expand its trade with other nations if the United States makes too many demands on the human-rights front. Yet the United States is China's biggest source of investment and technology and is the destination for 30 percent of China's exports. (Only 2 percent of U.S. exports end up in China.)

All this gives the United States plenty of negotiating strength. The Clinton Administration has used such leverage to force China to make concessions on economic issues that include intellectual property rights and market access. "There's a clear double standard," Mike Jendrzejczyk, the Washington director of Human Rights Watch/Asia, told journalist Ken Silverstein in 1997. "On human rights, the United States claims to be completely impotent, but in other areas it's willing to make use of leverage it supposedly doesn't have."

So who has benefited from freer trade with China? The most obvious winners are the elite group of huge corporations that head up the China lobby, especially AlliedSignal; AT&T; Boeing: Cargill, Inc.; Caterpillar, Inc.; Motorola; and the Big Three automakers.

Led by those firms, U.S. investment in China has climbed from $358 million in 1990 to $6.9 billion in 1996. Mattel, which has fired thousands of American workers in recent years, makes most of its Barbie dolls in China. The Christian Industrial Committee, a Hong Kong-based labor-rights group, visited a Mattel factory in China and found workers making twenty-five cents an hour with only two days off a month.

Although China desperately wants to maintain its most-favored-nation status, it spends little on direct lobbying in the United States. That is because Corporate America has been getting the job done on its own. As a 1997 report by the Congressional Research Service reads: "Chinese officials apparently decided that Beijing's interests would be better served by allowing U.S. business groups to speak for themselves, rather than be seen as part of some coalition of forces led by the Chinese Embassy officials."

U.S. corporations have pooled resources to underwrite such groups as the U.S.-China Business Council, which has a $4 million annual budget and offices in Washington, Beijing, Shanghai, and Hong Kong. Corporate firepower has been further augmented with hundreds of lobbyists from practically every powerhouse firm in Washington. The China lobby includes Patton, Boggs, which in 1996 had nine of its guns trained on the China MFN campaign, among them Thomas Hale Boggs, Jr., the son of the late House Speaker and a frequent dinner companion of Bill Clinton's, and Darryl Nirenberg, former chief of staff to North Carolina Senator and Foreign Affairs Committee Chairman Jesse Helms; Hogan and Hartson, whose roster boasts Warren Maruyama, a former associate general counsel of the Office of the U.S. Trade Representative; and the Dutko Group, which employs Frances Norris, a former aide to Senate Majority Leader Trent Lott. Many of these officials have money at stake in China, although this fact is rarely noted when they shill for Beijing.

Take, for example, former Secretary of State Henry Kissinger, who now heads Kissinger Associates, a consulting firm that opens doors for U.S. companies seeking to do business abroad. Following the 1989 massacre of pro-democracy demonstrators at Tiananmen Square, Kissinger appeared on ABC News and voiced strong opposition to economic sanctions against China.

Many of Kissinger's clients have huge investments in China. In 1997, Walt Disney Company hired Kissinger to smooth Beijing's feathers, which were ruffled over Disney's production of *Kundun,* a motion picture, released later that year, that took a critical look at China's occupation of Tibet. Chinese anger over the movie threatened the company's plans to open a theme park outside Beijing.

Brent Scowcroft is another former U.S. government official who plies the China trade. As a member of the National Security Council, Scowcroft traveled to Beijing in 1989 shortly after the crackdown at Tiananmen Square for consultations with Chinese leaders (who commemorated his arrival by dispatching security forces to pummel a group of student demonstrators). Scowcroft now heads the Scowcroft Group, a consulting firm that develops "market entry strategies" for companies seeking opportunities in China and other countries. In October 1996, Scowcroft traveled to Beijing, joining Dean O'Hare, the chairman and chief executive officer of Chubb Corporation, at a meeting with Premier Li Peng. According to an account in the Chinese press, Li "expressed his appreciation for the prolonged efforts Scowcroft has made in helping to develop Sino-U.S. relations."

None of this has stopped Scowcroft from offering himself up as a dispassionate analyst of U.S.-China relations.

With polls showing that Americans overwhelmingly put human rights above trade with China, corporations have also spent lavishly to influence public opinion in the United States. "The companies [with big investments in China] all face PR difficulties," Kenneth DeWoskin, a professor at the University of Michigan Business School and a consultant to several automakers that do business in China, told the Center. "That requires an ongoing effort to educate the public and make people feel positive about U.S. investment there."

To that end, a coalition of Fortune 500 companies—including Boeing, AlliedSignal, ConAgra, Motorola, TRW, Nike, General Electric, Dresser Industries, and IBM—launched a public-relations campaign informally known as the China Normalization Initiative. They hired big PR firms like Hill & Knowlton. They retained pro-China academics to draft newspaper commentaries, speak at public events, and produce Panglossian brochures that laud China and urge an expansion of U.S. trade with Beijing. They commissioned a video called "New Faces of China," which *The New York Times* described as "a remarkably dewy-eyed depiction of China— no repression of dissidents, no sales of automatic weapons to gangs in Los Angeles, no nuclear proliferation, but plenty of Chinese enjoying American goods." The companies underwriting the campaign distribute such material to Members of Congress, the news media, and even to community organizations like Rotary International.

Everybody is getting rich on China, it seems, but American workers. During recent years, thousands have lost their jobs as U.S. companies head for China in search of cheap labor.

One such casualty is Lynette McCall, who for twelve years worked for Lockheed Corporation in Meridian, Mississippi, doing subassembly work on its C-130 transport plane. In August 1995, she and another 100 or so employees were laid off. McCall had been earning about $17 an hour. Lockheed replaced her and her coworkers with Chinese workers who have to work about ten days to make $17.

After two years on unemployment, McCall was rehired by Lockheed. The call back to work came after she had used up her life savings, about $57,000. "There were a lot of gaps to fill in— the mortgage and household expenses—so my family had to rely on my pension money," McCall told the Center. "I don't know how these companies expect the American people to get by. They're going to have trouble one of these days because there's not going to be anybody to purchase their products if we don't have jobs."

Although McCall got her job back, her family continues to feel the impact of Congress's unwavering support for free trade. During the period that McCall was unemployed, her daughter, Sharita Whitehead, was forced to drop out of the University of Alabama at Birmingham, where she was studying to be a nurse. After moving back to Mississippi, Whitehead took a job at Delco Remy International, Inc., which makes starters for General Motors Corporation.

Not long after her mother went back to work, Whitehead lost her job when Delco Remy announced that it was moving its operations in Meridian to Mexico. She now works at a Dillard's department store, where she makes $8 an hour.

18

||||||●|||||

The Turn of the Screw

IN 1978, AFTER HAVING A DOUBLE MASTECTOMY, MARIA STERN, A U.S. Forest Service employee in Salinas, California, sought to restore her self-esteem through silicone breast implants. The surgery was a common procedure: Thousands of American women were getting implants each year, some to enhance their appearance, others to cope with the disfiguring effects of cancer. When told that the implants would safely last a lifetime, Stern had no reason to be doubtful. As she told a reporter in 1992, she believed she would "live happily ever after" with her implants.

Instead, a year after the implant surgery, Stern began to feel ill. Her fingers became swollen, she lost her sense of smell and taste, her hearing failed, and her hair started falling out. Before long, she was experiencing pain so "bone-shattering" that she could not get out of bed. Her doctors were mystified. By 1981, her five-foot-four-inch body had shrunk from 120 to eighty-seven pounds and she had begun to suspect that something was wrong with her implants. Doctors, on removing them, discovered that Stern's suspicions were correct: The sacs of silicone had developed holes, and their contents were leaking into her body.

Stern proceeded to file a lawsuit in federal court against Dow Corning Corporation, the Michigan-based manufacturer of the implants. In the course of the lawsuit, her attorney, Dan Bolton, obtained internal company memos that documented quality-control problems in the manufacture of the implants and a lack of scientific evidence that the implants were safe.

As a result of those damning revelations, in 1984 a federal jury in San Francisco decided that Dow Corning had committed fraud and had failed to warn Stern of the implants' potential to cause severe side effects. It awarded Stern $1.5 million in punitive damages and $211,000 in actual damages. More important, by exposing the hazards of silicone breast implants, Stern had struck a blow to protect the health of thousands of other women.

Or so it might have been. Instead, Dow Corning appealed the verdict and, as often happens in lawsuits, made an offer to settle the case. Desperately ill and in need of money, Stern accepted the offer. As part of the settlement, a protective order issued by the court prohibited Stern's attorney and expert witnesses from revealing information about the potential dangers of implants to anyone—including other women who might have thought twice about having implants, had they known of the risks. Stern and her legal team were not even allowed to share what they knew with the Food and Drug Administration (FDA), the regulatory agency charged with ensuring that medical devices such as implants are safe. In 1988, when the FDA held hearings to investigate the safety of silicone implants, Bolton could not provide the documentation he had used to prove the dangers of implants in his case.

Finally, in 1992, some of the documents Bolton had obtained were leaked to FDA commissioner David Kessler.

During the 1980s and 1990s, corporate litigants began pushing the envelope in terms of legal discretion—routinely asking federal judges to place under seal many, and sometimes all, of the documents they were compelled to reveal during the discovery phases of cases.

That information quickly convinced him to put a moratorium on implants. But because of the delay, nearly 1 million women had received implants throughout the 1980s without knowing of the potential risks. "They became the unwitting participants in a human medical trial. . . ." Sybil Niden Goldrich, a breast-implant activist, said. "The court, with its intransigence about secrecy orders, allowed it to happen."

Unfortunately, the hazards of silicone breast implants are not the only secrets that companies have kept from the American public with the cooperation of the courts. At least as far back as the 1940s, courts began sealing documents in cases, initially to protect trade secrets whose disclosure stood to harm companies' fortunes. While that sort of confidentiality seems justifiable, during the 1980s and 1990s, businesses began pushing the envelope in terms of legal discretion. While companies often seek secrecy in local and state proceedings, some of the most extreme examples of the quest for corporate secrecy have occurred in the federal courts. Blithely ignoring the spirit of federal court rules—which ostensibly are supposed to allow as much public access as possible to court records and proceedings—more and more corporate litigants routinely asked federal judges to place under seal many, and sometimes all, of the documents they were compelled to reveal during the discovery phases of cases. In addition, they increasingly seek to include in settlements the promise that documents and information gathered during the litigation will remain sealed, and that the terms of the settlements themselves will be confidential.

In some instances, companies sought to virtually erase the lawsuits from the public records, as if the suits had never happened. "Often after a case is over," Joan Claybrook, the president of the consumer-advocacy group Public Citizen, told members of the House Judiciary Committee in 1997, "defendants will destroy—or require the plaintiffs to destroy—discovery materials so that plaintiffs in similar cases, particularly against common defendants, lose access to this information." And in a 1995 law-journal article, Fordham University law professor Jill Fisch descries the practice of "post-settlement vacatur," in which the parties in a lawsuit agree to settle on the condition that the verdict be erased, "as if the judgment had never been rendered at all." Indeed, in some cases even the names of people or companies involved in a suit have been kept secret, with the court record titled "Sealed vs. Sealed."

Judges, faced with dockets clogged by long, drawn-out corporate litigation, often take the simplest way out. Federal court rule 26(c) traditionally has given federal judges considerable leeway to decide what constitutes a legitimate need for secrecy. "Limiting the discretion of district judges could result in burdening the parties with unnecessary expense of duplicative discovery or, in some instances, slowing down the process with numerous rulings on contested issues of confidentiality," Federal Appellate Judge Joseph Weis, Jr., the chairman of the congressionally created Federal Courts Study Committee, said in testimony to the House Judiciary Committee in 1992. But faced with sifting through the mountain of pretrial testimony and documents in cases to determine which had a legitimate claim to confidentiality, judges sometimes took the easy way out and simply rubber-stamped companies' requests for blanket secrecy.

Defense attorneys for corporations argue that such confidentiality is necessary to protect secrets—a revolutionary manufacturing process, for example, or the plans for marketing next year's product line—that competitors might dig up and use to gain an unfair advantage. And they argue that companies, like individuals, have a right to privacy. "The courts are supposed to solve disputes between private parties," Alfred Cortese, Jr., a corporate defense lawyer and a partner in the Washington office of Pepper, Hamilton & Scheetz, told *Legal Times* in 1995. "The courts shouldn't be an information clearinghouse. The public's right to know has to be equally balanced with a person's right to privacy." In many instances, those concerns are no doubt legitimate. But sealing corporate documents and compelling silence as a condition of settlements has also served other purposes that are harder to justify.

In the early 1980s, seven chemical companies—Dow Chemical Company; Diamond Shamrock Corporation (now Ultramar Diamond Shamrock Corporation); Hercules, Inc.; Monsanto Company; T. H. Agriculture and Nutrition Company; Thompson Chemical Company; and Uniroyal, Inc.—obtained protective orders to block the release of documents they had turned over to plaintiffs in lawsuits dealing with Agent Orange, the defoliant that some Vietnam veterans and others claim has caused serious health problems for those exposed to it. One such settlement, in 1984, actually called for sensitive documents to be returned to the chemical manufacturer. It took another three years of litigating

||||||||||||||||||||||||||||||||||||||||||||||||||||||||||||||||||||||||||||

Court secrecy has enabled companies that make unsafe products to keep them on the market—sometimes years after their lethal flaws were uncovered—without the public or even government regulatory agencies learning about the problem.

for the Vietnam Veterans of America, alleging a cover-up, to get a federal appeals court to lift the protective order for good.

In 1986, after 123 patients died when their mechanical heart valves failed, Shiley, Inc., a subsidiary of pharmaceutical giant Pfizer, Inc., took the valves off the market. Over the next few years, the parent company reportedly settled at least thirty lawsuits around the nation, in each instance exacting an agreement to put both key documents and the terms of the settlement under seal. Eventually, thanks in part to documents leaked by a Pfizer employee to Public Citizen—which in turn made them available to the FDA and subsequently offered a 2,000-page package of Pfizer documents, news articles, and other information to attorneys interested in filing lawsuits against the company—Pfizer's efforts to head off a reckoning were unsuccessful. In 1992, the company paid out $215 million to settle a massive class-action suit.

During his career at General Motors Corporation, engineer Ronald Elwell gave more than sixty depositions and testified in more than a dozen trials, serving the company as an expert witness who could verify the safety of GM vehicles. Eventually, however, Elwell became disenchanted with his employer—by his account, following his discovery that the company had withheld from him the results of unfavorable crash tests. In 1991, Elwell gave a deposition in a suit against GM, in which he said that the location of gas tanks outside the frame of pickup trucks was unsafe. After Elwell's testimony in an Atlanta case resulted in a $105 million verdict against GM, Elwell started getting calls from plaintiffs who had been injured or had a family member killed in a GM truck accident. GM, in turn, fought to silence Elwell in courtrooms around the country, obtaining a protective order against him in Michigan that said he was violating a confidentiality agreement he had signed as a condition of his retirement from GM. After a federal appeals court sided with GM, the case went to the U.S. Supreme Court, which in January 1998 ruled that a state court could not gag an expert witness from testifying elsewhere in the nation.

In 1995, a federal judge in Pennsylvania denied a motion to unseal documents in a liability case dealing with the pedicle screws used to stabilize the spine in fusion surgery, even though the plaintiffs argued that the information would show that some of the authors of an FDA study on the effectiveness of the devices had a financial interest in the company that manufactured the product.

On occasion, the corporate right to court secrecy has taken precedence over the First Amendment. In 1995, *BusinessWeek* magazine was set to publish a story about a federal lawsuit in which Procter & Gamble Company sought nearly $200 million in damages from Bankers Trust Company, which P&G accused of not adequately informing the public of the risks involved with certain complex investments. Hours before the magazine was to go to press, U.S. District Court Judge John Feikens in Cincinnati ordered *BusinessWeek* not to publish the story, saying that the magazine had used information from documents that were under seal. Even though *BusinessWeek* had obtained the information from a source outside the courts, it was forced to comply. "This was the first time in our sixty-six-year history that we have ever been forced by the government to pull a story," *BusinessWeek*'s editors wrote. Although the judge relented and unsealed the documents in question, the case was another example of just how potent the corporate claim to secrecy could be.

Businesses have even been able to compel the federal government itself to keep their secrets. In 1991, for example, when federal regulators negotiated a $49 million settlement of the failed Silverado Savings and Loan in Colorado, the details of the settlement were sealed by a federal judge.

Court secrecy has enabled companies that make unsafe products to keep them on the market—sometimes years after their lethal flaws were uncovered—without the public or even government regulatory agencies learning about the problem. And the ability to keep potentially damaging information under seal can give a big company a powerful advantage against any injured consumer who tries to sue it for damages; the company can force that person's lawyer to fight a long, hard, and costly battle to obtain the same information that the company already has revealed in previous lawsuits by other injured consumers.

Companies have justified all this in the name of protecting proprietary data and preserving their competitive advantage, even when it is clear that their opponent is not a competitor but rather an injured customer. Cancer patient Sybil Niden Goldrich suffered through four surgeries in an attempt to correct problems with her breast implants in the mid-1980s; doctors later discovered that silicone had leaked and contaminated her uterus, ovaries, and liver. When she finally decided to file a lawsuit in 1986, she ran into a brick wall of secrecy. "Manufacturers zealously fought my attorney's attempts at discovery of the documents by claiming that trade secrets would be revealed," she told members of the Senate Judiciary Committee in 1994. "Although I'm not a competitor, and although there were many ways the documents requested could have been redacted to maintain true trade secrets, entire categories of documents were withheld."

Goldrich was handicapped in her lawsuit because she did not know about the Maria Stern case, let alone have access to its sealed secrets. Instead, she struck back in other ways: She wrote an article for *Ms.* magazine to publicize the problems with implants, and she joined forces with Kathleen Anneken, a fellow victim of implants, to form the Command Trust Network, a nationwide organization that disseminated information about implant problems and that grew to develop a 16,000-person mailing list. After the Stern documents were divulged to the FDA, Goldrich finally got a measure of retribution: Victims joined in a class-action suit, and in 1992 the judge in that case lifted all of the long-standing protective orders that guarded implant manufacturers' secrets. Ultimately, the manufacturers were forced to settle the class-action suit for a staggering $4.75 billion, the largest such settlement up till then.

Thanks to the efforts of activists such as Goldrich, revelations about the hidden horrors of breast implants caused a backlash against court-imposed secrecy. Trial Lawyers for Public Justice, a national public-interest law firm, began to file suits and motions challenging court secrecy around the nation. States began to pass laws limiting the sealing of records at the local level. In the early 1990s, legislators in Florida and Washington State passed laws barring judges from sealing records in lawsuits that involved a public hazard; the Texas Supreme Court decreed that plaintiffs seeking protective orders had to demonstrate that the damage they would suffer from disclosure outweighed the secrecy's potential harm to the public.

At the federal level, however, Congress was slow to follow. In 1988, as Pfizer fought to cover up the problems with its artificial heart valve, Senator Howell Heflin, a Democrat from Alabama, and then-Representative Dan Glickman, a Democrat from Kansas and a member of the Judiciary Committee, introduced legislation to keep foreign recipients of the heart valves from suing in U.S. courts. Congress, for the most part, seemed more interested in so-called "tort reform"—that is, making it more difficult for individuals to sue companies. (Not surprisingly, Fortune 500 companies contributed at least $182 million to congressional campaigns from 1987 through 1996 by way of their PACs, while "soft money" contributions to both parties over the same period added up to more than $73 million.)

But there were a few exceptions. In 1992, Representative Larry Smith, a Democrat from Florida, introduced the Sunshine in Litigation Act, which would have prohibited federal judges from issuing protective orders that concealed public hazards. "Today courts can still prohibit the disclosure of certain information, even if that information could save another person's life," Smith told the House Judiciary Committee. "I believe that secrecy agreements should be the rare exception to open judicial proceedings." (Smith, unfortunately, had his own problems with disclosure. He pleaded guilty to evading income tax and misusing his campaign account and, after leaving office in 1992, spent three months in federal prison.) Representative David Skaggs, a Democrat from Colorado, introduced legislation, the Federal Court Settlements Sunshine Act of 1991, that would have barred the courts from sealing any documents in cases where federal regulators had settled lawsuits, unless the trial judge determined that "a compelling public interest" required secrecy. The Bush Administration opposed both bills. Steven Bransdorfer, a deputy assistant attorney general in the Justice Department's Civil Division, testified that restricting secrecy would endanger companies' trade secrets. The legislation went to the House Judiciary Committee, where ultimately both measures died.

In the Senate, Herbert Kohl, a Democrat from Wisconsin, took up the cause of unsealing the court system and waged a lonely three-year battle to pass legislation restricting the granting of protective orders in federal court. "Far too often," he said in 1996, "the court system allows vital information that is discovered in litigation—and which directly bears on people's health and safety—to be covered up, to be shielded from mothers, fathers, and children whose lives are potentially at stake and from the officials we have appointed to watch over our health and safety."

|||||||||||||||||||||||||||||||||||||||

In 1996, Congress passed the Small Business Jobs Protection Act, which for the first time made victims of workplace mistreatment pay tax on emotional and punitive damage awards as if it were pay for work and not damages for injury or injustice.

|||||||||||||||||||||||||||||||||||||||

In August 1993, Kohl introduced his own version of the Sunshine in Litigation Act. Kohl wanted to alter the law so that judges would be required to determine beforehand that a protective order would not cover up a threat to the public's health or safety. He wanted to place the burden of proof on the party that sought the protective order, requiring it to show that its need for confidentiality outweighed the public's right to know. Kohl also sought to bar parties in a lawsuit from entering into any agreement to keep information from regulatory agencies. After that bill did not make it out of the Judiciary Committee, the following year Kohl tried again. The Senate rejected his amendment by just a single vote.

In 1995, Kohl reintroduced the Sunshine in Litigation Act, but once again he couldn't get his bill out of the Judiciary Committee. The federal courts seemed to be moving in the opposite direction; some judges actually favored making secrecy restrictions easier to obtain. That same year the Judicial Conference of the United States, the official policymaking body of the federal judiciary, considered revising the law to eliminate even the meager requirement that judges had to find "good cause" to seal documents. Instead, under the proposed change, judges would have been allowed to issue a protective order in any case where the plaintiff and defendant both agreed to it. After Kohl led four other Democratic members of the Senate Judiciary Committee in opposing the bill—including, somewhat surprisingly, the same Howell Heflin who seven years earlier had introduced legislation on behalf of Pfizer, maker of the problematic artificial heart valve—the Judicial Conference opted not to change the rule.

In 1996, Kohl gave his Sunshine in Litigation measure one more try. He managed to get it attached as an amendment to the Federal Courts Improvement Act, an appropriations bill. This time it passed and became law. Although his modest legislation laid out better guidelines for determining whether records should be open or sealed, even Kohl recognizes that excessive secrecy is still an issue. At a hearing in October 1997, for example, he asked a judicial nominee he supported to affirm that he would deliberate over the need for secrecy before issuing a protective order. "Altogether too often," Kohl said, "secrecy agreements prevent the real dangers to public safety from being disclosed."

Given the continuing fervor in the GOP-dominated Congress for "reform," however, it is unlikely that legislators will take more aggressive steps to prevent future Maria Sterns from suffering the same sort of tragedies.

From the time the issue emerged in the mid-1980s, it was nearly a decade before lawmakers took action to curb court secrecy. But Congress's slowness in dealing with the issue is just one part of the larger story. In recent years, instead of working to improve the legal system so that it might better protect the public from fraud or unsafe products, Congress has focused on protecting companies from lawsuits and on making it more difficult for the public to seek help from the courts. For example:

- Congress has protected companies from being held accountable by their investors. In 1995, legislators overrode a veto by President Clinton and passed the 1995 Private Securities Litigation Reform Act, supposedly to curb a plague of frivolous class-action suits against high-tech companies. The act hinders groups of investors who want to sue for damages after they have lost money because a company's "forward-looking" statements turned out to be wrong. Unhappy shareholders now have to wait until a judge rules that their case has merit before they can conduct discovery and subpoena the large numbers of company documents that might be necessary to prove their allegations. In addition, the company's Wall Street underwriters and accountants are shielded from any liability. Investors sought to avoid those obstacles by seeking justice in local state courts where the law did not apply. In October 1997, Senators Phil Gramm, a Republican from Texas, and Christopher Dodd, a Democrat from Connecticut, introduced additional legislation that would compel groups of twenty-five or more investors to use the federal court system.

- Congress has discriminated against victims of civil-rights abuses. In 1996, Congress passed the Small Business Jobs Protection Act, which for the first time made victims of workplace mistreatment pay tax on emotional and punitive damage awards as if it were pay for work and not damages for injury or injustice. As critics noted, a plaintiff who claims emotional distress from whiplash in a car accident now receives more favorable treatment under the law than a person who was sexually harassed on the job or denied a promotion because of race. The legislation reduced legal protections for discrimination victims that Congress had created just five years before.

- Congress has sought to shield companies from being held accountable for unsafe products. Since the mid-1980s, business advocates in Congress have sought to enact "tort reform" legislation that would override laws in the fifty states and replace them with a single federal standard, under which the public would have a more difficult time suing companies and damage awards would be greatly reduced. In 1995, both chambers of Congress finally passed "tort reform" bills—the Product Liability Fairness Act in the Senate and the Common Sense Product Liability and Legal Reform Act in the House—and agreed on a joint version in March 1996, only to have it vetoed two months later by President Clinton. A scaled-down version of the legislation, the Product Liability Reform Act, was reintroduced in the

Senate and sent to the Senate Commerce Committee in May 1997. The bill would protect companies who show "conscious, flagrant indifference to the safety of others" by capping their punitive damages at $250,000 or two times compensatory damages, whichever is greater. The legislation would also establish a two-year statute of limitations from the moment a person discovers that he or she has been harmed by a defective product and would essentially bar suits against products eighteen years after their purchase, unless they contain toxic chemicals.

Will any of these "reforms" do much to relieve the crowded dockets in courts across the nation? Probably not. In 1993, a study of Fortune 1000 companies by University of Wisconsin sociologist Joel Rogers and RAND Institute for Civil Justice senior researcher Terence Dunworth showed that 43 percent of lawsuits in federal court—the single largest category—were companies filing lawsuits against one another, as the result of contract disputes. *The National Law Journal* reported in 1995 that business cases make up a third of the federal-court backlog of cases that take more than three years to resolve. Personal-injury and product-liability claims made up just 10 percent of the federal total. In state courts across the nation, medical malpractice cases amount to less than 1 percent of all civil filings.

> **In 1993, a study of Fortune 1000 companies showed that 43 percent of lawsuits in federal court—the single largest category—were companies filing lawsuits against one another as the result of contract disputes.**

"There is a growing perception that there is a litigation explosion occurring in our court system, that our courts are backlogged due to the filing of meritless cases by greedy lawyers," Senator Barbara Boxer, a Democrat from California, told the Senate Commerce Committee in 1995. "The increases . . . are the result of businesses suing other businesses."

Little wonder that consumer activists and others argue that Congress has been barking up the wrong tree.

19

IIIII•IIIII

Third-Class Citizens

Matthew Garvey will never forget his fourteenth birthday. He had just started working at Quality Car Wash in Laurel, Maryland, where he loaded a big machine that sucked the water from wet towels. After a long, hot day feeding towels into the machine, Matthew took a break on top of the dryer to catch a cool breeze rising from its whirling fan blades.

"While I was sitting there," Matthew recalled, "another boy that worked there was using his cigarette lighter to burn the hair on my legs." Matthew instinctively pulled away from the flame, but to his horror, his leg was sucked into the dryer. "It was spinning me around, and I remember trying to push myself out of the machine. Then I was thrown from the machine and landed in the driveway outside the car wash."

Matthew tried to get up but couldn't. "I looked up and saw that my leg was gone. I was lying on the ground, and I could hear my leg thumping around in the machine."

The dryer that took Matthew Garvey's leg was operating that day without a safety lid. The machine was not supposed to run without the lid, but it had been rigged to do so anyway. The car wash was initially slapped with a fine of $400—until a public outcry caused it to be raised to $730—for operating defective equipment. (Matthew Garvey later settled with the car wash's insurance company for nearly $600,000.)

Matthew told his tale to a Senate subcommittee considering a child labor bill that might have prevented similar tragedies by imposing tighter restrictions on when, where, and how long American children can work. But the bill, introduced by Democratic Senators Howard Metzenbaum of Ohio and Christopher Dodd of Connecticut in 1991, was later defeated.

The simple truth in Washington is that children do not vote and do not lobby. They do not contribute to political campaigns or pay for candidates' trips. They do not go to parties, and they never do lunch. About the only thing children do for a politician is provide a photo opportunity.

And what do they get in return for offering a chubby cheek at a campaign rally? Child labor laws that go unenforced. Classrooms with peeling paint, leaky roofs, no heat or air conditioning, broken or boarded-up windows, electrical systems unable to handle computer networks. Cutbacks on food assistance programs that will send millions of them to the soup line. And cutbacks in immunization programs that will doom many before their lives even get started.

Here are a few snapshots of the problems facing America's largest class of disenfranchised citizens:

> The simple truth in Washington is that children do not vote and do not lobby. They do not contribute to political campaigns or pay for candidates' trips. About the only thing children do for a politician is provide a photo opportunity.

- Children under eighteen are the nation's poorest age group, accounting for 27 percent of the population but 40 percent of the poor. The poverty rate for children is higher than for any other age group—20.5 percent in 1996, a figure that has remained at 20 percent or more since the early 1980s.
- The number of children without health insurance in the United States continues to grow. The Census Bureau found that, in 1996, some 10.6 million young people—15 percent of their ranks—were uninsured.

- More and more children are being raised by someone other than their parents. An estimated 462,000 children lived in full-time foster care, kinship care, or residential care in 1994, up from 276,000 in 1985. And it is estimated that 80,000 healthy children will have been orphaned by AIDS before the year 2000, with a third of them likely to enter a dysfunctional child-welfare system.
- Every day at least three children—most of them under five—die as a result of abuse or neglect, usually at the hands of a parent or caregiver. A 1996 Justice Department report found that children under eighteen were the victims in nearly 20 percent of the violent crimes committed by criminals now in state prisons and that more than half of the child victims were twelve or younger. The number of child murders increased from 1,463 in 1984 to 2,660 in 1994.
- In 1997—under the new, stricter standards of the 1996 welfare law that allow children to receive benefits only if they have "marked and severe functional limitations"—Congress and President Clinton cut off disability benefits for more than 95,000 children, most of whom suffer from mental disorders. As many as 55,000 additional children who now receive disability benefits could be cut off as well.

Across the United States, children are suffering for no greater reason than because Congress has failed, time and time again, to protect them from their exploiters, who wield a much heavier hand in Washington. "Congress has shown no interest in reforming labor law to make sure that workers can actually exercise the rights they supposedly have," Joshua Freeman, an associate professor of history at Queens College, has observed. "By cutting funds for enforcing laws regulating child labor, hours of work, and health and safety conditions, Congress has contributed to the reemergence of conditions once thought to have been eliminated forever: slave labor, child labor, grossly unsafe sweatshops, and coerced, uncompensated overtime."

Most people think that child labor is a relic of the past or a scourge of developing countries where children are forced to stitch basketball shoes, soccer balls, or rugs all day. But child labor is alive and well in the United States.

Nowhere is it more prevalent and more tolerated than in agriculture. According to the Farmworker Justice Fund, Inc., an advocacy group for migrant farmworkers, at least 200,000—and perhaps as many as 800,000—children work in agriculture today. The Fair Labor Standards Act of 1938 outlawed child labor in most industries except agriculture. It took Congress another thirty-six years to impose any age limits on child labor in agriculture.

In most industries, fourteen- and fifteen-year-olds can work only after school hours. Teens must be sixteen before they can be employed by anyone other than a parent for unlimited time periods, and they must be eighteen before they can work in hazardous conditions—even in businesses owned by their parents.

But agriculture has its own child labor rules. For example, a child sixteen or older is allowed to do hazardous work on a farm, such as operating a tractor, even during school hours. Children who are twelve or thirteen can do farmwork with the consent of a parent or guardian. There are also exemptions for children under twelve if they are employed by a parent or guardian on a farm owned or operated by the adult.

Many large farms exploit an exemption designed for small farms by hiring dozens of farmhands and their families through independent contractors. Children, working side by side with their parents in the field, end up exposed to such hazards as farm machinery, pesticides, and highway traffic.

The American Farm Bureau Federation strongly opposes closing this gap in child labor laws. "Our position is supportive of the law," C. Bryan Little, its director of governmental relations, told the Center. "Most of the exemptions are there so that kids can work on their parents' farm."

Children under eighteen are the nation's poorest age group, accounting for 27 percent of the population but 40 percent of the poor.

But Mull says that the small-farm exemption has turned into a big loophole, mainly for large fruit and vegetable growers. "The owner's kids," she says, "are not out working in the fields."

Agriculture is the second-most dangerous line of work in the United States, in part because of pesticide exposure. The Environmental Protection Agency estimates that hired farmworkers suffer up to 300,000 acute illnesses and injuries a year from exposure to pesticides. A General Accounting Office study found that children are at greater risk than adults from the dangers of pesticides. The reasons: They absorb more pesticides per pound of body weight, and their nervous systems and organs are still developing. What is more, children are more likely to ingest dirt or crops contaminated with pesticides.

But pesticides are only part of the problem. Each year, a 1993 study estimated, 27,000 children age nineteen and under who both live and work on farms suffer injuries, and an additional 300 die from work-related accidents. It is no wonder, when children work with tractors, farm machinery, knives, ladders, and pesticides.

Consider the tragic case of five-year-old Jacob Rubina, who was helping his mother, Rosa, grade and pack watermelons in the fields of Tifton, Georgia, when his hand got caught in a conveyor belt and was torn off. Jacob was rushed to the hospital, but surgeons were unable to save his hand.

Jacob's story reveals another side of farmworker life: children who work with their parents becase their labor is needed to help support the family. According to the Census Bureau, 46 percent of all farmworkers live below the poverty line. With average annual earnings of $6,500 for backbreaking work, most farmworkers, unable to afford day care, bring their children along with them to the fields.

The National Child Labor Committee estimates that at least 100,000 children work illegally on farms. The Labor Department has been ill-equipped, however, to do much about the problem. In 1989, it had 1,000 labor-law compliance officers, whose enforcement duties included far more than just child labor law violations; by the mid-1990s, it had fewer than 800.

Agriculture, of course, is not the only industry that uses children as workers. The Labor Department slapped Pizza Hut, Inc., with a $194,400 fine in April 1997 for violating child labor laws by having minors operate razor-sharp slicers and dough mixers in twenty-six restaurants. Pizza Hut has contested the charges. In January 1997, a Kenny Rogers Roasters restaurant in Indianapolis was fined for violating similar laws.

Congress has aided and abetted businesses, big and small, in their efforts to use children as low-wage workers. And not surprisingly, businesses have thanked supportive lawmakers on Capitol Hill with large campaign contributions. The American Farm Bureau Federation, one of the nation's most powerful lobbying organizations, has repeatedly opposed further restrictions, as have allied farm organizations, restaurants, automobile dealers, and others.

Testifying before the same Senate subcommittee on child labor as Matthew Garvey—the boy who lost his leg in the car-wash accident—James Coleman, the general counsel of the National Council of Chain Restaurants, called for relaxing the child labor laws that restrict work after seven o'clock on school nights. "We question both the reasonableness and the necessity of the seven P.M. time limit, given the other daily and weekly hour restrictions—for obvious reasons due to the dinner rush," Coleman said. "Frankly, we fail to see the substantive difference between a fifteen-year-old working after school from three P.M. until six P.M. and the same individual working from six P.M. until nine P.M. In either case, the total work is limited to three hours."

And the restaurant industry puts its money where its mouth is. In 1996 alone, the National Council of Chain Restaurants spent at least $140,000 lobbying Congress to weaken the 1938 Fair Labor Standards Act, which includes child labor protections, and to head off a raise in the minimum wage. The 33,000-member National Restaurant Association spent at least $770,000 in 1996 alone to lobby Congress on the Labor Department's appropriation budget and other issues. And it paid Capitol Hill lawmakers more than $381,000 in speaking fees from 1986 to 1996.

"There are so many industries desperate for workers, they're looking to younger and younger workers," Darlene Adkins, the coordinator of the Child Labor Coalition, part of the National Consumers League, told the Center. "There is a continuous effort to relax fourteen-year-olds' work-hour restrictions."

In 1990, the Labor Department began investigating the use of child labor in the food and retail industries as part of its Operation Child Watch. It found thousands of minors working in violation of federal law and assessed millions of dollars in penalties in 1990. Among the businesses cited were supermarkets and grocers that had ignored a rule banning teenagers from loading such hazardous machinery as paper balers and compactors. Many of them—including A&P Corporation; Food Lion, Inc.; Winn-Dixie Stores, Inc.; and Grand Union Company—settled their cases for reduced fines. Stung by the violations, the grocers fought back in time-honored tradition: They lobbied Congress to get the Labor Department off their backs and to relax child labor protections.

||||||||||||||||||||||||||||||||||||||||||

Most people think that child labor is a relic of the past or a scourge of developing countries. But child labor is alive and well in the United States. Nowhere is it more prevalent and tolerated than in agriculture.

||||||||||||||||||||||||||||||||||||||||||

Mission accomplished. In 1995, Representatives Thomas Ewing of Illinois and Larry Combest of Texas, both Republicans, spearheaded an effort to allow children under eighteen to load wastepaper into mechanical balers and compactors. They enlisted more than fifty of their colleagues as cosponsors of what came to be known as the Baler Bill. "They got the bill nailed down in a two-week blitz," Jean Hutter, a lobbyist for the United Food & Commercial Workers International Union, told the Center. "We did the best we could with a bad situation. We were being rolled."

Never mind the warnings of Tom Lantos, a Democrat from California, who worried that the legislation would result in more tragedies like the one he had investigated as the chairman of a House subcommittee—the death of a seventeen-year-old boy crushed while operating a paper baler at the direction of his supervisor. The Baler Bill ultimately became law. Meanwhile, the industry leaned on Congress to cut the Labor Department's budget—a hedge against funds being expended to enforce the under-eighteen age restriction.

Among those leading the charge to gut the child labor law was the Food Marketing Institute, which in 1996 spent at least

$80,000 to help get the job done. But this was pocket change compared with the money spent that year by the Labor Policy Association, which counts nearly 250 of the nation's largest corporations among its members. The association was concerned about no fewer than nine child labor bills, along with the Labor Department's budget, and ran up a lobbying tab of at least $1.38 million.

Founded in 1939 by corporate executives who were worried about the labor laws ushered in with the New Deal, the Labor Policy Association uses its ample war chest to curry favor on Capitol Hill. It paid Members of Congress more than $80,000 in speaking fees from 1986 to 1996. In March 1996, for example, it gave Senator James Jeffords, a Republican from Vermont, and Republican Representative Charles Stenholm, a Democrat from Texas, all-expenses-paid trips to Williamsburg, Virginia, to participate in a panel discussion on "The Congressional Agenda Ahead." Jeffords was a member of the Senate Committee on Labor and Human Resources, where the Baler Bill was sent and, in July 1996, unanimously passed. Stenholm was a cosponsor of the Baler Bill.

The president of the Labor Policy Association, Jeffrey McGuiness, is a partner in the Washington lobbying firm of McGuiness & Williams, which also counts something called the Flexible Employment Compensation and Scheduling Coalition among its clients. The coalition, whose mission is to replace overtime with "comp" time, is one of the food industry's biggest front organizations.

The food industry is a fearsome force on Capitol Hill because it includes three of Washington's most powerful trade associations:
- The Food Marketing Institute, which lobbied on behalf of the Baler Bill, gave more than $1.8 million to congressional candidates from 1987 to 1996.
- The National Restaurant Association gave more than $3.1 million to congressional candidates from 1987 to 1996. And that does not even include the more than $5.9 million in other contributions that restaurant owners gave on their own to congressional candidates.
- The National American Wholesale Grocers' Association gave more than $524,000 to congressional candidates from 1987 to 1996.

Lantos's Young American Workers' Bill of Rights, which

would have strengthened child labor laws, attracted twenty-four cosponsors and was sent to the House Economic and Educational Opportunities Subcommittee on Workforce Protections, where it died a quiet death. The Labor Policy Association, according to disclosure forms filed with the Senate and the House, lobbied Capitol Hill lawmakers on nine child labor bills in 1996. One of them was Lantos's bill.

The food industry is not alone in pushing for changes in labor laws that would allow businesses to employ younger children and have them work longer hours or perform more dangerous tasks.

Senator Slade Gorton, a Republican from Washington, introduced a bill in 1995 that would allow sixteen- and seventeen-year-olds to drive vehicles as part of their job, as long as doing so was not their primary duty. The law currently allows only incidental and occasional driving. Representative Randy Tate, also a Republican from Washington, sponsored similar legislation in the House. Gorton introduced the so-called Dealer Bill after the Labor Department cracked down on automobile dealerships in his state that were using teenagers beyond the allowable limit to park cars and drive them off their lots to get gasoline. Gorton said that his bill would be "better for car dealerships and better for kids who want to work."

The National Automobile Dealers Association gave $8,000 to Gorton in the 1994 election cycle and $15,000 to Tate in the 1994 and 1996 election cycles. It spent approximately $900,000 to lobby Congress to change the restriction and permit teens to drive more, among other issues.

But allowing teenagers to drive more may result in additional work-related accidents and deaths. According to the Labor Department, motor-vehicle-related accidents are the leading cause of teenagers killed at work.

Not satisfied with rolling back one child labor protection, Combest is picking up where Gorton and Tate left off by setting his sights on helping the auto dealers get teenagers to drive more on the job. In July 1997, Combest introduced a new Dealer Bill for another round to change the child labor law.

*   *   *

The redbrick building looks more like a small factory than an elementary school. Located in the trouble-plagued Southeast quadrant of Washington, D.C., Shadd Elementary School features dingy, yellow-stained windows that block the sun from classrooms. Steel gratings cover the bottom row of windows to deter vandals. Throughout the building's interior are signs of water damage from a leaky roof. Only some classrooms have air conditioners. The chain-link fence surrounding the grounds is rusted and dented. But crowning Shadd Elementary School is a bright new copper roof, a sign that the crumbling school may yet see better days.

"My official title is roof fixer," Charles Williams says as he pokes at the debris of roofing material left in Shadd's parking lot. "I've seen enough roofs. I dream about them." A retired general with the Army Corps of Engineers, Williams is in charge of replacing the roofs of more than forty of the most troubled schools in the nation's capital. Every Tuesday and Thursday he tours the schools to inspect how the repairs are going.

They do not always go well, as evidenced by the developments of August 1997: More than 70,000 students and their families were sent scrambling for day care when it was announced that all schools would be starting three weeks late because the roof replacements were not done on time.

After decades of deferred maintenance, crumbling infrastructure problems have hit schools in the District of Columbia hard. But the city would not even be replacing roofs if it were not for a 1992 lawsuit that a parents' group filed, forcing officials to conduct fire-code inspections. When the fire department found more than 11,000 code violations, city leaders decided to replace the roofs rather than do more patchwork.

> **A third of the nation's schools, the General Accounting Office found, need extensive repair or replacement of one or more buildings, a problem that affects 14 million children.**

Washington, D.C., is not the only city with crumbling schools. From the South Side of Chicago to the suburbs of New Mexico, the nation is facing a school-infrastructure crisis.

"When the Mississippi River floods over, we attack that as a national issue," Williams said. "The public got into this problem by improper management and a lack of funding. The real issue now is: How do we get out of it?"

The General Accounting Office (GAO) estimated in 1995 that we get out of it by spending $112 billion. A third of the nation's schools, the GAO found, need extensive repair or replacement of one or more buildings, a problem that affects 14 million children. Almost 60 percent of the schools report at least one major building feature in disrepair or requiring extensive repair, overhaul, or replacement. Although the problem stretches across urban and suburban school districts, it is worst in the nation's largest cities, where schools are decades old.

About 31 percent of the nation's 84,000 schools were built before World War II, and 43 percent were built during the Baby Boom of the 1950s and 1960s. New York City needs $7.8 billion to bring its schools into overall good condition. Chicago needs $2.9 billion, while Washington, D.C., and New Orleans each need $500 million.

Ironically, as politicians, unions, lobbyists, and education advocacy groups push for more programs and technology for children, the walls are literally crumbling around them. Three-fourths of the schools surveyed by the GAO reported having sufficient computers and televisions but not the system or building infrastructure to use them; computers cannot be connected or networked in these schools. More than 14 million children attend the approximately 40 percent of schools without adequate facilities for laboratory science or large-group instruction.

Senator Carol Moseley-Braun, a Democrat from Illinois, has led the charge to fix the nation's schools, but she has found little support from Congress or the White House. In April 1994, she introduced the Education Infrastructure Act, which became law as part of the Improving America's Schools Act of 1994. President Clinton initially supported the act and earmarked $100 million for it, but he later rescinded the money. In July 1996, Moseley-Braun and Clinton stood outside the White House and announced a new proposal to commit $5 billion in federal spending for school improvements. The following spring she introduced yet more legislation to address school infrastructure repair, including a $5 billion amendment to the 1998 budget.

Republicans swiftly attacked the initiative on the Senate floor. "From what I understand of this amendment, the amendment would be paid for by, once again, reducing the level of net tax reductions allowable for the American people," Republican Pete Domenici of New Mexico said on the Senate floor in May 1997. "It seems to me that every time we turn around, somebody wants to say, 'We want to give the American people less of a tax cut.' We have this great need for something, so we will just take it out of the tax-cut package." Domenici urged his colleagues to vote against Moseley-Braun's amendment, despite the fact that his home state reported 30 percent of schools with at least one inadequate building and 69 percent with one inadequate building feature, such as a leaky roof. The Senate killed the amendment.

But Moseley-Braun wasn't finished. A month later, she introduced yet another amendment, this one to provide $1 billion in tax credits for construction or renovation projects. It was later defeated on a voice vote.

"We have hundreds of billions of dollars in tax cuts, disproportionately going to the top five percent of the population," Senator Paul Wellstone, a Democrat from Minnesota, told his colleagues. "What kind of priorities are these? We have not invested anything in rebuilding crumbling schools."

What voices are raised in protest?

"Children don't vote," Delabian Rice-Thurston, the executive director of Parents United, which filed the lawsuit against Washington, D.C.'s schools, told the Center. "There's no percentage for supporting things for children."

Nathan Timothy missed the chance to play Little League baseball. He missed his first day of school and his graduation. He missed running into the kitchen and asking his mom what was for dinner. He missed his first car and cool breezes on fall days. He missed his first kiss and his first prom. He missed being the best man at his friend's wedding, and he missed countless birthday parties.

Nathan missed all those things and more by seven days. The

eleven-month-old boy was just beginning to walk when he came down with a high fever and a rash. He developed encephalitis and pneumonia—both brought on by measles—and died in July 1989. The cause of death was respiratory failure.

Nathan Timothy should not have gotten sick at all. His parents had followed the rules and scheduled an appointment for his measles shot. But he contracted the illness a week before the appointment. "[It] was just bad timing," Bobbie Owens, Nathan's mother, told a reporter.

Actually, it was more than bad timing. Nathan was a victim of a failed immunization policy—one mired in complacency, cost, concern over product liability, delivery and access problems, system barriers, and a lack of critical information. Congress's on-again, off-again commitment to the immunization program had miserably failed him—and uncounted others.

Nathan's was one of forty-one deaths from measles in 1989, the highest number in this country in seventeen years. More than 18,000 cases of measles were reported to the Centers for Disease Control and Prevention that year, and the number grew in 1990 to more than 25,000. After the outbreak struck, the government dispensed $30 million worth of free vaccines through public clinics. But it was too little, too late. The death toll reached sixty.

Nearly a decade later, Congress has yet to recognize that constant, sustained pressure is needed to fight infectious diseases. Its nearsightedness over how to fight infectious diseases is exemplified by the current struggle over funds for two immunization programs—a dispute that may destroy recent immunization success rates and lead to a resurgence in diseases such as measles.

In 1993, President Clinton launched the Childhood Immunization Initiative in response to undervaccination of preschool children. Its goals included increasing vaccination coverage levels among two-year-olds to 90 percent or more through a new program called Vaccines for Children. The initiative aimed to keep private physicians from shunting poor or underinsured children to public clinics by providing them with inexpensive vaccines.

Vaccines for Children prompted Congress to cut funds from the Section 317 program of the Public Health Service Act, which had provided states with low-cost vaccines for poor children and had funded their efforts to reach underimmunized populations.

Since 1996, Section 317 funding has been gradually reduced, leaving states with less money for outreach programs like computer databases that track when children need shots. As a result, those outreach efforts are now in jeopardy. At stake is the health of all children—poor, middle class, and rich.

"The Vaccines for Children program and Section 317 work in a complementary fashion," Christopher Atchison, the director of public health for the state of Iowa, told the Center. "The infrastructure funds allow states and communities to develop multifaceted strategies for bringing children to the vaccine and in some cases bringing the vaccine to the child." Atchison testified in defense of Section 317 funding before the Senate Subcommittee on Public Health and Safety in May 1997.

"The cuts that happen this year will hit hard next year," Claire Hannan, the Association of State and Territorial Health Officials' project director for immunizations, told the Center. "States will have to decide what to cut, whether to cut proportionately over everything or eliminate staff or programs, but they won't be able to maintain programs at the same level. I hope it doesn't mean that fewer children will be immunized."

"We've been able to achieve tremendous gains, from fifty percent immunization rates [in Iowa] to eighty-eight percent in a short period of time," Atchison told the Center. "To take away one of those arms now—I'll use a sports analogy: It's hard to hit without both hands on the bat."

Heidi Flores spends her days trolling through the food pantries of New York City, looking for enough food to feed her three hungry children. The young mother pounds the pavement of countless blocks in her search. "I spend a lot of time during the week going from pantry to pantry," she told a reporter for the *Village Voice*. "That's how I get by."

For an increasing number of families in both inner cities and small towns, scavenging for food is becoming a way of life. Second Harvest, the nation's largest food bank, expects those numbers to grow in the wake of welfare reform.

Hunger in the United States is a serious and pervasive problem. More than 25 million Americans—about one in ten—rely on food pantries, soup kitchens, homeless shelters, and other emergency feeding programs served by the Second Harvest network. More than four of every ten fed are seventeen or younger. The number of American children under twelve who are hungry or at risk of hunger is estimated at 13.6 million.

Despite these trends, Congress has cut federal food-assistance programs that reach children.

IIIIIIIIIIIIIIIIIIIIIIIIIIIIIIIIIIIIIIIII

Cuts in food stamps will mean 18 million fewer people who could have been fed three meals a day.

IIIIIIIIIIIIIIIIIIIIIIIIIIIIIIIIIIIIIIIII

Almost half of the spending reductions in welfare reform, for example, come from the food-stamp program. Welfare reform includes a $23.1 billion reduction in food stamps over six years, according to the Congressional Budget Office, as well as $2.9 billion in cuts in federal child nutrition programs. The reductions will slash food-stamp benefits by almost 20 percent, the equivalent of reducing the average food-stamp benefit from its current level of eighty cents per person per meal to sixty-six cents, according to a report by the Center for Budget and Policy Priorities. Such reductions will affect all food-stamp recipients, including the working poor, the elderly, and the disabled.

A 1997 study by the Tufts University Center on Hunger, Poverty, and Nutrition Policy calculated that the cuts in food stamps will mean approximately 23 billion pounds less food served to hungry Americans over the next six years and 18 million fewer people who could have been fed three meals a day.

The only thing that keeps some Members of Congress from doing away with the program altogether is the fact that it pumps more than $25 billion a year into farm-state economies. During the welfare-reform debate, Republican Pat Roberts of Kansas, the chairman of the House Agriculture Committee, told *The New York Times* that the program was "the ultimate social safety net." In truth, however, it is a safety net not only for the poor and hungry, but also for agribusiness.

Although some Capitol Hill lawmakers say that private institutions can make up for the reductions in government food assistance, Christine Vladimiroff, the president and chief executive officer of Second Harvest, does not think it is possible. "Our resources were depleted even before passage of this law," she said in July 1997. "There is no way even all private agencies combined can make up for the loss of twenty-four billion pounds of food over the next six years."

Congress and the President have sent America's poor and hungry on a long and tortuous march in which children are the hardest pressed to keep up and the most susceptible to falling by the wayside. Undernutrition forces the body into a triage state that sends resources to the most important parts of the body and cuts off the rest, according to a report by Dr. Larry Brown, the director of the Center on Hunger, Poverty, and Nutrition Policy at Tufts University. Children who suffer from undernutrition are stunted in growth, thin, and not as bright as other children their age.

Hunger has lost its cachet on Capitol Hill. The Select Committee on Hunger was formed in 1984 to focus on this problem and its solutions. Its members used their influence to get legislation through other committees and to influence bills and appropriations for hunger-relief programs. "If there were a shortfall for the Women, Infants, and Children program, the select committee members could try to fill in the cracks in other committees like Appropriations," John Morrill, the executive director of the Congressional Hunger Center, told the Center.

In a 1993 budget-cutting effort, Congress eliminated the Select Committee on Hunger, along with other select committees on aging, children and families, and narcotics. Representative Tony Hall, a Democrat from Ohio, waged a hunger strike for twenty-two days to protest the elimination of the select committee. In response, Congress authorized the establishment of the Congressional Hunger Caucus. The goal of the caucus was to ensure the federal food-assistance programs were adequately funded. In 1995, Congress eliminated it as well.

20

IIIIIII●IIIIIII

Reclaiming What's Ours

I<small>N THE LAST MONTHS OF HIS LIFE, THE</small> D<small>ANISH PHILOSOPHER</small> S<small>ØREN</small> Kierkegaard wrote in his notebook:

> If the conditions at a certain time are such that almost every-
> one knows privately that the whole thing is wrong, is untrue,
> while no one will say so officially; when the tactic used by the
> leaders is: Let us simply hold on, behave as though nothing
> had happened, answer every attack with silence, because we
> ourselves know only too well that everything is rotten, that we
> are playing false: then in that case the conditions are eo ipso
> condemned, and they will crash. Just as one says that death
> has marked a man, so we recognize the symptoms which un-
> questionably demand to be attacked. It is a battle against lies.

Kierkegaard believed that something was rotten in Denmark—
namely, the situation of the Protestant Church there in the mid-
nineteenth century—but he could just as easily have been writing
about the institutional corruption that has beset the U.S. political
system in the late twentieth century. From public-opinion polls
and recent voting trends, we know that the American people have
enormous distrust of, and disgust toward, Congress and politicians generally. Deep down, lawmakers generally recognize how

rotten things are today, but with the exception of a few well-meaning reformers, they play false.

For anyone who is upset about the corruption of our political process, it is, to borrow Kierkegaard's phrase, a battle against lies. The President, the Senate Majority Leader, the Speaker of the House, assorted other congressional leaders, governors, state legislators—all tell us with furrowed brows that they are all for integrity in politics, and all tell us that they will clean up politics. It sounds almost like a mantra. But with very few exceptions, it is bunk, pure and simple. The reality is that our political leaders across the land say, "Show me the money" virtually every day and, not so coincidentally, public policy is promulgated to the narrow advantage of the favored few. Along the way, the "pay-to-play" system continues to grow.

As a people, we do not really know what to do, where to go, whom to trust. It is a real dilemma for our democracy. Most of our political heroes are long dead or over time have developed feet of clay. Letters to politicians result in unctuous, insincere, "I feel your pain" replies signed with an autopen. As the last decade of the last century of the second millennium draws to a close, there is a significant disconnect between the American people and our elected representatives. The public feels disenfranchised and incidental to the political system, which seems to place a premium on wealth and influence.

Politicians, on the other hand, lament that the American people have little respect, and even contempt, for them, and they do not really know how to change that attitude. They rationalize that ultimately they have no choice but to raise big money to get their political message out—and you do not raise that kind of money from neighborhood raffles. The public might not like their representatives' campaign money to come from special interests, but Republicans and Democrats alike cannot survive without the cash. So the worst that can happen is that some people do not vote. When it comes to the legislative votes cast, our politicians realize

> Most of our political heroes are long dead or over time have developed feet of clay. Letters to politicians result in unctuous, insincere, "I feel your pain" replies signed with an autopen.

that most Americans have no idea how they vote or what they have done for some fat-cat donor. Indeed, most politicians accurately comprehend that they are largely anonymous to the body politic in the 1990s—unknown by name, face, word, and deed.

In 1991, following extensive survey research, the Kettering Foundation issued a report that observed: "Many Americans do not believe that they are living in a democracy now. They don't believe 'we the people' actually rule. . . . [They] describe the political system as impervious to public direction, a system run by a professional class and controlled by money, not votes." The report concluded: "Americans have [not] 'turned their backs' on politics, they do not want to participate . . . Americans are abstaining from politics . . . until they believe they can make a difference."

If there is one message you should take away from *The Buying of the Congress,* it is that abstaining from politics is the most counterproductive thing you can do. Make no mistake: What Congress does directly and powerfully affects our daily lives. Consequently, to opt out of the democratic process is to relinquish control and surrender our fate to the special interests.

Revolutionary leader and author of *Common Sense* Thomas Paine said, "Those who expect to reap the blessings of freedom must undergo like men the fatigue of supporting it." In recent years, fully one-half of this nation has reaped the blessings of freedom without undergoing the fatigue of supporting it. It is time for greater vigilance and citizen involvement, not less. Two decades after the double betrayals of Vietnam and Watergate, we may never trust again. Perhaps it was inevitable that members of the Baby Boom generation would lose their innocence and their certainty, just as their parents lost theirs in the Depression and World War II. And so, over the years, all of us have learned to be cautious, discerning, and sober-minded about most things. Just as we comparison-shop before making a major consumer decision—let the buyer beware—we increasingly must analyze the political landscape. It is, as you have just read, not a pretty sight.

That is part of the legacy of Vietnam and Watergate. As political accountability and our access to information increased in the wake of these national calamities, we learned more about our

"I am a firm believer in the people," Abraham Lincoln said. "If given the truth, they can be depended upon to meet any national crisis. The great point is to bring them the real facts."

government than ever before. Today we have more information and insight about current events, but the disadvantage is that we know more than ever about the motives and machinations of our leaders. Watching the sausage being made has lessened our appetite for sausage.

One of the few men to serve at the highest level of all three branches of the federal government, former Congressman, judge, and White House counsel Abner Mikva told us that he worries about the effects of this new scrutiny on the public's attitude toward government. Mikva believes there have been drawbacks from "opening up the room and clearing out the smoke and letting the people see what's going on inside. The more you do that, the easier it is to disparage the product. That's really what's happening . . . Who cares what the Congress is doing? They do such a lousy job that nobody is particularly scandalized when they find out that somebody is doing something wrong."

Somehow we must get over the disillusionment that has numbed us since the 1970s. As the late historian Barbara Tuchman once asked, "Where's the outrage? . . . We have lost a sense of respect for serious, honest conduct. If we are moved merely by greed, and there's no longer any respect for decent or honest government, then we will suffer the results." The decisions illuminated in this book all affect our daily lives, and whether or not the current political milieu is appealing to us or the latest ethical imbroglio is surprising to us, the people we elect work for us. They are our employees, and it is up to us to remind them of that.

Our credo at the Center for Public Integrity is a quote by Abraham Lincoln: "I am a firm believer in the people. If given the truth, they can be depended upon to meet any national crisis. The great point is to bring them the real facts." Simply stated, information is power, and we cannot have too much of it. There is so much we do not know about our government, our corporations, our labor unions, and other large institutions that affect our lives, information that we are entitled to know but are not told.

Beyond seeking the "real facts," what can we do?

Nonparticipation and low voter turnout by the public only embolden the special interests and their favorite lawmakers. Today's and tomorrow's citizens need to be better informed, to read newspapers and magazines, to watch local and national television news, to surf the Internet for information about politics and current affairs. What you don't know can actually hurt you. The more we know, the more engaged we are, the more we vote, and the more our presence is felt.

More specifically, citizens must arm themselves with information about elected officials, their career patrons, their voting patterns, their public statements. Most Americans know more about their toasters than about their public servants, even though they can be badly burned by both. If politicians say they are for "reform" of anything, what exactly are they talking about? Do they offer straightforward answers to questions or mouth so much gobbledygook?

Armed with knowledge and a sense of whom your representative really represents, the next level of commitment and engagement is to attend a town meeting, a community rally, an interactive exchange via the Internet, and listen to the responses. Better still, ask a question: "Representative Smith, why have you taken $125,000 from the toxic-waste industry over the past five years and voted against new, tougher environmental laws?" "Senator Jones, how can you sit on the Transportation Committee and accept six trips last year to three continents paid for by the airline industry? Isn't that a conflict of interest?"

Our politicians need more questions like these—from the public, from the news media, and from their own colleagues. In *The Buying of the President,* we put questions for the presidential candidates on our Internet Web site, for the public and journalists to ask. Based on this book, we have posed questions to various Members of Congress about their entanglements with their patrons. Today's politicians sneer and say contemptuously that no one ever asks them about their money. Maybe it is time that they start responding to these questions.

Finally, get involved directly in the struggle for the soul of America. There are dozens of advocacy organizations around the nation fighting to clean up politics—whether by voluntary public financing of all federal elections, improved regulations, or free television advertising time for candidates. Our Web site contains the names and addresses of organizations throughout the United States, should you wish to enter the fray.

Retired Democratic Representative Andy Jacobs represented his Indiana district for thirty years and established an impeccable record of integrity and honor in public service, even going so far as to give part of his salary back to the Treasury. When I asked him if there is a strong economic interest today that is not well represented when it comes to congressional decisions, he replied, "There's a very large economic interest—it's called the public interest."

Jacobs believes that Congress is absolutely capable of re-forming its own practices and campaign finance system. "They say Congress is not responsive," he told us. "That is not true. In my view, the Congress is one of the most responsive institutions in the United States. They respond to anything the public wants."

Jacobs, like most current Members of Congress we inter-viewed, believes that on the subject of cleaning up politics, the people have not yet spoken up. Therefore, nothing has changed, and the grip of the entrenched interests has become tighter.

On December 5, 1955, in the Holt Street Baptist Church in segregated Montgomery, Alabama, with 1,000 black Americans jammed inside and another 5,000 outside listening to loudspeak-ers, a twenty-six-year-old pastor named Martin Luther King, Jr.— who had just led the victorious campaign against segregated seat-ing in the city's buses—walked to the lectern. Without notes and surrounded by television cameras, King delivered the speech that first drew national attention to him.

"There comes a time, my friends," he said, "when people get tired of being plunged across the abyss of humiliation, when they experience the bleakness of nagging despair. There comes a time when people get tired of being pushed out of the glimmering sunlight of last July and left standing amid the piercing chill of

an Alpine November. We had no alternative but to protest. . . .
One of the great glories of democracy is the right to protest
for right."

History demanded both the leadership and the protest that
became the American civil-rights movement. Today, at another
time and in another kind of crisis, there is no leadership or protest
against our subjugation to the powerful economic interests that
have captured our Congress and our politics.

We are tired, and there is no alternative but to protest.

Acknowledgments

||||||||||||

Imagine a group of respected, expatriate journalists—unbowed by political considerations, corporate timidity, or social friendships—dissecting vital public-policy issues or systemic, institutional problems in our democracy, naming names and writing it all in a responsible but accessible way. Imagine that these journalists have access to the most advanced technologies, including on-line computer databases, hardware, and software, and that they are relatively unfettered by time or space limitations. Each investigative project is original and broad in scope, its findings released as a mass-media news event, at a press conference in the nation's capital.

In the eight years since it was founded, the nonprofit, nonpartisan Center for Public Integrity has produced nearly thirty investigative reports. To my knowledge, nowhere else in the world are so many people involved in investigative research projects about public-policy issues. For example, in 1990, the Center's very first study, *America's Frontline Trade Officials*—which found that half of the White House trade officials who left government over a fifteen-year period had gone to work for foreign governments and corporations, and which helped prompt congressional hearings, a General Accounting Office study, a Justice Department ruling, and a presidential executive order—had seven researchers. In 1992, the Center's 110,000-word *Under Fire: U.S. Military Restrictions on the Media from Grenada to the Persian Gulf* was accomplished with fourteen researchers in three cities. Our 1994 work, *Well-Healed: Inside Lobbying for Health-Care Reform*—described by journalists David Broder and Haynes Johnson as "the most authoritative" look at that subject—was produced by a team of twenty people. The Center's 1996 book, *The Buying of the President,* had six reporters, sixteen researchers, and 103 undergraduate and graduate student database researchers working for more than a year.

Which brings me to *The Buying of the Congress.* We employed more experienced journalists on this daunting project than on any previous Center endeavor, with ten writers (counting me), two editors, two senior researchers, and twenty-three researchers. The members of "The Investigative Team" are listed in the front of the book on page vii, and I gratefully acknowledge the tireless efforts of all these curious, determined, dedicated individuals. Only through such an elaborate collaboration could a work of this investigative breadth be completed or even attempted.

Four people deserve special mention and thanks for the extraordinary burden and leadership roles they carried throughout 1997 in getting us to the finish line. First and foremost, the Center's director of investigative projects, Bill Hogan—a nationally respected reporter and editor who shepherded our acclaimed exposé of the chemical industry, *Toxic Deception,* to its 1997 publication—brought his amazing blend of innate investigative instincts, Washington wisdom, collegial compassion, and editorial perfectionism to this undertaking. As for Bill Allison, the Center's chief of research, now I fully understand what two-time Pulitzer Prize-winning investigative reporter Jim Steele meant when he told me Allison "sees things that other people don't" and is the best researcher he and his partner, Don Bartlett, ever worked with in their more than two decades of peerless journalism at *The Philadelphia Inquirer.* William O'Sullivan, a gifted editor, left his imprint everywhere and helped us get to the finish line on time. Finally, "wunderkind" is an overused word, but whatever you call him, David Engel—a recent Phi Beta Kappa graduate of Stanford University—organized and constructed our astonishing lobbying, travel, and financial-disclosure computer databases. And that is in addition to keeping computer-frustrated Center employees from jumping out our ninth-story windows almost daily.

We learned from scores of impressive books about Congress, both academic and journalistic. We were determined not to write another political-science tome about the decision-making process or a "behind closed doors" account of how Congress works. How, we wondered, could we produce an important new work about a subject that has been as carefully studied and investigated as Congress? There have been, by the reckoning of the Library of Congress, more than 4,800 books on the subject.

This ambitious endeavor, of course, occurred not in a vacuum, but in a city reeking of more scandal than at any time since Watergate. The one thing lost in all of the campaign-finance Sturm und Drang of 1996 and 1997 was how the hundreds of millions of special-interest dollars pouring into congressional war chests directly affect ordinary citizens. With that in mind, we identified subjects we believed average Americans care about, as chapter themes, with the investigative task then to examine and analyze precisely what Congress did or did not do.

Determined to leave no stone unturned, we perused tens of thousands of secondary sources (stories in newspapers, magazines, newsletters, and on-line publications, as well as wire-service reports and transcripts of radio and television broadcasts) about the activities of Congress over the past decade. This simply would not have been possible without the miracle of Lexis-Nexis, the commercial, on-line computer database.

We began systematically examining primary sources, namely tens of thousands of federal government records, including transcripts of congressional hearings and all manner of material in the *Congressional Record*; campaign-spending reports filed with the Federal Election Commission; lobbying registration and reporting forms filed with the Senate and House of Representatives; and financial-disclosure reports filed by Members of Congress and their senior aides, including the monthly trip reports now available.

One of the most popular features of *The Buying of the President* was the "Top Ten Career Patrons" of presidential candidates that we identified for all the major presidential candidates. It marked the first time that anyone had identified the presidential candidates' most important, favorite special-interest sponsors before the election, and the information was moved nationwide by the Associated Press, *The New York Times,* and *The Washington Post,* among others.

For this book, we have identified the "Top Ten Career Patrons" for thirty-two of the most important Members of Congress (sixteen Senators and sixteen Representatives), based on a decade of political contributions (1987 through 1996), and have listed them on page 357. It has always seemed odd to us that Members of Congress served on committees with jurisdiction and enormous power over various industries and that they accept campaign contributions from those industries. We systematically and exhaustively studied the contribution patterns for lawmakers serving on twelve key committees in the Senate and thirteen in the House, and our findings are interspersed throughout the book.

None of these compilations would have been remotely possible without the generous assistance of the Center for Responsive Politics, whose computerized analyses of money in politics at the federal level are simply the best in the nation. Former executive director Kent Cooper, current executive director Larry Makinson, and project director Sheila Krumholz could not have been more gracious.

How do you measure influence? Besides "following the money" in the ways I have described, we also studied very closely the financial-disclosure forms filed by Members of Congress and top congressional employees over a six-year period (1991 through 1996); as part of this process, we built the first-ever computerized database of the reports filed by staff members. We put the travel reports that have been filed since the beginning of 1996 into another relational database, so that, for instance, we can type in a geographical destination such as "Paris" or an industry trip sponsor such as "tobacco" and generate a comprehensive set of records including that key word. We built yet another database of the lobby registration records. Although the documents have their limitations, we can quickly ascertain how many lobbyists— from what firms and at what price—have been retained by which clients to influence Congress. The fruits of all these labors can be seen throughout the book.

Time is money, especially in Washington, and we were fortunate to be able to spend hundreds of hours with the people who know the most about Congress. We conducted more than 1,200 on-the-record interviews with current and former Members of Congress, congressional aides, journalists who have covered Congress as an institution, and political scientists, as well as hundreds of other sources at trade associations, labor unions, and public-interest organizations. Every such individual who consented to be named as a source is identified on the Center's Web site (www.publicintegrity.org). Every current Member of Congress received at least two letters from us in 1997, seeking answers to a set of questions.

Although we were able to interview more than fifty current and former Capitol Hill lawmakers using broadcast-quality type recorders, several of the most powerful Members of Congress declined to talk to us, despite repeated requests throughout much of 1997. Our questions about Congress were met by the sounds of silence from Senate Majority Leader Trent Lott, Senate Minority Leader Tom Daschle, House Speaker Newt Gingrich, House Minority Leader Richard Gephardt, House Majority Leader Dick Armey, and House Majority Whip Tom DeLay.

I want to extend special thanks to legendary journalists Jack Anderson and Morton Mintz; veteran investigative reporter Sheila Kaplan; and Ken DeCell, senior editor of *The Washingtonian* magazine. Invaluable insights also came from William Schneider of the American Enterprise Institute for Public Policy Research (who is also a member of the Center's Advisory Board), Thomas Mann of the Brookings Institution, Paul Light of the Pew Charitable Trusts, Kathleen Clark of the Washington University School of Law, and Ellen Miller, a veteran campaign-finance expert and former executive director of the Center for Responsive Politics.

Special thanks also to our editor at Avon Books, Rachel Klayman, and to our perceptive and supportive attorney, Marc Miller. We are especially grateful to the Arca Foundation and Alida R. Messinger for supporting this project. Earlier in 1998, we published *Congress and the People,* a series of Center studies funded by a grant from The Pew Charitable Trusts. We are deeply grateful to our major, general Center supporters, including the Carnegie Corporation of New York, the Hafif Family Foundation, Cecil Heftel, the Rockefeller Family Fund, the John D. and Catherine

T. MacArthur Foundation, the North Star Fund, the Open Society Institute, the Florence and John Schumann Foundation, the Streisand Foundation, the Town Creek Foundation, Inc., and a Rockefeller family member. The Center for Public Integrity does not accept contributions from corporations, labor unions, and governments. Contributors are listed on our Web site.

We amassed far more data than this book—or any book—could contain. Auxiliary information complementary to *The Buying of the Congress* can be found at our Web site, including a complete set of footnotes for the book, computer database lists with updated figures, the statement of our findings presented at our Washington news conference, audio interviews with current and former Members of Congress, and so forth.

Finally, on a more personal note, I want to thank the Center's Board of Directors (especially Charles Piller, who was present at its creation) and the Advisory Board members who have been magnificently supportive over the years. Former Board member and former Center managing director Alejandro Benes was helpful in getting this large project on Congress off the ground. I am indebted to Bill Moyers and John Moyers of the Schumann Foundation for their trenchant insights and steadfast encouragement.

And no one has provided more sustenance to me in my "send-a-straitjacket" dream of the Center for Public Integrity than my family: my parents, Charles and Dorothy Lewis; my sister and brother-in-law, Mary Lewis and Randy Fisher; my daughter, Cassandra Lewis; and my wife, Pamela Gilbert, whose astute knowledge and savvy about Capitol Hill were quite valuable for this book.

Charles Lewis
April 1998
Washington, D.C.

Top Ten Career Patrons
of Congressional Leaders
|||||||||||||

STROM THURMOND
Republican, South Carolina
Senate President Pro Tempore

1.	**NationsBank Corporation**, Charlotte, N.C.* (commercial banking)	$48,944
2.	**Fluor Corporation**, Irvine, Calif. (global engineering, construction, coal)	30,500
3.	**Lockheed Martin Corporation**, Bethesda, Md.* (aerospace and defense)	25,000
4.	**Colonial Life & Accident Insurance Company**, Columbia, S.C.	22,500
5.	**American Bankers Association**, Washington	22,000
6.	**American Medical Association**, Chicago (physicians)	20,000
7.	**Northrop Grumman Corporation**, Los Angeles* (aerospace and defense)	20,000
8.	**McNair Law Firm**, Columbia, S.C.	19,800
9.	**The Boeing Company**, Seattle (aerospace and defense)	18,000
10.	**Scana Corporation**, Columbia, S.C. (utilities)	17,500

*Includes merged entities.

Notes: Based on analysis of contributions to Thurmond from 1987 to 1996. Thurmond also received $336,414 from the Republican National Committee over the same period.

TRENT LOTT
Republican, Mississippi
Senate Majority Leader

1.	**National Association of Realtors,** Washington	$367,498
2.	**Auto Dealers & Drivers for Free Trade,** Jamaica, N.Y. (Japanese cars)	332,126
3.	**National Security PAC,** Washington (defense industry advocacy)	58,202
4.	**Marine Engineers Beneficial Association,** Washington (labor union)	42,000
5.	**National Rifle Association,** Fairfax, Va. (gun advocacy)	33,864
6.	**Federal Express Corporation,** Memphis, Tenn. (delivery service)	33,000
7.	**Lockheed Martin Corporation,** Bethesda, Md.* (aerospace and defense)	31,000
8.	**The Southern Company,** Atlanta* (electric utilities)	31,000
9.	**Friedman, Billings, Ramsey & Company, Inc.,** Arlington, Va. (brokerage)	30,000
10.	**Litton Industries, Inc.,** Woodland Hills, Calif. (information systems)	27,000

*Includes subsidiaries and merged entities.

Notes: Based on analysis of contributions to Lott from 1987 to 1996, and contributions to his PAC, the New Republican Majority Fund, from 1995 to 1996. Includes independent expenditures made on Lott's behalf.

CONNIE MACK
Republican, Florida
Chairman, Senate Republican Conference

1.	**Auto Dealers & Drivers for Free Trade**, Jamaica, N.Y. (Japanese cars)	$339,550
2.	**National Right to Life PAC**, Washington (antiabortion advocacy)	56,353
3.	**National Security PAC**, Washington (defense industry advocacy)	50,790
4.	**Holland & Knight**, Lakeland, Fla. (law firm)	45,110
5.	**Flo-Sun, Inc.**, Palm Beach, Fla. (sugar)	40,500
6.	**Barnett Banks, Inc.**, Jacksonville, Fla. (commercial banks)	38,200
7.	**Moore Capital Management, Inc.**, New York (investment firm)	33,000
8.	**JM Family Enterprises, Inc.**, Deerfield Beach, Fla. (car dealers)	26,750
9.	**Marine Engineers Beneficial Association**, Washington (labor union)	25,313
10.	**Harris Corporation**, Melbourne, Fla. (electric systems)	25,313

Notes: Based on analysis of contributions to Mack from 1987 to 1996, and contributions to his PAC, the Adam Smith PAC, from 1995 to 1996. Includes independent expenditures made on Mack's behalf.

PAUL COVERDELL
Republican, Georgia
Secretary, Senate Republican Conference

1.	**National Rifle Association**, Fairfax, Va. (gun advocacy)	$95,806
2.	**King & Spalding**, Atlanta (law/lobbying firm)	46,150
3.	**Flowers Industries, Inc.**, Thomasville, Ga. (baked goods)	35,000
4.	**Jones, Day, Reavis & Pogue**, Cleveland (law/lobbying firm)	30,900
5.	**Waffle House, Inc.**, Norcross, Ga. (restaurant chain)	25,850
6.	**The Coca-Cola Company**, Atlanta (soft drinks)	24,850
7.	**Parker, Hudson, Rainer and Dobbs**, Atlanta (law firm)	24,476
8.	**AFLAC, Inc.**, Columbus, Ohio (supplemental health insurance)	23,500
9.	**Amresco, Inc.**, Dallas* (financial consultants)	23,300
10.	**Travelers Group, Inc.**, New York† (consumer lending)	22,790

*Includes subsidiaries and merged entities. Most contributions came from Atlanta-based BEI Holdings, Inc., which Amresco, Inc., acquired in 1993.
†Includes subsidiaries.

Notes: Based on analysis of contributions to Coverdell from 1991 to 1996.

DON NICKLES
Republican, Oklahoma
Senate Majority Whip

1.	**Phillips Petroleum Company**, Bartlesville, Okla. (oil and gas)	$38,381
2.	**UST, Inc.**, Greenwich, Conn. (tobacco products)	28,000
3.	**AT&T Corporation**, Basking Ridge, N.J. (telecommunications)	25,000
4.	**Kerr-McGee Corporation**, Oklahoma City (oil and gas)	24,200
5. (tie)	**Council of Insurance Agents & Brokers,** Washington	24,000
	Koch Industries, Inc., Wichita, Kan. (oil and gas)	24,000
6. (tie)	**Fluor Corporation**, Irvine, Calif. (global engineering, construction, coal)	22,000
	Massachusetts Mutual Life Insurance Company, Springfield, Mass.	22,000
7.	**Occidental Petroleum Corporation**, Los Angeles (oil and gas)	19,500
8. (tie)	**American Airlines, Inc.**, Fort Worth, Texas	19,000
	The Prudential Insurance Company, Newark, N.J. (life, health insurance)	19,000
9.	**Duke Energy Corporation**, Charlotte, N.C. (electrical service)	18,500
10.	**Federal Express**, Memphis, Tenn. (delivery service)	16,500

Notes: Based on analysis of contributions to Nickles from 1987 to 1996 and to his PAC, the Republican Majority Fund, from 1993 to 1996.

LARRY CRAIG
Republican, Idaho
Chairman, Senate Republican Policy Committee

1.	**National Association of Realtors,** Washington	$139,363
2.	**National Rifle Association,** Fairfax, Va. (gun advocacy)	78,771
3.	**Boise Cascade Corporation,** Boise, Idaho (lumber)	36,800
4.	**American Medical Association,** Washington (physicians)	29,984
5.	**Contran Corporation,** Dallas, Texas (sugar)	29,800
6.	**Morrison Knudsen Corporation,** Boise, Idaho (engineering and design)	26,550
7.	**American Institute of Certified Public Accountants,** Jersey City, N.J.	25,000
8.	**Potlatch Corporation,** San Francisco (paper and lumber)	24,394
9.	**American Bankers Association,** Washington (commercial banks)	22,500
10.	**National Association of Life Underwriters,** Washington (life insurance)	22,500

Notes: Based on analysis of contributions to Craig from 1987 to 1996. Includes independent expenditures made on Craig's behalf.

MITCH MCCONNELL
Republican, Kentucky
Chairman, National Republican
Senatorial Campaign Committee

1.	**Ashland, Inc.**, Ashland, Ky. (oil and gas)	$54,050
2.	**National Right to Life PAC**, Washington (antiabortion advocacy)	48,605
3.	**Columbia/HCA Healthcare Corporation**, Nashville, Tenn. (hospitals)	38,500
4.	**Philip Morris Companies, Inc.**, New York (cigarettes)	31,500
5.	**Foremost Maritime Corporation**, New York (shipping)	30,000
6.	**Addington Resources, Inc.**, Lexington, Ky. (coal)	28,250
7.	**Deloitte & Touche**, Wilton, Conn. (accounting firm)	26,110
8.	**UST, Inc.**, Greenwich, Conn. (tobacco products)	25,500
9.	**Union Pacific Corporation**, Bethlehem, Pa. (oil, gas, and mining)	21,999
10.	**RJR Nabisco, Inc.**, New York (cigarettes)	21,250

Notes: Based on analysis of contributions to McConnell from 1987 to 1996 and contributions to McConnell's PAC, the Bluegrass PAC, from 1991 to 1996.

WILLIAM ROTH
Republican, Delaware
Chairman, Senate Finance Committee

1.	**MBNA Corporation**, Wilmington, Del. (consumer lending)	$143,839
2.	**E. I. du Pont de Nemours & Company**, Wilmington, Del. (petroleum, chemicals, plastics)	84,526
3.	**Merrill Lynch & Company, Inc.**, New York (securities brokers and dealers)	37,400
4.	**American International Group, Inc.**, New York (multinational insurance)	30,400
5.	**Richards, Layton & Finger**, Wilmington, Del. (law firm)	27,287
6.	**Association of Trial Lawyers of America**, Washington (lawyers)	20,000
7.	**National Automobile Dealers Association**, McLean, Va. (auto dealers)	20,000
8.	**Rollins Truck Leasing Corporation**, Wilmington, Del	19,600
9.	**Advanta Corporation**, Horsham, Pa. (financial-services holding company)	19,000
10.	**Skadden, Arps, Slate, Meagher & Flom**, New York (law/lobbying firm)	8,950

Notes: Based on analysis of contributions to Roth from 1987 to 1996.

ALFONSE D'AMATO
Republican, New York
Chairman, Senate Banking Committee

1.	**Andrews Group, Inc.,** New York (comic books, toys, entertainment)	$250,000
2.	**Goldman, Sachs & Company,** New York (investment banking)	180,400
3.	**Fisher Brothers Management Company,** New York (real estate)	151,300
4.	**MBNA Corporation,** Wilmington, Del. (consumer lending)	118,500
5.	**D. H. Blair & Company,** New York (stockbrokers)	118,250
6.	**Bear, Stearns & Company,** New York (securities brokers and dealers)	117,001
7.	**CS First Boston Corporation,** New York (investment banking)	111,754
8.	**Sanford C. Bernstein & Co., Inc.,** New York (investment management)	102,000
9.	**David H. Feinberg,** New York (real estate)	100,000
10.	**Travelers Group, Inc.,** New York* (consumer lending)	86,100

*Includes subsidiaries and merged entities.

Notes: Based on analysis of contributions to D'Amato from 1987 to 1996 and contributions to his PACs, New York Salute 1992 from 1991 to 1992, New York Salute 1996 from 1995 to 1996, and Renew America PAC from 1995 to 1996.

TOM DASCHLE
Democrat, South Dakota
Senate Minority Leader

1.	Salomon Brothers, Inc., New York (financial services)	$36,750
2.	E. & J. Gallo Winery, Inc., Modesto, Calif.	28,000
3. (tie)	Vitas Healthcare Corporation, Miami (home health care)	23,000
	Joseph E. Seagram & Sons, Inc., New York (distilled spirits)	23,000
4.	Wine Institute, San Francisco	22,517
5.	Todhunter International, Inc. West Palm Beach, Fla. (alcoholic products)	20,000
6. (tie)	Archer Daniels Midland Corporation, Decatur, Ill. (agribusiness)	18,500
	Occidental Petroleum Corporation, Los Angeles (oil and gas)	18,500
7.	Invacare Corporation, Elyria, Ohio (medical supplies)	18,000
8.	Chicago Mercantile Exchange, Chicago (commodities investing)	17,250
9.	Cassidy & Associates, Washington (lobbying)	15,804
10.	The Prudential Insurance Company, Newark, N.J. (life, health insurance)	15,750

Notes: Based on analysis of contributions to Daschle from 1987 to 1996.

WENDELL FORD
Democrat, Kentucky
Senate Minority Whip

1.	**Akin, Gump, Strauss, Hauer & Feld,** Washington (law/lobbying firm)	$14,599
2.	**Philip Morris Companies, Inc.,** New York (cigarettes)	14,598
3.	**American Council of Life Insurance,** Washington (insurance companies)	13,999
4.	**Marine Engineers Union,** Washington (labor union)	13,500
5.	**Ashland, Inc.,** Ashland, Ky. (oil and gas)	12,950
6.	**BAT Industries, PLC,** London (cigarettes)	12,376
7.	**Humana, Inc.,** Louisville, Ky. (managed health-care plans)	12,000
8.	**Duke Energy Corporation,** Charlotte, N.C. (electrical service)	12,000
9.	**Joseph E. Seagram & Sons, Inc.,** New York (distilled spirits)	11,750
10. (tie)	**Brown-Forman Corporation,** Louisville, Ky. (distilled spirits)	11,500
	Delta Air Lines, Inc., Atlanta	11,500

Notes: Based on analysis of contributions to Ford from 1987 to 1996.

HARRY REID
Democrat, Nevada
Co-Chairman, Senate Democratic Policy Committee

1.	**Circus Circus Enterprises, Inc.**, Las Vegas, Nev. (hotels and casinos)	$68,000
2.	**Reid & Priest**, New York (law firm)	66,750
3.	**Auto Dealers & Drivers for Free Trade**, Jamaica, N.Y. (Japanese cars)	65,000
4.	**Lionel, Sawyer & Collins**, Las Vegas, Nev. (law firm)	37,716
5.	**Hilton Hotels Corporation**, Beverly Hills, Calif. (hotels and casinos)	32,877
6.	**Del Webb Corporation**, Phoenix, Ariz. (real-estate development)	29,500
7.	**Lady Luck Gaming Corporation**, Las Vegas, Nev. (casinos)	29,000
8. (tie)	**Harrah's Entertainment, Inc.**, Memphis, Tenn. (hotels and casinos)	27,500
	Sierra Health Services, Inc., Las Vegas, Nev. (life and health insurance)	27,500
9.	**Interface Group, Inc.**, Needham, Mass. (casinos)	26,500
10.	**Horseshoe Holdings**, Las Vegas, Nev. (casinos)	26,000

Notes: Based on analysis of contributions to Reid from 1987 to 1996.

JOHN KERRY
Democrat, Massachusetts
Chairman, Senate Democratic Steering
and Coordination Committee

1.	**Mintz, Levin, Cohn, Ferris, Glovsky & Popeo,** Boston (law/lobbying firm)	$106,996
2.	**Time Warner, Inc.,** New York (entertainment and telecommunications)	80,450
3.	**Massachusetts Teachers Association,** Boston (labor union)	62,315
4.	**Hale and Dorr,** Boston (law firm)	48,650
5.	**MacAndrews & Forbes Holdings, Inc.,** New York (investment firm)	47,000
6.	**Foley, Hoag & Eliot,** Boston (law firm)	42,650
7.	**AFL-CIO,** Washington (labor unions)	38,583
8.	**The Beacon Companies,** Boston (real estate)	37,750
9.	**American Federation of State, County, & Municipal Employees,** Washington (labor union)	36,502
10.	**Thermo Electron Corporation,** Waltham, Mass. (monitoring instruments, biomedical products, research and development)	35,500

Notes: Based on analysis of contributions to Kerry from 1987 to 1996.

BOB KERREY
Democrat, Nebraska
Chairman, Democratic Senatorial Campaign Committee

1.	**PaineWebber Group, Inc.,** New York (investment banking)	$58,450
2.	**Healthsouth Corporation,** Birmingham, Ala. (rehabilitation services)	42,050
3.	**US West, Inc.,** Denver (communications)	37,585
4.	**National Committee to Preserve Social Security and Medicare,** Washington (fund-raising and advocacy)	34,159
5.	**Allen Holding, Inc.,** New York (investment banking)	30,250
6.	**Printon, Kane Group, Inc.,** Short Hills, N.J. (investment banking)	30,000
7.	**AFL-CIO,** Washington (labor unions)	29,175
8.	**Salomon Brothers, Inc.,** New York (financial services)	27,750
9.	**Air Line Pilots Association International,** Washington (labor union)	26,000
10.	**Marine Engineers Beneficial Association,** Washington* (labor union)	25,500

*Includes affiliates.

Notes: Based on analysis of contributions to Kerrey from 1987 to 1996.

DANIEL PATRICK MOYNIHAN
Democrat, New York
Ranking Minority Member, Senate Finance Committee

1.	**National Committee to Preserve Social Security and Medicare**, Washington (fund-raising and advocacy)	$72,570
2.	**American Express Company**, New York* (consumer lending)	65,075
3.	**American Federation of State, County, & Municipal Employees**, Washington (labor union)	58,526
4.	**Triarc Companies, Inc.**, New York (liquefied petroleum gas)	58,526
5.	**CS First Boston Corporation**, New York (investment banking)	47,050
6.	**Willkie, Farr & Gallagher**, New York (law firm)	46,950
7.	**Goldman, Sachs & Company**, New York (investment banking)	45,050
8.	**Continental Corporation/CNA Financial Corporation**, Chicago (insurance)	38,312
9.	**E. M. Warburg, Pincus & Company**, New York (venture capital)	28,000
10.	**Citicorp**, New York (bank holding company)	27,474

*Includes subsidiaries.

Notes: Based on analysis of contributions to Moynihan from 1987 to 1996.

ROBERT BYRD
Democrat, West Virginia
Ranking Minority Member,
Senate Appropriations Committee

1.	**AFL-CIO**, Washington (labor union)	$22,509
2.	**Lockheed Martin Corporation**, Bethesda, Md.* (aerospace and defense)	22,500
3.	**United Transport Union**, Cleveland (labor union)	20,026
3.	**Associated General Contractors of America,** Washington (construction)	21,000
4.	**Northrop Grumman Corporation**, Los Angeles (aerospace and defense)	20,000
5.	**American Bankers Association**, Washington (commercial banks)	19,000
6.	**National Committee to Preserve Social Security** **and Medicare,** Washington (fundraising and advocacy)	17,146
7.	**Laborers' International Union of North America,** Washington (labor union)	17,000
8.	**United Mine Workers of America**, Washington (labor union)	16,506
9. (tie)	**Association of Trial Lawyers of America,** Washington	16,000
	Credit Union National Association, Washington	16,000
	National Association of Home Builders, Washington	16,000
10. (tie)	**American Federation of State, County, & Munici-** **pal Employees,** Washington (labor union)	15,000
	American Electric Power, Columbus, Ohio (electric utilities)	15,000
	National Association of Realtors, Washington	15,000
	National Coal Association, Washington	15,000
	International Brotherhood of Teamsters, Washington (labor union)	15,000

*Includes subsidiaries and merged entities.

Notes: Based on analysis of contributions to Byrd from 1987 to 1996.

NEWT GINGRICH
Republican, Georgia
Speaker of the House

1.	**Terry and Mary Kohler/Windway Capital Corporation,** Sheboygan, Wis. (holding company, kitchen utensils, boat building)	$816,107
2.	**Capital Formation Counselors, Inc.,** Belleair Bluffs, Fla. (investment firm)	385,513
3.	**Milliken Family/Milliken & Company,** Spartanburg, S.C. (textiles)	370,300
4.	**Gilder, Gagnon, Howe & Company,** New York (brokerage firm)	363,650
5.	**Schwan family/Schwan's Sales Enterprises, Inc.,** Gary, S.D. (frozen-food sales)	300,755
6.	**Philip and Elizabeth Gelatt/Northern Engraving Corporation,** La Crosse, Wis. (metal engraving, automobile parts)	239,300
7.	**Jesse and Sylvia Thompson/Clermont Development Company,** Charlotte, N.C. (real estate)	230,000
8.	**K. Tucker and Karen Andersen/Cumberland Associates,** New York (investment firm)	227,000
9.	**Alfred Lee and Virginia Loomis,** Bluffton, S.C.* (investments)	222,000
10.	**Golden Rule Financial Corporation,** Lawrenceville, Ill. (life insurance)	213,110

*Alfred Lee Loomis died in 1994.

Notes: Based on analysis of contributions to Gingrich from 1987 to 1996, contributions to his PAC, GOPAC, from 1987 to the first quarter of 1995 (Gingrich relinquished control of GOPAC on May 1, 1995), and contributions to Monday Morning PAC from 1995 to 1996.

RICHARD ARMEY
Republican, Texas
House Majority Leader

1.	**Raytheon Company**, Lexington, Mass.* (defense electronics)	$48,201
2.	**Garvey Family/Garvey Enterprises, Inc.,** Wichita, Kan. (oil, real estate)	31,800
3.	**American Medical Association**, Washington (physicians)	30,450
4.	**National Automobile Dealers Association,** McLean, Va.	29,400
5.	**Bass Brothers Enterprises, Inc.,** Fort Worth, Texas (oilfield services)	26,250
6.	**Texas Utilities Company**, Dallas* (electric utilities)	24,500
7.	**American Airlines, Inc.,** Fort Worth, Texas*	23,550
8.	**SBC Communications, Inc.,** San Antonio, Texas* (telecommunications)	22,654
9.	**Americans for Free International Trade,** Alexandria, Va. (import auto dealers)	22,500
10.	**United Parcel Service of America, Inc.,** Atlanta (delivery service)	20,500

*Includes subsidiaries and merged entities. Most Raytheon contributions came from two of its subsidiaries, E-systems, Inc., and Electrospace Systems, both of which are in Texas.

Notes: Based on analysis of contributions to Armey from 1987 to 1996 and contributions to his PACs, the Policy Innovation PAC, from 1988 to 1991, and the Majority Leader's Fund, from 1995 to 1996.

TOM DELAY
Republican, Texas
House Republican Whip

1.	**Enron Corporation,** Houston (diversified energy)	$51,550
2.	**American Medical Association,** Chicago (physicians)	44,650
3.	**Aircraft Owners and Pilots Association,** Frederick, Md.	35,400
4.	**Fluor Corporation,** Irvine, Calif. (global engineering, construction, coal)	34,000
5.	**National Association of Realtors,** Washington	33,100
6.	**Coastal Corporation,** Houston (oil and gas)	32,000
7.	**National Automobile Dealers Association,** McLean, Va.	31,100
8.	**Michael Stevens Interests,** Houston (real-estate development)	30,000
9.	**Dow Chemical Company,** Midland, Mich. (plastics, chemicals, metals)	29,235
10.	**RJR Nabisco, Inc.,** New York (cigarettes)	28,750

Notes: Based on analysis of contributions to DeLay from 1987 to 1996 and contributions to his PAC, Americans for a Republican Majority, from 1993 to 1996.

JOHN BOEHNER
Republican, Ohio
Chairman, House Republican Conference

1.	**Cincinnati Financial Corporation,** Cincinnati (insurance)	$36,650
2.	**Ameritech Corporation,** Chicago* (communications)	34,523
3.	**American Medical Association,** Chicago (physicians)	32,900
4.	**Crown Equipment Corporation,** New Bremen, Ohio (forklift trucks)	32,700
5.	**AK Steel Holding Corporation,** Middletown, Ohio* (steel)	30,875
6.	**BellSouth Corporation,** Atlanta* (communications)	29,932
7.	**National Association of Realtors,** Washington	29,350
8.	**National Automobile Dealers Association,** McLean, Va.	26,100
9.	**RJR Nabisco, Inc.,** New York (cigarettes)	22,300
10.	**Federal Express Corporation,** Memphis, Tenn. (delivery service)	22,000

*Includes subsidiaries and merged companies.

Notes: Based on analysis of contributions to Boehner from 1990 to 1996 and contributions to his PAC, the Freedom Project, from 1995 to 1996.

JOHN LINDER
Republican, Georgia
Chairman, National Republican Congressional Committee

1.	**American Medical Association,** Chicago (physicians)	$30,800
2.	**Hanna Family,** Atlanta (investments)	29,000
3.	**Ernst & Young,** New York (accounting firm)	28,550
4.	**United Parcel Service of America, Inc.,** Atlanta (delivery service)	28,050
5.	**American Dental Association,** Chicago (dentists)	26,499
6.	**National Rifle Association,** Fairfax, Va. (gun advocacy)	24,546
7.	**American Bankers Association,** Washington	24,000
8.	**Sheet Metal and Air Conditioning Contractors National Association,** Vienna, Va. (plumbing and air-conditioning contractors)	22,500
9.	**National Right to Life PAC,** Washington (antiabortion advocacy)	22,494
10.	**AFLAC, Inc.,** Columbus, Ga. (supplemental health insurance)	20,030

Notes: Based on analysis of contributions to Linder from 1989 to 1996.

WILLIAM ARCHER
Republican, Texas
Chairman, House Ways and Means Committee
Chairman, Joint Committee on Taxation

1.	**PanEnergy Corporation**, Houston* (natural-gas transmission and sales)	$12,000
2.	**Todhunter International, Inc.**, West Palm Beach, Fla. (alcoholic products)	9,000
3.	**Pilgrim's Pride Corporation**, Pittsburg, Texas (poultry slaughterer/processor)	8,000
4.	**White & Case**, New York* (law/lobbying firm)	7,500
5.	**MCG/Dulworth & Company**, Houston (executive benefit planning)	7,722
6.	**Massachusetts Mutual Life Insurance Company**, Springfield, Mass.	5,150
7.	**Murphy Baxter**, Houston (independent oil operator)	4,000
8.	**Comiskey-Kaufman Inc.**, Houston (life-insurance marketing)	3,900
9. (tie)	**Liddell, Sapp, Zivley, Hill & Laboon**, Houston, Texas (law firm)	3,500
	McGovern Allergy Clinic, Houston	3,500
	Timmers Chevrolet, Inc., Pasadena, Texas (auto dealer)	3,500
10.	**Longmont Group**, Houston (insurance)	3,136

*Includes subsidiaries and merged entities.

Notes: Based on analysis of contributions to Archer from 1987 to 1996. During the ten-year period, Archer accepted no PAC contributions. He ran unopposed in four of the last five elections. Nonetheless, he raised $904,996 in campaign contributions during those ten years.

JOHN KASICH
Republican, Ohio
Chairman, House Budget Committee

1.	**Worthington Industries, Inc.,** Columbus, Ohio* (steel)	$48,850
2.	**The Limited, Inc.,** Columbus, Ohio (apparel)	36,400
3.	**Huntington Bancshares, Inc.,** Columbus, Ohio (bank holding company)	35,491
4.	**National Automobile Dealers Association,** McLean, Va.	32,850
5.	**The Ohio Company,** Columbus, Ohio (investment banking)	28,450
6.	**Nationwide Mutual Insurance Company,** Columbus, Ohio (auto insurance)	27,387
7.	**AT&T Corporation,** Basking Ridge, N.J. (telecommunications)	25,993
8.	**American Medical Association,** Chicago (physicians)	22,650
9.	**Banc One Corporation,** Columbus, Ohio (bank holding company)	20,100
10.	**National PAC,** Washington (pro-Israel advocacy)	20,000

*Includes subsidiaries.

Notes: Based on analysis of contributions to Kasich from 1987 to 1996 and contributions to his PAC, Pioneer PAC, from 1995 to 1996.

THOMAS BLILEY
Republican, Virginia
Chairman, House Commerce Committee

1.	**Philip Morris Companies, Inc.,** New York* (cigarettes)	$69,815
2.	**AT&T Corporation,** Basking Ridge, N.J. (communications)	53,475
3.	**American Institute of Certified Public Accountants,** Jersey City, N.J.	44,300
4.	**National Cable Television Association,** Washington (cable system owners)	36,000
5.	**American Bankers Association,** Washington	31,650
6.	**RJR Nabisco, Inc.,** New York (cigarettes)	31,100
7.	**American Medical Association,** Chicago (physicians)	30,209
8.	**National Automobile Dealers Association,** McLean, Va.	29,550
9.	**UST, Inc.,** Greenwich, Conn. (tobacco products)	25,700
10.	**Bell Atlantic Corporation,** Philadelphia* (communications)	25,670

*Includes subsidiaries.

Notes: Based on analysis of contributions made to Bliley from 1987 to 1996 and contributions to his PAC, Fund for a Responsible Future, from 1995 to 1996.

ROBERT LIVINGSTON
Republican, Louisiana
Chairman, House Appropriations Committee

1.	**Lockheed Martin Corporation**, Bethesda, Md.* (aerospace and defense)	$29,800
2.	**Textron, Inc.**, Providence, R.I. (aerospace technology)	23,000
3.	**Diagnostic/Retrieval Systems, Inc.**, Parsippany, N.J. (signal processing and display systems)	22,500
4.	**Northrop Grumman Corporation**, Los Angeles* (aerospace and defense)	21,900
5.	**Trinity Industries, Inc.**, Dallas (metal products)	21,700
6.	**Avondale Industries, Inc.**, Avondale, La. (shipbuilding and machinery)	20,200
7.	**National Association of Realtors**, Washington	18,700
8.	**General Motors Corporation**, Detroit (automobile manufacturer)	18,450
9.	**Entergy Corporation**, New Orleans* (electric services)	17,040
10.	**Raytheon Company**, Lexington, Mass. (defense electronics)	17,050

*Includes subsidiaries and merged entities.

Notes: Based on analysis of contributions to Livingston from 1987 to 1996.

RICHARD GEPHARDT
Democrat, Missouri
House Minority Leader

1.	**Anheuser-Busch Companies, Inc.,** St. Louis. (beer)	$215,300
2.	**Thompson Coburn,** St. Louis. (law firm)	177,939
3.	**Bryan, Cave,** St. Louis. (law firm)	128,850
4.	**McDonnell Douglas Corporation,** St. Louis. (aerospace and defense)	107,325
5.	**International Brotherhood of Electrical Workers,** Washington (labor union)	101,944
6.	**United Automobile Workers,** Detroit, Mich. (labor union)	100,000
7.	**Independent Insurance Agents of America,** Washington	94,999
8.	**National Education Association,** Washington (labor union)	91,000
9.	**Philip Morris Companies, Inc.,** New York (cigarettes)	90,948
10.	**International Brotherhood of Teamsters,** Washington (labor union)	89,500

Notes: Based on analysis of contributions to Gephardt from 1987 to 1996 and to his PACs, the Effective Government Committee, from 1987 to 1996; the Majority Leader's Victory Fund, from 1993 to 1994; the Democratic Leader's Victory Fund, from 1995 to 1996; and the Gephardt Dinner Committee, from 1995 to 1996.

DAVID BONIOR
Democrat, Michigan
Democratic Whip

1.	**Marine Engineers Beneficial Association,** Washington (labor union)	$52,500
2.	**Ameritech Corporation,** Chicago* (communications)	50,403
3.	**International Brotherhood of Teamsters,** Washington (labor union)	50,250
4. (tie)	**Air Line Pilots Association,** Washington (labor union)	50,000
	National Education Association, Washington (labor union)	50,000
5.	**United Brotherhood of Carpenters and Joiners of America,** Washington (labor union)	46,000
6.	**AFL-CIO,** Washington (labor unions)	45,880
7.	**International Association of Machinists & Aerospace Workers,** Upper Marlboro, Md. (labor union)	45,000
8.	**United Food & Commercial Workers International Union,** Washington (labor union)	44,100
9. (tie)	**American Postal Workers Union,** Washington (labor union)	44,000
	KidsPAC, Cambridge, Mass. (children's-rights advocacy)	44,000
10.	**Bell South Corporation,** Atlanta (communications)	43,500

*Includes subsidiaries and merged entities.

Notes: Based on analysis of contributions to Bonior from 1987 to 1996. Bonior also received $75,566 in contributions from six different Michigan State Democratic Party committees.

VIC FAZIO
Democrat, California
Chairman, House Democratic Caucus
Ranking Minority Member, House Appropriations Committee

1.	**American Medical Association**, Chicago (physicians)	$302,085
2.	**National Education Association**, Washington (labor union)	68,967
3.	**National Association of Realtors**, Washington	64,534
4.	**Human Rights Campaign**, Washington (gay and lesbian rights advocacy)	58,000
5.	**American Federation of State, County & Municipal Employees**, Washington (labor union)	57,499
6.	**SBC Communications, Inc.**, San Antonio, Texas (telecommunications)	56,695
7.	**Communications Workers of America**, Washington* (labor union)	54,700
8.	**International Brotherhood of Electrical Workers**, Washington (labor union)	54,250
9.	**Foundation Health Corporation**, Rancho Cordova, Calif. (managed health-care provider)	53,575
10.	**United Automobile Workers**, Detroit (labor union)	51,850

*Includes subsidiaries and merged entities.

Notes: Based on analysis of contributions to Fazio from 1987 to 1996 and to his PAC, Victory USA, from 1992 to 1996. Includes independent expenditures made on Fazio's behalf.

MARTIN FROST

Democrat, Texas

Chairman, Democratic Congressional Campaign Committee

1.	**United Automobile Workers,** Detroit (labor union)	$55,500
2.	**American Federation of State, County & Municipal Employees,** Washington (labor union)	51,000
3.	**Association of Trial Lawyers of America,** Washington (lawyers)	50,943
4.	**International Brotherhood of Electrical Workers,** Washington (labor union)	48,200
5.	**International Brotherhood of Teamsters,** Washington (labor union)	48,000
6.	**National Association of Realtors,** Washington (real-estate agents)	46,000
7.	**Communications Workers of America,** Washington (labor union)	45,648
8.	**Transportation Workers Union,** Washington (labor union)	44,000
9.	**National Education Association,** Washington (labor union)	43,000
10.	**Textron, Inc.,** Providence, R.I. (aerospace technology)	42,000

Notes: Based on analysis of contributions to Frost from 1987 to 1996 and to his PAC, the Lone Star Fund, from 1991 to 1996.

CHARLES RANGEL
Democrat, New York
Ranking Minority Member,
House Ways and Means Committee

1.	**Goldman, Sachs & Company,** New York (investment banking)	$55,500
2.	**New York Life Company,** New York (life insurance)	50,450
3. (tie)	**Don King Productions, Inc.** (entertainment)	50,000
	Henry Van Ameringen, New York (cosmetics)	50,000
4.	**Metropolitan Life Insurance Company,** New York (life and health insurance)	46,795
5.	**Americhoice Corporation,** Vienna, Va. (health maintenance organization)	45,000
6.	**American Federation of Teachers,** Washington (labor union)	42,125
7.	**AFLAC, Inc.,** Columbus, Ga. (supplemental health insurance)	40,000
8.	**American International Group, Inc.,** New York (multinational insurance)	39,182
9.	**American Federation of State, County & Municipal Employees,** Washington (labor union)	38,596
10. (tie)	**Philip Morris Companies,** New York (cigarettes)	37,000
	International Brotherhood of Teamsters, Washington (labor union)	37,000

Notes: Based on analysis of contributions to Rangel from 1987 to 1996 and contributions to his PAC, the Charles Rangel Victory Fund, from 1995 to 1996.

JOHN DINGELL
Democrat, Michigan
Ranking Minority Member, House Commerce Committee

1.	**General Motors Corporation**, Detroit (automobile manufacturer)	$59,900
2.	**Ford Motor Company**, Detroit (automobile manufacturer)	59,125
3.	**Chrysler Corporation**, Detroit (automobile manufacturer)	55,950
4.	**International Brotherhood of Teamsters**, Washington (labor union)	47,700
5.	**American Federation of State, County & Municipal Employees**, Washington (labor union)	40,609
6.	**Ameritech Corporation**, Chicago* (communications)	39,820
7.	**United Automobile Workers**, Detroit (labor union)	37,591
8.	**Joseph E. Seagram & Sons, Inc.**, New York* (distilled spirits)	37,500
9.	**National Cable Television Association**, Washington (cable-system owners)	37,000
10.	**BellSouth Corporation**, Atlanta* (communications)	35,050

*Includes subsidiaries and merged entities.

Notes: Based on analysis of contributions to Dingell from 1987 to 1996.

DAVID OBEY
Democrat, Wisconsin
Ranking Minority Member, House Appropriations Committee

1.	**American Federation of State, County & Municipal Employees,** Washington (labor union)	$61,767
2.	**Association of Trial Lawyers of America,** Washington	51,913
3.	**Associated Milk Producers, Inc.,** Arlington, Texas (dairy products)	45,000
4.	**American Federation of Teachers,** Washington (labor union)	40,500
5.	**National Education Association,** Washington (labor union)	39,850
6.	**United Automobile Workers,** Detroit (labor union)	38,000
7.	**International Brotherhood of Teamsters,** Washington (labor union)	37,000
8.	**National Community Action Foundation,** Washington (community services)	36,750
9.	**Laborers International Union,** Washington (labor union)	33,000
10.	**American Medical Association,** Chicago (physicians)	27,500

Notes: Based on analysis of contributions to Obey from 1987 to 1996 and to his PAC, Committee for a Progressive Congress, from 1993 to 1996.

Top Twenty Third-Party Sponsors of Congressional Travel

||||||||||||

January 1, 1996 to June 30, 1997

	Sponsor	Number of Trips
1.	Aspen Institute	395
2.	Center for Market Processes	185
3.	Nuclear Energy Institute	104
4.	Heritage Foundation	68
5.	Chinese National Association of Industry & Commerce	63
6.	American Israel Public Affairs Committee (AIPAC)	62
7.	Empower America	49
8.	Securities Industry Association	45
9.	Florida Sugar Cane League	44
10.	Chung-Yuan Christian University	41
11.	Sugar Cane Growers Cooperative of Florida	39
12.	Chinese Culture University	36
13. (tie)	National Broadcasting Company	33
	The Tax Foundation	33
14.	New York Stock Exchange	31
15. (tie)	The Edison Electric Institute	30
	The Tobacco Institute	30
16.	American Bar Association	29
17. (tie)	Asia Pacific Exchange Foundation	27
	Harvard University	27
	Tax Coalition	27
18.	National Cable Television Association	26
19. (tie)	Sahara Fund	25
	Stanley Foundation	25
20. (tie)	Association of American Railroads	23
	MCI Communications, Inc.	23
	Soochow University	23

Source Notes

|||||||||||

As noted in the Acknowledgments for this book, the Center for Public Integrity conducted more than 1,200 on-the-record interviews for *The Buying of the Congress*. The name of every person who agreed to be named as a source may be found on the Center's Web site, www.publicintegrity.org, as can selected interview transcripts. The Web site also contains a comprehensive set of footnotes for each chapter of the book, a complete bibliography, and brief biographies of contributors.

Introduction

The campaign-contribution figures come from the Center for Responsive Politics, utilizing Federal Election Commission data. Overall child work-related injury data is available from the National Electronic Injury Surveillance System, cited in *Child Labor Research Needs*, National Institute for Occupational Safety and Health, U.S. Department of Health and Human Services, August 1997.

For overviews of additional trends affecting lower- and middle-income Americans, see Donald L. Bartlett and James B. Steele, *Who Stole the Dream?* (Andrews and McMeel, 1996) and William Julius Wilson, *When Work Disappears: The World of the New Urban Poor* (Vintage Books, 1997).

Details on the widening gap between rich and poor in America and other figures on the state of the economy are contained in John Ralston Saul, *The Unconscious Civilization* (The Free Press, 1995) and Michael J. Sandel, *Democracy's Discontent: America in Search of a Public Philosophy* (The Belknap Press of Harvard University, 1996).

1. The Death of Conscience

For more on the Roosevelt-era muckrakers, see John A. Garraty, *The American Nation Since 1865: A History of the United States* (Harper & Row, 1966).

For details of the Rostenkowski case, see Toni Locy, "Rostenkowski Fraud Brings 17-Month Sentence," *The Washington Post,* April 10, 1996.

The material on Williams is from Charles Lewis, "Senator John: A Remembrance," *Wilmington News-Journal,* February 21, 1988; John Barron, "The Case of Bobby Baker and the Courageous Senator," *Reader's Digest,* September 1965; and Fletcher Knebel, "The Man Who Broke the Tax Scandal," *Look,* December 18, 1951. See also Michael Beschloss, *Taking Charge: The Johnson White House Tapes 1963–64* (Simon & Schuster, 1997).

For early biographical information on Hart, see Michael O'Brien, *Philip Hart: The Conscience of the Nation* (Michigan State University Press, 1995).

2. Going, Going, Gone

For more on Fahrenkopf, see the Center for Public Integrity's *Place Your Bets,* June 1996.

The committee receipt information is from the Federal Election Commission Web site and is available at www.fec.gov/finance.demhard.htm and www.fed.gov/finance.rephard.htm.

For more on Bill Gradison and Ira Magaziner on the health-care-reform debate, see the Center for Public Integrity's *Well-Healed: Inside Lobbying for Health Care Reform,* 1994.

3. The Ways, the Means, and the Ends

For more on issue advertising, see Annenberg Public Policy Center, "Issue Advocacy Advertising During the 1996 Campaign: A Catalog," Number 16, September 16, 1997. See also Elizabeth Drew, *Whatever It Takes: The Real Struggle for Political Power in America* (Viking Press, 1997).

Marianne Gingrich's professional activities are detailed in an article by Margaret Ebrahim and Charles Lewis, "Contract with an American," *The Public i,* the newsletter of the Center for Public Integrity, March 1995.

Information on Tom and Randy DeLay comes from Frank Greve, "Brothers in the Hot Seat," *Akron Beacon Journal,* September 21, 1996, and Nurith C. Aizenman, "Breaking the Rules," *Washington Monthly,* June 1997.

Details about D'Amato's, Foley's, and Torricelli's investments in IPOs can be found in James K. Glassman, "Maybe IPO Really Means 'Ingratiating Political Offering,'" *The Washington Post,* June 22, 1994; Glenn R. Simpson, "Foley Says Investments in No Way 'Irregular,'" *Roll Call,* August 3, 1993; and Timothy J. Burger, "Torricelli to Sell Bank Stock, Deal Only in Mutual Funds," *Roll Call,* June 13, 1994.

For more on Citizen Action, see Leslie Wayne, "Watchdog Group Is Under Scrutiny for Role in Teamster Race," *The New York Times,* September 22, 1997.

Details about the Ripon Society and its trips can be found in Ruth Marcus, "Business Groups Paid for Lawmakers' Trip: Gift Limits Didn't Ban Prague Conference," *The Washington Post,* September 26, 1997.

A detailed description of Bonner & Associates can be found in Ken Silverstein, "Hello. I'm Calling This Evening to Mislead You," *Mother Jones,* November/December 1997.

Accounts of the debate surrounding the disaster-relief bill come from Miguel

Perez, "Flood Relief Blackmail," *The Record,* (Bergen, New Jersey), June 11, 1997; the editorial "Victims Must Wait for Congress," *Chicago Tribune,* June 2, 1997; Elaine Povich, "GOP Backs Off on Aid, Moves to Trim Down Disaster Relief Bill," *Newsday,* June 12, 1997; Eric Pianin, "How Business Found Benefits in Wage Bill," *The Washington Post,* February 11, 1997; the Center's interview of Warren Rudman on June 17, 1997; and the Center's interview with John Sweeney on November 4, 1997.

4. The Killing Fields

Sandra Mero's story and the battle over methyl bromide in California are detailed in Sharon Bernstein, "Use of Powerful Insecticide Fills Air with Controversy," *Los Angeles Times,* March 23, 1997, and Steve Berry, "Woman's Coma Studied for Links to Pest Killer," *Los Angeles Times,* March 22, 1997. See also Bob Johnson, "Political Pesticide," downloaded from www.metroactive.com, which details the California strawberry industry's use of the pesticide and its economic and health effects on the surrounding communities.

For an overall review of methyl bromide in the agricultural community and its effects on the environment, see Jeff Wheelwright, "The Berry and the Poison: Strawberries and Methyl Bromide," *Smithsonian,* December 1996.

The Environmental Protection Agency maintains a Methyl Bromide Phaseout Web Site, which contains frequently asked questions, telephone numbers, the science of methyl bromide, and alternatives to its use. The address is www.epa.gov/docs/ozone/. The site also contains information about other ozone-depleting chemicals.

For more information about methyl bromide's use near schools, see "Heavy Methyl Bromide Use Near California Schools" and "Pesticide Use in California: The Ag-Suburban Pesticide Exposure Zone," both by the Environmental Working Group, downloaded from www.ewg.org.

5. The Tainted Table

Nichols Fox's book *Spoiled* (Basic Books, 1997) provides a comprehensive survey of the meat-processing industry and the increase in foodborne diseases.

Mary Heersink, in *E. Coli O157: The True Story of a Mother's Battle with a Killer Microbe* (New Horizon Press, 1996), gives a firsthand account of dealing with a child's illness caused by foodborne bacteria and a parent's fight to prevent it from happening again.

Food Chemical News provides comprehensive news on food-safety issues and the industry.

Statistics of foodborne diseases are maintained and updated by the Centers for Disease Control and Prevention and published in *Morbidity and Mortality Weekly Report.*

For more on poultry processing and the spread of salmonella, see *Playing Chicken* by the Center for Science in the Public Interest, March 1996.

6. Cash Crop

For the most comprehensive history of the cigarette industry, see Richard Kluger, *Ashes to Ashes* (Alfred A. Knopf, 1996).

For reviews of more than 4,000 leaked documents from the files of Brown & Williamson and B.A.T. Industries, see Stanton Glantz et al., *The Cigarette Papers* (University of California Press, 1996) and Philip Hilts, *Smokescreen* (Addison-Wesley Publishing Company, 1996). Copies of these documents are available on the Internet at galen.library.ucsf.edu/tobacco/.

For a history of the lobbying behind the 1984 labeling battle, see chapters 2 and 3 of Michael Pertschuk's *Giant Killers* (W. W. Norton & Company, 1986).

For multifaceted coverage of the industry and its lobbying and advertising tactics, see *Mother Jones,* May/June 1996 (also available at www.mojones.com/mother.jones/ MJ96/).

For updated articles from newspapers such as *The New York Times, The Washington Post, Los Angeles Times, The Chicago Tribune, Minneapolis Star-Tribune, Richmond Times Dispatch,* and *Knoxville News-Sentinel*; reproductions of documents released by courts; copies of the settlement proposals; and other links to tobacco industry and advocacy Web sites, see www.tobacco.org.

7. The Gun Club

Data on gun injuries from 1979 to 1995 was downloaded from the Centers for Disease Control and Prevention's Web page, at www.cdc.gov/ncipc/osp/data.htm. On injuries in the home, see Arthur L. Kellermann, Frederick P. Rivara et al., "Gun Ownership as a Risk Factor for Homicide in the Home," *The New England Journal of Medicine,* October 7, 1993.

The Violence Policy Center has published numerous reports on gun policy and is a rich source of information about the NRA and other pro-gun groups. The group's Web site is at www.vpc.org. The Center for Public Integrity's analysis of corporate donors to the NRA Foundation is based on annual reports for 1994 and 1995, which were collected by the Violence Policy Center.

8. Prescription for Disasters

For information on medicines, including their use and side effects, see the U.S. Pharmacopoeia's Web site at www.usp.org.

Hearings on dietary supplements were first held under Senator William Proxmire in the 1970s. Hearings leading to the Nutrition Labeling and Education Act were held in 1990. Additional hearings were held at various times from 1992 to 1994. See, for example, the hearing chaired by Representative Henry Waxman, House Energy and Commerce Subcommittee on Health and Environment, July 29, 1993.

Hearings on off-label use of drugs were held by the Senate Labor and Human Resources Committee on February 21 and 22, 1996, and by the House Government Reform and Oversight Subcommittee on Human Resources and Intergovernmental Relations on September 11, 1996.

Dorothy C. Wilson testified before the House Commerce Subcommittee on Health and Environment, July 29, 1993.

For information on L-tryptophan and EMS, see, among others: Janet L. Vaught et al. v. Showa Denko K.K. et al., No. 96-20200, 5th Cir; Holmes et al. v. Showa Denko K.K. et al., No. 95-9201, 11th Cir., case closed November 6, 1996; and Creamer et al. v. Showa Denko K.K. et al., Nos. 96-8628 and 96-8677, 11th Cir., brief filed September 26, 1996. In all, at least nine lawsuits have been filed in Oregon, Texas, Arkansas, Georgia, and Florida. Information about EMS can be found on the Internet at National Eosinophilia-Myalgia Syndrome Network, www. nemsn.org.

9. The Grim Reapers

Homer Stull's story was gathered from news stories at the time of the accident and from interviews with his brother, Norman Stull, and his sister, Diann Clodfelter.

Information about the standards, rules, and history of OSHA were culled from interviews with officials of the agency. Workplace-injury statistics and fatalities are from Guy Toscano and Janice Windau, Bureau of Labor Statistics, "National Census of Fatal Occupational Injuries, 1995," from "Fatal Workplace Injuries in 1995: A Collection of Data and Analysis," and from "Occupational Injuries and Illnesses: Counts, Rates, and Characteristics, 1994," which contain the most up-to-date statistics on work-related injuries.

Information about Congress's efforts to curtail OSHA's enforcement of safety standards was derived from a variety of sources and interviews. *Occupational Hazards* and *CTDNews Workplace Solutions for Repetitive Stress Injuries* monitor news, businesses, politics, and trends in the area of worker injuries.

Information about the meatpacking industry comes from interviews with workers, trade groups such as the American Meat Institute, company officials, officials of the United Food and Commercial Workers International Union, and residents of meatpacking towns in the Midwest.

10. Fear of Flying

Information on the crash of USAir Flight 1016 comes from the National Transportation Safety Board aircraft accident report, "Flight into Terrain During Missed Approach, USAir Flight 1016," available from the National Technical Information Service (www.ntis.gov), NTSB accident docket number SA-509, and newspaper accounts of the accident published in the *Pittsburgh Post-Gazette*.

For Federal Aviation Administration information on the safety of the air transportation system, see the Aviation Safety System on the FAA Web site, at www.faa. gov/publicinfo.htm.

For more information on safety measures not taken by airlines, see David Nolan, "Airline Safety: The Shocking Truth," *Discover*, October 1986.

The NTSB report dealing with seats and other survivability issues is *Cabin Safety in Large Transport Aircraft* (Government Printing Office, 1981) and is available from the National Technical Information Service.

11. Your Money or Your Life

The story of Merle Davis's abuse at a nursing home came from her daughter Dorothy Garrison's 1995 testimony before the Senate Committee on Aging and from Sheryl Stolberg, "GOP Plan Opens Door to Nursing Home Controversy," *Los Angeles Times*, September 30, 1995.

For anecdotal evidence of abuses, see particularly Carol A. Marbin and Stephen Nohlgren's five-part series "A Dangerous Age," *St. Petersburg Times,* May 21–25, 1995. Enforcement statistics are from the Nursing Homes Branch of the Health Care Financing Administration's Division of Outcomes and Improvement, "Survey Activity Summary" from July 1, 1995, to June 30, 1997.

Alan Solomont's lobbying for the nursing-home industry was first reported by Michael Weisskopf, "The Good Provider," *Time,* February 10, 1997. Information on Beverly Enterprises came from a variety of news sources and the study "Bad Care in Beverly's Backyard" by the Food and Allied Service Trades of the AFL-CIO, January 1997. Information on Representative Dan Miller's nursing homes came from sources including Sara Langenberg, "Nursing Homes 'Superior' Despite Problems," *Sarasota Herald-Tribune,* May 25, 1996.

Details about the state of health care in the United States came from various news articles, as well as from the National Coalition on Health Care, Physicians for a National Health Program, and the Children's Defense Fund.

Lobbying by the medical industry is well documented. Noteworthy accounts include Ruth Marcus, "Lobbying's Big Hitters Go to Bat," *The Washington Post,* August 3, 1997; Daniel Franklin, "Tommy Boggs and the Death of Health Care Reform," *Washington Monthly,* April 1995; Timothy J. Berger, "First, Do No Harm (To Our Fees)," *Legal Times,* June 2, 1997; David Andelman, "Prescription for a Powerful Lobby," *Management Review,* February 1997; Ramon Catellblanch, "Legislation for Sale," *In These Times,* October 28, 1996; and the 1994 study by the Center for Public Integrity, *Well-Healed: Inside Lobbying for Health Care Reform.*

The anonymous medical-industry witness testified before the Governmental Affairs Committee's Permanent Subcommittee on Investigations on February 14, 1996. Accounts of involuntary commitment include Chris Adams, "Medicaid Madness," *The New Orleans Times-Picayune,* August 13, 1995, and Dolores Kong, Gerard O'Neill, and Mitchell Zuckoff, "Locked Wards Open Door to Booming Business," *Boston Globe,* May 11, 1997.

John David Deaton's story of abuse by National Medical Enterprises is from his testimony before the House Judiciary Committee in 1994 and from interviews with his attorney, Robert F. Andrews.

12. The Price Isn't Right

The Center asked Shelly McPhail and Jeffrey Kinnamon for all of their grocery receipts for the month of July 1997, which were then entered onto spreadsheets and analyzed.

The Environmental Working Group, an environmental advocacy group based in Washington, D.C., produced a series of reports on farm policy, based on analysis of U.S. Department of Agriculture databases; they are available at www.ewg.org/pub/home/farm/farm.html.

In 1989, the Associated Press produced a four-part series called "Cashing In on the Drought," by Fred Bayles, which, among other things, examined how farmers preferred disaster aid to purchasing crop insurance. For a legislative history of the crop-insurance program, see Ruth Gastel, "Crop Insurance," *Insurance Information Institute Reports,* October 1997. For a detailed explanation of the federal crop-insurance program, see General Accounting Office, "Crop Insurance: Opportunities Exist to Reduce Government Costs for Private-Sector Delivery," April 14, 1997, GAO/ RCED-97-70. The GAO has published numerous reports over the years on the failure of crop insurance and disaster payments, which are available online at www.access. gpo.gov/su_docs/aces/aces160.shtml. For Representative Joe Skeen's role in the crop-insurance funding debate, see a series of reports in *National Journal*'s "Congress Daily," from June to July 1997.

The Center on Budget and Policy Priorities has published a series of reports on the cost of infant formula in the Special Supplemental Food Program for Women, Infants, and Children.

For a synopsis on John Connally's role in the milk-fund scandal, see John Shelton Reed, "In History's Shadow," *Washington Monthly*, November 1993.

For background on the sugar program and the influence of campaign contributions, see "The Politics of Sugar," Center for Responsive Politics, 1995. See also General Accounting Office, "Sugar Program: Changing Domestic and International Conditions Require Program Change," 1993.

13. Department of Highway Robbery

For more on President Clinton's tax policies, see James Galbraith, "Reagan Rides Again," *The Texas Observer*, August 29, 1997.

For more on the unfairness of the Social Security tax, see Jonathan Rowe and Clifford Cobb, "The Worst Tax," *Washington Monthly*, July/August 1997, and Matthew Miller, "A Tax None Will Touch," *U.S. News & World Report*, August 4, 1997.

For a look at the successful 1997 political campaign to slash the tax on capital gains, see Annys Shin, "Capital Games," *In These Times*, April 28, 1997.

For more about the $21 billion of corporate tax cuts inserted in the 1997 minimum-wage bill, see John Judis, "Bare Minimum," *The New Republic*, October 28, 1996, and Julie Kosterlitz, "A Bounty for Business," *National Journal*, October 26, 1996.

Citizens for Tax Justice has produced a variety of studies on the shifting of the tax burden away from the wealthy and onto the backs of the middle and working classes. Its 1996 report, "The Hidden Entitlements," details 122 loopholes businesses use to reduce their tax payments.

14. El Dorado on the Potomac

The Motion Picture Association of America's private film screenings are described in a number of reports, including Michael Shain and Anthony Scaduto, "Inside New York," *Newsday*, March 31, 1995.

For details of the hike in cable prices after the new telecommunications law was enacted, see MM Docket Number 92-266, "Statistical Report on Average Rates for Basic Service," January 2, 1997. Information on the cost to consumers of telecommunications services is from the Bureau of Labor Statistics, U.S. Department of Labor. See also CS Docket Number 96-133, "Annual Assessment of the Status of Competition in the Market for the Delivery of Video Programming," January 2, 1997. Both are available for downloading from www.fcc.gov. Also good background for the consumers' position on the cable industry is testimony by Gene Kimmelman, codirector of Consumers Union, before the Senate Commerce, Science, and Transportation Committee, April 10, 1997.

15. Future Shock

Statistical information on the state of the Social Security and Medicare systems comes from the *1996 Green Book* (U.S. Government Printing Office, 1996) and from the 1997 Annual Reports of the Trustees of the Social Security and Medicare Trust Funds and the Final Report of the 1994–1996 Advisory Council on Social Security, both of which are available online at www.ssa.gov.

Information on privatization efforts comes from various newspaper and magazine accounts, especially John F. Wasik, "Will Social Security Be There for You?" *Consumer Reports,* March 1996, and from the Cato Institute's Project on Social Security Privatization, available online at http://socialsecurity.org.

Information on the federal pension system comes from the General Accounting Office, "Federal Pensions: Relationship Between Retiree Pensions and Final Salaries," August 1997, and from various newspaper articles.

For further examples of Medicare fraud investigations and more information on Operation: Restore Trust, visit the Web site of the Inspector General of the Department of Health and Human Services, at www.hhs.gov/progorg/oig/index.html.

Tax statistics are from the 1993 Statistics of Income Bulletin of the IRS. For a more detailed account of the regressivity of the payroll tax and its use in masking the size of the budget deficit, see Donald L. Barlett and James B. Steele, *America: Who Really Pays the Taxes?* (Simon & Schuster, 1994).

For further information on the future of job creation, see the Final Report of the Technical Panel on Trends and Issues in Retirement Saving, available online at www.ssa.gov. Bureau of Labor Statistics data on the distribution of future jobs comes from the "Occupational Outlook Handbook," available online at www.bls.gov.

16. The Return of the Trusts

For more information on the closing of the Breyers factory and its effect on the plant's employees, see Rita Giardano's occasional articles published in *The Philadelphia Inquirer* between October 28, 1995, and January 22, 1997. Information on Unilever comes from the company's annual reports.

For more information on the political and economic aspects of monopolies, trusts, and oligopolies, see Walter Adams and James W. Brock, "Revitalizing a Structural Antitrust Policy," *Antitrust Bulletin,* March 1994, and, by the same authors, "Areeda/Turner on Antitrust: A Hobson's Choice," *Antitrust Bulletin,* December 1996. See also the Web site of the *Antitrust Law and Economics Review,* at webpages.metrolink.net/~cmueller.

Statistics on antitrust enforcement come from the Department of Justice, Antitrust Division.

Information on Boeing and McDonnell Douglas comes from the companies' annual reports; 10-K forms filed with the Securities and Exchange Commission, available at www.sec.gov; Department of Defense procurement records; and various news accounts.

For more information on consolidation in the banking industry under the Riegle Neal Act, see David Holland, Don Inscoe, Ross Waldrop, and William Kuta, "Interstate Banking: The Past, Present and Future," available at www.fdic.gov/databank/bkreview. Information on individual banks is from annual reports, 10-K forms filed with the Securities and Exchange Commission, and from various news accounts.

For information on Microsoft's birth, growth, and dominance among computer operating systems, see James Wallace and Jim Erickson, *Hard Drive* (HarperBusiness, 1993). Information on Microsoft comes from the company's annual reports, 10-K forms filed with the Securities and Exchange Commission, and various news accounts, especially David Thielen, "How to Tame the Computer Beast," *The New Republic,* May 8, 1995.

17. Sold Out

The Center for Public Integrity interviewed workers who were fired because of cheap imports from Mexico and China. The accounts are also found in files of the U.S. Department of Labor's Employment Training Administration, where tens of thousands of petitions from displaced workers seeking employment retraining are piled up.

The National Labor Committee broke the story of how the U.S. government was encouraging American firms to move jobs overseas. For the full account, see the committee's report, "Paying to Lose Our Jobs," September 1992.

The U.S. corporate and Mexican government lobby for the North American Free Trade Agreement was detailed by the Center for Public Integrity in the 1993 study *The Trading Game: Inside Lobbying for the North American Free Trade Agreement.*

The power of the China lobby was discussed in Donald L. Barlett and James Steele, "Most Favored Lobby," *Washington Monthly,* December 1996. See also Ken Silverstein, "The New China Hands," *The Nation,* February 17, 1997.

18. The Turn of the Screw

The details of Maria Stern's experience with her breast implants and her lawsuit are from newspaper reports, especially Ursula Thomas, "Woman's Breast Implant Suit Started the Dominoes Falling," *Gannett News Service,* March 14, 1992. A thorough account of the legal issues surrounding Stern's suit, as well as other breast-implant cases, can be found in Alison Frankel, "From Pioneers to Profits," *The American Lawyer,* June 1992.

Testimony by Sybil Niden Goldrich before the Senate Judiciary Subcommittee on Courts and Administrative Practice, on April 20, 1994, offers further details on Stern as well as on Goldrich's own experience.

Attorney Jill Fisch's article explaining post-settlement vacatur is "Post Settlement Vacatur: A Case of Disappearing Decisions," *Trial Magazine,* February 1, 1995.

More information on the lawsuits against Pfizer regarding its mechanical heart valves can be found in Greg Rushford, "Lacovara's Risky Cure for Pfizer's Heartburn," *Legal Times,* April 4, 1988.

An extensive account of Ron Elwell's role in litigation against General Motors is contained in Terence Moran, "GM Burns Itself," *The American Lawyer,* April 1993.

For opinionated overviews of various challenges to protective orders, see Bob Gibbons, "Secrecy Versus Safety: Restoring the Balance," *ABA Journal,* December 1991, and testimony by attorney Dianne Weaver before the Senate Judiciary Subcommittee on Courts and Administrative Practice, March 15, 1994. An objective report on cases can be found in Paul M. Barrett, "Protective Orders Come Under Attack," *The Wall Street Journal,* August 31, 1988.

19. Third-Class Citizens

The account of Matthew Garvey's story is from his testimony before the Senate Labor and Human Resources Subcommittees on Labor and Children, Family, Drugs, and Alcoholism, March 19, 1991.

Many of the statistics on the condition of America's children, including foster care and kinship care, are from the Child Welfare League of America and the National Committee to Prevent Child Abuse, "Current Trends in Child Abuse Reporting and Fatalities: The Results of the 1994 Annual Fifty State Survey," 1995. On the condition of poor children in the nation, see the U.S. Census Bureau Web site, www.census.gov.

The information on child labor was culled from a variety of sources and interviews, including "Child Labor and Public Policy: Legislative and Administrative Issues Involving American Workplaces," *Congressional Research Service,* Library of Congress, April 11, 1997.

Information on the vaccination programs comes mostly from interviews cited in the text. Other sources include Centers for Disease Control and Prevention, "Status Report on the Childhood Immunization Initiative," *Morbidity and Mortality Weekly Report,* July 25, 1997. Nathan Timothy's story came from a news story at the time of the measles epidemic, Lanie Jones, "Measles Epidemic Claims 1st Local Death," *Los Angeles Times,* Orange County Edition, January 24, 1990.

Because hunger can be difficult to define, a variety of reports on hunger and children were cited to provide a range of the problem. Sources for these reports and other information on hunger in America were provided by the Congressional Hunger Center; the Food Research and Action Center; the Second Harvest network, in Chicago, Illinois; and the Tufts University Center on Hunger, Poverty, and Nutrition Policy.

20. Reclaiming What's Ours

The complete text of King's 1955 speech is printed in Brian MacArthur, ed., *The Penguin Book of Twentieth Century Speeches* (Penguin Books, 1994).

RELATED READING

Adams, James Ring. *The Big Fix.* New York: John Wiley & Sons, Inc., 1990.

Alexander, Herbert, ed. *Campaign Money.* New York: The Free Press, 1976.

Ashworth, William. *Under the Influence: Congress, Lobbies, and the American Pork-Barrel System.* New York: Hawthorn/Dutton, 1981.

Balz, Dan and Ronald Brownstein. *Storming the Gates: Protest Politics and the Republican Revival.* Boston: Little, Brown and Company, 1996.

Barone, Michael, and Grant Ujifusa. *The Almanac of American Politics 1998.* Washington, D.C.: National Journal, 1997.

Beschloss, Michael R. *Taking Charge: The Johnson White House Tapes, 1963–1964.* New York: Simon & Schuster, 1997.

Corrado, Anthony, Thomas E. Mann, Daniel R. Oritz, Trevor Potter, and Frank J. Sorauf, eds. *Campaign Finance Reform: A Sourcebook*. Washington, D.C.: Brookings Institution Press, 1997.

Drew, Elizabeth. *Whatever It Takes*. New York: Viking, 1997.

Etzioni, Amitai. *Capital Corruption: The New Attack on American Democracy*. New Brunswick, N.J.: Transaction Books, 1988.

Getz, Robert S. *Congressional Ethics: The Conflict of Interest Issue*. Princeton, N.J.: D. Van Nostrand Company, Inc., 1966.

Green, Mark, with Michael Waldman. *Who Runs Congress?* New York: Dell Publishing Co., Inc., 1984.

Hager, George, and Eric Pianin. *Mirage: Why Neither Democrats nor Republicans Can Balance the Budget, End the Deficit, and Satisfy the Public*. New York: Random House, Inc., 1997.

Kennedy, John F. *Profiles in Courage*. Memorial edition. New York: Harper & Row, 1955.

Maraniss, David, and Michael Weisskopf. *Tell Newt to Shut Up!* New York: Simon & Schuster, 1996.

McChesney, Fred S. *Money for Nothing: Politicians, Rent Extraction, and Political Extortion*. Cambridge, Mass.: Harvard University Press, 1997.

Mollenhoff, Clark R. *Despoilers of Democracy*. Garden City, N.Y.: Doubleday, 1965.

O'Brien, Michael. *Philip Hart: The Conscience of the Senate*. East Lansing, Mich.: Michigan State University Press, 1995.

Pearson, Drew, and Jack Anderson. *The Case Against Congress*. New York: Simon & Schuster, 1968.

Penny, Timothy J., and Major Garrett. *Common Cents*. New York: Avon Books, 1995.

Sabato, Larry J. and Glenn R. Simpson. *Dirty Little Secrets: The Persistence of Corruption in American Politics*. New York: Times Books, 1996.

Sabato, Larry J. *PAC Power: Inside the World of Political Action Committees*. New York: W. W. Norton & Company, 1984.

Schram, Martin. *Speaking Freely*. Washington, D.C.: The Center for Responsive Politics, 1995.

Stern, Philip M. *The Best Congress Money Can Buy*. New York: Pantheon Books, 1988.

Stern, Philip M. *Still The Best Congress Money Can Buy*. Updated and revised edition. Washington, D.C.: Regnery Gateway, 1992.

Thompson, Dennis F. *Ethics in Congress: From Individual to Institutional Corruption*. Washington, D.C.: The Brookings Institution, 1995.

Weaver, Warren. *Both Your Houses: The Truth About Congress*. New York: Praeger, 1972.

Weinberg, Arthur, and Lila Weinberg. *The Muckrakers*. New York: Capricorn Books, 1961.

Wilson, Woodrow. *Congressional Government*. Cleveland, Ohio: The World Publishing Company, 1956.

Index

||||||||||||

About The Center
for Public Integrity
||||||||||||

The Center for Public Integrity began operation in May 1990. It is a nonprofit, nonpartisan, tax-exempt educational organization founded so that important national issues can be investigated and analyzed over a period of months without the normal time or space limitations. Described as a "watchdog in the corridors of power" by *National Journal,* the Center has investigated and disseminated a wide array of information in more than thirty-five published Center reports since its inception. More than 3,000 news media stories have referenced the Center's findings or perspectives about public service and ethics-related issues. The Center's books and studies are resources for reporters, academics, and the general public, with databases, backup files of government documents, and other information available as well.

If you would like access to the most recent findings of the Center, including additional information about Congress not contained in this book, you can visit the Center's Web site at www.publicintegrity.org, or subscribe to *The Public i,* the Center's award-winning newsletter.

For more information or to become a member, contact the Center for Public Integrity:

The Center for Public Integrity
1634 I Street, N.W.
Suite 902
Washington, D.C. 20006

E-mail: contact@publicintegrity.org
Internet: http://www.publicintegrity.org

Telephone: (202) 783-3900
Facsimile: (202) 783-3906